FREEDOM AND CONSTRAINT
IN CARIBBEAN
MIGRATION AND DIASPORA

Delia Nichols
March 2009.

FREEDOM AND CONSTRAINT IN CARIBBEAN MIGRATION AND DIASPORA

Edited by
Elizabeth Thomas-Hope

Ian Randle Publishers
Kingston • Miami

First published in Jamaica, 2009 by
Ian Randle Publishers
11 Cunningham Avenue
P.O. Box 686
Kingston 6.
www.ianrandlepublishers.com

National Library of Jamaica Cataloguing in Publication Data

Freedom and constraint in Caribbean migration
    and diaspora/ [edited by] Elizabeth Thomas-Hope

p. ; cm.

    ISBN 978-976-637-351-1 (pbk)

1. Emigration and immigration – Economic aspects 2. Emigration and immigration –
Social aspects 3. Forced migration – Caribbean Area 4. Migrant labour – Caribbean
Area 5. Return migration

    1. Thomas-Hope, Elizabeth

304.8 dc22

Cover image courtesy of the Science and Society Picture Library.
Cover and book design by Ian Randle Publishers
Printed and bound in the United States

TABLE OF CONTENTS

◎

SECTION I: SOCIAL CONSTRUCTIONS OF RACE AND IDENTITY IN THE EXPERIENCE AND CULTURE OF MIGRATION AND THE DIASPORA

FOREWORD

◉

It gives me as much pleasure to write the foreword to this book, *Freedom and Constraint in Caribbean Migration and Diaspora,* as it did to give the opening address for the conference, 'Caribbean Migration: Forced and Free', at the Mona Campus of the University of the West Indies in June 2006, from which these contributions have been drawn.

Nothing in the intervening months since that academic gathering has lessened the importance of this subject; in fact, quite the reverse. The current immigration debate in the United States highlights some of the dilemmas thrown up by migration. It is also at the forefront of the political debate in Europe at the national level, and of critical concern for the future expansion of the European Union. Further, it exists in the fears generated by the attacks in New York of 9/11 and the discussions over international terrorism.

Migration has dominated the history of humankind and has often been at the root of military conquest, religious conflict and ethnic strife. One only has to recall the level and intensity of the convulsions which reverberate today — between Israel and Palestine, indeed throughout the entire Middle East, among the successor states of the former Yugoslavia (especially Bosnia and Kosovo), and on the continent of Africa, as in the Sudan (Darfur), Rwanda and Somalia.

Caribbean people know better than most what it means to be uprooted. The dehumanizing aspects of the slave trade, the bicentenary of whose abolition we celebrated last year (2007), can never be forgotten. It severed us from the roots of our social and cultural belonging and obliged us, as the dispossessed, to struggle against formidable odds in the search to regain our self respect and forge a new identity. Nor should we forget the conditions under which Indian and Chinese immigrants were brought to the

Caribbean. All of this forms the backdrop to our understanding of the modern migrations of our people: from the tobacco fields of Cuba, the building of the Panama Canal and the railways of Central America, to the post-World War II era and the 'Empire Windrush' generation.

The papers in this book remind us that the transnational communities which Caribbean people have evolved during the latter half of the twentieth century have not come about easily, or without cost to those migrant pioneers. Their struggles continue as new Caribbean dimensions of the international migration phenomenon emerge — trafficking, child labour and sexual exploitation.

Caribbean people were globalised long before the phrase was ever coined. Whether forced or free, we are a migrant people and take pride in our perseverance and adaptability. Today there must be no barriers between those who reside within our own borders and those who seek to pursue their living abroad, if we are all to realize fully our creative energies and harmonise our productive skills to enjoy our rich potential. Our future lies in forging a beneficial engagement between the Diaspora and our regional community, thereby securing mutual enrichment in a milieu of stronger connectivity.

This book, and the UWI conference which preceded it, point the way to that process and I commend it to a wide and critical readership both here and abroad.

The Most Hon. P. J. Patterson O.N., P.C., Q.C.
Prime Minister of Jamaica 1992-2006
Kingston, Jamaica
15 July 2008

FORCED AND FREE CARIBBEAN MIGRATION:
An Understanding of Modern Diasporas
HARRY GOULBOURNE

INTRODUCTION

The theme of this volume and the conference from which the papers are drawn — Caribbean migration: forced and free — appropriately describes a central aspect of the Caribbean region's history in the post-Columbian age. It also points to some major characteristics of the region's present condition, as the several themes suggest. The task here is to pose a few hypotheses or questions, which, to one degree or another, may touch on some of the themes addressed in this timely volume.

I had the privilege to be taught at the University of the West Indies (UWI) how better to understand my Jamaican and Caribbean heritage, and to draw upon the knowledge and wisdom that come from the little things we convey to each other in the course of our daily lives. The songs of Bob Marley and the poems of Louise Bennett (Miss Lou) sensitively captured some of these things and sent them across the world as part of the migration process. It is also part of my own biography as part of the narrative of post-World War II migration. I arrived in a cold, grey London of the late 1950s from the warm, green hills of Clarendon, Jamaica, where I had learnt the disciplines and rigours of early to bed and early to rise, barefoot to school after collecting water, feeding the animals, and remembering what I was taught the previous day (English grammar, spelling, times table, etc.); and in the evening, repeating the cycle of rural life, such as story-telling in an age when we had little exposure to radio and films, and none to television or the printed word beyond the *Bible*, the *Sankey Hymnal*, and, of course, the Leandro cartoons in the *Gleaner*. But this early life prepared me to appreciate the world into which I was suddenly thrown in London: a world of classical music and folk singing, the world of Shakespeare (myths, stories, magic, etc.); and the world of the Romantic poets. Thus, Wordsworth's *Michael* was not just a long, beautiful narrative poem about a nuclear family in the English Lake District; rather, it was for me a story about individuals, watery and mountainous places I had known, loved, and missed in Belcaras, Boonas, Ritches, Bellfield and Williamsfield on the borders of the parishes of Manchester and Clarendon. The opening lines of Goldsmith's *Deserted Village*

> Sweet Auburn! loveliest village of the plain
> Where health and plenty cheered the labouring swain ...

speaks not simply of the transition from agricultural to industrial England. Like so much more in British, particularly English, arts (music, painting and literature; humour and satire) this narrative poem, like so many others by the Romantic poets, speak also to the Caribbean transnational experience of the transition from ruritania to urbana; the relatively certain to the atomised and lonely life that Sam Selvon so poignantly captured in his *Lonely Londoners*. This is a point often left out of the accounts of our migration stories: that is, the loneliness, alienation and angst that accompany the opportunities and excitements of physical and social mobility.

These remarks serve as a partial explanation of this paper: Forced and Free Caribbean Migration: an Understanding of Modern Diasporas. My central assertion is that the Caribbean experience — whether within or outside, forced or free — is the pre-eminent collective experience from which to learn about the making of the modern world, particularly as we begin walking into, talking into, and thinking about, the twenty-first century.

MIGRATION: A DOMINANT NOTE IN THE CARIBBEAN AND ATLANTIC WORLD

While it is true that the movement of people across borders or boundaries — whether of a geographical/physical nature, or of a political or social nature — is to be found in all regions of the world, perhaps there is nowhere that this truism is more evident than in the experience of people of Caribbean backgrounds. This experience of movement has taken place exclusively in the modern world; that is, during the era since the late 15th century, when the Italian Cristóbal Colón — Christopher Columbus — (financed and supported by the emerging European superpower, Spain) brought Europe to what today are called the Americas. So, from the beginning of its modern history, the Caribbean has been locked into the greater American sweep of diverse experiences involving the movements of people of different racial and cultural identities; the making of new cultures; and the destruction of peoples and cultures. Contrary to the message contained in the title of Orlando Patterson's novel, *An Absence of Ruins*, there are paths back to a pre-Columbian past that the novels of Wilson Harris bravely attempt to reconstruct as part of a regional legacy.

These changes have been mediated by the experience of emigration and immigration. For most of the region's history (history perhaps partly defined in a Hegelian sense: written history), this has been the main story. Following Columbus, people were drawn into the region from Europe (principally: Spain, France, Britain and Ireland, but also the Netherlands and Denmark, and later of course the USA, and these have defined the linguistic boundaries of the region today); from Africa (principally: West Africa — a vast sub-region now organised according to nation-states, from a nation-state in-formation called Spanish Sahara to Angola, and beyond); vast regions of Asia (principally: what is today India, China and parts of the Middle East, such as Lebanon and Syria). The peopling of the post-Columbian Caribbean world has been continuously added to by individuals and families from these and other parts of the contemporary world as major events occurred elsewhere — for example, the break up of the Soviet bloc in the 1990s; the return of Hong Kong to China, marking the end of empire for

Britain; and the new patterns of return home from the mother-land(s), particularly Britain. These events are bringing the circle fully around in the post-World War II period, ie., from mother-land to settler-colony to mother-land, and then back to *back-home*, as Jamaicans, Barbadians, St Lucians and others from this region now living in British cities say amongst themselves — particularly when the going gets tough, but also when there's prosperity.

In-between, there have been people coming into the region over the last half millennium from a variety of places. And these complex movements of people not only reflected and continue to reflect the rhythm of human migration but have also created a unique dance of the movements, mixing and combining of people that somehow the theorists of social and cultural pluralism in the 1950s and 1960s failed satisfactorily to grasp — including one of my mentors and intellectual heroes — the Jamaican anthropologist M.G. Smith. I sometimes teased him by saying that his theory of social and cultural pluralism — where people meet and mix but do not combine — was borne out by my experience in East/Central Africa, and that it was a pity he had not conducted research in these regions of Africa. When I ventured to say that his influential theory did not hold water in the Caribbean (as so many Caribbeanist theorists have pointed out), the great man was gracious and would explain complex matters to a reluctant and slow student.

My main point here, however, is that the Caribbean during the course of its post-Colombian era has been a significant destination for the world's population — for settlement, colonization, nativising and, of course, for visits and for gazing (as tourism has become the world's main industry in a search for the realization of Jeremy Bentham's utilitarian dream of elevating pleasure over pain).

Second, and presently far more importantly: the movement of people has been almost equally marked by emigration of Caribbeans to some of the lands from which today's Caribbean people came to this region, and to other parts of the Americas. The first publication in which Elizabeth Thomas-Hope and I participated was an issue of the journal *Oral History* (1980): her contribution stressed the integrity of the migration experience for Caribbeans, while I asserted that no sooner had immigration into the Caribbean entered a tailing-off than emigration of Caribbeans commenced: the British Atlantic slave trade ended in 1807 (and understandably 2007 is a big year across the Atlantic world), the institution of slavery in the British Empire in 1838 (USA: 1864; Brazil 1888). But while indenture started in 1840 (from Madeira, China and most importantly, from India) and continued to 1917 (from India), the *outward* movement gathered pace with the building of Ferdinand de Lessep's Panama Canal (mid-1880s) and the need in war-torn Europe for Cuban sugar during WWI — both of which acted as pull factors for intra-Caribbean migration in those decades. By the boom years of the 1920s, Caribbeans were living cheek-by-jowl with new European migrants in some of the great cities of the USA, particularly New York. Of course, we could go back to the age of Alexander Hamilton in the eighteenth or Edward Blyden in the nineteenth centuries, or others from the period of the first British and French empires to find individuals and a degree of fluidity between North America and the Caribbean, between the region and European destinations, as well as African destinations particularly along the Continent's western hump.

In the twentieth century and presently in the new millennium we may want also to consider the experiences of a Claude McKay and Marcus Garvey in North America and Europe, the reactions of a Harold Cruise (in his *Crisis of the Negro Intellectual*) and recently the more sober re-visitation by Winston James or Perry Mars, asking us to appreciate the impact of Caribbeans on the making of contemporary North American society.

The long first phase of entry into this region marks the *forced* movement of people into the region: slavery and indenture: West African slaves, English poor, Cromwell's defeated Irish; Madeirans, Chinese and East Indians (South Asians). The times of *exit* from the Caribbean region have been characterised largely by *free* movement of each of these categories of people back to points of the old worlds of Africa, Asia and Europe, as well as North America, in search of perceived cultural and racial roots, or, more dynamically, in search of material opportunities for themselves and their offspring.

Of course, when we speak of Caribbean migration we very much have in mind different parts of the diverse Caribbean world: in North America (all Caribbeans: English-, French- Spanish- speaking); in Europe (the Commonwealth Caribbean, The Netherlands Caribbean, and less contentiously the French-speaking islands — because Martinique and Guadeloupe are departements d'outre-mer).

The docking of SS *Empire Windrush* at Tilbury, southern England, in 1948, symbolically marked the beginning of sizeable Caribbean migration to the UK, and thereafter the flows into the USA (particularly from the 1960s) and Canada again became the main destination for Caribbean migrants. Today, we are seeing a continuing flow of people from the region to both Europe and North America. As hinted earlier, there is also a 'return' flow of people from these regions to the Caribbean, just as there was a flow back to Europe from the region during periods of dramatic change, such as the end of slavery in the nineteenth century, during decolonization, political and natural crises in the twentieth century (Guyana, Grenada, Jamaica, Haiti as well as Montserrat).

So, what is new in the narrative or story of post-Columbian Caribbean people? What can we learn from this mixed and complex set of experiences of the movements of different people in different directions? There are several things to be highlighted here and to be learnt and applied to our present situation. There are three aspects or things in particular that we may want to observe about this common experience, which are of relevance to this volume. They are: first, the racio-ethnic dimension; second, the challenge to the nation-state; and, third, the challenges or implications for our notions of community in a globalized, transnational world.

THE RACIO-ETHNIC DIMENSION

The movement of people in the post-Columbian Caribbean world and across the Atlantic has been marked by social action being underscored by racial and ethnic identities and solidarities. If, for example, Europeans came to the Americas to escape religious persecutions and bigotry (the forces of Protestantism versus those of the Inquisition; the forging of Europe's modern nation-states, etc.), they brought with them a powerful discovery:

the discovery of racial differentiation, that is to say, phenotypical differences between human beings (body structures, shapes, and most powerfully, colours of skin). Arguably, this 'discovery' has been as important as the celebrated European 'discovery' (actually, exploration) of the Americas. The 'discovery' of human variation as reflected in our shapes and our structures, or in our colours and our diverse cultures has been a vital part of modernity, and for most of its history over the last three or four centuries modernity's project has exhibited some of the most malignant moments in recorded history. I have in mind here Atlantic slavery; the treatment of Africans and aboriginals in the Americas and Australia by European conquerors; the Holocaust; recent events in the states of former Yugoslavia (Bosnia, Serbia, Kosovo); and in Central Africa (Burundi and Rwanda) by Africans to Africans. There are numerous other examples in all regions of the world.

But modernity's project has also exhibited or presented the occasions for the benevolent transformation of the human condition, and to revolutionise our perceptions and behaviour with regard to human diversity or pluralism. In both instances, the Caribbean region and Caribbean folks across the Atlantic have been central (not marginal) to the story: we have participated in the sufferings as well as in the creation of a better and more tolerant world in which difference or diversity is taken as normal and is celebrated.

There is a second sense in which the racio-ethnic dimension is relevant to this discussion: the Atlantic — at least the North Atlantic — world is no longer one entirely controlled or underscored by the dominant interests of an apparently homogenous European perspective, or world view. The participation of black individuals in the decision-making processes and representations of power in the Atlantic world is making a difference to how subsequent generations may see our times, and this will also have significant implications for the re-interpretation of our pasts. I believe this re-interpretation of our pasts is presently being represented in film and literature as post-colonial and cultural studies emerge as distinct disciplines across the humanities and social sciences, as well as in the kinds and levels of participation in political and economic life hitherto excluded. The end result is that the dual (black/white) racial representation of humanity in the Americas that came with the Atlantic connections of Europe, the Americas and the Caribbean, is being replaced by something of a spectrum of racial identities. What has long been known in the Caribbean about these matters is becoming more widely recognised.

Let us take our most minute social institution, the family: in my work on Caribbean families over the last decade or so, the thing that impresses me most is the evidence of diversity, making it difficult to find Caribbean families who are not racially diverse in their memberships, particularly when we consider our wider kinship connections, and if we were to include friendship networks the picture would be even more diverse.

This, however, sets up an interesting tension: some of the most mixed individuals go in search of a mythical singular ancestry, deny their diversity, and appear lost in the very world of modernity that their forebears were active in forging. In other words, the world's first *de-tribalised* people sometimes seek to be *re-tribalised* — thereby reversing a powerful historical trend (modernity). In so doing, tendencies within the development of what it means to be Caribbean, also include a refusal to use the social and human capital with which our rich and diverse heritage endow us for life in a twenty-first century characterized by the acceptance of diversity.

My assertion here is that the diversity of humans in the Caribbean transnational experience comes out of the region's history of entry, departure, and return; a constant cycle of movement as many Caribbeanists have observed.

THE CHALLENGE TO THE NATION-STATE

A second major aspect of Caribbean migration is that it poses a significant challenge to the integrity of the nation-state. The post-World War II settlement rested on the existence of the nation-state as the basic unit through which sovereignty has been exercised. The process of de-colonization, starting with the independence of India and Pakistan in 1947, followed by Ghana's a decade later, and came to a comparatively rapid end by its demise in the 1960s. To be sure, some European colonies lingered on into the 1990s — Hong Kong (UK) or Macau (Portugal), but on a whole, the European empires ended more with a bang than a whimper, as the poet T.S.Eliot may have said. A world of nation-states became the corner-stone of the United Nations, and unlike the League of Nations after World War I, laid the foundations for the recognition of a number of generalized principles that have made our contemporary world. These include the *relative* rule of law across borders established by the assertion of collective self-determination, or aggregate identity enshrined in the Versailles settlement of 1919; and, the generalised acceptance of the principles of human rights as part of the post-1945 settlement that has taken us to the crisis of security in our present world.

The questions I am posing here are the following: has the contribution of nationalism in Africa, Asia and the Caribbean — a major feature of the last century — spent its progressive force? Are we living in a moment when there is a need to assert a new universalism that transcends the nationalist call for boundaries? Expressed another way: Do we need to ask whether the blossoming of national flags, songs, symbols, currencies, passports, and so forth, have gone on uncritically beyond their healthy *sell-by date*?

Migration — the movement of people across their customary boundaries (internal migration), but particularly the crossing of citizens of one nation-state into the jurisdiction of another nation-state (international migration) — stakes out the ground of a challenge to the world order established on the foundations of the nation-state. For example, as the British Caribbean colonies gained their independence in the 1960s, migrants to Britain had to decide on their citizenship: Would they be Jamaicans, Trinidadians, Barbadians, etcetera, or register and become British (island) citizens? Many refused to register because they held that they had always been British, and had travelled across the Atlantic on a British passport (under the 1948 British Nationality Act). More importantly, the crossing of state boundaries within the Empire and Commonwealth defeated a fundamental principle of the 1948 Act: To have a universal British citizenship, followed by specific citizenships for each political domain, as the then Home Secretary (Chuter Ede) stressed to Parliament.

Paradoxically, however, migration in the age of globalization is significantly undermining the barriers firmly erected by nationalism after World War I and World War II. How is this being done? First, through the search for regional entities that can address large aggregate matters that are beyond the capacities of individual nation-states, and issues that the nation-states still cannot release and allow the United Nations to deal with (indeed, the institutions of the UN as presently constituted are unable adequately to tackle these problems). They include such issues as security against global terrorism (that is, non-state aggression against non-military, civil society) — particularly following Nairobi and Dar-es-Salaam in the 1990s, 9/11, Bali, Madrid, and more recently the London bombings on July 7, 2005; the search for peace; the free movement of labour as well as material labour; the free flow of technological and other forms of knowledge; the management of water sources; depleting natural energy sources. A crucial addition to this list is the movement of human and social capital across national boundaries. In all developed economies a key example of this is the demographic imbalance between ageing populations, declining birth rates, the building up of new and massive social and economic problems such as work and the labour force reproduction, longevity, pensions and care provisions. In much of the developing world the problems of poverty, population growth, rising expectations and so forth, present another kind of imbalance in the world system. These issues and the human urge to find solutions to felt needs are questioning the relevance of the boundaries of the nation-state. Consequently, regionalism as expressed through the European Union, the African Union, North American Free Trade Area, the expansion of CARICOM in this region, reveal a global urge substantially to remould or modify the sanctity of the nation-state as the bedrock of the global order.

Second, these developments amount to a major challenge of the marriage of the nation and the state (the folk/community/people and political authority) expressed by what we perhaps inadequately describe as transnationalism and globalization. A key aspect of this that I have not mentioned is the fact that groups of people have transgressed state boundaries, while being able to maintain their folk/people/community integrity. In other words, de-couple or divorce the marriage of the nation and the state, and we still have people, nation, folk, maintaining their links, their bonds, their unity; *but* significantly fracturing their singularity of political loyalty that nearly all states insist upon from their citizens. This transnationalism has been made possible through the revolutions in technology and the continuing revolution that Marx foresaw, that is, the globalization of the planet through the spread of the forces of capitalism, suggesting that perhaps Plekanov and the Mensheviks were correct, where Lenin and the Bolsheviks were wrong, in their respective understandings of the transition from capitalism to socialism at the beginning of the last century.

Apart from racial and ethnic identities and social action, my research and intellectual concerns over the better part of the last two decades (since leaving Mona and returning to England) have been about issues of the aggregate community we call the nation-state and the most discrete social unit that we call the family. At both these levels of the socio-political spectrum we can observe the forces of transnationalism: the decline of the nation-state and, in several countries, the radical transformation of the family as an institution, allowing for greater freedom, social space and social democracy. But the main point to underline here is that the family unit (both the nuclear inner unit as well as the wider kinship network) is a unit that is emphasising, or groping for, the continuation of linkages across physical space and across state boundaries. This is not new. The rich or the well resourced have nearly always been transnational (take for example, the Medicis, the Rothschilds, the Windsors or the Murdocks). What is new is that inexpensive and accessible means of communications (travel, telephone and the internet, films and videos, common and universalised patterns of consumptions in food, clothing and living) have been increasingly available to ordinary people in a way that was historically not possible in past world systems. In this regard, the British sociologist Anthony Giddens is certainly right to stress that we humans are, for the first time, living in a truly global social order. The new facilities make it possible for us to maintain old communities as well as create new strands of our communities across state boundaries. Consequently, it is possible to be Jamaican in London as well as in New York, as well as in Kingston.

Indeed, this transnational communal situation makes it possible for us to be more in touch with groups of people across the globe than we are with our immediate neighbours. Transnational communities may therefore undermine neighbourhoods or neighbourliness; but this need not be the case: neighbourhoods (the physical space within which people lead their day to day lives) *may* and perhaps *must* exist side by side with our links across state boundaries, and this is emerging as another challenge to the integration of migrants and their offspring in existing communities found at points of destination.

The Caribbean transnational experience fits into what appears to be an evolving world situation. That is to say, the Caribbean experience is not unique, and we can learn from others as much as others can learn from us. What may be some of these lessons? I would point to three instances. First, some years ago, I interviewed a group of officials involved with resettling returnees in a major Commonwealth Caribbean country, and they told me two things that I found intriguing: They had records of Britain returning individuals who were mentally disturbed, criminals from the USA who were born in that country, and that Caribbean country also had to subsidise the pensions of some returnees. This was before that country was re-classified as a developed country. Second, in the major research project with which I am presently involved - families and social capital — one of my research colleagues, Elisabetta Zontini, has found that in one region of Italy (Trentino), the point of departure has become prosperous while some of the destinations of emigration (such as Argentina) Italians have become less prosperous. So today, Trentino sends aid to their communities abroad and tries to incorporate them into an Italian collective identity and bond of loyalty. Usually, it is the migrant who sends help back to the source of departure, or returns to the point of departure to add to the social capital of the source. My third example of the point of departure helping those who have moved, is that of the Jamaica National Building Society in London: the society attempts to draw upon the Jamaican community in the UK, but also tries to help with establishing links between people of Jamaican descent and Jamaica.

CONCLUSION

These examples suggest that I should reassert the broader points I have tried to make. These are that Caribbean migration :

- Shows how the nation-state is being undermined as a valid unit for the exercise of political authority in the contemporary world; the notion of nationalism may have had its day. Issues of care and provision, crime, security and perhaps most importantly, community and individual identities, are cross-national or transnational.
- the community called *the nation* — the folk, the people — continues to thrive, and can do so across vast physical spaces. But community should not be conflated/confused with the imperatives of the nation-state, which may have outlived its usefulness.
- This makes the model of community depicted by the Diaspora one that is highly adaptable to the modern world, and, like the Jewish community across the globe over the last two millennia (following Titus' destruction of Jerusalem in AD 70), Caribbeans and others are learning to live across physical space, and therefore exercising freedom of movement (as against being forced to move).
- The communities of the North Atlantic world are *in-the-making,* so to speak, and Caribbeans are at the forefront of this creation within modernity. The forced migration that created the contemporary Caribbean has been incomplete: the second part of the story is the re-making of the Atlantic world as a whole. The nation-state is merely one of the building blocks of this creation.
- Caribbean migration points the way forward, because it suggests that one of the major projects of modernity — a world order in which humanity is neatly organised into fixed communities, each with its own discrete political authority (the state) — is somewhat absurd, because it is an un-realizable utopian dream. This may be an uncomfortable point for die-hard nationalists, but there has to be recognition of the dawning of a post-national age.

- These possibilities pose challenges for policy makers and politicians, for academics and intellectuals in the arts and other areas of human endeavours in which Caribbeans contribute to emerging world cultures.

These developments point to an important start in addressing the collective issues involved with this phase of the Caribbean's participation in the wider, global, re-moulding of the modern world of which we were once at the forefront — as Arthur Lewis hinted in his Preface to Gisela Eisner's seminal book, *Jamaica: 1830-1930*. In that statement Lewis tells us that in 1850 Jamaica (as a representation of the Caribbean) was more advanced than Japan or Australia, but by 1930 inhabited another world entirely, one that was to be described by a generation of distinguished scholars as a 'developing' society. The present challenge for the region, however, is whether we will work our way to the back or hold a position somewhere at the front of the march of modernity. There is a point not far from the Mona Campus of the University of the West Indies called Cross Roads and another called Half-Way Tree: These are telling nomenclatures and metaphors suggesting the paradoxes of the Caribbean condition in the modern, diasporic world.

INTRODUCTION

◉

CULTURES OF FREEDOM AND CONSTRAINT IN CARIBBEAN MIGRATION AND DIASPORA

ELIZABETH THOMAS-HOPE

INTRODUCTION

Freedom and coercion in Caribbean migration is an enduring theme in a region where migration, under both of these circumstances, has characterized the construction of the region's societies and cultures. Modern Caribbean societies were created through the forced migration of Africans and Asians under conditions of slavery and indenture. Other groups, including Europeans and Arabs, also migrated to the Caribbean under varying conditions of coercion or the search for freedom. Subsequent movements from and within the region, including those of the present time, reflect motivations based not only on the freedom to move, but on migration as a resource in the pursuit of freedom. The dialectic of coercion and freedom is one that permeates the migration dynamic and is reflected in the ongoing movements outwards from the country of birth and, for some, back again, or in an ongoing cycle of transnational mobility.

Forced migrations still occur. Many persons are trafficked within and from the region to other parts of the world under conditions that deprive them of their human right to personal freedom. Caribbean persons in the USA and the UK are currently deported involuntarily back to their country of birth in significant numbers. Others move from their homeland due to political pressures and persecution. But these are among the more overtly forced movements of the present time. The coercions and freedoms in the migration process are in most cases covert and embedded in socially constructed inequalities of migrant identities – chiefly those based on race and the process of racialization conditioned by class status and national stereotypes. At the destination these factors are further complicated by the circumstances of migrant arrival in combination with the pre-existing, or even newly emerging, perceptions of the identity of the migrants leading to various levels of receptivity in the host society. However, this seemingly common migration framework, offering freedoms and coercion, opportunities and constraints, must not mask the real differences between forced and voluntary movement. The forced movements of individuals and peoples induced by war, economic deprivation, political repression or environmental disaster, who seek refuge elsewhere, are fundamentally different from the freedoms and constraints experienced in the mobility of those who move outwards and back again without any compulsion, simply to expand their horizons and to engage new environments of opportunity.

Viewed both from the behavioural and the historical-structural theoretical perspectives, and within the colonial and post-colonial contexts, there is good reason to interpret the characteristics of Caribbean migration in terms of freedom and constraint. This applies to the selectivity of the migration process as well as the subsequent relationship of the migrants with the host society, as also with the home society. Further, freedom and constraint underpin the identities and the perceptions which are embedded in the various constructions of the migrant as the 'other' and, on the part of the migrant, in the sense of self and the livelihoods they can pursue. It therefore affects the contribution the migrant can make to the culture and life at both migration source and destination.

Yet, the common conceptualizations of the migration process and explanations of the movements and experience at the destinations have subsumed the significance of freedom and coercion. Instead, the paradigms have been dominated by materialist interpretations of movement, and consequently a theoretical framework entirely comprised of periphery-centre alignments and relative advantage (the so-called migration 'pushes' and 'pulls' of popular discourse). At one level, individuals make decisions to migrate based on the differential advantages of perceived opportunities, and in this sense the competitive material nature of globalization ascribes relevance to the migration environment. But many interpretations remain at this most superficial of the various layers of exploration, leading to the conflation of reason for, and explanation of, migration. Such interpretations miss the importance of the selectivity of migrants and the ways in which they navigate the complexities of their destinations. Certainly, there is more than one level and scale of engagement involved, as well as the existence of multiple strands and layers of meaning in the texture of overall migration culture.

Likewise, there is no simple black or white in terms of the freedoms and constraints of Caribbean migrants in their host societies, even those of North America and Europe. These and other binary constructions are simplistic and severely limit explanation. The identity and social constructions of migrants at their destinations reflect and, at the same time, determine the freedoms and constraints of the host society. Thus the lack of freedoms in the host society is not necessarily or solely due to biological characteristics of race. It is contingent, relative to the specific circumstances at any particular place and time, including which other groups are competing within the same space.

Furthermore, the patterns, perceptions and identities formed in the context of circumstances in the past become part of the corporate memory of the present, both of the potential migrant as well as in the societies to which the migrants go. Thus to be a Haitian migrant today is to be tinged by the entire history and predicament of the Haitian people since the country's independence in 1804. The way that these events have been judged from the outside have reinforced the victimization of the victim. The Haitian migrant on Cuba's sugar plantations in the early twentieth century was viewed no differently, and had no greater freedom in the migration arena, than they have at the present time throughout the Caribbean region, as in the USA and Canada (Carr 2003). The Haitians have not yet been able to live down the legacies of their past, just as other Caribbean nationals have been caught in a mind-set determined by the history of colonialism worldwide and the ongoing cultural and intellectual imperialism that it spawned.

National differences and the racialization of migrants abroad are therefore associated with a deeply embedded intellectual and cultural imperialism which is internalised by people of the source as also the destination. Imperialism, as pointed out by Edward Said (1993), created a globally interdependent community, while at the same time allowing people to believe that they belonged to only one part of that community as Whites, or Blacks, Orientals, Westerners (Skeldon 1997). The experience of intellectual and cultural imperialism that dominates national images and identities and constructions of 'the other' deprives the migrant of many freedoms as they attempt to establish themselves at the destination. This deeply affects the contribution that the migrants can make.

To look beyond the implications of the materialist aspects of globalization in seeking explanation for migration and beyond the phenotype definitions of race is not to deny their significance, but to acknowledge the importance of historical and place specific aspects of migration, its paradoxes and its relatedness to Caribbean culture. Furthermore, it questions the sole South-North nature of diaspora discourses and raises questions about the heterogeneity and plurality of the Caribbean Diaspora. These levels of interpretation and examination are important in order to influence the theoretical perspectives and paradigms within which Caribbean migration and diaspora studies are positioned, and thereby the nature of the questions that are asked.

FREEDOM AND CONSTRAINT IN OUTWARD MIGRATION

The value of migration to the emancipated slaves in the context of the pursuit of freedom has been discussed elsewhere (Thomas-Hope 1978). This was especially the case in the Anglophone Caribbean where migration opportunities were first sought at a time that represented the early development of the post-slavery society of the nineteenth century. Emancipation could not guarantee freedom from the plantation system as there was no other means of livelihood than agriculture, nor any prospect of escape from the low status accorded ex-slave populations within the plantation system. Migration permitted persons to obtain the material capital (thus the ability to purchase land and house and to marry) and the symbolic attributes (for example, experience of the 'outside' world) that were associated with status that all in the society would recognize.

The ability of the former slaves to move away, not only from the plantation but from the country of birth and later to return, was also symbolically a fundamental dimension of the identity of a person as free agent, rather than merely as a victim of events and circumstances. By the end of the nineteenth century, migration had become an endorsement of freedom and a right of passage. In so doing it gradually became integral to the strategy for altering one's place in the society and negotiating the avenues to the achievement of personal goals, facilitation of mobility and enhancement of status in the otherwise racially and socially restrictive plantation system. Migration thereby contributed in fundamental ways to the cultural construction and ideology of personhood that ensued in the aftermath of slavery.

Moving away from one's place of birth takes on special meaning when that place is a small island (Thomas-Hope 2003). The sense of opportunities being limited and freedoms restricted by small islandness has meant that new horizons always had to be elsewhere, and elsewhere has always been another country. The power of the concept of restricted economic and social freedoms associated with small islands is both literal (or physical) and metaphorical, associated with parochialism and narrow mindedness pejoratively used to describe people even though living in large countries.

The need and perceived need to move away from the home country, even to another Caribbean island, in order to circumvent the institutional constraints to achieving status and mobility, and to use migration as a means of achieving these in the end, explains the high propensity for migration in the early years following Emancipation. It further explains why, even when the labour of the ex-slaves was needed on the plantations, the workers nevertheless sought out, and readily responded to opportunities to move away from their island in order one day to return with enhanced status. Besides, the early migrations had lasting implications for the continuing dependence upon migration as freedom from any constraints — domestic, economic, social or political — through departing and then returning when the conditions were considered to be right (Thomas-Hope, 1978).

The *Colon Man*, that literary depiction of the West Indian in Panama (Frederick 2003; Lamming 1983; Walrond 1983), epitomized the successful migrant at a time when remittance flows back to families were high, and in many cases formed the economic basis for personal mobility as well as inter-generational mobility through the education it afforded. Additionally, it portrayed the return of the migrants with all the material trappings that proved their success. This entered the collective consciousness as the model of migration to which others have continued to aspire — and around which other social institutions, such as those of the family and the care of children, the gendered division of labour and responsibility, the acknowledged avenue to success and 'having arrived', — have all accommodated migration and return. Thus the societal context in the Caribbean enhanced the freedom and diminished the constraints to movement at the migration source. This was not necessarily the case at the destinations, where the prime concern has been recurrently that of selecting migrants to provide a labour force of a specific type at a particular place and time.

TRAVERSING THE MIGRATION LANDSCAPE – RESOURCE AND RESOURCEFULNESS

Crossing borders carries with it the power to transform one's circumstances. But migration is a scarce resource. While globalization in terms of the distribution of the power of capital produces the international and national landscape of labour supply and demand, not all persons or groups are empowered by circumstance to traverse across it in the same directions or with the same degree of facilitation. The selectivity of immigration regulations at the destinations introduces freedoms for particular groups to enter a particular country based upon specific criteria. This creates channels of relative freedom across the migration landscape that last for a finite period. The freedom is extended only to those who meet the criteria. Others must resort to informal and illegal means of passage and entry if they are determined to move to another state.

At the migration destination, the competitive nature of the labour force as also the social constructions of identity, are reflections of the relative power of the states from which the migrants move and to which they go. These provide the criteria for social access versus exclusion, and thus condition the relationship of the migrants with the host. On this depends the contribution that the migrants as a group can make, and whether it is solely confined to contribution to the labour force or also to the culture and the social dynamic of the host society. However, freedom and constraint are not necessarily, or usually, fixed. Each have conditions that permit negotiation and exist at different levels of intensity and rigidity based on the social capital of the migrants and how they are constructed as the 'other'.

Social capital, in the context of migrants at their destinations, has been used to explain different outcomes of national groups, especially the relationship between group members and the groups' expectations and norms. (Cordero-Guzman et al. 2001). Social capital, whether gained through the political process, education or economic power, is therefore instrumental in gaining access to the group in which the migrants are interested or wanting to identify. These attributes then supersede the biological features associated with racial difference in terms of importance (Thomas-Hope 2005).

But what are the issues that lead immigrants to strategize in a particular way? Immigrants of various types and racial and class characterizations have to define themselves within the framework of the existing racialization processes and the perception of the dominant native groups — since the host society is not homogeneous either. Some migrants deliberately distance themselves from certain native groups, aligning themselves to other, 'whiter' native groups. In recent decades, Caribbean migrants have found benefit in emphasizing their culture, to gain advantage economically and politically. This is evident from the increasing popularity of Caribbean carnivals and other cultural events in cities of the Diaspora (Ho and Nurse, 2005).

Up until the 1960s, assimilation was the dominant approach to the analysis of migrants at their destinations. The main weakness, as Cordero-

Guzman, Smith and Grosfoguel point out, was in the underlying assumption that the assimilation of the immigrant groups was entirely based upon their capacity and willingness to integrate into the mainstream. This perspective ignored the limited freedoms and many constraints in the system of the host society, quite apart from the disposition or otherwise to assimilate. Effort was made on the part of the host society to appear to be neutral, as in the USA, by upholding the notion of 'free country', 'level playing field', 'anyone can come in and do well'; or in the case of the UK, the notion of 'being British' (that is, a British subject from the Commonwealth) and British 'fair play'. The logic of these slogans freed the host society from responsibility for creating blockages in the way.

Racialization processes proceed differently at different levels of social life. In politics they can work in one way and in the labour market another and in schools or social areas — or marriage — yet another (Cordero-Guzman et al. 2001). As groups have improved their situation in politics, the economy and the professions, they have become 'whiter', as in the case of Irish, Italians, Jews and Poles. But all members of the group do not assimilate at the same rate, or in the same way, and this distinction is largely determined by the nature of the racialization of the group and the disparate issues of identity surrounding race, which include, but are not confined to, phenotype. In New York, the site of the development of a sophisticated stratification system where racial phenotype, immigrant status and ethnicity and nationality all combine in creating racializing hierarchies which have evolved as the definitions of whiteness and blackness, and other categories, have changed. These categories matter, for once they are established they influence the freedoms and constraints in the life chances and trajectories of future generations of migrants.

RACIALIZATION OF THE MIGRANT IN CONSTRUCTIONS OF THE 'OTHER'

There is no migrant population that is not affected by the language that defines it within its particular context and in relation to the host society's sense of themselves. Thus the world and its possibilities at various places for various national groups are all contingent and thereby differences are constructed. These include differences of race in which the language is deliberately charged with values of superiority and subordination, and thus with freedoms and constraints that reflect the parameters of the economic, geographical and social spaces in which they can operate and establish livelihoods.

Phenotype is only one facet in a complex of economic, class, gender, and ethnic characteristics that shape Caribbean migration experiences and group identity and belonging. The varied constructions that relate to the migrant as the 'other' are critical. This opens up a framework for the analysis of the freedom and constraints in migration and the cultures of the Diaspora based on the variability of those constructions. The coercion and freedom inherent in the roles and identities embedded in race, class, gender and nationality, shaped by the migration process now and in the past, influence the ways in which national groups are represented in the language, especially that of the public arena. The way in which the national group is constructed as 'other' influences the ways and extent to which they can contribute to the development of new hybrid and creole cultures at their destinations.

Thus the concept of otherness is based on racialization of the migrant, which then becomes the determinant of his/her identity and is further associated with a gamut of stereotypes. The imagery is usually of a negative nature, including ignorance, ugliness, criminality and, in the Haitian case, oftentimes also the demonic. Some imagery is positive based, for example, on the notion of exoticism in the case of the 'Latin' migrant within the Caribbean region, but even this has its negative connotation associated with sensuality and prostitution. The imagery attached to different groups of migrants either reduces or enhances their freedom to be treated equitably in the host society or even to be understood on their own terms, in their own language. Where such freedoms are denied, metaphors of exile, namely alienation, isolation and anomie, together with the pressures of proving material and social success, which is associated with the migration experience, become burdens that only the most resilient can withstand.

The irony of racialization of the 'other' in intra-Caribbean migrations is that freedoms and constraints do not differ significantly from the migration to countries of the North. Migration studies have hardly touched the issue of the complexity of the Caribbean Diaspora, determined and conditioned by similar factors in its various locations, and fragmented by global capital in various ways within the overall globalization landscape (Puri 2003).

Racialization and identities of otherness and un-belonginging, xenophobia and deportation, are not confined to migrations from South to North. The continued migration, whether from the region outwards or within the region, results in similar forms of social exclusion. For example, the Haitian migrant faces the same types of social exclusion whether in Curaçao, Guadeloupe, the Bahamas, the Turks and Caicos Islands or the Dominican Republic. Recently, negative labels have been used to categorize the Guyanese in Barbados or the Jamaicans in the Cayman Islands. The unequal balance of power of states thereby creates the freedom to determine selectivity and rejection of immigrants, and forms the basis for social exclusion and, increasingly evident, the criteria for deportation from the USA and the UK.

The social construction of place is also an important part of the migration process; migration alters both the characteristics and meaning of place as the migrants become part of the new space. Not only are the demographic and labour-force profile and economic niches of place altered by migration, but so also are the culture, the social rhythm and the perspective of self and other. But the migrants change the characteristics of place depending upon the freedoms and constraints of their integration. Thus the characteristics of the places from which migrants leave, as also those to which they go, are always in process, being constructed and reconstructed to provide meaning in the particular context. For in the post-colonial city, Chambers observes, the '. . . metropolitan figure is the migrant: she and he are the active formulators of metropolitan aesthetics and life styles, reinventing the languages and appropriating the streets of the master' (Chambers 1994: 23). This process of changing identities also plays a role in class restructuring within the migrant community itself, and brings about social transformations in the localities at all the major points or centres in the transnational networks.

RETURN MIGRATION AND TRANSNATIONALISM

Migration is not simply the movement of people between places but the individual's relocation in relation to the social space that s/he occupies and within which their identities are fashioned and livelihoods developed. New livelihoods, identities and relationships of 'self' and 'other' thus define the migrants' incorporation into each country in the migration process (Ho, 1999; Nyberg Sorensen and Olwig 2002). The transnational experience varies with the migrant group and between individual migrants of each group so that adjustments have to be made accordingly. For location at any one point in the environment conditions how the individual relates to the rest of the space. The individual invariably is forced to experience and develop changes, sometimes dramatic changes, in livelihood, identity and sense of identity at each new location within the transnational space. Above all, while at one location the migrant never loses the experience of the previous locations, their relevance changes and their dominance and roles in the total livelihood of the individual at each move become characterized by a new dynamic (Chambers, 1994).

At the migration destinations, the initial migrants, in contrast to the subsequent generations born abroad, tend to see themselves as transient, still with a sense of belonging to their country of birth. They are, therefore, not impacted in the same way by circumstances at the destination; including the exclusivities of race and nationality, except where they have no social capital and even lose the vital connections and psychological support of home and family. Transnational livelihoods permit strategies of escape from the control of the societal systems of both states. The return migrants or transnational persons avoid racism, social exclusion and other possible negatives at the destination, while enjoying the economic and experiential/training benefits of work in the centres of global capital or elsewhere. Furthermore, the transnational person's objective is to return to the locus of emotional security and social comfort levels of 'home' while retaining the citizenship status and access to the material facilities of a country elsewhere. (Thomas-Hope 2002; 2006).

The emancipatory character of transnationalism is usually, if not always, counter-hegemonic (Guarnizo and Smith 1999). Studies have shown that transnational practices and livelihoods can be used for purposes of capital accumulation, as effectively as for the purpose of contesting hegemonic narratives of race, ethnicity, class and nation (Mitchell 1993; Ong 1996). Therefore, transnationalism may be interpreted as a form of resistance from below and the means of personally negotiating the benefits of migration from the point of view of the migrant.

Yet another irony of the migration process is that, despite the freedoms of the transnational space, returning migrants are initially denied full incorporation in their Caribbean home country. On their return, many migrants are identified with the foreign country where they had previously lived. For example, some returnees from Britain are called 'the English' and other labels based on their different accents and other cultural traits acquired abroad. Imagery of the returnee invariably refers to eccentricities of behaviour and dress or to excesses in the design of their houses. They generally feel misunderstood and surprised that they are identified with the foreign country in which they had lived and thus are not immediately reincorporated into the 'home' society at all levels (Byron 2005). This is part of the wider dilemma and duality of Caribbean culture and its contradictions. Some find this landscape too hard to negotiate — too stressful, so they think about shifting their main location of residence back to the country overseas. The longer they had stayed away in the first place the more difficult is the process of reintegration. In contrast, others stand firm and assert the legitimacy of their belonging. In an effort to counter what they view as a mis-representation of their identity and the suggestion of otherness and non-belonging in their own home country, the returnees recount stories that attest to their heroism in the face of what they endured in the migration experience standing up to the white man.

PARADOXES OF FREEDOM AND CONSTRAINT IN THE CONSEQUENCES OF CARIBBEAN MIGRATION

The very culture of migration, and the accepted norms associated with it, produce the consequences — positive and negative — of the movements themselves. In that migration is an ongoing process in the Caribbean, deeply embedded in the mind-set of all — whatever the gender, ethnicity or social class — influencing the lives and livelihoods of those who go and those who stay, it could not be without fundamental and lasting implications.

Whatever scholars or policy makers may interpret to be the reason for migration, there are so many specifics to the picture that the more important issue is the extent to which it is interpreted as an event in the life of an individual, or a way of life that incorporates many strategies for survival and support for mobility. Migration creates a mosaic comprised of a complex pattern of movement of persons and all forms of capital in various directions in a network of interactions. If this were not so, there would be a distinct start and finish in terms of time, place and individual. The reasons would be straightforward and simple and the impact direct. But for many migrations, there is no start or finish. Migration perpetuates itself leading to the movement of other persons, and for each individual it leads to ever-changing relationships with the external world and evolving forms of transnationality. These forms of transnationality provide the framework within which the non-migrant is also affected. The transnational space that evolves is continually in process, leading to new but changing horizons both within a single generation and with inter-generational continuity. This is reflected in the transnational nature of livelihoods and identities at the individual level as also the transnational nature of households, families and communities and entire island states and cultures at all levels.

The loss of human capital through emigration is not only experienced in the health and education systems through current high levels of nurse and teacher migration, but it is part of a wider depletion of human capital from the region as from other regions of the South (Sives et. al. 2007; Thomas-Hope 2001). More significant than that, it is part of a migration that perpetuates itself. Teachers, nurses and other young professionals take full advantage of the freedoms of the migration opportunities, and the cultural norms of the society offer few constraints on the creation of livelihoods that span two countries. Ironically, the migration of some workers creates the very situations, such as staff shortages, that nurses and teachers claim exacerbates the poor working conditions that they view as being unsatisfactory and likely to cause their own migration. In addition, the apparent success of the migration of those who go, and the stories they tell while they are living abroad, are usually remarkably positive and typically contain no significant reports of alienation, victimization or racialized exclusionary categorizations of otherness at the destination.

The predominantly positive personal reports of migration, accompanied by the material symbols of success, the building of the networks of friends, relatives and even professional colleagues, all help to perpetuate the movement and to facilitate the navigation of the migration landscape. Newly arriving migrants move into the same neighbourhoods as those of their friends and family, and nurses and teachers obtain employment in the same hospitals and schools as those of their predecessors. Additionally, the social construction of the return migrant as outsider designed to guard positions in the local labour force, reduces the contribution that return migrants can make. This leads to the irony of those who had not migrated guarding the very jobs that they will later vacate when they themselves have the opportunity to go.

Similar contradictions occur within the family. Children are left behind with relatives when their parents migrate as part of the very societal system that encourages them to do so in order to provide for the material requirements of the family. Society's prioritizing of migration over and above almost all else, including the responsibilities of daily parental supervision and interaction, lies in stark contradiction to the need of material resources for their survival, which frequently falls upon the single mother in the Caribbean family. The societal freedoms, including the family and gender roles and responsibilities that allow parents to go abroad as the solution to constraints at home, themselves become part of the problem.

ORGANIZATION OF THIS VOLUME

This collection brings together perspectives of intra-Caribbean and extra-Caribbean movements, so that some of the variability as well as the commonality in the cultures of migration and the Diaspora are demonstrated. These perspectives are presented within the context of freedom and constraint encountered across the migration landscape. The relatively high level of freedom at the source in terms of the social norms and accommodation of outward movement are followed by the challenges of navigating the complexities of the migration landscape in the countries of destination. Bridging national borders in the development of transnational livelihoods based on a pattern of single or multiple return, requires the negotiation of yet more freedoms and constraints consequent upon the constructions of the identity of self and the language of 'otherness' on the return. Finally, it is proposed that what are commonly regarded as the impacts of migration are inherently part of the paradoxes and contradictions in the freedoms and constraints of the migration culture.

Section I is comprised of chapters that demonstrate the centrality of race and the racialization of migrants in the varied constructions of the 'foreigner' and the 'other'. The meaning and implications of race, mediated by class and the homeward orientation of the intended return, are reflected in the variability of the Diaspora and raises the issue of the heterogeneity of migrants as well as of migration experience in different Diaspora situations. This determines the identity and thus the freedom of migrants to negotiate their position, as in the case of Curaçao shown by Rose Mary Allen. The social distance resulting from the identity of foreigner versus Curaçaoan was the basis of policies that shaped the opportunities or freedoms of foreign workers in general. The negative image of the Haitian migrants in Curaçao and similarly in the case of Guadeloupe, as demonstrated by Marie-Gabrielle Hadey-Saint-Louis, was also determined by the legacy of racio-ethnic characterization of Haitian migrants in the past and even up to the present time. The constraints that Haitians face to migrating legally has led to the undocumented nature of much of their movement within and from the region and this reinforces the often low social status with which they are identified. This has greatly constrained the freedoms of the migrants and the cultural impact in their region. In contrast, the positive racial images of 'Latin' migrants lead to easy accommodation of persons from the Dominican Republic in Curaçao as also demonstrated in relation to Venezuelans in Trinidad and Tobago, the theme of the chapter by Michele Reis. The student status and 'Latin' ethnic identity provides freedoms to settle and acculturate, but raise other issues because of their desirability from a gendered perspective — also on account of their Latin ethnicity — to work in clubs as dancers and as commercial sex workers.

While negative images reduce the freedom of negotiation at the destination, Kathleen Valtonen discusses ways in which civil society can provide avenues for the migrants accumulating social capital, and thereby negating some of the stigma associated with their identity as foreigners. Political affiliation provides an example of the use of civil society in the acquisition of social capital, which is then used to negotiate the place of the migrants in the society. The constructions of race in the Metropolitan localities of the Caribbean Diaspora are demonstrated by Carol Archer in relation to Caribbean migrants in New York City, and the ways in which they use the political system to attempt to change the landscape of power and obtain greater freedoms in the host society.

The linkages maintained with the home society and family are critical in providing support to the migrants abroad. This plays a major role in compensating for the negative effects of the migration experience, the internalization of the hostilities embedded in their racialization and construction by the host society as 'outsider' or 'other', together with lack of social capital in the new location. The case studies of persons diagnosed with schizophrenia in Birmingham, UK, discussed by Hilary Robertson-Hickling and Frederick Hickling, highlight the problems that arise at the personal level. This situation was compounded by the misinterpretation of the individuals' behaviours leading to mis-diagnosis and inappropriate treatment that removed their freedom in the society on a permanent basis.

Grappling with identity and belonging reflects many of the contradictions and the paradoxes of race as vividly shown in Andrea Levy's novels discussed by Kim Robinson. The effects of immigration on the lives of the characters in the novels – both of the immigrant and those of 'small-island mentality' with whom they interacted in post-World War II Britain — led to the hybridization of British culture that was testimony to the restricted social freedom, and thus to many painful experiences of those who were part of the process.

In contrast, the confidence of those for whom their racialization and ethnic identity are mediated by their upper middle class status, together with the psychological freedom from racialization based on their homeward orientation and intended return, is discussed in relation to a group of Jamaican students in the USA by Mikaila Brown. Their own sense of identity runs counter to that from the perspective of young African-Americans of similar educational background.

Marcia Burrowes presents the narratives of returned Barbadians of their experiences in Britain in the 1950s and 60s, focusing on the ways in which they dealt with the treatment they received in relation to how otherness was socially constructed in the UK. However, on their subsequent return to Barbados, ironically, they had to re-claim their place and belonging in the very country, their homeland, with which they had been identified as they suffered the indignities of racial exclusion abroad. This is followed by a chapter by Dwaine Plaza and Frances Henry which gives an overview of return migration, highlighting the context of transnationalism within which the return takes place, and the incorporation of the wider society in its morphology and consciousness.

The eleven chapters of Section II highlight paradoxes of the freedoms and constraints of Caribbean migration viewed from the perspective of some of its attendant impacts and implications, themselves embedded in the migration culture.

The need for counselling of children who were part of transnational families with parents resident abroad is highlighted by Audrey Pottinger, Angela Gordon Stair and Sharon Williams Brown. A further negative circumstance of the migration process is the deportation of migrants, even those who are legal residents in the destination country. The removal of freedom inherent in the involuntary return of persons to their country of birth is, as already pointed out, a situation not confined to the deportation of persons from the USA, but occurring at a number of locations within the Caribbean itself. Clifford Griffin's chapter on the de-integration of Caribbean persons deported from the USA and their re-integration into their 'home' society is conditioned by the criminalization inherent in the social constructions of these migrants. This is followed by Suzette Martin Johnson's discussion on the role of civil society in the reintegration process of persons deported from the USA to Jamaica and the Dominican Republic. She discusses the stigma that leads to their suffering the effects of otherness in the country of their birth, to which they have been involuntarily returned and, therefore, without the social capital necessary for their proper reintegration.

Simultaneously the depletion and accumulation of material and human capital are paradoxes of migration evident in the sending of remittances by migrants abroad, and the loss of human capital due to the emigration of professionals and other skilled persons from the Caribbean. Remittances as material proceeds of migration are an important source of foreign exchange for Caribbean countries. Remittances are the themes of the following three chapters. Mark Figueroa places remittance behaviour within the framework of different types of migration. Ransford Palmer examines the remittance profile of Jamaican migrants in the USA, demonstrating the change that takes place based on length of stay at the destination, and discusses its impact on economic growth. Amani Ishemo takes a micro-level approach to the evaluation of remittances, focusing on the changes that occur in terms of small farm management and its role in maintaining the viability of farming under the challenging conditions of poor infrastructure and recurrent environmental hazards relating to flooding and landslides and limited financial resources.

The emigration of human resources, especially of the skilled and highly trained, is the theme of the next two chapters. An assessment of the impact of the migration from Jamaica is made by Pauline Knight, Easton Williams and Steven Kerr, who demonstrate the extent of the emigration of persons with tertiary level educational qualifications. In the following chapter, Natasha Mortley demonstrates some of the circumstances surrounding the migration of nurses and its impact with special reference to Jamaica and St. Lucia.

Discourses of what the solutions might be relate to the need for policies to manage, or at least mitigate, the negative aspects of migration. Policy thus becomes a resource in attempting to identify ways of maximizing the benefits and minimizing the costs of migration at the level of the state. Jason Jackson raises the possibilities for turning loss into gain in terms of human resources in the context of comparisons with Asian cases of economic success. The development of policies at the regional level between states of the CARICOM Single Market and Economy (CSME) is shown by Sophia Whyte Givans to be faced with the challenge of promoting the freedom of movement of desirable migrants, and strengthening the constraints to movement of the undesirable. The final chapter, by Peter Jordens, raises critical policy issues of migration within the current era of neoliberal economic and political structures.

CONCLUSION

The chapters comprising this volume address issues relating to the freedom and constraints of Caribbean migration within the context of the heterogeneous nature of the meaning and culture of migration. This is associated with the heterogeneity of Caribbean Diasporas; the various identities associated with race, mediated by class, gender, nationality as well as the homeward orientation and social capital of the migrants individually and collectively. The impacts and implications of migration are reflected in both the depletion and accumulation of capital of various kinds, the solving of problems and, at the same time the creation of others. The freedom inherent in transnationalism and return migration coexists with the challenges of reincorporation into the migrant's country of birth. These all reflect the intense contradictions inherent in the freedoms and constraints of migration and the paradoxes whereby the one masks the other.

Migration and the associated shifts in livelihood and identity, marginality and centrality, provide a critical perspective on cultural formation. This underlines the themes of Diaspora. The dispersal of cultures associated with contemporary migration is in contrast to the overarching themes of post-colonialism, namely that of the nation state, identities determined by marginality and centre, and the hegemony of metropolitan cultures. Migration merges and blends the individual and corporate identities based on these constructs, creating new ones that are more consistent with the hybrid cultures of post-colonialism, not only in the global periphery but also at the Metropolitan centres.

The extent to which the present-day migrants are victims of the post-colonial story or also producers of the modern cultures and societies of North America and Europe, as well as that of the Caribbean region itself, raises issues concerning the freedoms and constraints of migration and the landscapes that the migrants have and continue to navigate and change. These migration landscapes are both extra-regional and intra-regional and continue to be the reflection of modern Caribbean societies in continuing transition. By raising issues such as these, one situates the Caribbean in relation to globalization in such a way that the heterogeneity of the migrations and Diasporas can be seen, and the part played by migration better understood in terms of the specifics of place and historical experience. In so doing one highlights the centrality of migration, its paradoxes and contradictions in the ongoing dynamic of Caribbean cultural formation and change.

REFERENCES

Byron, Margaret. 2005. 'Expanding Narratives of Emigration and Return'. In *Caribbean Narratives of Belonging*, eds. Karen Fog Olwig and Jean Besson, 206-221. London: Macmillan.

Carr, Barry. 2003. 'Identity, Class, and Nation: Black Immigrant Workers, Cuban Communism, and the Sugar Insurgency, 1925-1934'. In *Marginal Migrations: The Circulation of Cultures within the Caribbean*, ed. Shalini Puri, 78-108. London: Macmillan.

Chambers, I. 1994. *Migrancy, Culture, Identity*. London: Routledge.

Cordero-Guzman, Hector R., Robert C. Smith, and Ramon Grosfoguel, eds. 2001. *Migration, Transnationalization and Race in a Changing New York*. Philadelphia: Temple University Press.

Frederick, Rhonda D. 2003. 'Mythologies of Panama Canal Migrations: Eric Walrond's *Tropic Death*'. In *Marginal Migrations: The Circulation of Cultures within the Caribbean*, ed. Shalini Puri, 43-76. London: Macmillan.

Guarnizo, Luis Eduardo and Michael Peter Smith. 1999. 'The Locations of Transnationalism'. In *Transnationalism From Below*, ed. Michael Peter Smith and Luis Eduardo Guarnizo, 3-34. New Brunswick, New Jersey: Transaction Publishers.

Ho, Christine. 1999. 'Caribbean Transnationalism as a Gendered Process'. *Latin American Perspectives* 26, 5:34-54.

Ho, Christine and Nurse, Keith. 2005. *Globalization, Diaspora and Caribbean Popular Culture.* Kingston: Ian Randle Publishers.

Lamming, George. 1983. *In the Castle of My Skin.* New York: Schocken Books.

Mitchell, K. 1993. 'Multiculturalism or the United Colors of Capitalism?', *Antipode,* 25:263-94.

Nyberg Sorensen, Ninna and Olwig, Karen Fog. 2002. 'Introduction'. In *Work and Migration: Life and Livelihoods in a Globalizing World,* eds. Ninna Nyberg Sorensen and Karen Fog Olwig London and New York: Routledge.

Olwig, Karen Fog. 2007. *Caribbean Journeys: An Ethnography of Migration and Home in Three Family Networks.* Durham: Duke University Press.

Ong, A. 1999. *Flexible Citizenship: The Cultural Logics of Transnationality.* Durham: Duke University Press.

Plaza, D. and F. Henry, eds. 2006. *Returning to the Source: The Final Stage of the Caribbean Migration Circuit.* Kingston, Jamaica: University of the West Indies Press.

Puri, Shalini, ed. 2003. 'Introduction: Theorizing Diasporic Cultures: The Quiet Migrations'. In *Marginal Migrations: The Circulation of Cultures within the Caribbean,* ed. Shalini Puri, 1-16. London: Macmillan.

Said, Edward. 1993. *Culture and Imperialism.* London: Chatto and Windus.

Sives, Amanda, John Morgan, Simon Appleton, and Raquel Bremmer 2006. 'Teacher Migration from Jamaica: Assessing the Short-Term Impact', *Caribbean Journal of Education,* 27, 1: 85-116.

Skeldon, Ronald. 1997. *Migration and Development: A Global Perspective.* London: Longman.

Thomas-Hope, Elizabeth. 1978. 'The Establishment of a Migration Tradition: British West Indian Movements to the Hispanic Caribbean in the Century after Emancipation', in *Caribbean Social Relations,* Colin G. Clarke, ed. Liverpool, University of Liverpool, Centre for Latin American Studies, Monograph Series, no. 8, 66 – 81.

———. 1993. 'Small Island Environments and International Migration: The Caribbean' *Scottish Geographic Magazine,* 109, 3:142-151.

———. 'Caribbean Skilled International Migration and the Transnational Household', *Geoforum,* 19, 4: 423-32.

————. 1995. 'Island Systems and the Paradox of Freedom: Migration in the Post-Emancipation Leeward Islands', in *Small Islands, Large Questions: Society, Culture and Resistance in the Post-Emancipation Caribbean,* ed. K. Fog Olwig, 161-179. London: Frank Cass.

————. 1998. 'Globalization and the Development of a Caribbean Migration Culture.' In *Globalized Identities,* ed. Mary Chamberlain, 188-200. London: Routledge.

————. 2001. *Skilled Labour Migration from Developing Countries: The Caribbean Case.* Geneva: International Labour Organization (ILO).

————. 2002. 'Transnational Livelihoods and Identities in Return Migration to the Caribbean; The Case of Skilled Returnees to Jamaica', in *Work and Migration: Life and Livelihoods in a Globalizing World,* eds. Ninna Nyberg Sorensen and Karen Fog Olwig, 187-201. London and New York: Routledge.

————. 2005. 'Caribbean Migration and the Transnationalization of Social Capital', in *Le Monde Caribe: Défis et Dynamiques* Vol I *Visions Identitaires, Diasporas, Configurations Culturelles* ed. Christian Lerat, 337-353. Bordeaux: Maison des Sciences de l'Homme d' Aquitaine.

————. 2006. 'Maximizing Migration: Caribbean Return Movements and the Organization of Transnational Space', in *Returning to the Source: The Final Stage of the Caribbean Migration Circuit,* eds. Dwaine Plaza and Frances Henry, 167-187. Kingston, Jamaica: University of the West Indies Press,

Walrond, Eric. 1954. *Tropic Death.* New York: Collier Books.

SECTION I

*Social Constructions of Race and Identity
in the Experience and Culture of Migration
and the Diaspora*

1

MIGRANTS VERSUS THE *YU DI KÒRSOU*:
Race, Class and Identity in Curaçaoan Society

ROSE MARY ALLEN

INTRODUCTION

This chapter investigates Curaçaoan culture and the role that migration has played in shaping it. It looks at the ways in which Curaçaoan identity is affirmed in the discourses on who is and who is not considered a *Yu di Kòrsou* (translated as *Child of Curaçao*). The late Curaçaoan sociologist, René Römer, linked the question of cultural identity in Curaçao to the concept of *Yu di Kòrsou*. The concept of *Yu di Kòrsou* is present in the discourses about the cultural impact of the immigrant groups (both those in the past and the newly arrived) on the island. By the end of the twentieth century Curaçao began to play an important role in the present-day intra-regional migration. There has been a large increase in immigrants from societies such as Haiti, the Dominican Republic, Jamaica, Guyana, and Colombia. At the same time, Curaçaoans have emigrated in large numbers to the Netherlands due to the deteriorating economic situation, some of whom are currently returning. Finally, two key issues are addressed in the investigation of Curaçaoan culture: the discussions on cultural differences of the emigrants in Curaçaoan society, and how these discussions contribute to Curaçaoan identity.

'These foreigners are living as pigs together.'
'They are grabbing all our jobs.'
'They don't want to learn our language.'
'Latin American women are snatching away all our men.'

'They want to take over our island.'
'All Colombians are hit men.'

These are just a few expressions presently heard in Curaçaoan society regarding the new immigrants who have established themselves on the island.[1] They show the existing public perceptions about these newcomers in terms of their alleged involvement in criminality, labour market competition with the locals, as well as intra-ethnic female rivalry between local and new immigrant women.

Immigration is a complex phenomenon and has great impact on the demography, economy, politics and culture of the receiving as well as on the sending society (Meyers 2000, 1245). While each of these considerations warrants certain scholarly attention, this chapter looks at one neglected aspect: the continuing role of intra-Caribbean migration in the construction of cultural identities in the region. The Curaçaoan situation is used as a case study.[2] Being both a recipient as well as exporter of migrant labour over the past century, Curaçaoans have been in contact with people coming from all the language areas in the Caribbean.

The Curaçaoan case shows the dynamics of cultural formation and transformation that arises from movements of people without and within society. Intra-Caribbean migration research has yet to focus much more attention on the islands with a Dutch colonial history. In this chapter I examine how the discussions on cultural differences of contemporary migrants in Curaçaoan society today contribute to the reaffirmation of Curaçaoan identity and have delineated the ideal of being Curaçaoan. The data for this study derive among others from radio talk shows, newspaper clippings and editorials.[3]

First, a short overview is presented of the migration movements to and from Curaçao over the past 150 years. Next, the characteristics of contemporary Caribbean migration are compared with that underway at the beginning of the twentieth century. The third section analyses how the contemporary discourse about immigrants continues to redefine who is and who is not Curaçaoan. The conclusion offers broader remarks on the relevance of immigration for shaping contemporary cultural identity on the island.

EMIGRATION AND IMMIGRATION IN CURAÇAOAN SOCIETY

In a pattern similar to other Caribbean societies, migration is also rooted in Curaçaoan history. It is an event in which elites and non-elites, women as well as men, have fully participated. After emancipation from slavery in 1863, Curaçaoans joined the labour force of other Caribbean people (freed in even earlier decades), who followed work opportunities throughout the region. This was especially evident in the late nineteenth and early twentieth centuries. In semi-arid Curaçao climate also played a role in migration. Migration increased in periods when there was little rainfall. Migrants went to the Dominican Republic but also to mainland circum-Caribbean countries such as Venezuela, Panama, Colombia, Costa Rica and Suriname (van Soest 1977, 20; Koot 1979, 44, 54; Dekker 1982, 98; Pietersz 1985). Cuba was the destination of the last massive migration. Between 1917 and 1921, fifty per cent of the male labour force left Curaçao temporarily to work in the Cuban sugarcane fields (Paula 1973).

The long-standing pattern of intra-regional emigration that had characterized Curaçao changed in the mid-twentieth century to one of immigration to the island. The establishment of the oil-company in 1915 created ancillary economic activities, which made Curaçao a destination for migrants seeking employment. These workers came from Venezuela, the Netherlands, Portugal and Madeira and Suriname. Migrants from other parts of the globe also arrived. These included Syrians, Jews from Eastern Europe, Indians and Chinese. Their principal economic activity was commerce. Caribbean workers were also imported to supply the oil company. They initially came from the Dutch West Indies and later, the British West Indies.[4] A noticeable aspect in the British West Indian immigration to the island was the large group of young women who came to do domestic work after the 1940s. These women were known as the so-called '*sleep-in maids*' as they worked and lived in the homes of the (principally Dutch) staff of the oil-company and members of the traditional elites who were specialized in commerce.

When economic opportunities declined in the 1950s, the (principally) male migrants with their families returned to their countries of origin. Some of the British West Indian female migrants remained working in the homes of some families on the island; they are now senior citizens.

Curaçao continued to play a very important role in the intra-regional migration by the end of the twentieth century. The last immigration to Curaçao from the rest of the Caribbean region actually took place during the international migration of Curaçaoans to the Netherlands. Many Curaçaoans were affected by the severe economic crisis coupled with high rates of unemployment on the island. The wave of migration to the Netherlands started in 1998 and reached a peak in 2000, when 13,867 people left the island to settle there (Maduro 2003:2).[5]

At the same time, workers from other Caribbean islands were drawn to Curaçao as a result of the comparatively better economic conditions and greater employment opportunities compared to their own countries. They arrived on tourist visas, seeking work and overstaying the period allowed to them and eventually continuing as illegal immigrants on the island.[6]

Eytan Meyers[7] identifies two ways to see the migration policies that shaped foreign workers in general. The first concerns the rules and procedures that regulate the admission of foreign workers. The second way is to examine the work and housing policies that govern the conditions under which resident immigrants were assimilated into the broader society (Meyers 2000:1246). When comparing the intra-Caribbean migrations to Curaçao at the beginning of the twentieth century with that at its end, one significant point can be made, which is the shift from legal to illegal migration among immigrants. The second perspective identifies the lack of proper conditions for employment and workers rights as well as appropriate housing. By the century's end, few rules guide the presence of undocumented migrants on the island. As a result there are not many legal procedures to guide their rights as workers. Figure 1 shows that recent immigrants are principally illegal, unlike those who arrived on worker contracts earlier in the twentieth century.

Figure 1.1
Comparison of immigration characteristics in contemporary
Curaçao with that of the beginning twentieth century

Migration beginning twentieth century	Migration end twentieth century
Legality of entry, residence and work	General legal entry, illegality of residence and work
Some social and legal rights; Work in the oil company and oil refinery and related companies	No social and legal rights Dispersed work areas

Because many are undocumented, there is little data on the numbers, or working and living conditions of these new immigrants. People disagree about their number. Sometimes the debate on numbers is used to stir emotion and to indicate how big the problem is. This again has an influence on the perceptions of people and the actions by the government to take more stringent measures for dealing with undocumented immigrants. While it is not possible to give an exact data of their number, estimates for the non-documented range between 5,000 and 10,000. Most of these migrants come from the Dominican Republic, Colombia, Haiti, and Jamaica and are unskilled labourers.

Table 1.1 gives an overview of the different nationalities living in Curaçao at the time when the census was taken in 2001. Those falling under the category of Dutch nationality are both Dutch people born in the Netherlands and those born on the islands of the Netherlands Antilles and Aruba. Among people of other nationalities there are some who are undocumented, as during the census no question was asked whether they had a legal residence permit or not.

Table 1.1: Total population by nationality, age group and sex in Curaçao in 2001

Nationality	0 – 14			15 - 64			65+			Total		
	Male	Female	Total	Male	Female	Total	Male	Female	Total	Male	Female	Total
Chinese	44	23	67	118	108	226	7	7	14	169	138	307
Colombian	106	110	216	327	887	1,214	7	21	28	440	1,018	1,458
Dominican Republic	154	181	335	368	1,382	1,750	9	45	54	531	1,608	2,139
Guyanese	16	16	32	60	84	144	1	-	1	77	100	177
Haitian	27	26	53	215	183	398	3	4	7	245	213	458
Indian	28	27	55	144	114	258	5	4	9	177	145	322
Jamaican	34	43	77	54	284	338	-	3	3	88	330	418
Dutch	14,928	14,372	29,300	36,515	42,495	79,010	5,708	7,891	13,599	57,151	64,758	121,909
Portuguese	22	22	44	146	155	301	71	77	148	239	254	493
Suriname	40	49	89	155	165	320	5	7	12	200	221	421
American (U.S.)	34	26	60	58	74	132	6	18	24	98	118	216
English (U.K.)	3	4	7	27	36	63	8	29	37	38	69	107
Venezuelan	78	86	164	246	289	535	21	29	50	345	404	749
Others	57	43	100	298	310	608	30	51	81	385	404	789
Not reported	96	98	194	200	210	410	30	30	60	326	338	664
Total	15,667	15,126	30,793	38,931	46,776	85,707	5,911	8,216	14,127	60,509	70,118	130,627

Source: *Population and Housing Census 2001, Central Bureau of Statistics, Netherlands Antilles*

Table 1.2 compares the increase in the two census years of the number of household heads from the countries in the Caribbean, where most undocumented migrants come from. As these are census data, it is not possible to determine whether these are documented people or not.

Table 1.2: Place of birth head of household 1992 and 2001

Place of birth	1992	2001	Increase in percentage
Colombia	259	545	110.4%
Dominican Republic	837	1,322	57.9%
Haiti	33	221	569.6%
Jamaica	17	134	688.2%

Source: *Population and Housing Census 2001 and 1992, Central Bureau of Statistics of the Netherlands Antilles*

A better view of the number could be gathered based on the registration done in 2002, when the lieutenant governor instituted a period in which people with an undocumented status could apply for an official residence permit on the island. The reason why most came to the island was in search for work. Another motive was family reunion.

Table 1.3: An overview of the top 10 registered nationalities with undocumented status

Nationality	Total	Labour	Other motives
Haiti	1,798	1,743	55
Colombia	1,539	1,305	233
Dominican Republic	1,295	1,161	134
Jamaica	752	641	110
Venezuela	560	183	273
Suriname	392	151	238
Guyana	205	153	52
China	65	58	7
Ecuador	24	24	0
India	19	18	1
Total	6,649	5,254	865

Source: *Rapportage IT & Plaatselijk hoofd van Politie 26/ 11/ 2002*

The legal status of an estimated 10,000 of the new immigrants remains an unresolved but major problem on the island. The fact that these migrants are undocumented is also reflected in the discourses and opinions expressed about them in talk shows and newspaper editorials. They are accused of taking away jobs, adding to the cost of medical care when they are ill and, as some of them also produce children, they are believed to impact the educational sector.[8] However, these discourses express other underlying ideologies that refer to issues that go beyond their status as undocumented immigrants. There are also discussions on how Curaçaoans, especially Afro-Curaçaoans, view otherness and how they make space for other Caribbean people in their society.

INTRA-CARIBBEAN MIGRATION: WE VERSUS THEM

Traditional social studies on migration focus on the high levels of labour migration that occur from less developed nations to wealthier ones, such as the European countries, the United States and Canada (Pastor 1985). The impact of these migrations on developed countries are analyzed in several studies that address assimilation and integration (Chamberlain 1995, Thomas-Hope 1992, 1998). With regard to the migration from the Caribbean to the Netherlands, there are also several studies describing the migration processes and related problems which have taken place there. In the beginning these studies dealt with the social processes of integration of the Surinamese group, which were the first from the Caribbean to settle in the Netherlands in the years before their independence in 1975 (Bovenkerk 1987; Oostindie 1988). With the current influx of people of the Dutch Antilles to the Netherlands, research and debates are now addressing the complexity of inter-ethnic relationships resulting from this and the integration process, especially of young Curaçaoan males in Dutch society (Van Hulst 1993, 1997; Muskens 2005).[9]

Against this background of migration from Curaçao to the Netherlands, there are comparatively few migration studies that examine similar issues within the Caribbean and specifically, from other islands to Curaçao. This is significant for several reasons. There is a long-standing tradition of intra-Caribbean labour migration to Curaçao. Understanding its historical context offers the possibility to illuminate a broader understanding of race, class, and identity within the island. The process of social acceptance of Caribbean immigrants to Curaçao promises to inform a more general theorization of how these issues influence the construction of identity in black-majority societies in the Caribbean. In most cases the development of identity and culture in the Caribbean is analysed within the complexity of inter-ethnic group relationship of the nineteenth century, but neglects the role of inter-Caribbean immigration in this totality.

At one level Curaçaoan society shows similarities to what is observe for the rest of Caribbean. While Curaçao was not a monoculture plantation society, it certainly shares features characteristic of the slave societies defined by Elsa Goveia for the English-speaking Caribbean. The historical basis for Curaçao dates to the seventeenth century, when various ethnic groups settled on the island. They established a firm hierarchical social order based on race, class, gender and culture. In the eighteenth and nineteenth centuries the top eschelon of the society was dominated by white Protestant and Jewish slave masters; at the bottom there were enslaved Blacks. In between were the free descendants of the offspring of these two groups. This diversity, as elsewhere in the Caribbean, left a national identity that remains complex throughout the region. In the twentieth century Curaçao even became more culturally and ethnically complex due to the large influx of migrants to the island.

The sociologists Harry Hoetink and René Römer, who were the first to have examined the sociocultural complexity of Curaçao, have linked the island's cultural identity to the concept of a segmented society. By this they mean a society that consists of several groups of people of different races and cultures, each with its own social institutions and rank in the societal structure, even though the whole is governed by just one of these groups. Skin colour and ethnic descent determined the socio-economic power and position of different social groups in the society. This has for long characterized the interaction between the island's social groups as well.

The Curaçaoan philosopher and sociologist Alejandro Paula takes this discussion a step further by analysing the effect of race, colonialism and class on Afro-Curaçaoan self-perception. Paula describes an Afro-Curaçaoan identity that is shaped by an internalization of standards for self-judgment that white elites set forth as norms over time for subordinate groups. In this way, he argues, the particular group developed negative perceptions of self-judgment. The process resulted in the deep-seated internalization of social inferiority, which extends to Afro-Curaçaoan culture and cultural identity (*Paula* 1967, 31-32). The anthropologists Valdemar Marcha and Paul Verweel (2003) describe how this type of inferiority leads to 'a culture of fear'. What they mean is a reticence to express contrary views and to assert one's own cultural identity and that of others considered subordinate. In their view, this process of internalizing inferiority is an instrument of prevailing power relations that is integral in the process of socialization and that is transmitted from old to young, generation through generation.

Intra-Caribbean migration has unfolded within this social hierarchy and matrix of self-perception; a process that now has complicated and still complicates social acceptance, especially of Caribbean immigrants in the society.

Chamberlain (1995) has drawn attention to another important feature of migration. Aside from moving across geographical borders, migration calls into question the patriotic basis of identity. She referred in particular to the people who are leaving their countries. However, her statement is also applicable for those living in the places where the migrants are settling themselves. Migration sets in motion the search for an answer by both the migrants, as well as the population of the receiving country, to the questions posed the most in affirming identity which are: Who are we and who do we want to be?

The great influx of migrants to Curaçao that took place in the beginning of the twentieth century led to both social and cultural changes. The society became more ethnically and culturally diverse than it had ever been before. The black, white and mixed race people of Curaçao witnessed an influx of South Asians, Chinese, Middle Easterners and Caribbean Blacks and new religious expressions. Thus began the broader discussion of who is an authentic Curaçaoan and the popular term *Yu di Kòrsou* became one to mark who belonged to the island and who did not (Römer, 1974:49-60; Marks, 1976;

Eikrem, 1999, Benjamin 2002). In particular the Afro-Curaçaoans have used this term *Yu di Kòrsou* to demarcate themselves from the other ethnic groups in the society. In popular discourse, the term *Yu di Kòrsou* distinguish them from the other ethnic categories such as the Jewish group and the Dutch who also shared a long history in the society (Römer, 1974: 53, Oostindie, 1996: 223, Benjamin, 2002).[10]

With the arrival of immigrants in Curaçao, the popular discourse on who is the authentic Curaçaoan continued to be conceptualized in the term *Yu di Kòrsou*. Now it became one applied to exclude those newly arriving immigrants. Curaçaoans again used ethnic and racial categories to parallel the longstanding segmented character of their society. It infiltrated the discourse surrounding the acceptance of new immigrants by the local population; it also mediated the way migrants were accepted. It certainly operated to regulate the social esteem accorded to migrants who at times differed in phenotype, language, religious practices and beliefs. Regarding the migrants coming from the English-speaking islands of the Caribbean, this discourse on identity and its assimilation of these immigrants include the issue of race and culture, by which Curaçaoans assert their cultural primacy and place themselves in opposition to twentieth-century Caribbean migrants. Especially the early twentieth-century migrants coming from the English-speaking Caribbean were often poor and of the black working class, and some of whom did the most menial and inferior work and therefore occupied the lowest tier of the island's existing class-colour stratification.

The flow of contemporary migrants from the rest of the Caribbean to Curaçao has again sparked the discourse of the *Yu di Kòrsou* versus the non-*Yu di Kòrsou*. Once again we see that these poor immigrants also figure in a renewal of the process of redefining the *Yu di Kòrsou* concept. Public opinion labels these migrants, who come predominantly from the Caribbean, as being culturally different and their cultural influence as negative. The contemporary discourse is being expressed and reinforced in the media, through editorials and talk shows. The effect is to reinforce social differences between them and us: the *Yu di Kòrsou* and the non-*Yu di Kòrsou*. These are all demarcations produced by locals to formalize division and to claim authenticity on the Curaçaoan identity.

These discourses offer a paradoxical view of the society as well. The migrants from Haiti on one hand experience some acceptance by the host-society, as they are considered enterprising, strong work orientated, hard working, and willing to learn the Papiamentu language. On the other hand, they perform manual jobs which are not done by the locals. Their work in the host society has been termed *trabou di Haitiano* (Haitian work), which, over time, has come to have a low status connotation.

Skin colour differentiation is also an important criterion used to distinguish these migrants as well. Haitians are not racially distinguishably from most members of the host society. Nevertheless, they are considered primitive, black and ugly people. This paradox is also reflected in the approach of female migrants from the Dominican Republican. The discourse that evolves around them is being determined by race and ethnicity, but by gender as well. As these women approached the somatic ideal, there are liked in particular by the local males, who find them very attractive.[12] But at the same time, because of this preferential position, they are disliked by the local female population and seen as rivals.

There are some forms of cultural interaction as well. They manifest themselves in different areas of life. In the area of food, the so-called *aroz moro* (rice and peas) introduced by the people from the Dominican Republic is now available in all popular restaurants. In the area of music, the meringue and the bachata have become genres of music to be heard on the radio and elsewhere. People when confronting emotional problems would visit Haitians who are knowledgeable on the area of voodoo. These are just a few examples of the cultural influence which these migrants have on the society.

This cultural paradox expressed in the discourses and manifested in social behaviour towards migrants from other Caribbean countries also pose the question of Caribbeanness in Curaçao. It shows how Curaçaoans, predominantly those of African descent, perceive themselves and identify themselves as Caribbean people.

CONCLUSION

Migration is not just an economic issue. As presented earlier in this chapter, the sending and receiving characteristic of Curaçaoan society has reinforced greater contact with societies of different languages. It offers therefore a rare window through which the role of intra-regional migrations and cultural formation in the Caribbean can be studied. For the Caribbean migrants, emigration has meant — and stills means — questioning poverty and its historical roots in race and inequality. In that way they challenge existing institutions.

Also for the local population of Curaçao, migration means a confrontation with self. The discourse on migrants in Curaçao shows some parallel features with those in other places. For example, people believe that the presence of undocumented immigrants is a prime cause of the country's high unemployment rate and that they play an important role in the increase in crime, etc.

However, the fact that they are undocumented, is not only the main issue here. There is also the view of how the other is being seen and judged. In opposition to the migrant's issue in Europe, the 'other' in the Caribbean is not only judged by race, but by the shade of skin colour. It continues to play a very important role in the distinction and demarcation of who is Curaçaoan and who is not. For the purpose of comparative migration studies, the Curaçaoan case offers an interesting angle through which the constant constructing and reconstructing of culture in the Caribbean can be analyzed.

NOTES

1. An island of about 444 square kilometers, Curaçao is near the coast of Venezuela. Along with Aruba, Bonaire, St Maarten, St Eustatius and Saba it formed part of the Kingdom of the Netherlands. The three last-mentioned islands are situated near the island of Puerto Rico.

   In the Dutch part of the island of St Maarten migration of undocumented people is also a much discussed issue and therefore also needs special attention.

2. At the moment there are several talk shows on different radio stations to which people can call and express their opinions on different societal matters. The

arrival of the new migrants has been a recurring topic. However, the theme of undocumented migration warrants further in-depth research.

3. In this chapter, the British West Indian refers to the English-speaking Caribbean. The migration of this group came in different waves. The first one was in 1924 when 2,000 men came from Jamaica, Barbados and Haiti to help set up the oil company. The West Indian immigration came to a halt during the Depression years of 1930-1935, when immigration from the British West Indies temporarily stopped. During the Second World War, due to the increase need of oil by the Allied countries, again workers were imported.

4. These women were brought in by their employers, who were responsible for their work and residence permit. Oral history shows that these women often experienced vulnerable personal and work conditions. They were required to do any kind of work in the household day and night.

5. Caribbean undocumented workers were noted to have entered the United States as far back as the 1970s (*Pastor* 1985, 9).

6. Specialist in international immigration policy and author of *International Immigration Policy: a Theoretical and Comparative Analysis*. New York: Palgrave Macmillan, 2004.

7. Their children, who are born on the island and who are also undocumented, must receive school education. Another problem arises when an undocumented person dies and he or she must be buried by the state.

8. One third of young people under 45 migrated to the Netherlands for employment and for the better social security arrangements than they can obtain there. A section of this age group is unemployed and highly represented in the criminal justice system.

9. René Römer resisted this view in several of his publications and argued that, in Curaçaoan society, the Creole language Papiamentu is a central feature of Curaçaoan national identity, and the main social marker that distinguishes the 'Yu di Kòrsou' and non 'Yu di Kòrsou'. This distinction is socially inclusive as the language Papiamentu differs from other Caribbean Creole languages in that it is equally recognized and used as a medium of communication by all social classes. In this way, the intellectual discourse of being of Curaçao did not challenge the racial or economic legacy that shaped (and continues to shape), the island nation.

10. Hoetink introduced the term somatic distance, that is, the degree to which certain shade of skin colour and phenotypes are idealized as they match the dominant somatic norm image (*Oostindie* 1996:6).

RADIO PROGRAMMES

Perspektiva *Ilegalnan: kon nos pais ta atendenan'* Z-86, 15 March 2001.
Radioprogram van Radiostation Direct, Angelica Parris and Glen Thomas, 19 July 2002.
Ellen Maduro-Jeandor and Rose Mary Allen. Radioprogramma CBS, Z-86, 28 October
2002.

NEWSPAPERS

Nobo, 28 May 1997
Randy Neuman. Overheid, word wakker. *Amigoe*, August 25, 2006.
Velen aanhoudingen in illegalen controle. *Amigoe*, 5 January 2006
Overleden Jamaicaanse was illegaal op Curaçao. *Amigoe*,19 October 2007.

REFERENCES

Allen, R.M. 2001.*Ta Cuba mi ke bai. Testimonio di trahadónan ku a emigrá for di Kòrsou
bai Cuba na kuminsamentu di siglo XX.* Zaltbommel : ICS Nederland/Curaçao.
———. 2003. Acceptatie of uitsluiting. Enkele belangrijke invalshoeken voor de discussie
over beeldvorming over immigranten uit de region en over de Curaçaoënaars. In*:*
Allen, R.M., Coen Heijes, en Valdemar Marcha eds. *Emancipatie en acceptatie.
Curaçao en Curaçaoënaars. Beeldvorming en identiteit honderdveertig jaar na de slavernij.*
Amsterdam: Uitgeverij SWP, 72-90.
———. Coen Heijes, en Valdemar Marcha eds. 2003 *Emancipatie en Acceptatie. Curaçao
en Curaçaoënaars. Beeldvorming en Identiteit Honderdveertig jaar na de Slavernij.*
Amsterdam: Uitgeverij SWP.
Benjamin, A. 2002. *Jews of the Dutch Caribbean: Exploring Ethnic Identity on Curaçao.*
London: Routledge Harwood Anthropology.
Bovenkerk, F. 1987. 'Caribbean migration to the Netherlands : from elite to working
class'. In Barry Levine (ed.) *The Caribbean Exodus*, New York: Praeger, 204-13.
Bovenkerk, F., Mieke Komen en Yücel Yeoilgöz. 2003. *Multiculturaliteit in de
Strafrechtspleging,* Den Haag: Boom Juridische uitgevers.
CBS, Population and Housing Census 2001, Central Bureau of Statistics, Netherlands
Antilles, Curaçao.
Cross, M. and Hans Entzinger eds. 1988*, Lost Illusions. Caribbean Minorities in Britain
and the Netherlands.* London: Routledge.
Eikrem, O. November 1999. 'Contested identities. A study of ethnicity in Curaçao, the
Netherlands Antilles' Department of Social Anthropology, The Norwegian University
of Natural Science and Technology.

Heiligers, B. 2001. *Samenleven.* Curaçao.

Hoetink, H. 1958. *Het Patroon Van de oude Curaçaose Samenleving. Een Sociologische studie.* Assen: Van Gorcum [Reprinted in 1987, Amsterdam: Emmering.]

———. 1962. De Gespleten Samenleving in het Caribisch Gebied. Bijdrage tot de Sociologie der Rasrelaties in Gesegmenteerde Maatschappijen. Assen: Van Gorcum. 1962.

Hulst, H. van en Jeanette Bos, 1993. *Pan I Rèspèt = Brood en respect : aard en omvang van de criminaliteit van geïmmigreerde Curaçaose jongeren van 12-24 jaar in drie politieregio's in de periode 1989-1991.* Utrecht: onderzoeksbureau OKU.

Hulst, H. van. 1997. *Morgen bloeit het diabaas : de Antilliaanse volksklasse in de Nederlandse samenleving.* Amsterdam: Het Spinhuis.

Kempadoo, Kamala ed. 1999. *Sun, Sex and Gold. Tourism and Sex Work in the Caribbean.* Lanham, MD: Rowman and Littlefield Publishers, Inc.

Koot, Willem, Varina Tjon-A-Ten, Petrien Uniken Venema. 1986. 'Processes of ethnic identification among Surinamese children in the Netherlands'. In *The Caribbean in Europe: Aspects of the West Indian Experience in Britain, France, and the Netherlands,* London: Cass. 166-187.

Levine, B. 1987. *The Caribbean Exodus.* New York: Praeger.

Maduro-Jeandor, E. 2003. 'Met bijdragen van Francis Vierbergen en Mike Jacobs. Schets van de sociaal-economische situatie in de Nederlandse Antillen'. *Modus,* jrg.5, number 1, special edition.

Marcha, V. and Paul Verweel. 2003. *De cultuur van de angst. Paradoxale ketenen van angst en zwijgen op Curaçao.* Amsterdam: SWP.

Meyers, E. 2000. 'Theories of international immigration policy: a comparative analysis' *International Migration Review,* 2000.

Muskens, George, medew. van Suzanne Huender. 2005. Antillianenbeleid in zeven gemeenten, 2001-2004 : eindrapportage over de rijksbijdrageregeling Antillianengemeenten, opgesteld voor de Directie Coördinatie Integratie Minderheden van het Ministerie van Justitie. Doca Bureau.

Oostindie, G. Caribbean Migration to the Netherlands: a Journey to Disappointment. In Malcolm Cross and Hans Entzinger, eds. 1988. *Lost Illusions: Caribbean Minorities in Britain and the Netherlands.* London: Routledge. 54-72.

Paula, P. 1972. *From Objective to Subjective Social Barriers. A Historico-philosophical Analysis of Certain Negative Attitudes among the Negroid Population of Curaçao.* Curaçao: De Curaçaosche Courant.1972.

———. 1973. *Problemen rondom de emigratie van arbeiders uit de kolonie Curaçao naar Cuba, 1917-1937.* Curaçao: Centraal Historisch Archief.

Pastor, R. ed. 1985. *Migration and Development in the Caribbean: The Unexplored Connection.* Boulder, COL: Westview Press.

Pelligrino, Adela. 2000. *Trends in International Migration in Latin America and the Caribbean.* Oxford: Blackwell Publishers.

Philipps, A. 1988. 'Labour and migration in the Caribbean; Britsh West Indian domestic servants in Curaçao, 1940-1960' (Master's Thesis, University of Leiden).

Pietersz, Jorge A. 1985. *De Arubaanse arbeidsmigratie 1890-1930: drie studies* over *de trek van arbeiders* in het *Caraïbisch* gebied voor de *Tweede Wereldoorlo*g. Leiden: Caraïbische afdeling K.I.T.L.V.

Rapport deelname Nederlandse Antillen aan het Symposium on international migration in the Americas, San Jose, Costa Rica 4-6 september 2000; an expert group meeting on intra-regional migration, Port of Spain, Trinidad and Tobago, 9-10 november 2000. Willemstad, Permanente Commissie voor Bevolkingsvraagstukken, Population Unit.

Rapòrt integral pa barionan di Kòrsou; plan di urgensha i kontinuidat/Integrale ontwikkeling van de Curaçaose buurten: urgentieplan en voor continuïteit. 2001. Grupo di Konsulta Tripartite, Barionan, base pa un nashon. Curaçao.

Römer, R. 'Het 'wij' van de Curaçoënaar'. *Kristòf* 1, no. 2 (1974) 49-60.

———. *Un pueblo na kaminda. Een sociologisch historische studie van de Curaçaose samenleving.* Zutphen: De Walburg Pers, 1979. [PhD dissertation, University of Leiden, 1977]

Bar-Tal, C.F. Graumann, A.W. Kruglanski and W. Stroebe, eds. *Stereotyping and Prejudice: Changing Conceptions* New York: Springer-Verlag, 1989.

Thomas-Hope, Elizabeth. 1992. *Explanation in Caribbean Migration: Perception and the Image. Jamaica, Barbados and St. Vincent.* London: Macmillan.

———. 1998. *Emigration Dynamics in the Anglophone Caribbean.* In *Emigration Dynamics in Developing Countries,* vol III, *Mexico, Central America and the Caribbean* ed. Reginald Appleyard, 180-229. London: Ashgate.

———. 2000. Trends and Patterns of Migration to and from Caribbean Countries. In *Rapport deelname Nederlandse Antillen aan het Symposium on international migration in the Americas.* Willemstad: Permanente Commissie voor Bevolkingsvraagstukken, Population Unit.

Van Soest, J. 1977 *Olie als water. De Curaçaose economie in de eerste helft van de twintigste eeuw.* Zutphen: De Walburg Pers.

2

REFUGEES AND ASYLUM SEEKERS IN THE FRENCH OVERSEAS DEPARTMENTS:
The Case of Guadeloupe

MARIE-GABRIELLE HADEY-SAINT-LOUIS

INTRODUCTION

The people of Haiti have had a lengthy history of crossing borders and living abroad. The result of this continuous emigration is the existence of a Diaspora estimated between 1.5 to 2 million compared to a population of 8 million at home. How can one account for such mass displacement? Reasons for leaving are complex and varied, but from the Duvalier era to the present, Haitians have emigrated mostly in reaction to political and economic situations: political opponents seeking refuge abroad, and people fleeing poverty and natural disasters.

From 2001 to 2005, political violence forced thousands of Haitians to leave their country. In December 2002, the independent expert on human rights in Haiti, Louis Joinet, in his report to the UN Commission on Human Rights, observed a considerable increase in daily violence, violence aimed at specific sectors such as the press, political parties and their organizations, human rights' defenders (Joinet L). The 2003 report was very similar; in 2004 the emphasis was placed on the deterioration of the situation, and the expert deplored the fact that political violence between the pro- and anti-government militias continued to create victims. In 2005, Joinet stressed once more the question of impunity for human rights violations and noted that: '… the government continued to be surrounded by gangs, which seemed to wish to exterminate each other.' Parallel to this violence and the general lack of security that prevailed in the country or, perhaps, because of them, the state of an already weak economy worsened, leaving thousands of people little alternative but to flee. They went to the United States, the Dominican Republic, the Bahamas and, more recently, to Guadeloupe. They sought refuge in Guadeloupe for many reasons, the first one being the facility to enter the territory, being French-speaking, and the second one the relatively high standard of living.

The major issue facing France in its overseas departments, confronted as they were by the arrival of thousands of Haitian boat people, was to distinguish the asylum seeker from the economic migrant. This was of concern to human rights groups, especially considering the current trend to close doors to immigrants, including asylum seekers, due to the rise of xenophobia and racism and also to the fact that, in the public mind, asylum seekers had become synonymous with illegal immigrants. The tendency to deny minimum rights to asylum seekers in their process of applying for asylum, and also after they have been granted refugee status, was also noted.

This chapter gives an account of the plight of Haitian refugees in Guadeloupe and to demonstrate how this overseas department can be viewed as a laboratory for the French government's general policy on immigration. In the first section, an overview is given of the new immigration laws in France and their implementation in the French Overseas Departments. Secondly, the situation in Guadeloupe is analyzed: in 2005, only 2.3 per cent of those seeking the right of sanctuary were granted refugee status in Guadeloupe, whereas in France 12.4 per cent of the applications were accepted.

IMMIGRATION LAW IN FRANCE AND THE EUROPEAN UNION

The issue of immigration and asylum seeking has become a sensitive one since September 11, 2001, and the terrorist attacks on the United States. The dilemma European countries have to face is how to guarantee human rights while protecting the integrity of their people. Guaranteeing internal security implies reinforcing border control in order to maintain stability within states, safeguarding human rights includes access to fair and just asylum procedures. European policy on this matter presents a two fold characteristic: an international and an internal one.

The 1985 Schengen Agreement and the 1990 Dublin Convention are the basis of the European policy on immigration and asylum. Members of *'Schengenland'* abolished border checks on the movement of people between their territories and agreed on a common visa policy for nationals from outside the European Union (EU). The Dublin Convention was designed to reduce the number of asylum applicants in the EU and abolished the possibility for refugees to claim asylum in more than one of the member states.

After World War II international human rights discourses led to the establishment of international human rights norms as enshrined in the 1951 Geneva Convention on Refugees and The European Convention of Human Rights (ECHR). Despite these supra-national framework stipulations, states can still prescribe the overall conditions under which refugee rights apply.

In May 2006, the French Minister of the Interior presented to the National Assembly his new bill reforming the Entry, Sojourn and Asylum Right Code (Code de l'entrée et du séjour des étrangers et du droit d'asile: CESEDA). This bill was based upon the latest dictum of the French government: 'immigration choisie plutôt que immigration subie' (chosen immigration rather than imposed immigration), 'imposed' referring to family reunification and asylum seekers. Since the November 2, 1945 Ordinance, migration policies in France have always established hierarchies among migrants. This stands with the prevailing French view of the foreigner as hostile, and with the two-fold character of migration policies: repressive on the one hand, utilitarian on the other hand. The French government openly proclaims utilitarianism. This bill tightened the conditions for entry and residency both for documented and undocumented foreigners. Under this new code it would become more difficult for a documented foreigner to bring his family to France: marrying a French citizen would no longer give automatic access to French nationality; and undocumented foreigners who have resided in France for at least ten years or more, would no longer automatically obtain a residence card. All these changes would inevitably curtail the rights of refugees.

The CESEDA law is, of course, applicable in the French Overseas Departments, but with special measures for French Guiana, Guadeloupe and Mayotte. In France, there are three forms of protection: refugee status, subsidiary protection and stateless person status. This chapter deals mostly with the first two forms.

THE OFFICE FOR THE PROTECTION OF REFUGEES AND STATELESS PERSONS (OFPRA)

In France, refugee status and subsidiary protection are granted by the French OFPRA, a public body under the authority of the Foreign Ministry, and an administrative court, the Refugee Appeals Board (CRR), which is placed under the supervision of the *Conseil d'Etat*. When the asylum seeker applies for permission to stay at the Prefecture, he does not have to specify the type of protection he/she would like (refugee status or subsidiary protection). Indeed, his / her application will be examined by the OFPRA officers; firstly in relation to refugee status, and only if it does not fulfil the conditions, in relation to subsidiary protection. If OFPRA refuses both refugee status and the benefit of subsidiary protection, he/she may appeal to the CRR.

During the procedure, the Prefecture issues the asylum seeker with a provisional stay authorization — *autorization provisoire de séjour (APS)* — showing the words 'with a view to the OFPRA procedure' valid for one month. The APS will be issued within fifteen days. The OFPRA form has to be written in French and the applicant has to answer all the questions on the OFPRA form being careful to : describe all the personal reasons that led him/her to flee their country and the reasons they are unable to return there. The time required for OFPRA to make a decision varies: 15 days for the priority procedure, (incomplete or late demands, undocumented persons in the detention centre), up to several weeks for the standard procedure (60 days).

If the asylum application is accepted, the asylum seeker is either :

- Recognized as a refugee by OFPRA, which in this case will give him the right to go to the Prefecture and, upon presenting the document, receive a residence permit application receipt (récépissé), which authorises a renewable 3-month stay, and allows him/her to work. The receipt is issued while waiting for a ten-year residence permit, which is renewable, by right.

- Given subsidiary protection by OFPRA, which will inform him/her of the decision. On presentation of this document, the Prefecture will, within 8 days, give a residence permit application that authorises a 3-month renewable work permit. The receipt is issued while waiting for a temporary residence permit, marked 'private and family life', which is valid for one year and can be renewed if all the reasons justifying subsidiary protection are still applicable.

The OFPRA's rejection decision is sent to the applicant by registered mail with acknowledgement of receipt to the last known address. The deadline is one month starting from the time they are notified of the rejection by OFPRA to register their appeal with the Refugee Appeals Board. If this term is exceeded, their appeal will be considered inadmissible, that is to say, it will be rejected without prior notice.

THE REGUGEE APPEALS BOARD (CRR)

The commission is made up of a president, a qualified person appointed by the UNHCR (United Nations High Commission for Refugees) and a person appointed by the French Council of State on the suggestion of one of the ministers sitting on the OFPRA governing body.

The CRR can:

- Cancel the OFPRA rejection and grant the refugee status or subsidiary protection.
- Confirm the OFPRA decision and reject the appeal.

The rejection by the Refugee Appeals Board ends the validity of the three month *récépissé*: the prefecture will then send a letter informing the asylum seeker that his stay is at an end and asking him to leave French territory within one month. If at the end of the one-month period, he is still in France, his stay becomes illegal and the Prefecture may issue a government order, which may be enforced at any time. The order may be accompanied by a transfer to a detention centre prior to the expulsion.

THE RIGHTS OF THE ASYLUM SEEKERS

Any asylum seeker is entitled to social security. Social security covers accommodation, financial assistance and health care. This aid, financed by the state, depends on the person's status, type of permission to stay and its validity. Across the whole French territory reception centres are found and are only available to asylum seekers and their direct family.

Every asylum seeker may benefit from universal health coverage (Couverture Maladie Universelle). This coverage is offered from the time they make their asylum application on presentation either of an appointment or a summons or a temporary stay document, accompanied by a certificate of domiciliation. It will cover them for all medical and hospital expenses of any nature without having to make any payment beforehand. Asylum seekers are generally not authorised to work. They may benefit from a welfare allowance. The welfare allowance is €290.67 per month per adult, paid for the whole period of the procedure. However, if their application is rejected by OFPRA (without being followed by an appeal) or by CRR, these payments will be cancelled.

THE ISSUE OF IMMIGRATION IN GUADELOUPE

In December 2006, there were 28,805 foreigners living legally in Guadeloupe, there were 28,117 in December 2005 and in 2004 they were 27,923. The number of illegal immigrants in Guadeloupe is estimated between 10,000-20,000 for a population of 440,000 inhabitants.

Today immigration is a key issue in Guadeloupe and politicians from all parties as well as the authorities are attempting to restrain the continuous flow of immigrants. They come from Dominica, the Dominican Republic, but mostly from Haiti. As the numbers of Haitian immigrants rose and unemployment levels increased on the island, a deep feeling of xenophobia arose in the population.

The high standard of living of this French overseas department makes Guadeloupe an attractive migrant destination; the minimum wage is 8 to 32 times that of the other independant Caribbean states. The second factor to be taken into account in this flow is the geographic particularity of

Table 2.1: Foreigners from the Caribbean living legally in Guadeloupe in December 2006

Country Of Origin	Numbers	% Caribbean Zone
Cuba	98	0.71%
Dominican Republic	1,537	11.30%
Dominica	3,035	22.30%
Grenadines	18	0.13 %
Haiti	8,448	62.05%
Jamaica	114	0.84%
St Christophe & Nevis	29	0.21%
Saint Kitts	107	0.80%
Saint Lucia	195	1.43%
Saint Vincent	14	0.10%
Trinidad	18	0.13%
Total	**13,613**	

Guadeloupe, an archipelago with seven islands and all together 700 km of coastline to guard. This is a unique feature in the French overseas departments.

Under the pressure of the local politicians, the Coast Guards were given new and faster boats, and specific measures of the new immigration law have been applied in Guadeloupe, such as the right to destroy traffickers' boats on the spot, the right of the police to check identity papers on their own initiative and to arrest people more than 1 km from the coast. They also have the right to expel an illegal immigrant within 48 hours, even if he/she has made an appeal. The French Government has put pressure on the Government of Dominica to require visas for Haitians and Dominicans. On March 9, 2006, the Prime Minister of Dominica, Roosevelt Skerrit, and then French Interior Minister, Nicolas Sarkosy, reached an agreement that gives to the people of Dominica the right to come to Guadeloupe without a visa, if their stay does not exceed fifteen days; in return the Government of Dominica will allow the foreigners who entered France via their country to return to Dominica.

ASYLUM SEEKERS AND REFUGEES IN GUADELOUPE

Haitians come to Guadeloupe because it seems easier for them to enter than the other Caribbean states: they generally travel by road to the Dominican Republic where they take a charter flight to Dominica. They are presented as temporary workers going to Roseau. There they spend a few days and after putting down a guarantee of US$400, which they will lose if they leave Dominica clandestinely, they are smuggled into Guadeloupe by boat in groups of 10–20. The crossing costs them US$500 to US$1,000. If everything goes well they land somewhere on the coast near Bouillante, Trois Rivières, Saint-Anne, or on Les Saintes or Marie Galante (small islands in the Guadeloupean archipelago); when things go wrong they are thrown over board and have to swim to the coast.

Landing zone in Guadeloupe

In 2005, with 4,718 applications, the Haitians became the main group of asylum seekers in France. They represented 12 per cent of the total number of applications in France, and 73 per cent of this total was in Guadeloupe.

Table 2.2: Main countries of origin of asylum seekers 2005 and 2004

	2005	2004	% change 2005 / 2004
Haiti	4,953	3,067	61.5%
Turkey	3,612	4,409	-18.1%
China	2,579	4,188	-38.4%
Serbia & Montenegro	2,569	2,378	8.0%
D.R. Congo	2,563	3,353	-23.6%
Russia	1,980	2,165	-8.5%
Moldavia	1,964	2,058	-4.6%
Sri Lanka	1,894	2,090	-9.4%
Algeria	1,777	3,702	-52.0%
Bosnia-Herzegovina	1,658	2,012	-17.6%
Other countries	17,029	21,125	-19.4%
Total	**42,578**	**50,547**	**-15.8%**

Table 2.3: First demands for asylum by month 2005

	Haiti	Dominican Republic	Others	Total Demands
January	440	1	16	457
February	313	2	10	325
March	278	3	17	298
April	336	2	17	355
May	516	20	14	550
June	653	34	24	711
July	484	3	10	497
August	426	11	21	458
September	490	13	11	514
October	475	12	22	509
November	315	4	21	340
December	227	8	20	255
Total	**4,953**	**113**	**203**	**5,269**

PROFILE OF THE HAITIAN ASYLUM SEEKERS.

Generally, the Haitian demands are linked to the violence and general insecurity that prevail in the country and the inability of the Haitian authorities to protect its citizens. The majority of the applicants are victims of this violence: they are traders, victims of racketeering, people who have been kidnapped or have seen members of their family kidnapped or murdered; they are political or associated activists, students, journalists, civil servants under the government of former President Jean Bertrand Aristide, policemen, judges; there are also members of violent gangs called Chimères, criminals who work mostly for either the Lavalas Party or the Convergence Party.

In 2005 the French Overseas Departments of Guadeloupe, Martinique and French Guiana registered a dramatic increase in the number of asylum seekers (a rise of 121 per cent between 2004 and 2005). In 2005 there were 3,799 demands, 92 per cent in Guadeloupe, 4.5 per cent in French Guiana and 3.5 per cent in Martinique.

At the end of 2004 the government responded to that increase by sending OFPRA's officers to Guadeloupe every two months for a two-week period to interview the applicants. In 2005 there were seven such missions. The OFPRA Officers and the interpreters had up to eight interviews per day instead of the usual four. And the decision time was 120 days. In 2005 there were thousands queuing at the Prefecture doors to apply. The Prefecture's immigration services were not prepared for such crowds, and it became impossible for French citizens and legal immigrants to access these services, for example to renew their identity cards or passports. The applicants were waiting outside, with no protection from the sun or the rain, impatient to get in and receive the papers that would give them an appointment with the immigration services. There were too few civil servants to cope with the situation and rioting almost broke out. All this was shown on television and the population was deeply shocked.

The issue of the Haitian asylum seekers became so sensitive that in January 2006, the French government, decided to open, for the first time outside continental France, a branch of OFPRA in Basse Terre. The objective was to bring down the decision time from 120 days to the normal 60

Asylum seekers at the prefecture gate, Basse Terre, Guadeloupe, 2005.

days. This agency in Guadeloupe also administers the applications from Martinique and French Guiana. Six months after its opening, the agency became the third most active in France (9.9 per cent) after the Île de France region (41.7 per cent) and the Rhône Alpes region (11.6 per cent).

Since the beginning of 2006 there has been a noticeable decline in the number of applicants for asylum: on December 2006 there were 1,042 demands, in 2005 at the same date the number was 4022. On the other hand, the number of people expelled has increased from 1,053 in 2004 to 1,200 in 2005 and 447 for the first term of 2006. These bi-directional trends are related and are due to various factors:

- The decline in the flow of boat people between Dominica and Guadeloupe.
- The right given to the police to expel an illegal immigrant within 48 hours.
- The opening of the OFPRA in Basse-Terre has supported all those measures. Indeed, the decision time has been reduced to two weeks compared to the two or three month delay that was the rule before.

But who are these immigrants? Are they mainly fleeing poverty, as is generally believed by the population and the local authorities, or are they, as they claim, fleeing insecurity and persecution? How can we account for the fact that only 2.3 per cent of these asylum seekers, men and women aged 22 to 40 are granted refugee status? They are mostly from Leogane, Croix des Bouquets, La Gonave, and are students, peasants, street vendors, members of grass roots organizations. Many are illiterate and mostly creole-speaking, aged between 20 and 40. They have all fled insecurity and persecution.

The major difficulty of the Haitian asylum seekers in Guadeloupe is, surprisingly, the language barrier. It took some time for the French authorities to realize that the creole spoken in Haiti is different from that spoken in Guadeloupe, not only in vocabulary, but also in syntax and cultural and historical references. The first task was to find qualified Haitian interpreters. The second task was to explain to the different governmental agencies the rights of the asylum seekers.

For the asylum seeker, the first obstacle is to fill in the application form, which is in French and must be filled out in French. They generally pay someone (€20-50) to do it for them.

In continental France, asylum seekers are taken under the wing of various associations and members of the Haitian community. The Haitians who make it to continental France are mostly important persons (former MPs/ members of the government or journalists) they have enough money to obtain a visa and take a plane, and thus arrive legally in France where they often have family. It should be noted that 12.4 per cent of these applications are accepted, whereas in Guadeloupe the acceptance rate is 2.3 per cent. In Guadeloupe there are no such associations; those in place are not set up to do this kind of work and have never dealt with refugees. The consequence of this is that the asylum seekers are not ready for their interview at the OFPRA, and sometimes do not know what to say or how to present their story. Some of them are still frightened and too traumatized to give the details of their stories. When they arrive for their interview, they have to deal with various stresses: the pain of reviving their memories, the fear of reprisals, and above all the burden of their lives in Guadeloupe. They all are miserable, lonely, malnourished; some are homeless or live in squalid conditions. If they are lucky enough to find a job (although their status of asylum seeker forbids them to work) they are exploited (€22-30 per day to work in a banana plantation instead of €50 per day).

According to the Code on Refugees and Asylum, any asylum seeker is entitled to financial aid of around €290 per month from the French state, as well as access to state medical insurance. In many state agencies some employees, thinking that it is their duty to fight illegal immigration, simply refuse to apply the law. So in Guadeloupe asylum seekers sometimes never get that financial aid, and if they do get it, they have it for only 2 to 6 months. As for universal health coverage, few were lucky enough to obtain it; even then some hospitals refused to take them. Moreover, in 2004/2005 the average length of time between the date asylum seekers applied for asylum at the Prefecture, and the final decision was between six months and a year, compared to 60 days in France. All this is carried out in a general climate of xenophobia fuelled by the media. Haitian asylum seekers feel deeply rejected, are constantly humiliated and belittled in their dealings with the French civil service: if they are creole-speaking the person systematically speaks to him/her in French, and if they do speak French, administrators respond in creole. They are often asked to wait for hours without any explanation.

According to the first article of the 1951 Convention on the Status of Refugees, to qualify for asylum the person must have a significant 'fear of persecution on account of his race, religion, nationality, membership of a particular social group or political opinion.' Article L. 712-2 c of the Ordinance n° 2004-1248 of 24th November, 2004, grants subsidiary protection 'because of generalised violence resulting from an internal or international armed conflict.' With the Haitian demands the OFPRA officers are confronted with a crisis with no clear parameters, because most of the times the cases do not fit into the general framework. The inability of the OFPRA officers to grasp the real meaning of the refugee's testimony, despite translation, poses problems. The asylum seekers' lack of knowledge of the law also poses problems: for them the term refugee only applies to those who have been persecuted by the government. Detrimental to them also is their inability to find the appropriate words to explain the specific character of their dramatic experience in the general climate of insecurity. They should also prove that the Haitian authorities were unable to protect them. All this, plus the fact that the OFPRA officers cannot take into account the general insecurity that prevails in Haiti - because it does not result from internal armed conflict- may explain their difficulty in reaching a favourable decision, and thus the acceptance rate of only 2.3 per cent.

THE OFPRA DECISION

Once the OFPRA has taken its decision, if it is negative, the asylum seeker has the right to contest the decision made by the General Director of the OFPRA by appealing to the Refugee Appeals Board (CRR). Here again Haitians encounter problems; their appeal must be written in French and has to be sent by registered mail within one month following OFPRA's decision. Again they have to pay someone to write their appeal, and some of them miss the deadline because they receive the OFPRA's decision late due to a change of address or because the person with whom they live does not give them the mail on time. They must justify their appeal with new information or new arguments, but generally they simply repeat the story that they have already told the OFPRA officer. Moreover the CRR holds an audience in Guadeloupe only once every two months, so in the meantime these persons live in dire conditions. Those living in Martinique, French Guiana and Saint Martin have to travel to Guadeloupe. Once more their lack of preparation and understanding of the system are detrimental. They are entitled to judicial assistance but they never ask for it, thinking they have to pay. In 2005, 2,554 decisions were taken by the CRR for Guadeloupe, Martinique and French Guiana with an acceptance rate of 3 per cent.[4]

What happens to those who fail to qualify as refugees? The rejection by the CRR ends the validity of the three-month receipts. The prefecture sends a letter informing them that their stay is at an end and asking them to leave French soil within one month. In this letter they are also informed that they may benefit from repatriation assistance to help them return to their country. This assistance is given by the National Foreigner's Reception and Migration Agency — Agence Nationale pour l'Accueil des Etrangers et des Migrations (ANAEM). In France the financial aid amounted to €2,000 for an adult, the plane fare with 30 kilos of baggage, in Guadeloupe the ANAEM gives them €153, the plane fare with 30 kilos of baggage. According to the Prefecture the majority of those rejected by OFPRA apply for a resident card under the criteria of the CESEDA: marriage or equivalent ties, parents of French children, health reasons. They do so with the help of local lawyers who charge them €400 to 600, even though they have no chance to get a resident's card once their appeals have been rejected.

For those who qualify as refugees, the long road to integration begins. Once the OFPRA gives its decision, the refugees normally get a temporary resident card and a travel document. With these documents they are entitled to all aspects of state assistance; every refugee receives an allowance of €10 per day and the right to bring their close family to France. This takes longer in Guadeloupe, as their documents are made in continental France; in the meantime they receive a three-month receipt. Because of the delay in receiving their documents they have great difficulty in their dealings with the various state agencies, for instance, to apply for housing allowance and open a bank account, they need the travel document and the ten-year resident card. Again the language barrier creates difficulties for the majority of the refugees in Guadeloupe in their dealings with the administration, or the social services.

CONCLUSION

In 2006, the tendency throughout the whole territory of France is towards a significant decline in the number of people asking for asylum. With respect to Haiti, the percentage of this downward trend is 63.5 per cent. Haiti now represents 6.3 per cent of the general asylum requests in France. The most spectacular decrease is the requests in Guadeloupe: from 3,491 in 2005 to 461 in 2006, a decline of 87 per cent. But parallel to this trend there is a significant increase of the number of appeals to the CRR from 396 in 2005 to 1,077 in 2006 (+172 per cent). This is due to the fact that the audiences of the CRR are now being held in Guadeloupe. Another point that should be stressed is the growing number of women asking for protection.

In Guadeloupe the demands from Haitian people represent 86 per cent of the applications for asylum, the Dominicans hold second place. In Martinique, all the demands are from Haitians; in French Guiana the number of applications is more balanced with respectively 54 per cent from Haiti, 14 per cent from Peru, 9 per cent Guinea-Bissau, 5 per cent from Senegal and 4 per cent from Colombia. For the three overseas departments OFPRA made 2,755 decisions, the percentage of people who were granted the refugee status rose to 6 per cent compared to 2.7 per cent in 2005.

The nature of the Haitian crisis and its impact in Guadeloupe prefigure the crises to come; the 2004 Ordinance on refugees although new, is already obsolete regarding the realities of the countries of origin. This crisis has also highlighted the fact that the 'well-founded fear of persecution' is not a sufficient criterion in the Haitians' case. Even if they were not directly persecuted, these people have left their homeland mainly because of the deterioration of the political situation and the violence engendered by it and its economic consequences.

The issue of Haitian refugees has also worked as a test of the commitment to human rights in Guadeloupe. Even if it is not always possible to distinguish an asylum seeker from an economic migrant, the fact remains that regardless of whether a person is a refugee or not, that person is entitled to a minimum of human rights. Unfortunately this has not always been the case in Guadeloupe.

Regional cooperation with Haiti, in the fields of education, agriculture and seasonal work, could be part of the solution to the problems posed by the flow of Haitian immigration in Guadeloupe. It may also help to prevent the ostracism of the asylum seekers and the whole Haitian community. This could benefit both islands and may curb the flow of illegal immigrants.

REFERENCES

Joinet, Louis. 2002. *Situation des droits de l'homme en Haiti*. Geneva, UNHCHR, December 2002.
Reports by Louis Joinet:
- E/CN.4/2003/116, 23 Décembre 2002
- E/CN.4/2004/108, 21 Janvier 2003
- E/CN.4/2005/123, 24 Janvier 2005
- E/CN.4/2006/115, 26 Janvier 2006
- A/HCR/4/3, 2 Février 2007
  http://www.unhchr.ch/
Office Français de Protection des Réfugiés et Apatrides. Repots of Jean Loup Kuhn-Delforge:
- Rapport d'activité 2005. Jean Loup Kuhn-Delforge, Avril 2006
- Rapport d'activité 2006. Jean Loup Kuhn-Delforge, Avril 2007
  http://www.ofpra.gouv.fr
Préfecture of Guadelope, Service des Etrangers, Juin 2007
Commissions des Recours des Réfugiés. Rapport d'activité 2006, 16 Avril 2007
http://commission-refugies.fr

3

CONTEMPORARY VENEZUELAN STUDENT EMIGRATION TO TRINIDAD

MICHELE N. REIS

INTRODUCTION

The linkages and affinities between Trinidad and Tobago and Venezuela are numerous and long established. There are four principal factors that account for this, which in some measure have contributed to migration patterns between the two countries. These are 1) geographical proximity, 2) a shared colonial past (Trinidad was once a Spanish colony), 3) cultural similarities reflected in the cuisine and music of the two countries and 4) common natural and economic resources (plantation agriculture, natural gas and petroleum). Thus, it is not surprising that early historical accounts of Venezuelan wars, insurrections and expeditions document migratory flows between Trinidad and Tobago and the Venezuelan mainland, in addition to the flourishing commercial trade and the fact that many Venezuelans sent their children to Trinidad to acquire proficiency in English. In the 1920s, the discovery of petroleum in both countries further fuelled migration of Trinidadians to Venezuela in substantial numbers until the 1980s, when Venezuela's economic and political climate worsened dramatically, making it less attractive to Trinidad migrants.

Within recent times there is a common perception that Venezuelan emigration to Trinidad has become more pronounced. While indeed more visible, this chapter will dispel the myth that Venezuelan presence is recent or even unprecedented. By a tracing the historical antecedents of the migratory flows between the two countries, it will become apparent that these flows have been constant, though more prominent at various times in the history of both nations.

The chapter will first trace the historical antecedents to the migratory flows between Venezuela and Trinidad and Tobago, before looking at the socio-cultural implications of this most recent influx of Venezuelans. It will include empirical data based on interviews conducted by the author with Venezuelan students. The study is timely, as the linkages between Spanish-speaking Latin America and the English-speaking Caribbean is both important and under-researched. The present research on the Venezuelan community is limited by the fact that there are no recent analytical or academic studies of the phenomenon. The lack of data on actual numbers of students makes it difficult to make a comparison with the early period of Venezuelan student migration to Trinidad.

For the most part, in general, Venezuelan migration to the island has been commonly linked to an upsurge in criminal activity, drug trafficking and prostitution. The current study is meant to stimulate two possible ideas for further research: (1) constructions of Venezuelans and Venezuelan migration in the Trinidad media; and (2) the role of language schools in encouraging Venezuelan-Trinidad migration and facilitating social integration. It will also comment briefly on the more positive aspects of the Venezuelan presence in Trinidad, as well as the benefits of the *rapprochement* between the two countries.

HISTORICAL ANTECEDENTS

There was interaction between Venezuela and Trinidad even prior to the 'discovery' of the two territories by Christopher Columbus in 1498 on his third voyage to the New World.[1] In the Orinoco Basin, the Warahoons and the 'Caribs' were the first migrants, setting the pace for the more contemporary waves of immigrants. That there were movements of people from the early exploratory expeditions of the sixteenth century to the present day is not difficult to imagine, given that only 10 miles of water between Güiria in Venezuela and Port of Spain, the capital of Trinidad, separate the two countries.

Trinidad has been aptly coined 'a gigantic Ellis Island', by the historian, Gerard Besson (Interview 2005). In fact, by dint of its Spanish rule for almost three centuries, its close proximity to Venezuela and the constant back and forth movements of people from both territories, Trinidad can be considered the most 'latinized' of the English-speaking Caribbean islands. Unlike most host countries in the North Atlantic, it is a major destination point for many other migrant groups, in addition to being simultaneously a point of departure.

The principal reasons that Venezuelans arrived in Trinidad were as a result of: people fleeing dictatorships and revolutions in Venezuela; a small movement of Sephardic Jews from Venezuela; the running of the cocoa industry; the settling of urban aristocrats; and people coming to learn English.

Early nineteenth-century civil wars on the South American mainland brought an influx of Spanish immigrants to Trinidad. Venezuelans were drawn to Trinidad because the island was situated near to the coast of Venezuela and provided a safe haven from revolutions and dictators, notably Gómez. Thus, there was always a strong impetus for Venezuelans to come to Trinidad, particularly in the immediate post-independence years when Venezuelan peasants became destitute. Even then, writes Moodie (1994: 3), 'the government was corrupt and autocratic.' The more wealthy immigrants usually brought their extended families and servants. Hence, names such as Pacheco, Pazos and Trujillo and others, hark back to an era where Venezuelans were escaping from revolutions.

Most Venezuelans that settled in Trinidad came from the eastern and north-eastern parts of Venezuela — Estado Sucre: Cumaná, Carúpano or Güiria and Margarita. This was facilitated by the fact that in the nineteenth century, Trinidad and the small islands off the Trinidadian coast were still a province of Venezuela. In the pre-independence era, arms were shipped through Trinidad and a vibrant to-and-fro of human cargo and ammunition flowed freely between the two territories. By the 1880s, Trinidad relied on Venezuela for foodstuffs and Venezuelans on finery and luxury items from Port of Spain. In fact 'contact between Trinidadians and Venezuelans was never lacking, especially in the areas closest to Trinidad, the Paria Peninsula,

San Félix, El Callao, Ciudad Bolívar, the flatlands of Los Caños with their rundown villages, Tucupita and Pedernales…'(Moodie 1994, 153). Early newspaper accounts record the indebtedness of Venezuelans to Trinidad for providing both logistical support and refuge during the Independence Wars (Ménendez 1996).[2]

The second most important arrival of Venezuelans in Trinidad relates to the small presence of Sephardic Jews from Venezuela in the 1790s and 1800s. They were quickly assimilated into Trinidad's white French creole society, in addition to settling 'alongside the existing local "Spanish" population' (Moodie 1994:4). Names such as Herrera, Perrera and Cádiz are indicative of this period. In the early 1800s, Venezuelans were also sought as an answer to the island's chronic labour shortage.[3] According to Moodie (1994:154), in 1817, there were 'fresh emigrations from Margarita, Carúpano, Río Caribe and Guyiria….' In November 1817, 'more of the inhabitants fled to Port of Spain, while about 600 people, probably slaves sought refuge in the forests of the Paria Peninsula.'

Then a much larger wave of Venezuelans arrived to develop Trinidad's cocoa industry.[4] This was a considerable movement of rural, peasant people who settled in the forested interior of Trinidad, primarily for the purpose of propagating cocoa lands. To this day, there are Spanish-speaking remnants of these *cocoa panyols* present in Rancho Quemado, Rio Claro, Mundo Nuevo, San Rafael, Gran Curucaye, Cerro de la Cruz, Siparia, Sangre Grande and Mamoral, among other places. They came principally from the '*Oriente*' — Eastern Venezuela: the Paria Peninsula, Carúpano, Río Caribe, the island of Margarita, the plains (*llanos*), Guayana region, Caracas and Lara, adjacent to the Andes and Colombia. These people were known as *mestizos* or *zambos*. They were a mixture of Amerindian and Spanish or Amerindian, Spanish and 'negro'. They were both Spanish-speaking and Catholic.[5]

The *gran cacao* possessed the money to buy the cocoa lands and were a distinctive class from the *cocoa panyols* who actually worked the land. The rural, uneducated Spanish-speaking peasantry who were nestled in the foothills of the cocoa-producing areas, were separate and 'distinct from the mostly upper class, professional, wealthy, Venezuelan exiles residing in Port of

Spain' (Moodie 1994, XII). In fact, there was a more urban movement of Venezuelans that came to Trinidad at the end of the nineteenth century and the beginning of the twentieth century. They came mainly from Maturín, Maracaibo and Angostura, which later became Ciudad Bolívar. Throughout the 1850s and 1870s there was a marked presence of urban Spanish people, who were the descendants of Don Antonio Gómez, Ramón Llanos and Ramón García. Until the early 1960s, prior to Trinidad acquiring independence, Trinidad was a land of exile for many Venezuelan revolutionaries and patriots. In fact, 'Trinidad hosted all kinds of Venezuelan refugees, Royalists and Patriots alike' (Toussaint 2000, 94).

Thus the presence of Venezuelan students on Trinidad soil is not a recent phenomenon. From the 1940s to 1961, Venezuelans came to Trinidad to learn English and were primarily boarders in convents. The influx of Venezuelan boarders halted in 1961, with the passing of the Common

The old Venezuelan Boarding School, currently occupied by Venezuelan students residing in St Joseph.

Source: *Special Edition Magazine: First Commemoration of the First Capital of Trinidad and Tobago-St Joseph, 2004: 8.*

Entrance Act, an examination to gain entry into the secondary school system, open only to nationals of Trinidad, which thereby restricted the eligibility of Venezuelans. It was quite *en vogue* that 'until the late 1950s, affluent Venezuelans had their children educated at Catholic boarding schools in Port of Spain and San Fernando. The less well-off sent their sons and daughters to learn English at private homes and self-styled language institutes…' (Moodie 1994, 55). These Venezuelan boarders were the early precursors of the contemporary wave of student migrants in private language institutions all across Trinidad. During the 1940s to 1960s Venezuelans sent their children to learn English in Trinidad in order to improve their chances of securing a good job in the oil industry, banks and as bilingual secretaries in multinational companies in Venezuela.

Language skills were also in great demand in the 1950s and 1960s in Trinidad as the Venezuelan clientele in Port of Spain's downtown shopping area was not negligible, so store-owners resorted to hiring bilingual store clerks. It was a common sight to see retail stores on Charlotte Street displaying signs *'Aquí se habla español'*. Today, more than the obvious geographical proximity of the two countries, the current political climate and socio-economic situation in Venezuela has further prompted Venezuelans to choose Trinidad as an alternative destination to the U.S.A. in order to become bilingual or further their education. The value of the *bolívar* as well as acute foreign exchange restrictions deter even well-to-do Venezuelans from going as far afield as North America or Europe to study.

Finally, the discovery of oil in both countries helped solidify bonds between Venezuela and Trinidad, as the same companies explored for petroleum in both countries — Royal Dutch Shell, Exxon and Standard Oil to name but a few. Between the 1940s and 1950s there were constant flows between Trinidad and Venezuela. Just as the discovery of oil in Venezuela in 1922 prompted one of the largest internal migrations in Venezuela's history since the Wars of Independence in the nineteenth century, the discovery of oil in Trinidad caused back and forth migrations between both countries. However, at that time more Trinidadians went to Venezuela than the opposite. In fact, those who went to Venezuela in the early half of this century did so to work in the gold mine at El Callao, and, later on, in the oilfields of Anzoátegui and Maracaibo which also attracted immigrants from many other parts of the Caribbean (Moodie 1994: 155). A substantial number of Trinidadians of Chinese descent went to Venezuela as cooks, or ran grocery stores, bakeries, laundries or haberdashery stores. The vast majority of these Trinidadian migrants went as labourers in the petroleum industry in all capacities.

THE RECENT WAVE OF VENEZUELAN STUDENTS

This section culls what is known about Venezuelan students in Trinidad based on findings of a survey conducted by the author in 2005 of approximately 100 Venezuelan students from various schools across Trinidad, as well as from journalistic reports. An almost equal number of males to females participated in the survey. Table 3.1 also shows that the 21-30 demographic was quite significant, followed by the 31-40 age group.

Given the fact that Caracas is only a half-hour journey from Port of Spain, it would seem most logical that the vast majority of Venezuelan student migrants to Trinidad would come from the state of Monagas. In reality, Venezuelan students interviewed came not only from Caracas in Monagas, but from Sucre, areas that are closest in proximity to Trinidad's west coast, but more significantly from remote areas across Venezuela from as far west as Maracaibo to the interior of Venezuela (El Tigre, Valera, etc). Students came from large towns and cities such as Mérida and Valencia in addition to rural and coastal villages (Anaco, Punto Fijo, Coro, etc). The survey indicated that students came from 14 of the 26 states in Venezuela (See table 3.2).

Table 3.1: Demographic and gender profile of Venezuelan students included in the study (2005)

AGE	Under 20	21-30	31-40	41-50	51-60
	13	61	22	6	1
SEX	Male	Female			
	52	51			

Table 3.2: Areas in Venezuela from which the students originated

Town/ City in Venezuela	State	Number of Students
San Antonio de los Altos	Miranda	1
Caracas	Miranda	20
Total		21
Puerto La Cruz	Anzoátegui	9
El Tigre	Anzoátegui	3
Anaco	Anzoátegui	3
Barcelona	Anzoátegui	1
Pariaguán	Anzoátegui	1
San José de Guanipa	Anzoátegui	1
Total		18
Maturin	Monagas	12
Caripe	Monagas	1
Total		13
Valencia	Carabobo	9
Güiria	Sucre	2
Cumaná	Sucre	4
Carúpano	Sucre	1
Total		16
Ciudad Ojeda	Zulia	1
Maracaibo	Zulia	5
Total		6
Punto Fijo	Falcón	3
Coro	Falcón	1
Paraguaná	Falcón	1
Total		5
Puerto Ordaz	Bolívar	2
Ciudad Bolívar	Bolívar	2
Total		4
Maracay	Aragua	4
Barquisimeto	Lara	4
San Cristobal	Táchira	2
Rubio	Táchira	1
Total		11

Table 3.2: (continued)

Town/ City in Venezuela	State	Number of Students
Margarita	Nueva Esparta	2
Los Robles	Nueva Esparta	1
Total		**3**
Valera	Trujillo	1
San Juan de los Morros	Guárico	1
Maiquetía	Distrito Federal	1
Vargas	?	1
Total		**4**

The phenomenon of Venezuelan students seeking Trinidad as an alternative destination to acquire proficiency in English has changed significantly from the early precursors, who were boarders in a handful of convents run by the St. Joseph of Cluny Sisters. Currently there are over thirty private language schools in Trinidad offering English classes. They are located in Port of Spain and its immediate environs – Woodbrook, Newtown and St. James. In the east, there are schools in St. Augustine, Curepe, Maracas Valley and Arima. In Central and South Trinidad, there are schools in Couva, Chaguanas and San Fernando. Given the fact that these schools are widely dispersed across Trinidad, the students themselves tend to be clustered around the areas where these language schools exist. Table 3.3 illustrates the areas in which Venezuelan students (in the survey) reside in Trinidad. This is a reflection of the general pattern for the larger Venezuelan student population.

Of great importance, is the educational level of students interviewed: 2 had only a primary education; 27 secondary, 54 tertiary and 19 professional training. A very high percentage (73 per cent) of the group had some level of tertiary or professional education and training. Many Venezuelan students remain in the country once their period of study is completed, although data are not readily available. This has important implications for potentially redressing the loss of educated groups from Trinidad, and points to the need for further research to ascertain the level of skills that South American migrants actually possess, so that they can be maximised and integrated into the host country.

Table 3.3: Areas where Venezuelan Students in the survey reside

Port of Spain	Number of Students	East Trinidad	Number of Students
St. James	20	Barataria	1
Woodbrook	9	Curepe	3
Petit Valley	3	Arouca	1
Westmoorings	2	St. Joseph	5
Victoria Gardens	1	Tunapuna	2
Diego Martin	10	St. Augustine	1
Carenage	1	Mt. Lambert	1
Maraval	6	Arima	4
Port of Spain	18	Champs Fleurs	1
Santa Cruz	1		
Belmont	1		
Cascade	1		
Total	**73**	**Total**	**18**
Central Trinidad		**South Trinidad**	
Freeport	1	St. Joseph Village	1
Perseverance Village	1	San Fernando	4
		La Romain	1
		Marabella	1
Total	**2**	**Total**	**7**

The demand for both semi-skilled and skilled labour in Trinidad has seen the transformation of the role of the Venezuelan Embassy in Port of Spain into an unofficial unemployment/placement agency to meet the demand for jobs in the Trinidad market. As the country approaches full employment, it is not surprising, for example, that the difficulty in filling job vacancies has caused the country's largest supermarket chain to offer jobs to Venezuelan students, despite the fact that student permits strictly prohibit their employment. Similarly, Radical Designs Ltd., one of Trinidad's largest clothing manufacturers, has hired a Venezuelan designer and has sought the assistance of the Venezuelan Embassy in locating additional designers among the Venezuelan nationals registered.

One noteworthy contribution of the influx in Venezuelans to Trinidad is the number of Latin dance schools and Latin night clubs that have also dramatically increased over the last few years, signalling a resurgence in interest in merengue and salsa, catering to both a local Trinidadian clientele but primarily the young Venezuelan students. Many Venezuelans network by socialising at the weekly treks to Port of Spain's Latin nightclubs. A few years ago some language schools and institutes even suspended English classes on Fridays to facilitate the popular Latin night on Thursdays at Pier 1 - one of the premiere entertainment establishments on the Western peninsula. By day, the Pier offers a weekly passenger service between Güiria and Trinidad (since 2000) making it a haven for the young Venezuelan student community. Most recently-opened establishments and others that have been in existence longer in and around the capital have Latino nights catering to the Spanish-speaking clientele: Latino Tuesdays and Thursdays at Sabor Latino in Maraval, a Latin evening at Nemo's in Mucurapo, an occasional Latin night at the popular 51 Degrees, Crobar, Squeeze, Tasca Latina, Pabloz, the latter being run by Venezuelans themselves.

The socio-cultural impact of Venezuelan emigration to Trinidad is insufficiently analysed or reported. This includes the fact that one language school in St. James organised a baseball team comprised of Venezuelan students to compete against a local Trinidadian baseball team. The National Library's registration form in Port of Spain is printed in both Spanish and English, in keeping with the initiative to make Spanish the first official foreign language of Trinidad.[6] These are more than just disparate socio-cultural facts. They are an indication of social transformations that are afoot in Trinidad due to the presence of Venezuelans. In fact, a local newspaper reports that '. . . in Trinidad alone, the influx of Venezuelans in the past decade has led to Latin music, dances and other entertainment, as well as Latin non-government associations, being established as weekly and social fixtures' (Mohammed 2004).

In addition to Venezuelans flocking to Trinidad as a cheaper and nearer destination for learning Spanish, it is interesting to note that many language-learning institutions across the country have recorded a marked increase in the requests for Spanish classes by Trinidadian nationals. This fact has been corroborated by Trinidad and Tobago's Minister of Trade and Industry at the launch of the Spanish as the First Foreign Language Initiative.[7] The rationale for bilingualism is that it will enhance economic performance of businesses by facilitating exchanges between local Trinidadian companies and their Latin American counterparts. Bilingualism is also equated with social and economic progress.

Since Hugo Chávez came to power in 1999, there has been a warming of relations between Trinidad and Tobago and Venezuela, both countries enjoying longstanding good relations. On July 24, 2006, in commemoration of Francisco de Miranda's achievement, the Government of the Bolivarian Republic of Venezuela erected a bust of him at the Chaguaramas Military History and Aerospace Museum. Venezuela and Trinidad held talks on joint security and anti-drug efforts along their shared maritime border in Carúpano in September 2005. The two countries are also expected to resume talks with the Chevron Corporation to develop two blocks in the Deltana Platform field, which straddles Venezuela's offshore border with Trinidad and Tobago. Any arrangement arrived at would create history as the two nations would share oil and gas resources of both the Manatee and Loran fields common to both countries.

There is growing evidence of Venezuelan socio-cultural influences on Trinidad's social landscape. There has also been ongoing cultural cooperation between the two neighbouring countries. In 2005, the Venezuelan Embassy assisted a local dance troupe in participating in a cultural festival in Maracaibo. Over the last few years Venezuelan and Trinidadian artistes have combined their talents to produce an opera that marries flamenco and song. Both Spanish and Venezuelan students from the Venezuelan Embassy undertook a project to create 12 creches from the various regions of Venezuela during Christmas 2005. The Hispanic Women in Trinidad and Tobago (HWTT) has been in existence in five years and comprises 30 members from Venezuela and other Spanish-speaking countries and islands of the Caribbean. Their fund-raising activities benefit various charities in the host country. Most recently, an ancient Hispanic festival — 'La Cruz de Mayo' (May Cross) was revived in Lopinot, a verdant valley in east Trinidad which was home to many Venezuelan cocoa planters in the nineteenth century. The May Cross Celebrations were reinstated through collaboration with the Trinidad and Tobago Parang Association and the Venezuelan Institute for Culture and Cooperation (IVCC).

VENEZUELAN RESIDENTS IN TRINIDAD

The Venezuelan Embassy currently has an official number of approximately 3,000 Venezuelan citizens who have registered voluntarily. These numbers are by no means indicative of actual numbers, which may be closer to 7,000 or even 10,000. Official numbers are not currently available from the Immigration Department.

For the purpose of this study, Venezuelans in Trinidad have been categorised accordingly: (1) residents with work permits who are either married to Trinidadians or who work with multi-national companies, such as in the oil and natural gas industries; (2) the student migrants who enter the country on student visas, some with the intention of staying, though many are transient and leave after the duration of study; (3) those involved in drug trafficking and other illegal activity; and (4) commercial sex workers.

Unfortunately media representation of Venezuelan migration is highly negative. The two final categories capture the most attention in the daily press. In fact, scores of articles regularly appear in the country's three major newspapers concerning arrests of Venezuelans on drug charges, prostitution and illegal docking of Venezuelans in Trinidad waters.[8] The growing presence of Venezuelan and Colombian prostitutes and dancers in night clubs has engaged the attention of certain sectors of the society, although young Venezuelan women who are incarcerated for prostitution and 'lewd dancing in public,' usually have valid work permits. The proliferation of establishments in Port of Spain, Woodbrook, Balmain, Couva and San Fernando is indeed a growing problem. Escort services, regularly advertised in the country's newspapers make specific reference to Latin American, Spanish or Venezuelan girls. In addition, this demand for sex workers from the Spanish mainland, is not only restricted to females, as there is a growing clientele for male Venezuelan strippers, masseurs and escorts.

Prostitution, like the trade in narcotics, should be of grave concern to officials on both sides of the Gulf of Paria. The city of San Fernando in the South is a major entry point for Venezuelan and Colombian sex workers, as well as drug traders. Trinidad's proximity to Venezuela and the increased contact with its sub-cultures makes Trinidad even more vulnerable as a stepping-stone to the Andean community and South America's drug trade while in turn giving these territories (Venezuela and Colombia) further access to CARICOM and Commonwealth countries. The isolated fishing villages on Trinidad's South-Western peninsula are known as a major entry point for illegal drugs. Interestingly, even in the 1800s these distant rural villages were

> also cause of concern to the British authorities, as 'the fishing village of Cedros, in which three quarters were located and which formed the south-western tip of Trinidad, was at the time so remote from the northern concentration around St. Joseph and Arima, that it seemed more closely associated with Venezuela than the rest of Trinidad. Its very isolation made it a base for illegal activities and a haven for would-be immigrants and emigrants' (Toussaint 2000: 93).

CONCLUSION

One can argue that ties between the two countries have become solidified informally through the widespread acceptance of the Hispanic population in Trinidad. In fact, it is more accurate to state that there has been a recent warming of relations between Trinidad and Tobago and the Chávez government in Venezuela, which can be considered a context for these migrations, as the two neighbouring Republics have signed a bilateral agreement waiving visa restrictions for Trinidadians and Venezuelans staying less than three months in either country.

This study has confirmed that Trinidad is becoming increasingly a popular destination for Central and South American students to learn English, because of the relatively low costs, proximity to Latin America and the ease of obtaining visas. However, there is still too large a disparity in the quality of the instruction the students receive, with some institutes offering an all-inclusive package with classes, lodging and meals provided, often advertised in Venezuelan newspapers. Because of the increasing number of students from Venezuela, as well as neighbouring Andean and Central American nations: Colombia, Guatemala, Ecuador, Mexico and Brazil, many students are forced to accept sub-standard lodging. In addition, there exists a Venezuelan underground economy that has become a survival mechanism, in which young females are often employed as babysitters or resort to working in night clubs, in retail stores or as cashiers in grocery stores.

The government of Trinidad and Tobago needs to have a clear policy with respect to student migration. Students interviewed spoke of the need to regulate the entry of Spanish-speaking students by having a bilateral agreement between the two countries to facilitate two-way student exchanges, particularly in the case of the less affluent students. Immersion programmes would be mutually beneficial to both Spanish teachers in Trinidad, as well as English teachers in Venezuela. Trinidad has much to gain by embracing its Hispanic minority. In fact, the Secretariat for the Implementation of Spanish (SIS) has already planned to enlist the assistance 'of the numerous Venezuelan students and citizens who have been in the past decade, making this country their permanent and temporary home, bringing with them their culture and language' (Mohammed 2004). One can anticipate that more attention will be paid to this phenomenon from which many have sustained a livelihood by running schools and Internet cafés, as well as providing lodging and other services.

NOTES

1. Toussaint (2000, 41) also asserts that, 'there has always been migration of persons between Trinidad and Venezuela.'
2. Similarly, in the foreword to Jaime Correa's (2004, 13) recent book, *Trinidad Through the Eyes of Francisco de Miranda's Correspondence,* reference is made to the pivotal role Trinidad played in Venezuela's quest for independence.
3. Toussaint's (2000, 41) thesis, also notes that 'following initial contact with Europeans, Trinidad suffered one type of labour shortage after another…'

4. 'A central figure in the development and cultivation of the crop was the local "Spanish" peasant' (Moodie 1994, 1). 'His origins were both in Spanish colonial Trinidad (1498-1797) and in neighbouring Venezuela…His culture was essentially Hispanic and his occupation was chiefly agriculture, with cacao as his special area of expertise.' (Moodie 1994, 2).

5. Moodie (1994, XI) notes in the foreword to her work on cocoa panyols in Trinidad that 'their language and customs were Spanish…They were peasants, not capitalists, so they were not allied to the French/ British planter elite.'

6. The government of Trinidad and Tobago has implemented the Secretariat for the Implementation of Spanish (SIS) to fast track making Spanish its first foreign language. The Initiative is part of the drive to have the country achieve developed country status by 2020 and dovetails with the bid to have Port of Spain as the headquarters of the FTAA.

7. According to Trinidad's Trade Minister, Kenneth Valley, 'the Centre for Language Learning at the University of the West Indies reports increased enrolment in Spanish language classes - as do the Venezuelan Embassy, Niherst and many private Spanish institutions and providers across the nation' (*Guardian* Newspaper, April 27, 2005).

8. Between 2004-2005, the *Newsday* carried such articles: 'Piparo Woman and Two Foreigners in $10M Drug Bust' (*Newsday* Dec. 7, 2004); 'Venezuelan Loses Marijuana Appeal' (*Newsday* Feb. 25, 2005); 'Venezuelan Sailor Gets 14 Years for Cocaine' (*Newsday* May 17, 2005); or 'Venezuelan Held in $2M Coke Bust' (*Newsday* Dec. 9, 2004).

9. Azócar, Hector. Outgoing Venezuelan Ambassador to Trinidad, Interview by author, February 2005.

REFERENCES

Besson, Gerard A. Interviewed by the author, February 2005.

———. 1995. *The Book of Trinidad and Tobago: Echoes of the Past,* ed. Desmond Charles Smith. Trinidad and Tobago.

Ménendez, Alfredo. 1996. *Correo del Orinoco: Selección de Episodios Navales.* Caracas, Venezuela: Naval de la Comandancia General de la Armada, Ediciones Facsimilar.

Mohammed, Sasha. 2004. 'Spanish For All…*Muy Pronto.*' *The Newsday.*

Moodie-Kublalsingh, Sylvia. 1994. *The Cocoa Panyols of Trinidad: An Oral Record.* London: British Academic Press.

Toussaint, Michael Ferguson. 2000. *Afro-West Indians in Search of the Spanish Main: The Trinidad-Venezuela Referent in the 19ᵗʰ Century.* PhD dissertation, UWI.

4

IN PURSUIT OF CITIZENSHIP:
Immigrants' Relations to Civil Society

KATHLEEN VALTONEN

INTRODUCTION

Immigrants are persons who have migrated, or moved from one society to another in order to settle. It has been customary to distinguish between 'voluntary' and 'forced' migrants. This distinction is based on individuals' reasons for departure from their country of origin, which generally determines how they are categorized in the destination country. However, the salience of this distinction might be decreasing with the increasing awareness that migration dynamics are complex and that migrants cannot be put into discrete categories.

'Settlement' refers to the range of activity undertaken by immigrants as they seek to become established in the new society. 'Integration' is a term that overlaps with settlement, but has, at its core, the notion that the individuals, their families and communities are gradually becoming a part of the social fabric of the new society (see Breton 1992). It embodies the idea that they are forging links and relations with the formal and informal institutions of the society. The term 'integration' will be used in this chapter, as it captures important purposeful, goal-oriented and qualitative aspects of the phenomenon.

My main argument is that immigrants' *participation in the community and society often takes place for extended periods in institutionally peripheral zones, rather than within the institutional mainstream.* Most empirical, theoretical and policy research on integration has focused on immigrants' relations to main institutions in the receiving society, for example, the labour market, educational institutions, political parties, etc. The chief concern of researchers, and often of practitioners, has been over their links to the so-called 'mainstream', which, in turn, is frequently conflated with market and state structures.

I arrived at the specific focus on 'civil society' in immigrant integration because the findings in my previous research indicate strongly that for immigrants and refugees, the achievement of full participation in mainstream resettlement society can be an extremely long-term project, especially if economic and social conditions in the receiving society are unfavourable, non-supportive or even hostile. Access to institutional participation can be blocked by structural obstacles, or delayed by the time needed by individuals to acquire appropriate levels of local qualifications (human capital), an information base, networks and those capacities that would enable them to use, or to identify, pursue and grasp opportunities to use to advantage any human and social capital which they develop. On the other hand, settlement can be significantly facilitated in an oblique fashion, by participation in civil society networks and activity. Immigrants' relations to civil society should not be underestimated, but identified, valorized and supported. For example, one outcome of participation in civil society is social capital, which represents a potential base of power residing in individuals, or in communities, which can be mobilized if and when needed. Linking into the formal and informal institutional networks can lead to an increase in immigrants' capacity and social resources for resettlement, and to opportunities for engaging more actively in the pursuit of equality.

The main data collection instrument was the semi-structured questionnaire. Participant observation and informant interviews brought a level of pre-understanding to the investigation. Social work practice with resettling populations in Finland also brings 'evidence-based' insight to the arguments presented in this chapter.[1] The work has significance for the areas of migration research that deal with regional and international flows, as well as the settlement of immigrants in countries of reception.

SETTLEMENT AND INTEGRATION IN THE LITERATURE

The integration-related literature shows that a broad range of determinants or implications of integration have been studied. These can generally be put into two classes: (1) individual characteristics and (2) environmental or structural elements. The former category includes demographic characteristics such as age, gender, religion and education level, but spans more individual attributes such as coping styles, social support circles, various forms of social capital, and cultural values. See, for example, Lindley (2002) on religion; Kloosterman, van der Leun and Rath (1998) on social capital.

Of late, scholars have directed considerable attention to the structural and societal context, and its impact on settlement and integration. This has required a macro-level approach and, in particular, scrutiny of policy implications and consequences. Weight is also given to the prevailing attitudes and pre-dispositions to immigration in the receiving populations. The impact of these types of social forces have been addressed, for example, by Reitz et al. (1999), who focus on education and labour market policy; Gran and Clifford (2000) on social rights; Soderling (1997) on the attitudes to immigrants and life management skills in the receiving population.

The progress of settlement and integration activity towards full participation and full membership in the society, depends on the nature and efficacy of immigrants' engagement with the societal institutions of the new home society. Institutions fall into the state, the market and civil society categories. Figure 1 shows this field of institutional engagement.

Individuals relate to the state as citizens with claims on the state, and bearing rights and duties. The scope and level of institutionalized rights varies in different States. 'Social citizenship' has been used as a frame for understanding the matrix of social, civil and political rights, which are embodied in the citizen's relation to the state (Marshall 1963). Scholars have pointed out that the concept and language of social rights are predominantly Western in origin, and question its general significance for non-Western countries (Mishra 1999). However, even though social citizenship might not be appropriate for evaluating the state of social rights and social welfare mechanisms across diverse societies, this concept is useful

Figure 4.1: Immigrant engagement with societal institutions

Immigrants/actors with particular characteristics: Demographic characteristics (e.g. age, gender, education level) Personal qualities (e.g. attitudes, social supports, coping styles)	**Environmental/structural institutions:** • The State, which grants to citizens: Social Civil Political rights Citizens relate as claimants on the State • The Market, locus of employment relations in the formal and informal sectors • Civil Society

for understanding one potential model of formalized relations between the state and its citizens

In the case of immigrants, engagement with the market is largely operationalized in the employment or self-employment relation. Through the process of 'commodification' of their labour, immigrants participate in the formal and informal labour market in a strongly reciprocal relation, selling their labour for economic remuneration. On the other hand, immigrants may remain unconnected to the labour market if their labour is not commodified, as in the case of many immigrant professionals who cannot practice their profession in the settlement country. Their participation in this institutional sector might also be hindered by barriers such as discrimination and other exclusionary processes. Labour market relations have, moreover, direct influence on the individual's ability to participate in the society in the role of consumer.

Studies of integration have also examined aspects related to the civil society arena, addressing themes such as political incorporation and participation (Klopp 2002; Fennema and Tillie 1999); the political rights of migrant workers (Layton-Henry 1990); ethnic community organization (for example, Zetter and Pearl 2000). The present study takes a more composite approach to immigrants' engagement with civil society, and examines how immigrants can engage in this arena along several dimensions.

CIVIL SOCIETY AS A CONCEPT

As a social construct, civil society is useful for scrutinizing a range of participation modes, which could lead to the increased control of immigrants over their own resettlement conditions. While some types of civil society activity (such as associational involvement) are not necessarily formalized, they may have strong salience for integration in the long term. I argue that civil society is a potentially important sphere, which facilitates the development of social resources that are critical to the eventual exercise of full citizenship. Through participatory activity in civil society, immigrants can also build their capacity, resources, network bases and strategies to influence policy in direct, indirect and collective ways. In this way, they can exert a degree of influence over their conditions of citizenship.

According to Brubaker (1992), citizenship is not only an instrument of participation and integration, but can also be a means of social closure and exclusion for some groups. The dynamics of social closure are inherent in the instituted process of citizenship (see Jacobs 1998: 143-157). Notwithstanding the propensity to exclusion present in the very systems of nationhood and citizenship, it is argued that within the fabric of civil society, solidarity action can be organized, based on common understandings of interest and commitment. Four areas or spheres of civil society are presented as offering such opportunities. These are the social solidarity base in civil society, the public sphere of rational/critical discourse that can inform public policy, the political arena and the community organization field. In the following sections, these areas are discussed in relation to their relevance for resettlement and integration processes.

AFFILIATION WITH THE SOCIAL SOLIDARITY BASE IN CIVIL SOCIETY

Civil society can be conceptualized as a sphere of society that is largely independent, not only of the narrowly political but also of the economic realm. This approach allows for social solidarity to play a prominent role in this arena. Alexander (1997: 118) speaks of the 'we-ness' of a national community, and the feeling of connectedness to 'every member' of that community that transcends particular commitments, narrow loyalties and sectarian interests. He argues that only this kind of solidarity can provide a thread of identity that would have the capacity to unite people who are dispersed by religion, class or race.

When civil society is understood as an arena of engagement founded on elements of social solidarity, it constitutes a very inclusive societal sphere from the perspective of the newly settling citizens. It should promote initiatives and actions characterized by the norm of universal participation. Furthermore, Shils (1997:85) argues that there must be a society-wide collective self-consciousness. This collective self-consciousness can coexist alongside the various sectional collective self-consciousnesses, and function to impose limits on the demand for the realization of the divergent ideals and interests, on occasion, even superceding them. Civil society is thus understood as anchored in the inclusive collective self-consciousness which can temper possibly opposing and contradictory forces in human relations in the citizenry. Extrapolating upon this idea, the social solidarity base can be understood as a locus of so-called 'promotive interaction' in which individuals can strive for mutual benefit. Promotive interaction incorporates the idea of working in shared interests, by assisting, helping, and encouraging each other's efforts to achieve. Promotive interaction may be contrasted with 'oppositional interaction' (individuals attempting to obstruct and frustrate each other's goal achievement), and no interaction (individuals ignoring — neither facilitating nor frustrating — each other's goal achievement) (Johnson and Johnson 2000).

Participation in the civil sphere is productive of mainstream linkages when resettling persons are established in solidarity networks and institutions, which are at the same time, contiguous and overlapping with the formal societal structure. Civil society can thus be a vehicle for 'voicing' concerns and advocating issues, especially in the early periods of settlement when 'newer' citizens have as yet little direct formal clout of their own.

THE PUBLIC SPHERE

The public sphere, like civil society of which it is a part, incorporates and recognizes the diversity of identities which people bring to it from their manifold involvements in civil society (Calhoun 1996). It follows that the structure-based threshold to participation should be low, even to the newest of citizens, who are a central group of stakeholders in immigration discourse. The public sphere, as elaborated here, is a social institution of discourse, a mechanism for communication, information dissemination and knowledge-management among citizens, working through the articulation, exchange, critique and development of ideas. As such, the public sphere can be identified with the spectrum of local and national arenas of discourse, including the media. The dynamics of the public sphere can move society towards change.

It is well recognized that majority-minority relations are sensitive to information distortion and arbitrary treatment in the media. The stereotyping, which may result, is very damaging to ethnic relations and the integration process as a whole. For instance, access to the labour market can be jeopardized if hiring practices are influenced by biased information sources.

It would be in the interest of immigrants to have a greater part in the discourse at public level in order to redress the imbalance of 'voice' on the public platform. Addressing issues of bias and prejudice directly, is one way of promoting equitable practices. This form of civil engagement usually remains undeveloped, or at best, there is a considerable time lag before the newer citizens come forward as actors in the public discourse. Difficulties in joining the public discourse on the part of immigrants, often relate to newcomer status, lack of language skill, and other pre-occupations, such as family reunification in the case of those who arrived as refugees.

ACTIVITY IN THE POLITICAL ARENA

When settling individuals take part in electoral activity, or stand as candidates, they are seeking to affect outcomes from the 'bottom up'. The right to vote in municipal elections is granted in many countries after a specified period of residence. The immigrant vote is incrementally developed and can generate critical leverage when the settling groups acquire a numerical base.

The political arena is closely affiliated with the issues of 'power'. In the process of relocating, immigrants do not easily transfer their bases of personal power with them to the receiving society.[2] They often lose their original reference groups, and cultural frames of reference. Resettlement is a pursuit of substantive citizenship, which is simultaneously a process of rebuilding the bases of power that fuel this undertaking. Engagement in the political arena brings the individual close to the competitive transactions in the public power distribution and redistribution process.

Participation in the political life of the receiving society depends to a great extent on the rate at which individuals become familiar with the sociopolitical arena. For a considerable period, the political 'centre' for settling persons may remain in the country of origin before being transferred to the new home society.

COMMUNITY ORGANIZATIONS

Organizational activity is perhaps the most easily recognized form of civil society linkages. It emerges often in the spontaneous formation of civil solidarity subsets, or subgroups. Organizations can thrive when communities grow to a viable size, and when circles of interest and commonality have coalesced. A critical prerequisite is a core of persons with the will and capacity to organize and invest commitment to collective activity.

Many immigrant organizations have some type of integration objective, that is, to facilitate the settlement process, to function in a bridging capacity between members and mainstream society, to promote the interests of their communities and the wider immigrant community. In order to pursue these goals effectively, however, the instrumental nature of activity has to be uppermost. In order for organizations to develop as interest groups, a base of consensus and support would be essential for legitimizing this form of collective activity. Instrumentally focused activity, such as interest group activity, which requires legitimized representation and consensus on chosen issues, is often a demanding mode of participatory activity for immigrants because of the heterogeneous nature, and extant lines of cleavage in many settling communities. An issue-oriented and inter-community style of organization could overcome this difficulty, and would be well in keeping with the 'solidarity' and 'common good' concerns of civil society. There is an ever-present danger that cultural and other forms of diversity inherent in settling communities can constitute a risk to an effective organizational agenda.

OUTCOMES OF CIVIL SOCIETY DYNAMICS

SOCIAL CAPITAL

Engagement in all the areas of civil society activity discussed above, can be seen as productive of social capital. Social capital refers to the mobilization of people through connections, social networks and group membership (See Peillon 1998). Of special significance in this context, is the notion of fungibility, or convertibility of the different forms of capital. Fungibility refers to the property of being exchangeable or replaceable, in whole or in part, for another form of capital. It is possible to convert a particular form into another although the extent and ease of convertibility is likely to be quite different in different contexts (Bourdieu 1986; Calhoun 1993: 68).

Social capital (contacts and connections) of immigrants would be crucial in the new society, because of its convertibility into valuable forms of assistance in specific situations, for example, into employment references, or insider information on cultural norms and expectations. Social capital would represent a potential base of power residing in individuals, or in communities, which can be mobilized if and when needed.

AGENCY AND ACTOR ROLES

Using the concept of a 'dense' civil society, we can understand civil society as a field of transactions and action (See Rosanvallon 1988). Citizens develop scope for exchange and mutual support, functioning as 'actors' and 'agents' rather than leaving issues to be resolved by the forces of the market and the state. Figure 4.2 illustrates how immigrants can link into the formal and informal institutional networks through a range of

Figure 4.2: The dynamics of immigrants' relations to civil society

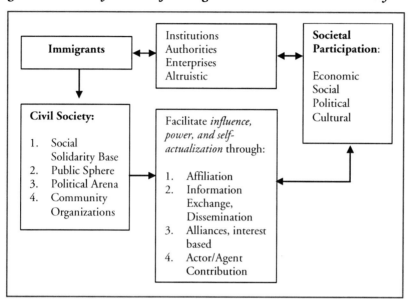

participatory modes, the outcome of which can be a rise in capacity and resources for resettlement.

Immigrants' involvement on the four dimensions in the civil society sphere can result in various types of affiliation, access to information networks, links into interest groups and opportunities for action, including collective action. Such activity generally has positive repercussions in other participatory spheres, which in turn draws newer citizens into the institutional fabric of resettlement society.

The gradual attainment of meaningful roles and positions in the community and society attest to progress in the integration process. The public discourse, political arena and community action forms are the established arena of contentious politics, and emancipatory struggles against hierarchies and inequalities. Immigrants' linkages with civil society make possible their participation as change agents in bringing about the very conditions that are critical for the integration process. This key activity can be operationalized more effectively through collaboration, partnerships and coalition building among groups of committed individuals both from newly settling communities and from the majority society. Civil society furnishes a prime forum for such collective action.

NOTES

1. The term 'evidence-based' is founded on a concept from health that implies a move towards a more rigorous and grounded research base to inform the planning and development of services (Brown and Loveridge 1999: 159).
2. See, for example, French and Raven (1959) on the bases of legitimate, coercive, referent, reward and expertise power.

REFERENCES

Alexander, J.C. 1997. 'The Paradoxes of Civil Society', *International Sociology,* 12, 2:115-133.

———. 2001. 'Robust Utopias and Civil Repairs', *International Sociology*, 164: 579-592.

Bader, V. 1997 'Fairly Open Borders'. In *Citizenship and Exclusion,* ed. Veit Bader. Basingstoke, Hampshire: Macmillan Press Ltd.

Bourdieu, P. 1986. 'The Forms of Capital'. In *Theory and Research for the Sociology of Education,* ed. J.G. Richardson, 241-8. New York: Greenwood Press.

Breton, R. 1992. 'Report of the Academic Advisory Panel on the Social and Cultural Impacts of Immigration'. Canada: Research Division, Strategic Planning & Research, Immigration Policy Group, Employment and Immigration.

Brown, L. and L. Loveridge, 1999. 'The politics of joint agency-university research'. In *The Politics of Social Work Research and Evaluation,* ed. Bob Broad, Birmingham: Venture Press.

Brubaker, R. 1992. *Citizenship and Nationhood in France and Germany.* Cambridge, MA: Harvard University Press.

Calhoun, C. 1995. *Critical Social Theory: Culture, History and the Challenge of Difference.* Oxford: Blackwell Publishers Ltd.

———. 1996. 'Social Theory and the Public Sphere'. In *The Blackwell Companion to Social Theory,* ed. Bryan S. Turner, Oxford: Blackwell Publishers Ltd.

Fennema, M. and J. Tillie, 1999. 'Political participation and political trust in Amsterdam: civic communities and ethnic networks', *Journal of Ethnic and Migration Studies* 25, 4: 703-726.

French, J.R.P. Jr. and B.H. Raven, 1959. 'The Bases of Social Power'. In *Studies in Social Power,* ed. D. Cartwright, Ann Arbor: University of Michigan, Institute for Social Research.

Gran, B.K. and E.J. Clifford, 2000. 'Rights and ratios: Evaluating the relationship between social rights and immigration', *Journal of Ethnic and Migration Studies*, 26, 3: 417-448.

Jacobs, R.N. 1998. 'The Racial Discourse of Civil Society: The Rodney King Affair and the City of Los Angeles'. In *Real Civil Societies: Dilemmas of Institutionalization,* ed. J. Alexander, London: Sage Publications Ltd.

Johnson, D.W. and R.T. Johnson, 2000 'The Three Cs of Reducing Prejudice and Discrimination'. In *Reducing Prejudice and Discrimination*, ed. Stuart Oskamp, New Jersey: Lawrence Erlbaum Associates, Publishers.

Kloosterman,R., J. van der Leun and J. Rath, 1998. 'Across the border: immigrants' economic opportunities, social capital and informal business activities', *Journal of Ethnic and Migration Studies*, 24, 2: 249-268.

Klopp, B. 2002. 'The political incorporation of EU foreigners before and after Maastricht: the new local politics in Germany', *Journal of Ethnic and Migration Studies* 28,2: 239-258.

Layton-Henry, Z. 1990. *The Political Rights of Migrant Workers in Western Europe.* London: Sage.

Lindley, J. 2002. 'Race or religion? The impact of religion on the employment and earnings of Britain's ethnic communities', *Journal of Ethnic and Migration Studies*, 28, 3: 427-442.

Marshall, T.H. 1963. *Sociology at the Crossroads and Other Essays*. London: Heinemann.

Mishra, R. 1999. *Globalization and the Welfare State*. Northampton, MA: Edward Elgar.

Peillon, Michel. 1998. 'Bourdieu's Field and the Sociology of Welfare', *Journal of Social Policy* 27, 2: 213-229.

Reitz, J.G., J.R. Frick, T. Calabrese and G.C. Wagner, 1999. 'The institutional framework of ethnic employment disadvantage: a comparison of Germany and Canada', *Journal of Ethnic and Migration Studies*, 25, 3: 397-444.

Rosanvallon, P. 1988. 'The decline of social visibility'. In *Civil Society and the State*, ed. J. Keane. London: Verso.

Shils, E. 1997. *The Virtue of Civility*. Indianapolis: Liberty Fund, Inc.

Soderling, I. 1997 Maahanmuuttoasenteet ja elamanhallinta (Attitudes towards Immigration and Life Management Skills). Helsinki: The Family Federation of Finland.

Stake, Robert.1995. *The Art of Case Study Research*. London: Sage Publications.

Zetter, R. and M. Pearl, 2000. 'The minority within the minority: Refugee community-based organizations in the UK and the impact of restrictionism on asylum seekers', *Journal of Ethnic and Migration Studies* 26, 4: 675-698.

5

CARIBBEAN IMMIGRANTS CHANGING THE POLITICAL LANDSCAPE OF NEW YORK CITY

CAROL DEAN ARCHER

INTRODUCTION

This study examines how various forms of identity are being negotiated by the Caribbean immigrant community in New York City. It also examines the relative roles of the political elites representing the Caribbean community, the mass constituencies in this process and the impact of this on the political landscape of New York City. It asks how this process of identity formation relates to political participation and tries to determine how the various forms of identity are used to access power and resources for the larger community. In addition, it examines the role of community-based organizations as vehicles for facilitating group identity formation and interaction within the group, with outsiders, or both.

This research highlights the disjuncture between the identity being forged by the leaders and that of the Caribbean community members. The two have quite different approaches to forming a group identity. In the context of New York City's political milieu, the leaders see developing a Caribbean identity as the most effective way to create political gains for the community as a whole, as well as for advancing their own interests in New York City and in their home country. For most residents, race seems to be more important in their identity formation. The research addresses the following questions:

- How does the racial context shape the process by which Caribbean immigrants are incorporated in New York City politics?
- What roles do political elites outside of the Caribbean community, particularly African-Americans, play in facilitating or impeding this incorporation?
- Are notions of group identity being forged by the elites and transmitted to the populace, or are they being forged among the rank and file and transmitted to the political elites?

THEORETICAL PERSPECTIVES

Understanding the development of group identity and its relationship to political participation among Caribbean immigrants is, and will continue to be, of significant theoretical concern for the field of political science and for the study of New York City politics. One aspect involves the political leadership or political elite representing the Caribbean immigrant community.

The question becomes, 'Who are the political elite and what are their strategies for developing an ethnic, national, and/or racial identity among Caribbean immigrants for greater political gain?' Another concern is the ability of the current political establishment of New York City, including the regular Democratic Party, to incorporate or shape Caribbean political participation, in ways similar to the Irish, in the latter half of the nineteenth century and Italian and Jewish immigrants in the first half of the twentieth. Key to this concern is the issue of race and the process of racialization.

It can be argued that Caribbean immigrants might assume a black identity in addition to, or instead of, a broader 'Caribbean' group identity based on historical, socio-political, and cultural commonalities of the people from that region. Furthermore, it can be argued that Caribbean immigrants might retain their separate national identities (that is, Jamaican, Haitian, Guyanese) and/or an 'American' identity in addition to, or instead of, a larger 'Caribbean/West Indian' or 'black' identity. This argument can be made based on the initial observation of the settlement patterns, the voting patterns, the rhetoric espoused by the political elites and the general population, and self identification of Caribbean immigrants over the years.

The arguments for the Caribbean immigrants adopting the 'American' identity are based on the 'straight-line' model of assimilation of earlier immigrants (Warner and Srole 1945). In essence, immigrants become 'Americanized.' Figure 5.1 illustrates the possible identities used by Caribbean immigrants as they negotiate the political landscape of New York City.

Figure 5.1: Factors influencing identity/possible political identity formation

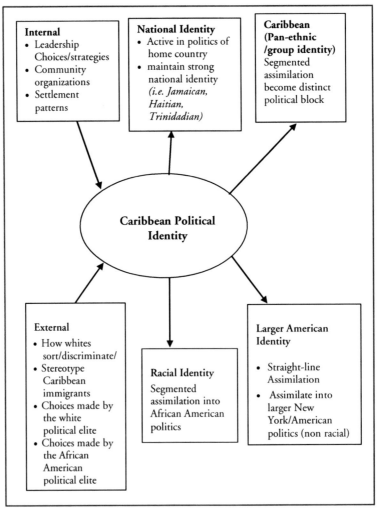

GROUP IDENTITY THEORY

Social scientists recognize the fluidity of group identities. Fox (1996) asserts that human identity is negotiable and is based on categories that individuals make up and/or others impose on them. The individual ability to identify with a larger group, especially an ethnic group, is forged early in life and is carried throughout the life cycle. This learned identity becomes second nature because early group identity is often built into self definition. Alban (1985) noted that this larger group identity, the particular ethnic identity 'cannot stand on its own because it is draped over the skeletal structure of inequality' (Alban 1985:12). In other words, group identity becomes pronounced when viewed from the context of power and the distribution of resources (Barth 1969).

Here, group identity is taken to go beyond individual and national identities. It submerges ethnic, national, and sometimes racial differences to encompass a more expansive identity based on a region of the world which would rest on cultural, social, economic, political, and historical factors.

ASSIMILATION THEORY

Dahl's theory of immigrant assimilation (Dahl 1961) is based on the notion that immigrant incorporation fosters greater equality, especially in terms of political and economic empowerment, weakens discrimination, increases individual freedom, and creates a more flexible society (Yinger 1994). These assimilationists fail to recognize that immigrants often have to abandon their cultural distinctiveness to become assimilated and this can often lead to alienation, especially from the political process. Limited assimilation may allow for the preservation of culture and reduce the feeling of alienation, thus allowing the immigrant to participate more in the political process.

On the other hand, Waters (1994) and Portes and Zhou (1993) argue that some post-1965 immigrants seem to adopt an identity similar to that of native minority groups or the underclass instead of the larger American society while others hold on to an immigrant identity to keep the larger society from classifying them.

Similarly, Kasinitz (1992) points out that Caribbean immigrants did not 'wait their turn' to enter the political arena as a distinct ethnicity. Instead, immigrants from the Caribbean promoted their 'Africanness or Blackness' and served as political leaders in the African American community from the 1920s until the 1970s. Green and Wilson argue that West Indian politicians embraced the 'Africanness or Blackness' because it was politically expedient to do so. It can be argued that the election of Una Clarke as the first 'Jamaican woman' to the New York City Council in 1993 and Yvette Clarke, in 2006, as the first Congresswoman of Jamaican ancestry runs counter to Kasitnitz's theory (Kasitnitz 1992). While there are questions about the identity which prevailed during these women's bid for office, it is safe to assume that Caribbean immigrants in general did not readily embrace the larger racial identity.

THEORY OF POLITICAL PARTICIPATION AND COMMUNITY ACTIVISM

Although Caribbean immigrants have participated at varying levels of politics in New York City since their arrival in the early twentieth century, like most immigrants to a new society, they have experienced periods of alienation. This alienation stems from several factors. First they are an immigrant group with a fairly recent history of voluntary migration to the United States, compared to the European immigrants who have at least 100 years of history in the United States and have helped to mould politics at the national, state and local levels. Most Caribbean immigrants, especially those who have migrated in the last major wave of migration (1976 to 1992) have not become citizens, cannot vote in most elections and are thus alienated from the political process. Second, the majority of the immigrants are of African ancestry and have experienced racial discrimination, which further alienates them. Third, American society sees them as poor and uneducated, with limited ability to influence the decision-making process at the local or national levels.

Nisbet (1978) posited a correlation between a group's alienation from the dominant political institutions and the rise of alternative forms of community and political activism rooted in group symbolisms. The assertion of such a group identity is seen as a renunciation of and/or challenge to the dominant political institutions. It is heightened when individual members (or the group as a whole) are not accepted by the dominant social group even though they have made significant economic, educational and social contributions to the host society.

The systematic exclusion of the majority of the Caribbean immigrants and African-Americans from New York City politics during this period, based primarily on race, allowed for the emergence of 'another kind of politics.' The new political force used street-side pulpits to advance their campaign against American racial, social, political, and economic injustice toward people of African ancestry. Marcus Garvey, founder of the Universal Negro Improvement Association (UNIA); Malcolm X, a second generation Caribbean immigrant; the Black Panther Party; and the Nation of Islam, have all used the soapbox or street-side preachers and group-based appeals to educate and encourage people of African ancestry to fight against political, social, and economic oppression in America.

While the soapbox orators used their verbal gift to bring issues to the Black public for analysis and discussion in the 1920s and 1930s; a middle-class leadership, who wanted to maintain the status quo, also arose in this period. They worked through various social and professional organizations to influence the political system. This leadership was most likely to be drawn from the doctors, lawyers, real estate dealers, and other successful business people in the community. They did not attempt to dismantle the status quo of New York City politics. They were, however, able to obtain several appointments in the judicial system and on various commissions throughout New York City. In the 1990s, although the legacy of the soapbox is but a memory, those with access to the print, audio, and visual media have emerged as leaders in the Caribbean community.

CARIBBEAN IMMIGRANTS IN NEW YORK CITY, 1980-1990

Jenkins (1990) argues that the Caribbean immigrants have asserted themselves in the cultural fabric of New York City to some degree, but more so in the communities in which they settled. She further argues that this assertiveness was achieved through social, cultural, religious and political community-based organizations. These organizations assisted the group in gaining access to vital services provided by the city. The organizations also served as advocates in the political and policy-making arena (Jenkins 1990).

Linda Basch has also analysed the relationship between the mainstream New York social and cultural organization and the Caribbean community (Bash 1987). From an anthropological perspective, Basch examined the role of voluntary associations in Caribbean immigrants' adaptation to New York City during the 1980s and found community organizations act as mediating forces between the immigrants and the new environment. They also served as a conduit for reproducing cultural institutions in the new environment and fostered links with the home country. From her studies, Basch concluded that these community-based organizations are developed in response to the inequalities and constraints imposed by racial and ethnic division in the city.

SETTLEMENT PATTERNS OF CARIBBEAN IMMIGRANTS 1990-2000

Traditionally, states such as New York, New Jersey, Connecticut were the largest receivers of Caribbean immigrants. However, the US 2000 Census shows that Caribbean immigrants are becoming more dispersed. In New York City, Brooklyn in general, and Central Brooklyn in particular, was the area with the largest concentration of Caribbean immigrants in the USA.

The data from the Newest New York shows that Caribbean immigrants are moving out of Brooklyn into the boroughs of Queens, the Long Island suburbs and the Bronx (City of New York Department of City Planning, 2005). Crown Heights, Flatbush, and East Flatbush saw declines or minimal growth in immigrants, primarily due to the out-migration of

Figure 5.2: The residential distribution of Caribbean immigrants

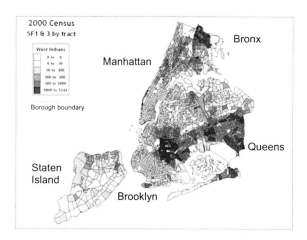

Source: *the Public Use Micro-sample for the 1990 and 2000 US Census data*

non-hispanic Caribbean groups to other parts of Brooklyn. (Source: *http:/ /www.nyc.gov/html/dcp/html/census/nny_exec_sum.shtml*). The pattern of residential change is in direct response to the availability of housing.

The Census also shows that in states such as Georgia, Virginia, Pennsylvania and North Carolina there has been marked increase in the Caribbean population, particularly Jamaicans and Haitians. In some instances the population grew by 150 per cent. Among the other Caribbean immigrants, Trinidadians, Guyanese and Barbadians still remain concentrated in Brooklyn. (Camarota and McArdle 2006).

CARIBBEAN IMMIGRANT POLITICAL PARTICIPATION 2000 AND BEYOND

Becoming a naturalized citizen is the first step in the political participation process in the United States for Caribbean immigrants. Recent research conducted by the Immigration Policy Centre (2003) and Lori Minnite (2005) show that Caribbean immigrants are being naturalized at a very high rate. This was the direct result of the passage of the 1996 immigration reform bill and the pressure placed on immigrants following the terrorist attack of September 11, 2001 ('9/11'). The 1996 Personal

Responsibility and Work Opportunity Act prevented immigrants from accessing health and education benefits, especially if they were not citizens. With the passage of this act federal government spending on welfare was cut by 40 per cent.

By the end the decade of the 1990s, an average of 767,000 immigrants were being naturalized every year. The average immigrant felt that being a citizen was the only way to access government benefits. Citizenship was also seen as a safeguard to deportation. Once the immigrants became naturalized, it allowed them direct access to the political process by being able to register and vote. In fact, many naturalized citizens are registered to vote on the spot as soon as they are naturalized.

As a result of the increased naturalization among Caribbean immigrants, there was a resultant increase in the number of them participating in elections. In an exit poll conducted in the 2004 Presidential election in New York City, 34 per cent of the 2,800 persons interviewed were Caribbean immigrants and more than 60 per cent of them had been naturalized within the previous ten years. The increasing number of naturalized Caribbean immigrants is significant because this is the only way that one can become a registered voter. Furthermore, Caribbean immigrants are not only registered voters but they are also active voters.

The 2000 Census indicates that in 1990 only 2.6 per cent of the Caribbean immigrants were registered voters and voted. This figure increased to 5.2 per cent in 2000 (see figure 5.3).

Caribbean immigrants are also moving away from 'home country' politics and focusing more on local level politics of the host society. Minnite (2004) showed that more than 59 per cent of the Caribbean immigrants who voted in the 2004 Presidential election indicated that job/economy mattered most in voting for the President. The second most important consideration was given to the war in Iraq. More than 42 per cent voted based on their concern about how the Presidential candidate would deal with the Iraqi war. Access to affordable healthcare was the third most important issue for the Caribbean immigrant.

Table 5.1

Decennial Census			Voting Age Citizen		Total
			No	Yes	
1990	West Indian (Incl. Haiti & Guyana)	No	2,504,799	4,448,605	6,953,404
			92.4%	97.4%	95.5%
		Yes	206,997	119705	326,702
			7.6%	2.6%	4.5%
		Total	2,711,796	4,568,310	7,280,106
			100.0%	100.0%	100.0%
2000	West Indian (Incl. Haiti & Guyana)	No	3,068,930	4,442,461	7,511,391
			92.5%	94.8%	93.8%
		Yes	248,492	244,876	493,368
			7.5%	5.2%	6.2%
		Total	3,317,422	4,687,337	8,004,759
			100.0%	100.0%	100.0%

(Source: *Public Micro Use Sample of the US 2000 Census*)

MAJOR FINDINGS ON CARIBBEAN IMMIGRANTS 1980 TO THE PRESENT

Caribbean elected officials are having some difficulty with the reformulation of New York's racial and ethnic political hierarchy. Many of the leaders of Caribbean descent, who have held elected office, run for office, or plan to run, note that they must move carefully. Their fear, they say, stems from the possibility that emphasizing a Caribbean political identity will come at the expense of black racial solidarity. Since a majority of the elected leaders have close ties with the African American political establishment, they worry about alienating the African Americans.

Community leaders and residents recognize that adopting a racial political identity might lessen their political power and group status. This belief originates from the perception that there are subtle, yet significant differences between Caribbeans and native-born African Americans. These differences are mainly associated with Caribbeans' conservative views on government support of social welfare programmes and their support of the Protestant work ethic. But it also stems from the perception that being grouped with the larger Black population would cause them to be subordinated to African Americans instead of getting a 'piece of the pie for themselves.' Furthermore, Caribbean immigrants' status as a 'model minority' would become suspect if they were grouped with African Americans who, as a group, are seen in a negative light by the wider American society.

The move by some leaders to encourage organizations representing Caribbean immigrants to focus on local issues, in addition to home-country issues, suggest that the community may be moving to use its social capital to create political capital. For example, groups such as the Sesame Flyers (a Trinidadian Cultural Group), and the Union of Jamaican Alumni Associations (UJAA), have received funding from New York City government, under the auspices of Council member Clarke, to conduct after-school programmes and develop a transitional institute for young Caribbean immigrants.

For many Caribbean immigrants national identity brings strength, status and power to the immigrants, but only in their country of origin. A number of Caribbean immigrants use their affiliation to New York City elected officials to increase their power and influence in their home country. Leaders and residents also gain political strength and status by working with country-specific organizations doing charity and/or political work in their home country. More often than not, however, this home country power and status has little impact in New York City. Unlike Irish or Jewish immigrants, Caribbean immigrants do not use the New York political arena to contest the politics of their home country, with the possible exceptions of Aristide's fight to regain office in Haiti and the US invasion of Grenada.

CONCLUSION

It is not enough to focus on a 'Caribbean' ethnic identity in analysing the integration of Caribbean immigrants in the USA through politics. The research indicates that Caribbean immigrants in New York use various forms of identity to navigate their political, social and economic landscape. By focusing on the various forms of identities imposed on and/or constructed by the Caribbean immigrant community and the relationship between these identities and political participation, it is shown how the

Caribbean immigrant community is pursuing social, cultural and political recognition from the larger US society.

This research raises a further question: namely, how can the Caribbean political identity that is forged by the leaders be institutionalized? In other words, how will Caribbean residents and the citizens of New York achieve the same kind of ethnic empowerment practiced by Italians on Staten Island or the Jews in Borough Park? One way is to encourage the second generation to adopt a Caribbean identity. There is some evidence that this is happening. John Sampson, who represents the Canarsie section of Brooklyn, appeals to his constituents by making constant reference to his Caribbean heritage. Assemblyman Denny Farrell and State Senator Basil Patterson have also found it strategic to highlight their Caribbean heritage. These appeals will become more potent as New York City's Black population becomes more Caribbean. The 1990 census data shows that New York City is experiencing a significant out-migration of African Americans, especially the middle class, and they are steadily being replaced by first and second generation US-born persons of Caribbean descent.

It is quite possible, however, that Caribbean identity will become more institutionalized in cultural rather than political terms. There are four reasons for this. First, the general population sees their identity as cultural rather than political. Second, the larger New York community also recognizes and has incorporated the various cultural aspects of the Caribbean community into its daily fabric. As a result, throughout New York City there are Italian Pizzerias selling Jamaican beef patties and popular television commercials trying to convince the public, with the hypnotic reggae or calypso music, to buy products ranging from cosmetics to vacation cruises. Third, the close proximity to the Caribbean and the immigrants' frequent contact will constantly renew this cultural connection. Finally, the federal government's and the courts' decision to limit the racial basis for redistricting may hamper the emergence of more Caribbean districts. In 1998, a federal court overturned Congresswoman Nydia Valasquez's district on the grounds that far-flung Hispanic neighbourhoods did not constitute a community of interest. Given that the 11th Congressional District (the largest Caribbean district in the United States) was redrawn to reflect its Caribbean population and the likelihood of a heated race between Owens and Clarke, African American political elites may try to hamper Caribbean immigrants' influence. These constraints remind us that, as always, the process of ethnic succession in New York City politics is far from smooth.

REFERENCES

Alban, B. (1985). 'The Effects of Socialization on Women's Managers Careers,' *Management Bibliographies and Review* 11 (3).

Barth, Frederick. 1969. *Ethnic Groups and Boundaries: The Social Organization of Culture Difference*. Boston: Little, Brown, and Company.

Basch, Linda. 1987. 'The Vincentians and Grenadians: The Role of Voluntary Organizations in Immigrant Adaptation To New York City.' In *New Immigrants in New York City,* ed. Foner, Nancy, New York: Columbia University Press. Camarota and McArdle (2006)

City of New York Department of City Planning. 2005. *The Newest New Yorkers: An Analysis of Immigration into New York City During 2000-2004*. New York: City of New York Department of City Planning.

Dahl, Robert Alan, 1961. *Who Governs? Democracy and Power in an American City.* New Haven: Yale University Press. Immigration Policy Center (2003).

Fox, Geoffrey. 1996. *Hispanic Nation: Culture, Politics and the Constructing of Identity.* Secaucus, New Jersey: Birch Lane Press.

Jenkins, Shirely. 1990. 'New Immigrants.' in Bellush, J. and Netzer, D., eds. *Urban Politics, New York Style*. New York: M.E. Sharpe. (Green and Wilson)

Kasinitz (1992).

Bottomore, T. and R. Nisbet, 1978. *A History of Sociological Analysis*, New York, New York, Basic Books.

Portes, Aldjandro and Zhou, Min. 1993. 'The New Second Generation Segmented Assimilation and Its Variants.' *Annals of the American Academy of Political and Social Science*. Vol. 530: 74-96.

Waldinger, Roger. 1996. *Still the Promise City? African Americans and New Immigrants in Post-industrial New York*. Cambridge, Massachusetts: Harvard University Press

Warner, Lloyd and Srole, Leo.1945. *The Social Systems of American Ethnic Groups*. New Haven: Yale University Press.

Waters, Mary. 1994. 'The Intersection Between Race and Ethnicity: Generational Change Among Caribbean Immigrants to the US' *International Migration Review*. Vol. 28 No. 4: 795-820

Yinger, Milton J. 1994. *Ethnicity: Source of Strength? Source of Conflict?* Albany, New York: State University of New York Press.

6

RISK AND RESILIENCE IN THE AFRICAN-CARIBBEAN COMMUNITY IN THE UK

HILARY ROBERTSON-HICKLING AND FREDERICK W. HICKLING

INTRODUCTION

The year 2008 marks the 60th year of the arrival of the SS *Empire Windrush* in the United Kingdom with 492 Jamaicans on board, and thus the beginning of the mass migration of West Indians to Britain as part of the rebuilding effort in the aftermath of the devastation of World War II. Their arrival and integration into British society in the face of racism and numerous other challenges, illustrate some of the risks involved in the process of migration, as well as the remarkable resilience which the Caribbean migrants displayed. This paper examines the dialectic nature of the risk and resilience factors encountered by this group of migrants from case studies drawn from public and private clinical settings in Birmingham and London, England; explores the causes and the consequences of these factors in the issues of mental health and African-Caribbean migration to the UK and concludes that risk and resilience are dialect antipodes for survival in a hostile, racist environment.

The risks to which the Caribbean migrants were exposed included possible criminalization and the development or onset of mental illness. Resilience results in survival, wellness, academic and personal success and the development and maintenance of healthy, wholesome relationships.

Garvey's (1967) 'A people without knowledge of its history is like a tree without roots' acknowledges that a complete understanding of the risk experienced by African-Caribbean people and their resilience to these experiences must begin with an insightful perception of the history of the forced and free migrations of African-Caribbean people in the latter part of the previous millennium. Hickling and Gibson (2005), and Hickling (2007) have suggested that the European invasion and genocidal colonization of the New World, the enslavement of the African people and the concept of the Euro-American psychosis, set the stage for the present day dilemma of Caribbean people. He suggests that the initial European colonizers experienced a delusion '…all that I see is mine, and all therein belongs to me…' that underpinned the conquest of the New World and continues to underscore the desire to expropriate all of the wealth and resources of the world for their use. A delusion is defined as a fixed false belief, impervious to rational argument, out of keeping with the cultural beliefs. The European delusion is the basis of the domination of the rest of the world by Europeans and Americans for the last five hundred years. Their thinking has had a negative impact on the migrants and subsequent generations who are forced into the role of the inferior and subservient other.

The rigours of the Middle Passage and the horrors of African slavery have been well documented (Williams 1970, Sherlock and Bennett 2000) and the seminal relationship of the development of contemporary capitalism and African slavery (Williams 1970) set the stage for the colonial 'devouring' of Africa by Europe in the late 1900's (Pakenham 1991). Embedded in the legacy of 350 years of African slavery was the forced migration of African people to the Caribbean and the Americas. The mass movement of people from Africa and Asia continued after the abolition of slavery in the form of indenture driven by the demand for cheap labour to fuel the voracious capitalist maw worldwide. The construction of the Panama Railway and Canal (1850-1914) provided a major source of employment for migratory Caribbean labour in the late nineteenth century, where the creation of a discriminatory glass ceiling between white workers - gold men - and black workers — silver men — (Newton 1984) was a common feature of European colonial social engineering.

Caribbean migration is the legacy of half a millennium of European-imposed slavery and colonialism. The past six decades since 1948 have provided an opportunity for us to examine the impact of migration on the West Indian community and its integration into British society. Researchers from many disciplines have contributed to our understanding of African-Caribbean migration and integration into British society including historians such as Fryer (1988), and sociologists Hall (1990, 1992, and 1996), and Gilroy (1992).

> '…When four hundred and ninety two Jamaicans disembarked from the SS [*Empire*] *Windrush* in 1948 they may not have been aware that they had opened a new chapter in history. They were the beginning of the largest mass migration of black people to come to England. Although to be black and British is nothing new, since there have been Africans in Britain at least since Roman times.' (Fryer 1988, 77).

The geographer Thomas-Hope suggests that for Caribbean migrants:

> …Mental images of places outside the home island incorporate as 'true' or 'real' not only what people have known, or thought they knew about the external world, but also what they believe… (Thomas-Hope 2002, 6).

Mental illness and the associated stigma present a worldwide challenge and are particularly evident in the African-Caribbean population in Britain. The community experiences the highest rates of mental illness of all ethnic groups in Britain. After a period of mass migration, beginning in 1948, thousands of hopeful West Indians migrated to Britain in search of a better life. Some succeeded in this quest, but many failed and some experienced a severe and enduring mental illness and its sequelae. Social isolation, loss of self, family and community, and racism as well as difficulties with the National Health Service, Social Service and the police continue to be the experience of some up till the present time. Ari Kiev (1965) was the first to identify the high rates of admission of African-Caribbeans to mental hospitals in the UK. Other studies in the UK identified the mental hospital admission rate for African-Caribbeans to be four to six times higher than that for British Whites. Ken Royes (1962) noted that the mental hospital admission rate of 148 per 100,000 in Jamaica was the same as for Whites in the UK. Hickling (1991) who reported a mental hospital admission rate 136 per 100,000 in Jamaica showed that there was a lower admission rate for schizophrenia in Blacks in Jamaica than for Whites in the UK. Studies shifted from admission rates to first contact incidence rates, using standardized diagnostic instruments such as the present state examination (Wing et al. 1974).

Studies by Harrison et al. (1988), and Wessely et al. (1991) reported risk ratio for schizophrenia 6-18 times higher for African-Caribbeans in the UK than for Whites. Hickling and Rodgers-Johnson (1995) investigated the incidence of first contact schizophrenia in Jamaica and identified a rate of 2.09 per 10,000, which was lower than that of Whites in the UK. This was a watershed study, which established unequivocally that the high incidence of schizophrenia in African-Caribbeans in the UK was not caused from factors in the Caribbean, but from factors in the migrant host country. This conclusion had been strongly suggested by previous studies by Burke (1984) and by Hickling (1991). Both Trinidad and Barbados (Bhugra et al. 1999 Mahy et al. 2000) reported incidence rates of schizophrenia in Blacks to be similar to that in Jamaica, and less than that of Whites in the UK. The high rates of schizophrenia reported in Blacks in the UK have been strongly contested. Sashidharan (1993) wrote a fierce critique on the methodological deficiencies in ethnic risk ratio studies of schizophrenia in the UK.

Aggrey Burke was the first Caribbean psychiatrist to identify racism as a cause of mental illness in African-Caribbean people in Britain (Burke 1984). Robin Murray and his colleagues (Sharpley et al. 2001) in the UK strongly countered the racism/social etiology, by positing biological causes for the high rates. These biological causes included genetic (predisposition of migrant Blacks to schizophrenia); viral (cross placental neuronal infection by influenza and other viruses; developmental (obstetric and perinatal risk factors). Hickling collaborated with colleagues (Hickling et al. 1999) from the Institute of Psychiatry in London to study the role of misdiagnosis by White psychiatrists.

RISK AND RESILIENCE

This chapter argues that risk and resilience are dialect antipodes for survival in a hostile racist environment and that the African-Caribbean community of Britain has displayed remarkable resilience in view of the risks and protective factors associated with racism. For this community to have overcome formidable odds such as those experienced by the persons described by the case studies is proof of their resilience.

Risk factors are defined as individual or environmental markers that are related to the increased likelihood that a negative outcome will occur.

Resilience (or 'psychological resilience') is a term used in psychology to describe the capacity of people to cope with stress and catastrophe. It is also used to indicate a characteristic of resistance to future negative events. This psychological meaning of resilience is often contrasted with 'risk factors'. (Wikepedia)

Protective factors are individual or environmental safeguards that enhance a person's ability to resist stressful life events, risks or hazards and promote adaptation and competence. An important but often overlooked aspect of protective mechanisms is that they only operate when a risk factor is present (Wikepedia). Risk and protective factors can exist both within individuals and across various levels of the environment in which they live. Diverse problems can share common risk factors. Risk factors often co-occur, and when they do, they appear to carry additive and sometimes expon ential risks. It is often the accumulation of multiple risks rather than the presence of any single risk factor that leads to negative outcomes.

These issues are examined utilizing the cases of four African-Caribbean persons, three of whom have experienced a severe and enduring mental illness in Birmingham, England. Birmingham, the second largest city in England has the second largest African-Caribbean population in the country. These persons have spent long periods of their lives in mental hospitals and now live in the community as a result of the policy of deinstitutionalization. Three of the cases are about African-Caribbean persons who succumbed to the risk of mental illness while the other is about a person who has been largely resilient and therefore better able to overcome the same risks. Important variables highlighted in the cases and presented here include, their place of birth, their parents, schooling and other experiences in the UK which have had a profound effect on their lives. These cases have been selected by the authors from a number of persons who were seen in public and private settings or interviewed during a series of focus groups as part of the research undertaken for a PhD thesis in Birmingham during the period 1995-2000. All of these persons gave written consent for their experiences to be shared. Our clinical experiences proved to us that misdiagnosis and racism are alive and well in British psychiatry. The following case illustrates some of the risks associated with migration.

CASE 1

An African-Caribbean, second-generation woman, age 42 was born in Leeds, England. She went to Jamaica when she was age 5, where she grew up in Santa Cruz, St. Elizabeth, with her mother. Her mother still lived in Santa Cruz where she was looking after her son. Her father lived in Leeds with her brother but she had no contact with them. She attended Lacovia Secondary School and left school at age 17. She had her first child, a son, soon after leaving school and then had another son at age 23. She started working in Kingston as a domestic worker. She was working in Kingston, Jamaica, when she met her husband, an Englishman man who looked 'white' but was of mixed race and was living on British income support in Jamaica. His father was a Black Jamaican, and his mother was a White English woman. She got married to him in Jamaica and then returned to England in 1990 at age 29. They lived in Wolverhampton where she had two children for him, who were subsequently put in care. She started to have trouble with him while they were living together, and he was very violent and abusive to her. She had never worked in the UK and had no history of serious physical or mental illness. Symptoms of depression were noted in a letter from her general practitioner in June 1991 when she was pregnant with her daughter. In December 1993, there are notes of her displaying outbursts of temper, breaking a window for no apparent reason, and talking nonsense. In April 1994 she was found wandering in Coventry in a confused state. It appeared that her husband had obstructed her access to social services and mental health services over these years.

She was likely to have been suffering from a post-partum psychosis of a schizophrenic nature, which arose after her last pregnancy. She functioned quite capably at home in Jamaica doing domestic and related activities and showed a significant degree of resilience and strength. In England her domestic skills were readily activated and actualized in a work rehabilitation programme, and she was encouraged to rebuild her life around suitable work activity and a secure emotional relationship. This case study demonstrates the destabilizing effect of moving between Jamaica and the UK without the appropriate support systems being in place. Hence when this woman was having marital problems and mental health problems associated with her pregnancy, she ran foul of the state authorities and ended up losing her children. The National Health Service provided less than adequate service as she was misdiagnosed and inappropriately treated. It required the culturally appropriate care at Servol Community Trust (a privately run African-Caribbean mental health service) to enable her to make significant progress.

CASE 2

This man, age 49, was born in Fairfield district, St. Catherine, Jamaica. He came to England at the age of 9 years old in 1964. He left school at the age of 17 with some CSE exams, and after a few short-term jobs, attended College. At the age 20, he attended University and eventually graduated in Mechanical Engineering in 1979. A large car manufacturing company employed him for about 3 years, before he was made redundant. He had no close relatives or friends, he had three half brothers and his mother lived in Jamaica. He saw his brothers occasionally when they came to visit him. He also visited one brother at his home on occasion. His mother communicated with one of his brothers and he read her letters but he did not communicate with her directly. He seemed to have lived a reclusive life since he had been made redundant. Concerns had been raised about his mental health after a neighbour reported to the police that he had made an unprovoked attack on the neighbour the previous day. No previous history of violence or mental illness was known. Social Services were aware of a two-year history of self-neglect, failure to pay bills and he was consequently facing an eviction order from his flat. He was also reported to be verbally abusive to his neighbours and would sometimes spit on them. He was reported to have told the Jamaican High Commission that he thought he was being persecuted and others were trying to kill him. His hospital assessment diagnosed paranoid schizophrenia characterized by mainly negative symptoms of lack of drive, motivation, volition and blunted affect. He was not open and concealed many of his personal concerns.

He moved to Servol Community Trust in 1994. During the time of his placement he was in complete denial about his illness and had lacked motivation to the extent that staff had to attend to his every need. He was diagnosed as having schizophrenia and started on anti-psychotic medication, which resulted in a marked improvement in his health. He spent most of his time at the library and kept abreast of developments in computer technology. He was also applying to do post graduate studies, then the teachers' qualification, so that he might become a lecturer. He was also diagnosed as suffering from severe identity problem and personality disorder, which made him feel superior to his fellow clients and deny his Black racial identity. It was suggested that he had a classical 'Roast Breadfruit Psychosis' which develops in persons who deny their Black identity and are faced with severe social stressors of racism and prejudice (Hickling and Hutchinson, 1999). After some years there were problems with his care during which he killed a policemen who tried to apprehend him. He was given a sentence of life imprisonment for murder.

This is a case study, which depicts the mental health problems of a brilliant, educated young man who lost his job and found himself unable to cope with the pressures of life. His situation was exacerbated by his isolation from his family and the identity problems which he experienced. He had had racist experiences, which affected him deeply. He was also struggling with problems of racial identity and seemed to be ambivalent about his 'Blackness', and did not have the anchor of the support system which was largely located in Jamaica; he had expressed a desire to visit his family in Jamaica.

CASE 3

An African-Caribbean second generation man, age 25 was born in London, England to a Black Jamaican mother and a White English father. His mother left her own parents and siblings in the UK and with her son returned to Jamaica where he was educated from primary school, and completed tertiary education at the University of the West Indies. He went to England to do postgraduate work in law and to reacquaint himself with his father and his newly discovered all-White family. He also maintained contact with his mother's family which encouraged him to overcome the adversities of racism and complete his studies. The experience of racism and social isolation at home and at the university in England caused him much pain and despair and contrasted with the privileged status conferred on him as a result of his mixed racial heritage and brown skin colour in Jamaica which allowed him various social advantages. He reported:

'...The more I tried is the more difficult that it became and it just caught up inside and over a period of a year it just got worse. Toward the end of the year I was just losing the plot, losing the plot completely. My head felt like it was going to burst, I felt like I had no one to turn to. I went to two of my exams in the first year and then I just walked out. I told the faculty that I was leaving, that I was pulling out; I got a ticket and went home to Jamaica. My mum didn't even know I was coming home, I just turned up. For days my head was just going like that, I didn't know if I was coming or going. For the first time in my life I started thinking about suicide, something like that, I felt that I had to leave before I did something really drastic.....Before I left I had visited some of my cousins in London, they were all black and I told them and they were surprised. They were saying to me,' You cannot give up and let them beat you. You have to show them that you are better than them .You can rise above whatever they throw your way...'

The evidence suggested that the well people had some prophylaxis that protected them from the social pressures in the UK. The most important elements seemed to be strong African-Caribbean roots and educational success outside of the UK, involvement in a church and the development of a strong and supportive family and community. This seems to allow young people to have great expectations and ambitions, and to pursue their goals despite the compelling burden of racism. This process involved the development of adaptive coping mechanisms in a society that had low expectations of African-Caribbean people and poor opportunities for healing in the community.

The risks mainly surround the issues of racism, unemployment and social deprivation i.e. the Jarman scales Top of Form.

CASE 4

This woman age 42 was born in Jamaica and migrated to the UK age six, grew up and was educated in London. She became a mother and after her daughter had experienced racism at school she decided to home-school her child, age 10. This resulted in a stand-off at her home with the social services and British police force, during which time she set the curtain at her home on fire in an attempt to 'bun out de pestilence'. She was arrested and charged with 'arson with intent' and sent to the Maudsley Hospital, where she was diagnosed with schizophrenia by the White British psychiatrists. Subsequently she was examined in 1993 by one of the authors whose diagnosis was that of depression, contrary to the findings of the British psychiatrists. A Jamaican-born African-Caribbean psychiatrist Dr. Aggrey Burke, who saw the lady at the same time, at the request of the Social Services, but unknown to the author, concurred with the diagnosis of depression. She was admitted to Broadmoor for life, on a charge of 'arson with intent.'

These four cases bore remarkable similarity to many other persons who we saw in the NHS or in a private organization based in the African-Caribbean community between1995-2000. Hickling worked at North Birmingham Mental Health Trust as a consultant psychiatrist to assist in developing a system for understanding the problems of mental illness in African-Caribbean's and helping to develop culturally safe appropriate services. The patients underwent similar problems experienced by many African-Caribbean patients in the UK National Health Service, including little access to talking therapies (psychotherapies), high doses of medication, the loss of their children into state care, racist experiences with the health and social care services as well as high rates of unemployment and deprivation. In addition, there was very little expectation of recovery on the part of the authorities, hence many patients or clients found themselves dependent on income support for the rest of their lives. We have worked to mitigate the risk and foster resilience in our work with African-Caribbean people in the Caribbean and in the United Kingdom. This work has been at the individual and organizational levels and has helped to restore people to health and also to prevent illness by facilitating individual achievement and organizational health.

Table 6.1. The triangulation process revealing the Risk/Resilience factors

Variable	Case #1	Case #2	Case #3	Case #4	Risk/Resilience Factor
Gender	Female	Male	Male	Female	Male/female
Birthplace	UK	Jamaica	UK	Jamaica	UK/Jamaica
Childhood socialization	Jamaica	Jamaica/ UK	Jamaica	Jamaica/ UK	Jamaica growth/ UK Growth
Migration to UK	Age 29	Age 9	Age 22	Age 6	Early migration/ Late migration
Parents	Black Jamaican	Black Jamaican	Black J F White UK M	Black Jamaican	Racial purity/ miscegenation
Schooling	Primary School Jamaica	University UK	University Jamaica	Secondary School UK	Low education/ High Education
UK Social encounter	Racism UK	Racism UK	Racism UK	Racism UK	Racism/ Low racial prejudice
Diagnosis	Depressive psychosis	Schizophrenia	None	Depressive psychosis	Mental Illness/ Mental health
Psychosocial response 1	Violent social behaviour	Violent social behaviour	None	Violent social behaviour	Violence/ Non-violence
Psychosocial response 2	Hopelessness	Murder	Completed Law degree	Despair	Non coping/ Adaptive coping
Psychosocial response 3	Incarceration in UK	Incarceration in UK	Successful lawyer in Jamaica	Incarceration in UK	State Custody/ Social Freedom

By the process of triangulation (Gribich 1999), the congruent and opposing themes of these four case studies have been teased out and the resulting risk/resilience factors identified. These have been expressed in table 6.1.

ANTIPODAL DIALECTICS OF RISK AND RESILIENCE IN AFRICAN CARIBBEAN MIGRANTS

By extracting demographic, social and psychological variables from the four case studies and comparing these variables between the cases, the process revealed a number of dialectic opposing themes representing risk factors and resilience factors. These are expressed graphically in figure 6.1. Emerging from the analysis is a cartwheel of dialectical antipodes of psychosocial risk and resilience factors related to migration of African-

Figure 6.1. Antipodal dialectics of risk/resilience factors in African-Caribbean migrants to the UK

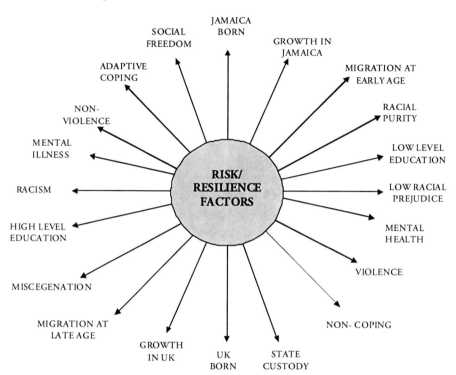

Caribbean people to the UK, that link racism, social dysfunction, mental illness and violent behaviour to early migration from Jamaica to the United Kingdom. The cartwheel illustrates the powerful array of competing and conflicting forces that African-Caribbean migrants to Britain encounter, and points the direction for the resultant vector of migrant survival in a hostile racial and political environment. The array also points direction for future research on migrant resilience in the African-Caribbean Diaspora.

DISCUSSION

Migration has characterized Caribbean life from the times of African enslavement by Europeans, of Asian indenture and of course, resulted in the mass migration to Britain, the USA and Canada in more recent times in history. Thomas-Hope (1992) and Chamberlain (1997) advance arguments supporting the pervasiveness of migration in the Caribbean. James (1992) provides a valuable platform for raising issues about Caribbean migration to Britain and the development of identity, especially when he notes the paucity of research on the topic:

> '...Although much had been written on the forces behind Caribbean migration to Britain, and on the social and economic conditions in which Black people live, precious little work has been done on the nature and ethnic identity of Caribbean's and their descendants here... It is now generally acknowledged that ethnicity and ethnic identity however defined, are not static and eternal in their constitution but are profoundly dynamic, always in the process of being made, unmade and remade. Moreover, it is evident, that the phenomenon of migration and the encountering of new challenges in a new environment quite often accelerates the process of such changes...' (James 1992, 232).

James provides the foundation for the historical and sociological integration of African-Caribbean migration to Britain, and has contributed to our understanding of the lives of African-Caribbean people in Britain. The recognition of the paradox of this migratory experience is important in understanding the ambivalence felt by many African-Caribbean people about Britain. There have been both costs and benefits to the experience, as has been revealed in the lives of many African-Caribbean people.

The *SS Empire Windrush* had provided the initial vehicle for Caribbean migration to the UK in 1948. In Britain today there is a continuing debate about 'Britishness' and the issue of citizenship especially in the age of terrorism. At this time Britain is grappling with the fact that it is a small group of British born citizens of Pakistani and other Islamic ancestry who have planted bombs and been engaged in terrorist activity, and that the war in Iraq and the problems in the Middle East have heightened conflict with Muslims in Britain and elsewhere. The issues of citizenship in Britain and in the European Union continue to be contentious and some of the same old issues from the time of African-Caribbean migration are still current. The role of the enigmatic politician, thinker, and maverick Enoch Powell (1912-1998) in the life of the West Indians who migrated to the

United Kingdom in the 1940's, '50s and '60s has been very important. His famous speech in 1964 prophesied that unchecked immigration by Black people, particularly West Indians, would cause rivers of blood to flow. His academic and oratorical prowess was employed in the service of Britain's right-wing politicians and racist extremists who believed that 'Enoch was right'. This chapter asserts that he was wrong, and that although there were risks in the immigration of the West Indians, their resilience would allow them to survive and even thrive in Britain. The paradoxical situation is that some West Indians had been recruited by Enoch Powell to work in the National Health Service and the transport system. The West Indian migrant would contribute to the development of a multicultural society in the main, not be a burden nor pollute the sacred concept of 'Britishness'.

Enoch Powell focused on the risks of migration, the development of a multi-cultural society with the possibility of miscegenation, the dilution of the British identity and a number of other so-called 'evils'. But the West Indians came to make a better life, to work and save money then return to the West Indies in a better socio-economic standing. They believed that they were coming to the 'mother country' which would welcome and take care of them.

The history of Caribbean migration to the UK has always been told by historians (Chamberlain), geographers (Byron, Thomas-Hope) and sociologists (Goulbourne). It is now time for the history to be told by psychologists, psychiatrists and other mental health workers, who can anticipate the problems, and are required to diagnose and treat persons who develop mental illness. They are also required to interpret mental illness for the law and other institutions in British society. Migration is a complex and multidimensional process. Participants and observers in the Caribbean and elsewhere must enrich the perspective of participants and observers in the UK. This is even more important as there is a popular myth held by those who have remained in the Caribbean 'that England makes people mad.'

Psychiatrists have contributed to our understanding of the risk factors for mental illness. The work of Rutter (1999) was groundbreaking in relation to childhood development and resilience. Not only have the psychiatrists provided an understanding of the issues in the metropolitan countries, which receive the migrants, but also in the Caribbean societies from which the migrants have come.

Psychologists like Mama (1995) have been examining the complex process of migration and delineating such issues as that of Black British identity. One critical issue identified is the impact of racism, although there is limited information about the impact of racism on this identity (James 1992). In addition, little information exists to identify the connection between identity, social exclusion and the negative experiences of African-Caribbean people in Britain. A multidisciplinary approach is necessary to provide all of the information required to make sense of the experience of migration. Writers like Samuel Selvon in his epic *Lonely Londoners, Moses Ascending* and *Moses Migrating* contributed to our understanding of the early period of mass migration and poets like Jamaican Louise Bennett have also contributed to our understanding.

Bennett (1982) aptly expressed the expectations of those who came in the *Windrush* period in her poem, 'Colonization in Reverse,' written in the Jamaican creole language. The following verse weaves the critical issues together:

What a devilment a Englan
Dem face war an brave de worse;
But ah wondering how dem gwine stan
Colonizin in Reverse (Bennett 1982).

This poem illustrates the high levels of excitement and expectations of high status jobs and prosperity with which many Caribbean people came to Britain.

With the excitement there was also a sense of caution and concern about the reversal of the historical process that would result in the coloniser being colonised. When the Caribbean migrants who were British subjects came to live in Britain, the seat of the Empire, concerns were felt by those who came and by those who were receiving them. It was one thing to live in the colonies out in the periphery, but quite another matter to come to live in the centre. The audacity and sense of belonging in Britain of the African-Caribbean migrants was met with horror, hate and fear by their hosts and set the stage for the difficulties which lay ahead. Black people are over-represented in the UK prison population where 17 per cent of male prisoners in England and Wales were from ethnic minority groups constituting 6 per cent of the general population. The rates of imprisonment for Blacks were 8 times higher than for Whites. Of Blacks over the age of 21, 51 per cent were serving sentences of over four years compared to 35 per cent of Whites.[1]

In the Mental Health Services, Black and ethnic minorities (compared to the 'White' majority community) are more often diagnosed as schizophrenic, and compulsorily detained under the Mental Health Act. In addition they are transferred to locked wards from open wards, are admitted to hospital as 'offender patients' and held by police under Section 136 of the Mental Health Act.[2] They are given high doses of medication and sent to psychiatrists by courts and are not referred for psychotherapy. In the education and schooling system there were a large number of permanent exclusions of Black pupils of compulsory school age. African-Caribbean children were excluded 4 times more commonly than White children.[3]

The significance of these statistics is that they show an overrepresentation of Black people in some of the major institutions like prison, mental hospital and under-representation in terms of scholastic and economic achievement. While there are risks to the health and well-being of the African-Caribbean community there is also tremendous resilience in the face of racism, deprivation, high levels of unemployment and a host of economic and social ills.

An Associated Press report quotes Sir David Calvert Smith, Director of Britain's Crown Prosecution,

> '... British society is institutionally racist ... London's Metropolitan police was branded institutionally racist in an official report on the bungled investigation of the 1993 killing of black teenager Stephen Lawrence. According to the McPherson Report: 'There is unwitting prejudice, ignorance and thoughtlessness

and racist stereotyping and the collective failure of an organization to provide an appropriate and professional service to people because of their colour, culture or ethnic origin...[4]

While it is important to understand the risk factors associated with racism it is also important that the concept of resilience is understood. This will allow for the development of more appropriate policies and interventions in health and social care and a better understanding of minority ethnic communities. This understanding can be applied to several contexts including that of the mental health system and the general community.

This chapter applies the concepts of risk and resilience to the African-Caribbean in Britain and suggests that racism generates many risk factors. There was a tendency of the mental health system to focus more on the risk and not enough on resilience. While the definition of health is physical, mental and spiritual wellbeing, it is recognized that when a person is chronically mentally ill the definition has to be adjusted. Indicators of health include the ability to live independently or in a warden-controlled flat, to remain on medication without having to be hospitalized, to establish and sustain healthy relationships, to attend college, get a job, and care for one's daily needs. These and other indicators of good health have been identified especially in terms of the lives of people who had lived in isolation, and idleness in a mental hospital where things seemed hopeless and the patients were no longer actively living in the world. In fact they had given up, felt that they were useless and that there was no future. If the therapies used do not result in improvements in health, patients will not comply in taking them. There are currently many problems for African-Caribbean patients who are rarely given talking therapies. Instead they receive very high dosages of medication and are too often misdiagnosed. Where the medication is prescribed and there are serious side effects, patients feel worse rather than better. There is also inadequate support for people who are experiencing mental health problems.

Many families have been pathologized in ways described by Robinson (1995) and have been undermined, yet when people are in trouble there is nowhere else to go. Although there are often valiant efforts made through the social services or the health services in providing community care and other support, it is frequently inadequate. The literature about the chronically mentally ill suggests that they often end up isolated, are not visited by relatives when they are in hospital and are generally without support systems. This is frequently the result of extended families being undervalued and undermined. It would also seem that the chaplaincy services available could be inadequate, inappropriate or even racist in character. So there is or was no relief for those in need of help and support.

In Britain as well as in the Caribbean there have been persons who have overcome the adversities identified here. Their experience points to the way forward and defies the logic of the Euro-American psychosis. With access to opportunities, African-Caribbean people have demonstrated success in politics, the academy, sports, religion and business. The Caribbean prime ministers and other graduates of the University of the West Indies and other universities, Caribbean Nobel Prize Winners, Derek Walcott, Vidia Naipaul and Arthur Lewis, and many others demonstrate the resilience which had been discussed here. There is a realization that the African-Caribbean community can contribute to its own development as well as that of the larger society and that good mental health can come from its own efforts. There is the need to focus on transnational multidisciplinary collaborative approaches, which draw upon resources in the Caribbean and in the UK.

NOTES

1. Home Office White paper Cm 3190, (1996).
2. A section of the UK Mental Health Act that authorizes a police officer to remove a person from a public place.
3. Department for Education and Employment News, 'Minority Ethnic Pupils in Maintained Schools by Local Education Authority Area in England.' Jan. 1997 (Provisional), 342/97-30th Oct., 1997.
4. The *Jamaica Observer* June 24 2002.

REFERENCES

Bagley, A. 1971. 'The social aetiology of schizophrenia in immigrant groups'. *International Journal of Social Psychiatry*, 17, 292 –304.

Bennett, L. 1982. 'Colonization in reverse' In *Selected Poems by Louise Bennett*. Kingston, Sangsters.

Bhugra, D., et al. 1996. 'Incidence of first contact schizophrenia in Trinidad'. *British Journal of Psychiatry* 169, 587-592.

Burke, A.W. 1984. 'Racism and psychological disturbance among West Indians in Britain' *International Journal of Social Psychiatry* 30:50-68,

Chamberlain, M. 1997. *Narratives of Exile and Return*. London: Macmillan.

Dean, G., Walshe D., et al. 1981, 'First admissions of native-born and immigrants to psychiatric hospitals in South East England'. *British Journal of Psychiatry* 139, 506-512.

Fryer, P. 1988. *Black People in the British Empire*. London: Pluto.

Garvey A.J. 1967. *The Philosophy and Opinions of Marcus Garvey*. London: Frank Cass.

Gordon E.B. 1965. 'Mentally ill immigrants'. *British Journal of Psychiatry* 111:877-887,

Grbich C. 1999. *Qualitative Research in Health: An Introduction*. London: Sage

Gilroy, P. 1987. *There Ain't No Black in the Union Jack*. London: Hutchinson.

Hall, S. 1978. 'Racism and Reaction'. In *Five Views of Multi-Racial Britain,* Council for Racial Equality. ed., London, BBC Publications.

Hall, S. 1992. 'New ethnicities in 'race' culture and difference', in eds. J. Donald and A. Rattansi *Open University Reader* London: Sage. 252-260.

Hall, C. 1996. 'Histories, Empires and the Post Colonial Moment'. In *The Post Colonial Question: Common Skies, Divided Horizons*, eds. I. Chambers & L. Curti, London, Routledge.

Harrison, G., Owens, et al. 1988. 'A prospective study of severe mental disorder in Afro-Caribbean patients'. *Psychological Medicine*, 18:643-657.

Hickling, F.W. 1991. 'Psychiatric hospital admissions in Jamaica 1971-1988'. *British Journal of Psychiatry,* 159, 817-821.

Hickling, F.W., K. McKenzie, R. Mullen, R. A. Murray 1999. 'Jamaican psychiatrist evaluates diagnoses at a London psychiatric hospital'. *British Journal of Psychiatry* 175: 283 – 285.

Hickling F.W. and P. Rodgers-Johnson 1995. 'The Incidence of first-contact schizophrenia in Jamaica'. *British Journal of Psychiatry* 166; 522-526.

Hickling, F.W. and G. Hutchinson, 1999. 'The roast breadfruit psychosis: Disturbed racial identification in African Caribbeans'. *Psychiatric Bulletin* 23:132-134.

Hickling, F.W. and R.C. Gibson, 2005. 'Philosophy and Epistemology of Caribbean Psychiatry'. In *Images of Psychiatry: The Caribbean,* eds. Hickling, F.W. and Sorel, E., Kingston: University of the West Indies Press.

Hickling, F.W. 2007. 'Psychohistoriography: A Postcolonial Psychoanalytic and Psychotherapeutic Model'. Kingston: CARIMENSA, University of the West Indies

James, W. 1993. 'Migration, Racism and Identity Formation'. In *Inside Babylon: The Caribbean Diaspora in Britain.* eds. Winston James and Clive Harris, London and New York: Verso.

Kiev, A. 1965. 'Psychiatric morbidity of West Indian immigrants in an urban group practice'. *British Journal of Psychiatry*, 111: 51 – 56.

Mahy, G.E., et al. 1999. 'First contact incidence rate of schizophrenia in Barbados'. *British Journal of Psychiatry,* 175: 28 – 33.

Mama, A. 1995. *Beyond the Masks Race, Gender and Subjectivity.* London and New York: Routledge.

Newton, V. 1984. *The Silver Men: West Indian Labour Migration to Panama, 1850-1914.* Mona, Kingston Jamaica: Institute of Social and Economic Studies, University of the West Indies.

Pakenham T. 1992. *The Scramble for Africa.* London: Abacus.

Robertson-Hickling, H. and F. Hickling, 2002. 'The Need for Mental Health Partnerships in Jamaica'. *Social and Economic Studies,* 51, No.3.

Robertson-Hickling, H. 2006. 'The Quest for Healing in the Black British Community. A Reflective Study of Mental Health Care in Birmingham, England'. PhD disseration, University of Birmingham.

Robinson, L. 1995. *Psychology for Social Workers: Black Perspectives.* London: Routledge.

Royes, K. 1962. 'The incidence and features of psychosis in a Caribbean community'. *Proceedings of the 3rd World Congress of Psychiatry* 2, 1121 - 1125.

Rutter, M. 1999. 'Resilience concepts and findings: implications for family therapy' *Journal of Family Therapy.* 21:119 -144.

Sashidharan, S. P. 1993. 'Afro-Caribbeans and schizophrenia; the ethnic vulnerability hypothesis re-examined'. *International Review of Psychiatry,* 5: 129-44.

Sharpley, M., G. Hutchinson, K. McKenzie, R. Murray, 2001. 'Understanding the excess of psychosis among the African-Caribbean population in England. Review of current hypotheses'. *British Journal of Psychiatry* 178 suppl. 40 2001, 18.

Selvon, S. 1972. *Lonely Londoners.* Port of Spain: Longman Caribbean.

———. *Moses Ascending.* London: Davis Poynter.

———. 1983. *Moses Migrating* Longman: Harlow.

Sherlock, P. and H. Bennett, 1999. *The Story of the Jamaican People.* Kingston: Ian Randle Publishers.

Thomas-Hope Elizabeth. 1992. *Explanation in Caribbean Migration: Perception and the Image – Jamaica, Barbados, St. Vincent.* London: Macmillan.

———— . 2002. *Caribbean Migration.* Kingston: University of the West Indies Press, (reprint of the London edition).

Wessely, S., D. Castle, G. Der and R. Murray 1991. 'Schizophrenia and Afro-Caribbeans: A case-control study'. *British Journal of Psychiatry* 159:795-801.

Wing, J.K., J.E. Cooper, and N. Sartorius, 1974. *The Measurement and Classification of Psychiatric Symptoms.* Cambridge: Cambridge University Press.

Williams, E. 1970. *Capitalism and Slavery,* Longmans, London.

————. 1970. *From Columbus to Castro: A History of the Caribbean.* New York: Vintage Books, Random House, Originally published by André Deutsch, London.

7

SMALL ISLANDS AND THE SPACE IN BETWEEN:
Exploring the Liminal World of Andrea Levy

KIM ROBINSON-WALCOTT

Inglan is a bitch
dere's no escaping it
Inglan is a bitch
dere's no runin whe fram it
— Lynton Kwesi Johnson, 'Inglan is a Bitch' (2002)

Jamaican-British dub poet Lynton Kwesi Johnson was emerging as an exciting new countercultural voice when I was at university in London in the early 1980s. During that time I had my first encounters with 'black Brits' — the descendants of those first pioneering West Indians who bravely boarded ships such as the SS *Empire Windrush*[1] seeking to better themselves in the 'mother country'. Two of my friends at college were such descendants — second-generation Jamaicans, first-generation Britons, still at that time an anomaly in the university setting: none of their classmates in each of their programmes was a black person born and/or raised in Britain — and in fact my friends may well have been the only two black Britons at the college altogether. At that time, black Britons were uncommon in elite tertiary institutions, but common in the Underground, on the buses, working as drivers, conductors; common on the street corners of Brixton.

wen mi jus come to Landan town
mi use to work pan di andahgroun

but workin pon di andahgroun
yu don't get fi know your way around
(Johnson 2002, 39)

I saw my two friends negotiating sometimes hostile physical and psychological spaces as they attempted to carve out an identity for themselves. With their thick London accents, they were still considered Jamaican by their white colleagues; considering themselves British, they still tucked into Sunday dinners of fricassee chicken and rice and peas cooked by their mothers. One of them had never been to Jamaica, and the other had been only once, and was in no hurry to repeat the experience. The descendants of the *Windrush* pioneers find themselves in an in-between space, identifying fully neither with the country of their ancestors nor with the country of their birth — and being fully accepted by neither.

'Where are you from, Angela?'
'I was born in this country,' I said, as I always said to this familiar question.
(Levy 1994, 186)

The question posed in the above extract from Andrea Levy's first novel *Every Light in the House Burnin'* is indeed familiar — to Levy's protagonist Angela, to her other protagonists in her other novels, and to black Britons generally. Levy herself is the child of a *Windrush* pioneer: her father was one of those who travelled on that ship in its maiden voyage as transporter of West Indian migrants to Britain in 1948 —— to be followed shortly after by Levy's mother.[2] Levy's protagonist Angela, like so many other offspring of these pioneers, is still inevitably othered, still considered to be not British by her white compatriots, despite having been born and raised in the UK.

The alienation experienced by young blacks of West Indian origin raised in Britain has been expressed in a number of works of fiction, including Velma Pollard's *Homestretch* (1994), and earlier, Joan Riley's especially bleak novel *The Unbelonging* (1985). Pollard's novel, centred on an elderly couple's return to Jamaica after 30 years in Britain, features the young woman Brenda who, transported to the UK by her father against her will at age

14, after spending three difficult years in the USA, has found it even harder to adjust in this new, stranger, colder place. Riley's protagonist Hyacinth, sent from Jamaica to join her father in the UK at the age of eleven, is severely alienated from her new environment, scarred by the racism that she encounters, both overtly ('Kill the wog!' [16]) and covertly ('the bland face, the insincere smile' [72]). Grappling with her otherness, her physical, social and cultural difference from those who surround her, Hyacinth develops a crippling self-hatred.

The dilemma of unbelonging experienced by Levy's Angela, however, is somewhat different. Unlike Brenda or Hyacinth, Angela was actually born in the UK, so that questions about her origins must be especially painful. And there is another dimension: to return to the extract quoted earlier, the question 'Where are you from, Angela?' is preceded by an observation:

> 'You look a little Italian. Are you Italian?'
> 'No,' I answered.
> 'Where are you from, Angela?'
> 'I was born in this country,' I said, as I always said to this familiar question.
> 'Yes, but what about your parents — are they Jewish?'
> 'No, they come from Jamaica.'
> 'Both of them?'
> 'Yes.' (186)

Angela's interrogator is understandably confused. For Angela's appearance does not conform to the stereotype of the black Brit: Angela is light-skinned, not dark-skinned, with hair which, when straightened, is 'hair like [her] friends — not different' (172).[3]

Like so many light-skinned Jamaicans, Angela would have to prove her right to claim Jamaica.[4] But the country she is wishes to claim is not Jamaica but Britain, the country of her birth. And she has to prove her right to claim that country also. The child Angela yearns to fit in to British society; she wishes her mother could cook real English food like that served in the homes of all her friends, delicious steak and kidney pie and 'chips, beans and fried spam fritters that left your lips glossy with grease' (44), meals which her English friends will agree to eat. 'But my mum cooked different things. She boiled rice in coconut with beans. She spiced chicken and meat until it was hot. She fried bananas. Everything she made tasted different' (45).

Yet at the same time, Angela recognizes her difference from the other West Indian Londoners, from 'people from the Caribbean like my mum and dad, only "real" black people with dark brown skin'. In the salon where everyone is black and female, Angela feels 'pale in this company, out of place, as white here as I felt black among the pasty-faced English' (166). In contrast to Angela's liminal existence, her mother does not appear out of place. She 'looked fair and white but her broad African features and Jamaican accent let you know she was among kin' (166). The thick Caribbean accents comfort each other in a hostile environment.

Angela's parents are reserved, taciturn, private in a peculiarly English way; Angela's knowledge of her parents' emotions, or even their histories, is limited. It is a family which prefers not to discuss matters which are close to the heart, or disturbing. So, for example, it is only when Angela is 25 that she is abruptly informed, firstly, that her father has a brother — and an identical twin at that; secondly, that he has been living not in distant Jamaica but in the Midlands; thirdly, that he has just died.

> 'It must have been awful, dad,' I said, feeling a tender moment.
> 'Well, it was a bit upsetting,' he said loudly, filling the kettle, 'but I'm all right now.'
> 'It was only last week!'
> 'I know, Anne, but I feel all right now. You can't let these things bother you.' (237)

Angela's parents do not allow 'these things' to bother them. And 'these things' include working long hours, living in a dingy council flat for most of their lives, dealing with the prejudices and racism of their neighbours, all without complaint, because they have been brought up to display dignity and reserve and good breeding in a manner that is grounded in the colonial values of their Jamaican past — Jamaican values which are supposedly English values yet are foreign to the working-class English people who surround them.

Angela's parents insist, at least to others, that their lives are much better in England. 'We hear awful things back home about how coloured people treated bad here. Living in one room. People not wantin' to give jobs if you from Jamaica. You find that?' Angela's aunt visiting from Jamaica asks. 'You find that,' her father replies, 'but we don't have any trouble. We just keep ourselves to ourselves. Don't let anyone know our business, you know' (126).

Among the values that Angela's parents have learned back in Jamaica is the 'stiff upper lip'. But perhaps more importantly, they have been taught to view the mother country as maternal caretaker, and even though they are somewhat disillusioned with it they retain a fundamental trust in it. So when Angela's father is diagnosed with cancer, both he and his wife trust that the National Health Service will take care of him. With stiff upper lips, they both face his illness. As his illness progresses, the nonchalance with which they are treated by the health service reveals fully the extent to which they are outsiders in the society. Only at the end does he break down, yelling for Lazarus in his pain-crazed dementia, and it is his abandonment of his English reserve that finally gives him peace — literally, in that the nurses are forced to notice him and give him an injection for pain relief. Yet that abandonment coincides with his death.

The dark elements in *Every Light in the House Burnin'* hint of the sinister underbelly of racism encountered more glaringly in works such as Riley's *The Unbelonging*. Indeed, the disillusionment of Angela's parents, and by extension of Angela, is not dissimilar to that experienced by the pioneer protagonists featured in other works of migrant fiction[5] (Caryl Phillips's disturbing *The Final Passage* [1990] here especially comes to mind) — though Levy's characters in *Every Light* perhaps acknowledge it less readily.

These dark elements are deepened in *Never Far from Nowhere* (1996), Levy's starkest novel. Two teenage sisters growing up in London, the daughters of a Jamaican migrant couple, find that their different physical features lead to entirely different lives. The narrator, Vivien, is light-skinned; and as the novel progresses she becomes increasingly alienated from her dark-skinned sister Olive, because it is easier for Vivien to pass for white and so assimilate into British society. Vivien is impatient with Olive's lack of interest in school or in her white English friends. Later Vivien finds herself socializing with a group of skinheads; and when their racism is exposed, Vivien chooses to conceal her own background and to deny her relationship to her sister in order to maintain their friendship. Vivien's superior marks enable her to go to college, where again all her friends are white, and where she again chooses to conceal her background. Olive, meanwhile, descends further by getting pregnant for and briefly married to a worthless (white) man. Nevertheless she is feisty and brave as a single mother on welfare. Only when Olive is subjected to the racism of police who plant marijuana on her after they stop her for breaking traffic lights does she lose her spunk. She calls her sister at college and asks if she can visit her for a few days: 'I mean, it's not that I'm not a strong black woman. I am. I am!' But: 'I feel . . . scared here.' (270) Vivien refuses. Later, Olive is advised by her solicitor to plead guilty: 'She didn't understand that I could be innocent. Oh no. I was born a criminal in this country and everyone can see my crime. I can't hide it no matter what I do. It turns heads and takes smiles from faces. I'm black' (272). Like Hyacinth in Riley's *The Unbelonging*, like Leila in Phillips's *The Final Passage*, like Angela and her parents in Levy's *Every Light*, Olive has been forced to confront the reality that the care and protection of its citizenry for which the British welfare state is renowned does not willingly include black people.

Olive decides that she is going to live in Jamaica:

> 'I'm going to live somewhere where being black doesn't make you different . . . Vivien thinks she's escaped, with all her exams and college and middle-class friends. She thinks she'll be accepted in this country now. One of them . . . But Vivien, one day she'll realize that in England, people like her are never far from nowhere. Never.' (272-3)

At the end of the novel, Vivien seems to understand her own unbelonging existence: when her mother prompts her to tell Olive where she belongs, suggesting that she belongs in England, and must make a life here rather than fleeing to Jamaica, Vivien 'answered [her] mum the only way [she] could: 'I don't know'' (281).

> Inglan is a bitch
> dere's no escaping it

Inglan is a bitch
dere's no runin whe fram it

Running away may indeed not solve the dilemma of unbelonging. Riley's severely alienated character Hyacinth in *The Unbelonging* eventually returns to Jamaica, only to find herself equally alienated there. The Jamaica that she dreamt about during all those years of suffering in England is just that: a dream, not reality. In contrast, Brenda in Pollard's *Homestretch*, who as a young adult in England finds herself murmuring 'Inglan is a bitch' 'over and over as if Kwesi Johnson had written the words specially for her' (74), sets out on a trip to Jamaica 'to find her Jamaican self' (51) and succeeds.[6]

The protagonist in Levy's third novel, *Fruit of the Lemon* (1999), also visits Jamaica. Faith, like Vivien in *Never Far from Nowhere*, seems well assimilated into white British life, and is taken aback when her parents, who moved from Jamaica to Britain before Faith was born and also have seemed perfectly comfortable there, suddenly announce that they plan to return home. For Faith, going back 'home' must surely mean back to Stoke Newington, the location of the council flat that they used to live in for ten years, and certainly not to Jamaica, a country of which her parents — like Angela's parents in *Every Light* — have rarely spoken, much less visited since they migrated to the UK. Yet it becomes apparent that Faith's parents (like the elderly migrant couple David and Edith in Pollard's *Homestretch*) have in fact been preparing for this return home ever since Faith can remember: their seemingly eccentric longstanding habit of saving boxes has been for this purpose. Faith's reaction, to her own surprise, is anger, even though they are not asking her to return with them.

> The question I wanted answering was, why Jamaica? Why is Jamaica home? I knew my parents had come from there . . . But what mum and dad really loved was snow and cold evenings after shopping, when we would all sit around a coal fire and eat muffins and drink cups of tea whilst watching Cilla Black and arguing over whether she could sing or not. My mum's mantra had always been, 'You couldn't get this in Jamaica.' . . . They had never been back to Jamaica . . . (45)

This news coincides with a series of incidents in Faith's life which, though at first seemingly innocuous and dismissed by Faith, accumulatively disturb her preconceptions about her self and her identity: incidents ranging from exposure to the racist comments of a flatmate's working-class family — which, they hasten to assure her, don't refer to her personally — to exposure to another flatmate's entirely different family setting, one located in the landed gentry, where the family, unlike Faith, can trace its lineage back several generations. Then there is the suspiciousness and nervousness with which Faith's brother and herself are greeted when they go to a white neighbourhood to look at a second-hand car advertised for sale; then, her exposure to racism in her place of work; and finally, her encounter of a black woman who has just been attacked by National Front hoodlums. 'The woman was black,' she says repeatedly to her white flatmates after relating the story, but they fail to grasp the full significance of the incident (156), until: 'But then I tipped my cup of tea slowly over the table. "Will you all just shut up. Just fucking shut up. It's not funny!" And there was complete silence as they stopped and stared at me' (158).

Faith (like Hyacinth in *The Unbelonging* and Leila in *The Final Passage*) suffers a nervous breakdown,[7] and her parents suggest that a trip to Jamaica may help her. 'Why?' she asks. Her mother replies: 'Child, everyone should know where they come from' (162). Whereas Faith had earlier ironically proclaimed, in response to being told at a job interview that her artwork had 'an ethnicity which shines through' (31), that she was born and bred in Haringey, her new fragility makes her agree.

The visit to Jamaica, though only for a few weeks, is revelatory. By meeting and learning about her previously unknown relatives, Faith begins to grasp the texture of her Jamaicanness, the complicatedness of the country's colonial heritage with its multi-ethnicity, its convolutions of race and class. Faith hears that her aunt Constance, the light-skinned one for whom the family had high hopes, was forced to eat lemons as a child because she was told that eating lemons was one of the ways of the English (312-13). However the perceived ways of the English (sometimes distorted as they cross the Atlantic) are not always palatable:

Lemon tree very pretty
And the lemon flower is sweet
But the fruit of the poor lemon
Is impossible to eat (xi)

Ultimately Faith learns that the history of her family did not, after all, start when her parents' banana boat sailed for England (321): she now can resist the taunts of those ignorant English people who tease her about her background, just as her parents resisted the racism they encountered when they first arrived in England because 'they knew where they came from and they knew where they wanted to go' (331). Unlike the first two novels, *Fruit of the Lemon* ends on a note of upliftment. Faith, somewhat like Pollard's Brenda, returns to England strengthened, energized and thankful for the gift of Jamaica.

Levy's fourth novel, *Small Island* (2004), turns to that generation who knew where they came from and where they wanted to go. Set in 1948, the novel's protagonists include Gilbert, who served in the RAF in World War II and, having gone back home to Jamaica after the war, decides to return to England to make a life for himself. Hortense, his wife, marries Gilbert shortly before he sails although she barely knows him, because marriage to him will enable her to escape inferior Jamaica for superior England.

Not surprisingly to Levy's readers, but surprisingly to at least one of her protagonists, Gilbert and Hortense face a difficult life in post-war London, where the city is not only still crippled from the blitz of the war but also struggling to come to grips with a new invasion, this time of West Indians. The haughty Hortense, a 'speaky-spokey' woman with delusions of grandeur and with fixed notions of the superiority of the culture of the mother country, must endure a series of shocks when she arrives in that promised land: 'Is this the way the English live?' (22) she constantly asks her beleaguered husband, reminding one of Faith's mother's comment in *Fruit of the Lemon*: 'I never thought English people lived like that' (9). Hortense's culture shocks range from the inferior standard of accommodation — lodgings consisting of one room, with defective heating, toilet five flights down, in a house shared with prostitutes (very similar to the conditions faced by Faith's parents in *Fruit of the Lemon*) — to more sobering reality checks, the worst being when she applies for a job as a teacher and is laughed at (455). So the so-called mother country reveals itself to be merely another small island, perhaps even more small-minded than the country Hortense left behind. Gilbert tries to shield her, having suffered his own painful disillusionment with the mother country from his exposure to English racism during and after his wartime experience, when he discovered that the efforts and sacrifices of his West Indian cohort in supporting the mother country in her war effort counted as close to nought.

These lessons are familiar: the pioneer migrants David and Edith in Pollard's *Homestretch* and Leila and Michael in Phillips's *The Final Passage* reel at the signs posted in rooming houses announcing no vacancies for coloureds. The lessons can be hard: Hyacinth's father in Riley's *The Unbelonging*, though grovelling publicly in deference to white authority, privately teaches his daughter to be terrified of treacherous white people, and her resulting fear of exposing his abuse leads eventually to severe emotional and psychological scarring; Phillips's Leila similarly is encouraged to distrust all white people, and in her consequent lonely despair and disillusionment quietly descends into madness.[8]

Gilbert has also had other lessons, however: for one thing, having returned to Jamaica after the war and attempted unsuccessfully to establish a business, he has concluded that he 'can't get a break' in Jamaica, and that 'the world out there is bigger than any dream you can conjure' whereas Jamaica is 'a small island. Man, we just clinging so we don't fall off' (207). For another, he has found that the English breed of racism is less vile than the American one; and despite the many examples of bigotry, narrow-mindedness and hypocrisy, there are still some English people — like their landlady Queenie, forced to take in West Indian lodgers when her husband fails to return from the war — who are fundamentally decent individuals, and who, despite the traumatic upheavals to their lives caused by the war, are courageous enough to make whatever adjustments to their lives and outlooks as are necessary to enable their survival.

And herein lies Levy's underlying message in this novel: the war and its aftermath, when the *Windrush* brought the first of many waves of West Indians to Britain, was a period of reconstruction not only of physical infrastructure but also of lives and livelihoods, not only for the West Indian immigrants but also for the British who had to remake their own lives as well as making room for the newcomers. By portraying the white Englishwoman Queenie and the black Jamaican Gilbert as equally vivid, equally likable characters — and in fact by portraying the black Hortense and Queenie's white husband Bernard as equally unlikable characters — all of whom have faced equal challenges in compromising and adjusting their lives to accommodate realities, Levy shows a maturity of vision in her understanding of her own history and in her quest to come to terms with her own position not only as a white-skinned black person, but as a dark-skinned Brit, not only as a second-generation Jamaican, but as a first-generation black Brit. 'I love having these wonderful levels of identities,' she said in a recent interview. 'I think they're coming from Jamaica, which has so many different people from different places' (Lev-Ari, 2006).

Levy's journey to self-discovery has in one sense been a circular one: starting with Angela's parents in her first novel who were nearly as much the focus of that novel as was Angela herself, and returning now, in the fourth novel, to examine the history and the motivations of that generation. In another sense the journey has been one of retracing, moving from the contemporary coldness of the black British unbelonging life of *Every Light* and *Never Far from Nowhere*, to the warmth of belonging found in Jamaican family history in *Fruit of the Lemon*, and finally to the warmth of an understanding of that initial relocation from the small struggling island of Jamaica to the small struggling island of Britain in *Small Island*.

> Inglan is a bitch
> Dere's no escaping it
> Inglan is a bitch
> Dere's no runin whe fram it

Immigration changes everyone's lives, Levy's website disingenuously proclaims. It continues that 'the second world war was the great catalyst that has led to the multi-cultural society Britain has become. For Andrea Levy, acknowledging the role played by all sides in this change is an important part of understanding the process so we can go on to create a better future together.'⁹ Rousing words; and perhaps a bit too new-age feel-good in terms of whitewashing the grim realities of the immigrant life revealed in Levy's novels and in other works; but perhaps the sentiment is fundamentally true. Ultimately, Levy's fourth novel, while maintaining that the small island England is indeed a bitch, is nevertheless celebratory, of past courage, compromise, mind broadening, generosity and accommodation. The hybridized lemon tree of the new multicultural Britain, then, may one day bear edible fruit.

NOTES

1   The SS *Empire Windrush* transported the first wave of post-1945 immigrants to the UK from the West Indies in June 1948. As Cecil Gutzmore relates in his article 'The SS *Empire Windrush*: Myths and Facts' (Gutzmore 2006), 'before the *Windrush*'s June 1948 voyage it had been almost impossible for civilians to get to the mother country from the colonies. There were hundreds, if not thousands, in the Caribbean who wanted to make this journey . . . The total number of expectant souls on board was 1,027' (p. 11). Gutzmore emphasizes that this voyage was not a UK-government-sponsored operation: 'However great her labour needs, the British government was not ready to organize the mass entry of black, largely male labour into the UK' (p.11). In fact, 'when ... news of the coming voyage spread . . . the role of the colonial labour department was mainly to sound warnings to workers against going to the UK. They were told to abandon high expectations of employment and accommodation in Britain (p. 11). Gutzmore further states that 'news of the coming of the *Empire Windrush* caused some consternation in the Labour government, civil service and media circles in Britain' (p. 12). That first wave was followed by what became regarded as 'a flood of "coloured immigrants"' which the authorities strove hard to stem. 'When in 1961 the first Commonwealth Immigration Act was finally passed, it was indisputably racist' (p. 13).

2   See http://www.andrealevy.co.uk/eca1.html. Levy's website states that 'Andrea Levy is a child of the Windrush . . . Her father and later her mother came to Britain in 1948 in search of a better life. For the British born Levy this meant that she grew up black in a very white England. This experience has given her an unusual perspective

on the country of her birth – neither feeling totally part of the society nor a total outsider.'

3   See http://www.andrealevy.co.uk/eca1.html, where *Every Light in the House Burnin'* is acknowledged to be semi-autobiographical. Those readers familiar with Levy's appearance, and seeing parallels between the description of Angela and the appearance of Andrea, will easily understand the confusion of Angela's interrogator.

4   I discuss the marginalization felt by white and light-skinned Jamaicans in the book *Out of Order! Anthony Winkler and White West Indian Writing* (Robinson-Walcott 2006).

5   In this essay I have not discussed Samuel Selvon's classic novel *The Lonely Londoners* (1956) which hilariously examines the adjustment, or lack thereof, of West Indian migrants to London in the 1950s. Notwithstanding the sidesplitting humour of the novel, many of the issues faced by Selvon's characters — for example, homesickness, alienation, racism — are similar to those encountered in the works examined here.

6   Pollard's book is in fact dedicated to Riley. This prompted me to ask Pollard whether her book was a response to Riley's, and she confirmed that she wanted to show the 'other side of the story' (conversation on 6 December 2007).

7   See note 7 below.

8   In *The Final Passage* Leila's husband Michael is warned by a West Indian co-worker about his new English boss: 'Well, you better know. He's a cunt and he's going to call you names, man, and you going to behave like a kettle for without knowing it you going to boil. It's how the white man in this country kills off the coloured man. He makes you heat up and blow yourself away' (Phillips 1990, 168). Leila's and possibly Hyacinth's fates, not to mention Faith's nervous breakdown in *Fruit of the Lemon*, bring to mind a common Jamaican folk belief: in her article 'Turning History Upside Down', Hilary Robertson-Hickling (2006) refers to the 'common myth that England "makes you mad"'(17). This myth is referred to in Pollard's *Homestretch* (1994): 'People round here say anybody go to England come back mad' (20). And it is worth noting that Frederick W. Hickling (2006) in his article 'Grappling with British Racism' relates his finding that the incidence of schizophrenia among African-Caribbean people in the UK was considerably higher than in the Caribbean, showing that 'if there was a schizovirus, then Britain was the host' (21).

9   See http://www.andrealevy.co.uk/eca1.html. The website also states that 'in *Small Island* Levy examines the conflicts of two cultures thrown together after a terrible war, but also the kindness and strength people can show to each other'.

REFERENCES

Gutzmore, Cecil. 2006. 'The SS *Empire Windrush*: Myths and Facts'. *Jamaica Journal* 30, no. 3 (December): 11-13.

Hickling, Frederick W. 2006. 'Grappling with British Racism: A Jamaican Psychiatrist's Struggles with Mental Illness in African-Caribbean People in the UK.' *Jamaica Journal* 30, no. 3 (December): 20-29.

Johnson, Linton Kwesi. 2002. 'Inglan is a Bitch'. *Mi Revalueshanery Fren: Selected Poems*. London: Penguin.

Lev-Ari, Shiri. 2006. 'A Different Tale of 1948'. Retrieved from www.haaretz.com, 09 March.

Levy, Andrea. 1994. *Every Light in the House Burnin'*. London: Review.

————. 1996. *Never Far from Nowhere*. London: Review.

————.1999. *Fruit of the Lemon*. London: Review.

————. 2004. *Small Island*. London: Review.

Levy, Andrea. http://www.andrealevy.co.uk/eca1.html

Phillips, Caryl. 1990. *The Final Passage*. London: Faber and Faber, 1985. Reprint: New York: Vintage (page references are to the reprint edition).

Pollard, Velma. 1994. *Homestretch*. Longman Caribbean Writers. Burnt Mill: Longman Group UK Ltd.

Riley, Joan. 1985. *The Unbelonging*. London: The Women's Press Ltd.

Robertson-Hickling, Hilary. 2006. 'Turning History Upside Down: How Jamaicans Colonised England in Reverse.' *Jamaica Journal* 30, no. 3 (December): 17-19.

Robinson-Walcott, Kim. 2006. *Out of Order! Anthony Winkler and White West Indian Writing*. Kingston: University of the West Indies Press.

Selvon, Samuel. 1956. *The Lonely Londoners*. London: Alan Wingate.

8

THE IMPORTANCE OF INTENT:
Understanding the Social Networks of Jamaican Migrants Abroad

MIKAILA BROWN

This chapter outlines the findings of research on the intentions, perceptions and behaviours of returned, middle class, Jamaican professionals who have received graduate degrees at American universities. Using information garnered from interviews and observations, the chapter explores the central question: How does the intention to return affect the migration experience of young Jamaicans educated in the United States?[1] It is hypothesized that for some returned, middle class, Jamaican graduates of US universities, the intention to return results in the selection of social networks that are perceived to aid in the maintenance of a continued identification with the home society, while at the same time encouraging access to opportunities available in the host country. More specifically, the chapter examines how the intention to return has resulted in the preference of some Jamaican migrants to socialize with other immigrants groups, white Americans, and fellow Jamaican migrants, rather than black Americans, by looking at the effects of three key positions:

Position 1: These Jamaicans attest to having consciously maintained the mores and values representative of the social structure and organization of their home country while abroad, even if it resulted in behaviours not representative of the culture of the host society.

Position 2: These Jamaicans tended to align themselves socially with the perceived academic and professional ambitions of white Americans, rather than those perceived of black Americans; while at the same time distancing themselves socially from the negative stigma attached to the native minority group.

Position 3: These Jamaicans tended to view black Americans as being hypersensitive about racial issues, and feel alienated by the expectation to share black Americans' racial consciousness,[2] which is perceived to be very different from their own.

The small number of professional Jamaicans, who utilized an education abroad as a means to maximize their professional potential in Jamaica, has been labelled a *transnational elite*. For one, their transnationalism is evidenced by the ways in which these informants simultaneously engaged with two societal frameworks simultaneously. While abroad, they straddle a liminal space between home and host society, involved in both, but not restricted to either. This allowed them to access the resources available in America, while simultaneously holding a place for themselves in Jamaica. In many cases, an experience in one space informed the experience in the other. Informants replicated and manipulated some of the same rules, beliefs and practices exhibited in their home society within the host country, especially when positioning themselves in relation to others. An example of this is how certain rules of conduct employed within Jamaica to distinguish themselves from those with a lower class status are likewise applied in the USA to distance themselves from the stereotypes of black American culture. This will be explored more thoroughly throughout this chapter.

A shortcoming of this research project is the lack of comparison between this study sample of returned professionals and other Jamaicans. Because of a lack of time and resources, this study is restricted to those that fit within the set study guidelines. This limited focus did allow for more time to conduct in-depth interviews, and deeper and more complex investigation of the issues specific to those researched. However, I acknowledge that an examination of the experience of those in this study against that of a control group would have revealed more of the study sample's distinct characteristics.

I also acknowledge that the use of snowball sampling as the primary means of gaining access to informants is limiting. For one, because the study sample is not random, it is not necessarily representative of all the individuals that fit within the description of the research group. Without a means to guarantee randomness, I acknowledge that my sample could be potentially biased toward those willing to share their experience. Additionally, considering social disconnection within the societal structure of Jamaica, especially between various socio-economic spheres, another limitation of this study is the fact that many of my informants are part of a specific and narrow network, excluding relative isolates from other communities (Erickson 1979). Recognizing this, I attempted to broaden my scope by employing cluster sampling (Bernard 2002), by targeting organized groups that catered to those that fit with the prescribed research characteristics.

IDENTITY POLITICS

To understand the experience of those this study theoretically, one must wed paradigms that focus on identity, as well as those that address how individuals engage with the wider social structure. The theory of structural symbolic interactionism posits that social roles gain their meaning through their relationship with 'counter-roles'. This means that individuals derive their primary understanding of who they are through the recognition of who they are not. The lenses through which they make these assumptions are based in stereotypes, normative characteristics, ideal qualities, and actual attributes of others and themselves (Burke 1980). Social roles do not stand on their own, but are formed within a particular societal framework.

Societies are a complex mosaic of relationships organized into 'an array of groups, organizations, communities, and institutions, and intersected by crosscutting boundaries of class, ethnicity, age, gender, religion, and other variables' (Stryker and Burke, 2000). These various cross sections develop social identities or categories that individuals identify with, and by which they are socially recognized by others as belonging to (White and Burke 1987). Social categories come with prescribed expectations of behaviours or roles (Parsons 1937, Merton 1957, Goffman 1969). These expectations are based in a hierarchy of standards that range from esteemed to pathologized.

Within highly stratified societies, like those of the USA and Jamaica, these social categories become significant in maintaining boundaries and affirming one's role/place within the society. As a result of this, social networks and individual self-awareness are based in cultural ideals specific to the society. The desired outcome for each group is to be perceived in a positive light, especially in relation to other groups. In the same manner as individuals evaluate their own personal attributes, they also evaluate the attributes of others. Relationships between groups are determined by these evaluations and if they support the most positive perception of all involved.

Katherine Ewing's work argues that one's own self perception and interpretation of others are not homogeneous, cohesive or one-dimensional. Building on the work of Hegel and Lacan, she argues that identities and self-representations are always changing and disconnected as determined by the many divergent discourses operating on the consciousness of people at any given time. Ewing asserts that often the meanings attributed to relationships are inconsistent and multivariate, mainly because there are so many 'others' that are simultaneously being reflected. Throughout this myriad of relationships, individuals are constantly attempting to maximize their advantage within each, which often results in a manipulation of a multiplicity of self-representations and a lack of universal loyalty to any particular one. An individual's perception of a given situation influences which identities are enacted at that time, as well as the salience she/he attributes to the identity as relevant to that situation.

When the variables of race, class and nationality are highlighted within this discussion, one can examine these nuances more concretely. The work of Brubaker et al. emphasizes the collective effort of these variables in shaping the ways that individuals interpret and experience the social world around them. They view ethnicity, race, nation, and class[3], not as closed, objective entities, but as integrated parts of a process of 'recognizing, identifying, and classifying other people, or construing sameness and difference' (Brubaker et al. 2004:47). This process of classification not only organizes the world into categories, but also results in the ascription of identities to social groups.

Often the expectations and assumptions attached to categorizations of social groups result in conflict; particularly when individuals overemphasize intragroup similarities and intergroup differences. Because individuals wish to be validated by others, affinity with a particular social group is based on how an individual esteems the characterization of that social group (Stryker 1980). If the characterization is perceived positively, then the individual is more like to be committed to it and assume the roles associated with it. The following sections focus on data obtained from 15 months of ethnography that exemplify the phenomena discussed above.

THE STUDY SAMPLE

Of the 36 individuals in the study sample, 18 were male and 18 were female. Their ages ranged from 25 to 55 years, with a majority in their early to mid 30s. Most had lived in the United States for an average of 10 years, and had been back in Jamaica anywhere from one month to 21 years. While all interviewed shared that they had considered remigrating back to the United States at one time or another, only eight had seriously given it thought, and none had taken any practical steps to actualize the move.

While all the informants had migrated to the United States primarily to obtain an education, seven individuals did stay after graduation to work for an average of 5 years before returning to Jamaica. All were presently working and/or residing in the Greater Kingston Metropolitan Area. Their occupations fell within the financial, business, academic, governmental and medical sectors of Jamaica. The majority held managerial or upper level positions within their companies. All those actively working in the medical field were doctors and had their own private practice. All but one of the academics interviewed were professors. There were two retired nurses in the study group.

All but four were raised primarily in the Kingston area, and only eight individuals were raised in working class families. Of those whose upbringing was middle class, all were raised in two parent homes, with at least one parent having received a tertiary education. Understandings of the social positioning of this study sample were based on information generated from interviews, life histories, and interviews with their families, friends, colleagues, and others with whom they had daily contact.

A majority of the research group attended tertiary institutions with a predominately white student body, with only four attending a historically Black college or university. Seven individuals attended Ivy League institutions. Of those who did not, many still attended universities with strong academic reputations; 18 went for graduate school only and 14 attended both undergraduate and graduate programmes in the United States.

THE EFFECTS OF INTENTION

Lloyd Braithwaite's (2001) study of foreign educated Caribbean nationals highlights their three major motivations to go abroad for education. The first major reason was the lack of suitable training facilities available within the region. Second, colonial powers encouraged certain sections of Caribbean society to be trained in the metropole as a way of developing a domestic leadership base. Finally, it was the opinion of many in the higher strata of society that education in the metropole was better than what was offered domestically. C.L.R. James argued that this belief was based on a colonial model of education, which instructed Caribbeans in the superiority of Western education (Makris 1997). Nonetheless, those in the middle and upper classes often made use of their financial advantage to access this presumed higher standard of education as a way to maintain their privileged status.

Based on the sentiments shared by those interviewed, very little has changed. Even with heightened globalization, which makes migration for education accessible to more sections of society, and the proliferation of domestic training institutions and universities, many Jamaicans still view education abroad as an opportunity to access a standard of education and training that is better than what is available locally.

Strategically, informants appeal to a Jamaican belief in the superiority of a foreign education. Some informants feel this is why immediately upon their return they were offered managerial positions at a national bank. They frame their memory of their intention around obtaining cultural capital[4] from their exposure abroad. As a result, informants' memory of their experience focuses primarily on their professional development and the competitive advantage that their degrees have provided. Going abroad was a way to guarantee success within Jamaica's professional banking sector, both because of the standard of training they received and the esteem it inspires. It was also an avenue to potentially greater earnings.

Because professional success is a major priority for this study sample, it was not a surprise that a major impetus to return was the fear of lay-offs, particularly for those working in the American investment and corporate sectors. These ideas were first expressed in 2003, on the heels of the Enron scandal, which resulted in a weakened global market and the heightened regulation of the American financial sector. There were also professional frustrations stemming from certain limitations informants' perceived were obstacles to a high level of success in the United States. They felt that within America's business sector there were many ceilings to their promotion due to their race and limited years of work experience. To them, these ceilings prematurely curtailed their potential professional growth, as well as their salaries.

Interviewees contended that in Jamaica these same restrictions did not exist, especially because their families' status allowed for guaranteed business connections and lowered competition for available professional opportunities. More than one informant stressed that in Jamaica, business relations were as socially based as they were professionally developed, which led to the monopolization of the market and its resources by a small percentage of the society. This minority was comprised of families with a history of being from a higher socio-economic status. Many informants felt that they could return and maximize the professional returns of their education abroad combined with their families' favourable societal situation. They also stressed that the decreased amount of competition in Jamaica ensured greater possibilities that one would be considered an expert within one's field.

The final and most common motivation to return when they did was a guaranteed position in a Jamaican based institution. However, even without the guarantee of a job, many felt reassured that they could return and readjust successfully because they knew that their family was willing and capable of financially supporting them until they were established well enough to support themselves. A third of them lived in homes and drove cars owned by their parents, or depended on their parents for additional financial support upon their immediate return. Returning to Jamaica immediately ensured access to a higher standard of life than they had ever enjoyed in the USA.

The intentions presented above represent some of the most salient values, beliefs, and meanings of this study sample. These individuals valued education and professional success. They also valued a middle class lifestyle, as well as living in Jamaica. They had a belief that the esteemed nature of a foreign education could guarantee them easier access to professional opportunities in Jamaica. They also believed that their families' social and financial position was sufficient to sustain a pre-retirement return to the island. For those in this study, the personal meanings that they attached to success were the ability to make enough money to enjoy a privileged lifestyle in Jamaica, while at the same time contributing to the development of Jamaican society, both professionally and socially. Coupled with a 'strategic flexibility' in life course decision-making, the behaviours that these individuals exercised while abroad were reflective of this rationality, and ultimately ensured their return (Conway 1988).

SOCIAL RELATIONSHIPS IN THE USA

In this section, it is argued that perceptions undergirded the behaviours exhibited throughout a migration experience. Through an examination of the social relationships of the sample while studying in the USA, this next section will bring together findings that show how intentions and perceptions were manifested within patterns of associations and disassociations.

COMMON ASSOCIATION IN THE USA

While abroad, informants primarily associated with other Jamaicans. Besides family members already living in the USA, informants acknowledged actively seeking out other Jamaicans with whom to socialize. The primary motivation for this was a presumption of familiarity and comfort based on a shared nationality, as well as a commitment to staying as connected to Jamaica as possible given the strong intention to return home.

While informants tended to know the Jamaicans students attending their universities prior to migrating, those friendships established outside of campus life were less familiar. These extramural relationships often felt as new as the new environment. Unlike the class based associations prevalent in Kingston, Jamaicans befriended at a cultural event, on a neighbourhood soccer field, or at a local reggae club, were typically from a different class background.

Those informants who forged friendships across class boundaries made this shift unconsciously. One informant did not even realize this inconsistency until our interview; he expressed his surprise:

> I just realized that I was hanging out with Jamaicans that I would never have socialized with in Jamaica…Jamaica is so segregated by class and where you live. I would never have even met them, let alone played football with them.

The group of Jamaican men, with whom he played a weekly football match, came predominately from rural parishes in Jamaica and were from working class backgrounds. Even those who grew up in Kingston lived in areas of the city that he never frequented. They had attended different high schools in Jamaica. They had migrated to New York to find jobs or to attend less prestigious schools. Though their differences were many, he said that it was never an issue.

These findings are an example of how the meanings attached to 'Jamaican' began to broaden in scope for these informants while they were abroad. The breaking down of class barriers proved that these informants not only increased the depth of their own personal identification with Jamaica, but also with others who claimed the same national identity. Ernest Gellner (1983:6-7) asserts:

> Two men are of the same nation if, and only if, they recognize each other belonging to the same nation . . . A mere category of persons (say, occupants of a given territory, or speakers of a given language, for example) becomes a nation if and when the members of the category firmly recognize certain mutual rights and duties to each other in virtue of their shared membership of it. It is their recognition of each other as fellows of this kind which turns them into a nation, and not the other shared attributes, whatever they might be, which separate that category from non-members.

Within this theoretical paradigm, the acknowledgement of affiliation and a kinship with other nationals is critically important for nationalism to exist. While informants felt a connection with other Jamaicans while in the Jamaica, it was not always universal. Living in a foreign environment, juxtaposed against individuals with foreign cultures, they are more able and willing to acknowledge the inclusive attributes of their nationality.

The second most common association of these informants was with other international students, particularly those from other Caribbean islands and Europeans. One informant explained why other immigrants were more comfortable companions than Americans. He shared, the following view:

> I think I connected more with Caribbeans and Europeans than any other group because we had the commonality of being 'foreign'. The fact that they were white or foreign never deterred me from being friends with them. I just wanted to get along with people, and make my stay on campus comfortable.

A major intention of this study sample group was to remain in the USA only until they had obtained the required training needed to be professionally competitive in Jamaica. Earlier, it was established that social relationships not only reinforce shared values, but also aid in the achievement of common goals. 'Comfortable' as expressed in the quote above, speaks to informants' motivation to establish relationships based on these shared values and goals. Therefore, an easy rapport was established with other Caribbean students because of regionally based similarities in the social, political and economic history of their countries to that of Jamaica. Caribbean students, like European students, were also commonly interpreted as having a similar motivation for migrating and, therefore, a shared value of education as well as a common expectation from the experience of being abroad.

The presumable temporary nature of this endeavour also influenced the types of associations informants engaged in whilst abroad. They were wary of any relationships that would ask them to compromise their commitment to returning, or assume allegiance to this new social context. Therefore, associating with other international students, whose national allegiance was also outside of the USA, complemented the informants' objective to remain sufficiently connected to Jamaica in order to ensure a comfortable return home. The class background of these migrants significantly influenced these reactions and actions.

The remaining sections of this chapter will focus primarily on the relationships that these informants had with the social categories of white and black Americans, while in the USA. This focus is important for a variety of reasons. Studies on race relations within the USA have highlighted black migrants, particularly those from the Caribbean, as able to navigate race relations very differently from their black American counterparts (Bryce Laporte 1972, Ogbu 1978, Kasinitz 1992, Waters 1999, Foner 2000, Rogers 2000). This research project will engage these works by highlighting the specific area of intent as a variable that affect the interactions of these groups.

THE INFLUENCE OF CLASS ON SOCIAL RELATIONSHIPS

Attending top tier schools results in student bodies comprised primarily of individuals from affluent backgrounds. Because these informants primarily socialized with fellow students, their social circles were very racially and ethnically heterogeneous, but less diverse along class lines. This correlates very strongly to their social circles in Jamaica.

Ethnic and racial diversity within Jamaican society is most evident within the middle class. Because all but eight of my informants grew up in middle class communities in Jamaica, Chinese, Syrians, Lebanese, Indians, whites, blacks, and a mix of these groups have always comprised their social networks. This cultural mix resulted in relationships that were never limited to strictly phenotypic commonalities. The strands of commonality that hold these social networks together were not based in a single racial or ethnic identity, but rather in a shared nationality and class background. Those in this study confirmed this comfort with socializing with people of different races and ethnicities is carried over while they are abroad. One informant stated:

> When I brought my [white American] boyfriend home, I honestly thought he could live in Jamaica …I did not worry about marrying interracially, because even if I had biracial kids in Jamaica . . . Jamaica is the perfect place to raise such kids; being brown is such *a privilege* and they would not have the burden of having to choose a side. Because the Uptown[6] crowd is already so mixed, they would be accepted as normal . . . if not in the wider community.

This is evidence that members of the Jamaican middle class acknowledged and celebrate their multiracialism and multiculturalism. They also use this diversity to their strategic advantage. Politically, those belonging to the Jamaican middle class use this multiculturalism as a tool to enlarge their numbers, knowing that to stand ethnically alone would limit their political significance (Payne 1988). Economically and socially, members of the middle class capitalize on the social privilege associated with their high-income bracket and obvious physical diversity. Ultimately, the basis for cohesion within the Jamaican middle class is the value for quality education and high levels of professional and economic success. This has been translated into a high standard of living.

These values are translated within an American context. A major implication of growing up in Jamaica within a system of social networks based on nationality and class, and not on race, means that it is very difficult for them to understand and assume race as a major influence over whom they associate with while in the USA. Therefore, not only do informants' social circles remain very ethnically and racially diverse, but they are also comprised primarily of those with affluent backgrounds similar to their own. Informants' friends in the US also come from families who value education and professionalism and have the means to access the highest standard of training.

ASSOCIATIONS WITH WHITE AMERICANS

Informants affirm that they were comfortable associating with white Americans, whom they described as exposed and open to a diversity of interests and cultures. This resonated with their upbringing. White Americans also allowed them to occupy the space of 'immigrant'. Because informants viewed their migration experience strategically as temporary, full integration into American society was never an intent or goal of these individuals. Informants felt that white Americans acknowledged this fact and never asked them to compromise it. One said:

> At that time [the duration of her graduate programme], my identity was primarily
> that of a foreign student. I had enough trouble adjusting to being

'international'…I couldn't understand anything else… I just wanted to get along with people and make my stay on campus comfortable.

Informants cited the predominately white demographic of their graduate cohorts as another major contributor to their ease with white Americans. For some, the unconventional nature of their graduate programmes meant that they were the only minority in their entire department. Therefore, the students they studied with, completed projects and assignments with, and commiserated with were often white Americans.

White Americans also made informants feel comfortable by continuously engaging with the informants on topics related to Jamaica. White Americans were perceived as interested in learning as much as they could about Jamaica. Though many had little knowledge of Jamaica outside of beaches and Bob Marley, they were open to understanding a way of thinking and behaving differently from what they were familiar with. Informants also felt that white people accepted them more enthusiastically because they felt less demonized by black Jamaicans than they did by black Americans. White Americans seemed pleasantly surprised to realize that not all blacks viewed them negatively. In his study on the racial consciousness of Haitian migrants, Woldemikael (1989) found that white employees of his informants preferred to hire black foreign workers because they felt that there would be less racially based, intra-office conflict and tension than if they hired a black American.

The fact that informants were not offended by the invalidation of the significance of their race within these attitudes of white Americans can be attributed to two significant variables. First, a 'successful' relationship is determined by an evaluation of whether the relationship promotes positive perceptions of all those involved (Stryker 1980). The positive attitude of white Americans towards black migrants, as compared to their black American counterparts, fulfills their need to be perceived favourably by others.

White Americans share this need to be approved of, which is achieved when black migrants do not automatically dub them as racist. The fact that Jamaicans are socialized in a predominately black country contributed to what Pitt (1974:47) terms as 'unrehearsed aggressiveness, naïve open mindedness, and thus, apparent easiness in the presence of whites'. It is their difference from black Americans that makes the relationship between white Americans and these informants work smoothly. One informant stated:

> I believe that with or without a reaction that these guys [white Americans] are racist, but I feel that I probably was 'acceptably black' to these guys because I was up against the ruler of black Americans. Even if black Americans did not react, they still would be the greatest evil.

In the minds of this informant, the variable of the black American saved him from having to assume the role of what he perceived was the most denigrated minority within American society.

Secondly, many black Americans feel that white America owes them reparations for a long history of mistreatment and inequality (Brown 1931). Because of the temporary nature of their involvement within American society, informants did not feel invested enough to warrant feelings of denial or deprivation due to racial discrimination. They also did not compare their economic or social success to the standard of white America. Rather, they continuously looked to Jamaica to set their standard of achievement. This absence of an expected entitlement to and competitive need for long term advancement within the USA, makes it easier for them to accept and engage with white Americans. Waters (1994) asserts that the identities of black immigrants are 'so strongly linked to their experiences on the island...their identity as an immigrant people precluded having to make a 'choice' about what kind of American they [are]' (p. 803).

DISASSOCIATION WITH BLACK AMERICANS

If informants viewed white Americans as open minded and culturally inquisitive, they viewed black Americans as provincial and culturally insensitive. Informants were alienated by the belief that black Americans use race as the normative measure by which they evaluate all of their experiences. These informants' understandings of the world around them are more multivariate. H.A. Miller argues in *Race, Nation, and Classes* (1924) that when race assumes a subordinate status within the overall societal framework, there results an extreme sensitivity to actions perceived to be potentially racist.

This is particularly true for societies, like the USA, where race is a prominent determinant of the social hierarchy. Because informants grew up in a society where class is a more prominent factor in social organizations than race, and their own racial and economic status was not subordinate within this societal framework, they lacked this sensitivity.

Another point of dissonance was the fact that black Americans appeared to use race as the major determining factor with which they associated. Most informants were very comfortable associating with a range of people were are not black. Many of their closest friends in Jamaican and the USA were non-blacks whom they considered to be unprejudiced. They were unwilling to deny or condemn these friends strictly on the basis of their race. Because of these relationships, they felt polarized from black Americans, who seemed to offer an ultimatum of 'them' or 'us'. This strict dichotomy between black and white Americans translated into a cultural provincialness that Jamaicans attributed to the ideologies and practices of black Americans.

If there was an expectation on the part of the black Americans that there was an assumed unity between themselves and black immigrants based on phenotype, these informants did not share this expectation. For them, the cultural gap nullified the phenotypic similarities. Even those who attended Black Colleges and Universites preferred to socialize with other students from Jamaica or the Caribbean over black Americans. As shown by the categorizations presented in the first half of the chapter, informants stereotyped black Americans as having different values, beliefs, and behaviours than their own.

William Brown explained this expectation for solidarity on the part of black Americans as a critical component of a racial consciousness. This solidarity resulted in a '...tendency towards sentimental and ideological identification with a racial group... [where] race becomes an object of loyalty, devotion, and pride. It becomes an entity, a collective representation' (Brown 1931: 90). According to Phillippe Wamba, who wrote about navigating an African and black American heritage within an American context in his autobiographical *Kinship: A Family's Journey in Africa and America*:

> Blacks all over the world often assume or expect to share enough with blacks
> elsewhere to build a significant sense of unity, and such unity is understood to
> be essential in confronting and combating racism around the world. This is
> such a powerful expectation that emotions tend to run high when we discuss
> it, or dare to critique it. And we often feel devastated or strangely disoriented
> and indignant when our expectations go unfilled (1991: 18).

All of my informants stated that they never 'took on the burden of racism' nor felt the need to combat it. This meant that they never let an incident of perceived racism make them angry or react. Most argued that they ignored all impoliteness and always kept an even keeled demeanour. As a result, they could not understand or relate to the defensiveness of most black Americans. And they did not like feeling obligated to join them in a 'cause' with which they did not identify. They attribute this noncommittal attitude to the fact that they knew their time in America was not permanent. An informant posited:

> While I was abroad racism bothered me, but I had the attitude that because my
> kids would never grow up in the USA, I did not have to take on the race fight
> to save them.

The ability of these informants to avoid internalizing the stigma associated with blackness while in the USA did not change the fact that they found black Americans to be too reactionary. As stated by another informant:

> Every black American I knew was preoccupied with identifying racism in every
> occurrence and constantly referencing a multitude of negative experiences
> from their past. I had no such history and, therefore, no such grudge.

These Jamaicans had not grown up in a society where issues of racism were explicit. Only nine informants believed that Jamaica was a racist society. And for those who did acknowledge racism, most felt it was not the 'same kind of problem' it was in America. They argued it was less obvious because of the smallness of the white community in Jamaica, coupled with the fact that this community is perceived to be only economically but not politically powerful. The fact that Jamaica is predominately black[4] also creates a social dynamic that is less based in racial differences. In the opinion of most informants, daily discrimination within Jamaica is perceived to occur more on the basis of shade rather than race.

Informants felt the presumption of racial solidarity was unfair, because black Americans seemed to make no effort to understand their Jamaican culture. Black Americans were interpreted to be unfamiliar with the diversity and complexity of Jamaican society. Informants shared stories of being associated with having many jobs, a cultural stereotype created by the 1990's popular comedy show *In Living Color*, or with living on the beach. Unlike their white American counterparts who seemed eager to learn about Jamaica, black Americans gave the impression that they expected all black immigrants to adopt their culture. However, for many black immigrants being black is not synonymous with being black American (Waters 1994).

Informants' inability to relate to the experiences of black Americans did not completely negate the fact that informants 'experienced' their own race differently while abroad. All encountered definite and obvious occurrences of racism. Male informants told stories of being questioned by police while visiting friends who lived in upscale neighbourhoods. Others were called pejorative names like 'nigger'. And while they did not agree with the ideologies of black Americans, they acknowledge that growing up in America might have changed this. Nevertheless, a majority of the informants still primarily viewed racism as an *American* issue.

However, from observations and conversations, subtle evidence was detected of the effects of being abroad. One poignant example was gained while spending time with a particular informant and his family. I often heard this particular informant complain that the problems of Jamaican society were caused by the 'dutty niggers' living in the country. His father also shared similar sentiments in my presence. These discussions often made me uncomfortable because of their privilege place within Jamaica due to their fair complexion and their upper middle class status. One day after hearing another diatribe about 'dutty niggers', I asked him whom he considered part of this construct, and if this was determined by shade or class. He answered immediately:

A 'dutty nigger' is anyone who behaved in an ignorant manner. I don't care about shade. I know I am black. I've lived in America.

Similarly, during another interview, another informant expressed a dilemma he has grappled with every since his return. He has a hard time reconciling the awareness that racism is still alive in the USA with his personal expectations of black Americans to get over it. He shared:

I wonder whether black Americans are right about racism and I am wrong. I mean, when you think about it...it's good that black America keep white America accountable for their racism and their perpetuation of it through things like media, education and other structural means.

These statements exemplify how understandings of blackness and race relations take on new meanings for these informants through their experience in the USA. Though these individuals may have begun to reconsider race after time spent abroad, there is no space to explore these issues within Jamaican society, because race is subsumed by a focus on class distinctions. As a result, many believe that their interpretation of Jamaican society was not altered significantly by their time spent abroad.

However, this tension is an example of the divergent and occasionally incongruous consciences of these informants. It is important to recognize that interpretations of self and others are neither homogeneous, nor one-dimensional. Identities and self-representations are always changing and disconnected as determined by the specific social context that the individual is engaging with at any given time. Therefore, understandings of certain social situations will not only vary across various social contexts, but also have multiple and at times contradictory meanings (Ewings 1990, 1997).

Another significant example of the multi-consciousness of the informants is the differences in the explanation for why these informants did not associate with black Americans. In the free association exercise, black Americans were described as lazy, irresponsible, and uneducated. These are all descriptors that stand in direct opposition with the self-perceptions of this group as hardworking and professional. Based on these findings, one would assume that those in this study did not associate with black Americans because of a lack of shared values. Previous research on this relationship has highlighted this observation as the explanation for the discord between Caribbean migrants and black Americans (Kasinitz 1992, Waters 1999).

However, within the first round of structured interviews, the informants attributed their alienation from black Americans to the highly racialized attitudes of black Americans. The assumption that black immigrants adopt the racial consciousness of black Americans is described as alienating and unfair. Racial consciousness, which uses race to inform the purpose and intention behind one's action (Pitts 1974), is antithetical to the expressed purpose and intention of this study sample. As one informant said, 'Mi nah count cows, mi only cum fi drink de milk'. This famous Jamaican idiom exemplified his belief that he did not come to tackle racism, but rather to get education and work experience and then return to Jamaica. Based on this, one would assume that a different set of ideologies and objectives are the primary reason that these informants did not associate with black Americans. However, this explanation and the one expressed above stand in opposition to each other.

This dissonance is important to acknowledge and understand. It can be attributed to many things. The first would be the affect that my presence as the interviewer had on the perceptions shared. Antoinette Errante (2000:17) argues that the identities that emerge out of an interview 'result [from] the interaction between historian (interviewer) and narrator (the informant)'. Because there are many ways of remembering an event or situation, taking into account the influence of the interviewer illuminates the reasons behind the selection of the version shared (Tonkin 1992, Fentress and Wickham 1992). I have argued above that the desired outcome for every individual is to be perceived in a positive light by others. An interview can be considered a relationship that operates under the same rules of participation. A belief that my upbringing in the USA would result in empathy and sympathy with the opinions of black Americans could have contributed to informants consciously relating their discord with black Americans in a light that cast them as the victim of cultural provincialism, rather than the perpetuator.

However, the explanation might be more multivariate and less pernicious. As Ewing emphasizes the incongruities within the discourse of her informants as an opportunity to address the divergent ideologies at play within their consciousness[7] (Ewing 1990, 1997), I argue that the explanation for the dissonance within the findings of this study is evidence that there are multiple, contradictory ideas and beliefs operating in the psyche of these highly transnational individuals. To assume that these informants view themselves and others in only one way, especially given their extensive exposure, is limiting. The arguments of Carola and Marcelo Suárez-Orozco (2004) agree that personal identities are fluid and context driven, and further complicated by exposure across geographic and ideological boundaries. The internationalization of education results in the process of racial and ethnic re-discovery and self-authority, where new identities are crafted through a process of continuous feedback between the subjective sense of self and what is mirrored by the new social surroundings. Simultaneously, attempts to maximize one's advantage within these multiple social frameworks result in a multifaceted consciousness.

CONCLUSION

Finally, I believe that while these two sets of findings appear paradoxical, they work together to inform the attitudes and behaviours of this study sample. While both black and white Americans are unknowledgeable about Jamaica, and make assumptions about the informants that were, at times, prejudicial and discriminatory, findings from the first round of interviews reveal that informants take offense at these behaviours and attitudes only when perpetrated by black Americans. Acts of ignorance, discrimination and prejudice committed by white Americans were often taken lightly and rationalized as being from a source other than racism.

The categorizations of a social group ultimately determine the lens through which its members actions are interpreted. Because informants' categorizations of white Americans were predominately favourable and more aligned with their own self-perceptions, the actions and attitudes of white Americans were interpreted through a positive light. This is complemented by the belief that white Americans allow them to occupy the space of sojourner, which ultimately serves the goals of their migration experience. Therefore, associations with white Americans are deemed to be strategically advantageous, and necessary to be maintained at all costs. Conversely, informants distance and separate themselves from black Americans because of the negative perceptions that they attach to the category of 'black American' and the assumption that black Americans want them to assume the racial burden of the United States. A disassociation from black Americans was also deemed to strategically complement the intentions of their migration experience. Ultimately, perceptions and intentions worked together to pervade the meanings attached to social relationships and inform the behaviours of these informants.

NOTES

1. For the purposes of this study, 'intention to return' refers to migrants that have clear and certain plans about the duration of time that they will spend abroad, largely determined by the objectives they set out to achieve prior to actually migrating. This goal should be able to be achieved in a fixed period of time (Gmelch 1980). This study is principally interested in the intention to return over the reality of the return, because it is interested in how the perception that one's stay is temporary influences behaviours while abroad.

2. Drawing on W.O. Brown's definition, the construct of racial consciousness refers to a tendency towards sentimental and ideological identification with a racial group (Brown 1931: 90).

3. Brubaker et al. focus on ethnicity within their work as a representation of a system of classification and categorization that is based in a perceived membership with a particular racial and national group. Class is absent from Brubaker et al.'s argument, but I have added it here not only because it is significant to this study, but also because I feel that it affects how individuals interpret and categorize the world around them.

4. Cultural capital is a concept developed by Pierre Bourdieu and Jean-Claude Passeron (1973) used to describe any form of knowledge, skill, or education that acts as an advantage for an individual by giving him a higher status in society.

5. Uptown is a Jamaican colloquial term that signifies someone from an affluent background.

6. Blacks comprise 90.9% of Jamaica society (*CIA World Factbook 2007*). https://www.cia.gov/cia/publications/factbook/geos/jm.html#People.

7. Consciousness is defined as 'a social product…purposive actions and interpretations of actions operating in social relationships' (Pitts 1931: 670)

REFERENCES

Alexander, Jack. 1997. 'The culture of race in middle class Kingston, Jamaica'. *American Ethnologist*. 4, 413-436.

Austin-Broos, Diane. *1984. Urban Life in Kingston Jamaica: The Culture and Class Ideology of two Neighbourhoods*. New York: Gordon Breach.

Bernard, Russell. 2002. R*esearch Methods in Anthropology: Qualitative and Quantitative Approaches,* Third Edition. New York: Altamira Press.

Bordieu, Pierre. 1979. *Distinction: A Social Critique of the Judgement of Taste*. Cambridge: Harvard University Press.

Braithwaite, Lloyd. 2001. *Colonial West Indian Students in Britain.*Barbados: University of the West Indies Press.

Broom, Leonard. 1954. 'The Social Differentiation of Jamaica'. *American Sociological Review* 19, 115-125.

Brown, W.O., 1931. The Nature of Race Consciousness. *Social Forces* 10, 90-97.

Brubaker, R. et al., 2004. Ethnicity as Cognition. *Theory and Society* 33, 31-64.

Bryce La- Porte, R. and D. Mortimer, eds. 1976. *Caribbean Immigration to the United States*. Washington DC: Research Institute on Immigration and Ethnic Studies, Smithsonian Institution.

Cerase, Francesco. 1974. 'Migration and Social Exchange: Expectations and Reality: A Case Study of Return Migration from the United States and Italy'. *International Migration Review* 8, 245-262.

Conway, Dennis. 1988. 'Conceptualizing Contemporary Patterns of Caribbean International Mobility'. *Caribbean Geography.* Vol. 2, 145-163

Domingo, W.A. 1925. 'The Tropics in New York'.*The Survey,* 53, 648-650.

Douglass, Lisa. 1992. *The Power of Sentiment: Love, Hierarchy and the Jamaican Family Elite*. Boulder: Westview Press.

The *Economist*, 2003. 'Brain Gain'. October 9, 48.

Erickson, Bonnie. 1979. 'Some Problems of Inference from Chain Data'. *Sociological Methodology*. Vol. 10, 276-302.

Eschbach, K. and M. Waters, 1995. 'Immigration and Ethnic and Racial Inequality in the United States'. *Annual Review of Sociology,* Vol. 21.

Ewing, Katherine. 1990. 'The Illusion of Wholeness: Culture, Self and the Experience of Inconsistencies'. *Ethos.* Vol.18, no.3 (Sept.), 251-278.

————. 1997. *Arguing Sainthood: Modernity, Psychoanalysis, and Islam*. Durham: Duke University Press.

Fentress, J. and C. Wickham, 1992. *Social Memory*. Oxford: Blackwell

Foner, Nancy. 1985. 'Race and Color: Jamaican migrants in London and New York City'. *International Migration Review* 19, 708-727.

————. 2000. *From Ellis Island to JFK*. New Haven: Yale University Press0.

Gellner, Ernest. 1983. *Nations and Nationalism*. Oxford: Blackwell Synergy.

Gerring, John. 1997. 'Ideology: A Definitional Analysis'. *Political Research Quarterly*. Vol. 50, no.4.

Gmelch, George. 1980. 'Return Migration' *Annual Review of Anthropology*, Volume 9,135-159.

Goffman, Erving. 1969. *Strategic Interaction*. Philadelphia: University of Pennsylvania Press.

Henriques, Fernando. 1953. *Family and Colour in Jamaica*. London: Eyre and Spottiswoode.

Hogg, M. et al., 1995. 'A Tale of Two Theories: A Critical Comparison of Identity Theory with Social Identity Theory'. *Social Psychology Quarterly*. 58,255-269.

Kao, G. et al., 2003. 'Racial and Ethnic Stratification in Educational Stratification in Educational Achievement and Attainment'. *Annual Review of Sociology*, 29, 417-42.

Kasinitz, Philip. 1992. *Caribbean New York: Black Immigrants and the Politics of Race*. Ithaca: Cornell University Press.

Lacan, Jacques. 1977. *Ecrits: A Selection*. trans. Sheridan A. New York: W.E. Norton.

Leo-Rhynie, E and Hamilton, M., 1983. 'Trends in Class and Migration. Women: Equal or Not'. *Caribbean Quarterly 9*, 70-85.

Makris, Paula. 1977. 'Beyond the Classics: Legacies of Colonial Education in C.L.R. James and Derek Walcott'. *Revista Iberoamericana*. Vol. 31.

Merton, Robert. 1957. 'The Role-Set: Problems in Sociological Theory'. *The British Journal of Sociology*, 8,106-120.

Miller, Herbert. 1924. *Race, Nation, and Classes: The Psychology of Domination and Freedom*. Philadelphia: JB Lippincott Company.

Ogbu, John. 1978. *Minority Education and Caste*. New York: Academic Press.

Parson, Talcott. 1937. *The Structure of Social Action*. New York: Free Press.

Philpott, Stuart. 1973. *West Indian Migration: The Monserrat Case*. London: Anthlone Press.

Pitts, James. 1974. 'The Study of Race Consciousness: Comments on New Directions' *The American Journal of Sociology*. 80, no.3, 665-687.

Robinson, William. 1996. *Social Groups and Identities: Developing the Legacy of Henri Tajfel*. Oxford: Butterworth.

Rogers, Reuel. 2006. *Afro-Caribbean Immigrants and the Politics of Incorporations: Ethnicity, Exception, or Exit*. Cambridge: Cambridge University Press.

Sowell, Thomas. 1975. *Race and Economics*. London: Longman.

Stryker, Sheldon. 1980. *Symbolic Interactionism: A Social Structure Version*. Menlo Park: Benjamin Cummings.

Suarez-Orozco, M. and Qin-Hilliard, D. 2004. *Globalization Culture and Education in the New Millennium*. Berkeley: University of California Press.

Tajfel, H and J. Turner, 1986. *The Social Identity Theory of Intergroup Behaviour*. Cambridge: Cambridge University Press.

Thomas-Hope, Elizabeth. 1982. 'Identity and Adaptation of Migrants from the English-Speaking Caribbean in Britain and North America' In *Self-Concept, Achievement and Multicultural Education*, eds.Gajendra Verma and Christopher Bagley, London: Macmillan, 227-239.

————. 1992. *Explanation in Caribbean Migration — Perception and the Image: Jamaica, Barbados, St. Vincent*. Warwick University Caribbean Studies Series. London: Macmillan.

————. 1995. 'Return Migration and its Implications for Caribbean Development'. In *Migration and Development in the Caribbean: The Unexplored Connection*, ed. Robert A. Pastor, Boulder, COL: Westview Press, 157-172.

Tonkin, Elizabeth. 1992. *Narrating Our Pasts: The Social Construction of Oral Histories*. Cambridge: Cambridge University Press.

Wallace, Walter. 1999. 'Rationality, Human Nature, and Society in Weber's Theory'. *Theory and Society* 19, 199-223.

Wamba, Philippe. 1991. *Kinship: A Family's Journey in Africa and America*. New York: Dutton.

Waters, Mary. 1999. *Black Identities: West Indian Immigrant Dreams and American Realities*. Cambridge: Harvard University Press.

White, C. and P. Burke, 1987. 'Ethnic Role Identity among Black and White College Students: An Interactionist Approach'. *Sociological Perspectives*. Vol. 30, no. 3, 310-331.

Woldemikael, Tekle. 1989. 'A Case Study of Race Consciousness among Haitian Immigrants'. *Journal of Black Studies*, Vol. 20, no.2, 224-239.

9

COLLECTING THE MEMORIES:
Migrant Voices in the Barbadian–UK Migration Project

MARCIA BURRROWES

INTRODUCTION

This chapter presents some of the early findings of the Migration Oral History project undertaken by the disciplines of History and Cultural Studies at the University of the West Indies, Cave Hill Campus, Barbados. The project was initiated by the migrants themselves who wanted their voices to be heard as they told their stories of migration. They felt strongly that current research and publication on migration did not fully speak to their experiences in the UK They named their project 'The Journey' as they sought to emphasise the continuum of the experience of departing Barbados, living and working in the UK, and returning to their native land. Their anxiety to capture these narratives was made all the more urgent by the realization that many of them were retirees in the 70+ years age group who had limited time left to share their experiences. Interviews were conducted in Barbados with those individuals who had migrated to the United Kingdom before 1970 and who had subsequently returned to live on the island.[1]

Though the project itself cast a wide net of questions to capture all areas of interest, this chapter places emphasis on responses that spoke to socio-cultural issues, such as cultural practices and race relations. Attention will be paid to the key areas that the migrants chose to highlight in their discourse, and events that they especially remembered when they reflected on their lived experience in the UK.

'THE JOURNEY'

During the decade of the 1990s, many Barbadian migrants returned to their native land after having lived and worked in the UK Seeing themselves as *Bajans*² returning home, they had to grapple with, among other things, the designated label of being a *Returning National*. This form of identification was perceived as alienating them from within the main embrace of the society. These Barbadian migrants found themselves embroiled in a discourse which dismissed their claims to a home within Barbados and to a sense of belonging to the island.

On the other hand, during the thirty years or more of living within the United Kingdom, these first generation migrants had used the name and concept of Barbados as home not only as a mantra, but as a beacon in the dark. Their understanding of being Barbadian gave them solace and meaning within the space/s of their exile. And the majority had remained in touch with home, whether through visits to the island, and/or by receiving visitors from the island, and/or through the tangible contribution of remittances to relatives and friends in Barbados. They saw themselves as Barbadian and Barbados as home. As one respondent states:

> The first time when I got on the plane and I knew I was coming back for good. I felt really good. Sad in a sense, but I knew, well, that's it. You feel bad because you leaving your kids behind as such, but I knew I was coming back to Barbados, some place that I always wanted to be any way. I didn't know when I was going to, but I always have a vision that if God gives me health and whatever, I want to come back, so I just made it back and I thank God for that.

Having now returned they learnt that though they had kept up a spiritual and real vision and vigil of home, the inhabitants on the island had not kept a similar narrative of and for them. The majority of the populace had forgotten them, or were uninformed about their experiences. Little or no attempt was made to teach their history/ries in the schools and universities and there was hardly any public discussion on migration, until they were seen to be arriving as retirees in the 1990s. As a result, the perception held by some Barbadians was that these returning nationals were upstarts, or even outlaws, returning (or perhaps turning up from nowhere?) to claim the fruit of the land.

It is in this way that questions of identity became critical to the process of resettlement. At the very core of the discourse lay the issue of the historical narrative, of what they as Barbadian migrants had endured and experienced in the UK, and how they would construct their individual and collective identities now that they were, once again, living in their native land. As Stuart Hall advises, 'identities are about questions of using the resources of history, language and culture in the process of becoming rather than being.' The historical narrative serves to provide not only an understanding of our roots, but also a coming-to-terms-with our routes.[3] For the migrants, recounting the historical narrative would provide a forum for discussion of the migrant experience. It would allow them to engage in the process of re/shaping their identities back in their native land.

Consequently in 2001, a group of Barbadian migrants who had returned from the UK to live in Barbados formed a committee known as *The Journey*. Their desire was to design ways of informing the Barbadian public of their experiences. They hoped that the dissemination of this information would provide bridges of understanding between the migrant community and the Barbadian people. Led by Sylvester Jones, Erma Jones, Jeff Hunte and Owen Eversley, all of whom had lived in London, and arising, (somewhat ironically, in view of their experiences with the Church in the UK), as a result of encouragement by Bishop the Rt. Revd. Dr. John Holder and Dean the very Revd. William Dixon of the Anglican Church, the committee was convened. At the time, its core membership came from within the Anglican Church and the majority of its members were migrants, although one of them, Benita Medford, was not.

In the ensuing months the Bishop remained its patron though the committee moved away somewhat from its original church moorings. It reached out to other migrants and individuals in the community to assist it in its cause. By 2002, Aubrey Deane, who had lived in Bradford, joined the committee and quickly became one of its most active members. The committee also chose to expand its membership by inviting historian Trevor Marshall and cultural studies specialist Marcia Burrowes on board to provide assistance.

From its inception, *The Journey* committee opted to use the Town Hall format as their main means of communicating with the migrant population and the Barbadian public. For example, in September 2002, they held a Town Hall meeting at Solidarity House, the headquarters of the Barbados Workers Union. They invited Professor Keith Hunte, historian and former Principal of the Cave Hill Campus, to deliver the feature address. They also invited Eric Lynch, third generation Barbadian living in Liverpool, to speak to the issues of Caribbean and African migration in Liverpool. At this Town Hall meeting, as at the others, all present were encouraged to provide the committee with their details, such as their name, address and telephone number. In this way the committee continued to create a pool of resources for their research.

By the beginning of 2003 the migrants were ready to commence the second stage of their project, that of recording their narratives. Though they understood the importance of all migrant experiences, including the observations of Barbadian migrants in the United States, they opted to place their initial focus on the Barbadian-UK migrant experience. They argued that this migration to the centre of the former British Empire needed a special focus and indeed was the one least known about by the Barbadian public:

> When you speak the English accent will come out and you would be classified as 'Black Bajans from Britain' or 'you English'… They used to call me Mrs. Thatcher and things like that but I didn't really (care). That was like water off a duck's back. I tried as best as I could to be adaptable to adjust. I made a decision to come back and it was a case of having to make the most of the situation here. I felt, well when I first went to England I had to adjust and adapt to the way of life in a foreign country, now I am coming back thirty something years later I would have to adjust and adapt this way of life.

It was these perceived tensions within the Barbadian society and the seeming rejection of the presence of Barbadian-UK migrants on the island that led them to their decision. These Barbadian migrants felt strongly that there was a marked difference in the public's attitude to Barbadian-UK migrants as against Barbadian-US migrants. They argued that because there were substantial differences between the two experiences it was all the more important to maintain a separate focus, especially in the initial stages of the research. Furthermore, they also believed that the knowledge of the UK experience would assist in changing those attitudes.

With this mandate in mind *The Journey* committee approached the University of the West Indies, Cave Hill Campus, for assistance with their enterprise. A new committee comprising of University lecturers Marcia Burrowes and Anthony Phillips and Barbadian-UK migrants Sylvester Jones, Aubrey Deane, Jeff Hunte and Meagan Applewaite was formed, all of whom had been members of *The Journey*. Oral History specialist Aviston Downes and Sociology PhD. candidate Kenneth Walters formed part of the team.

The project was renamed 'Collecting the Memories: the Barbados/UK Migration Experience'. It received funding from the Department of History and Philosophy and the Campus Research Funds of the Cave Hill Campus. From August 2003 onwards a series of interviews were held with Barbadians who had migrated to the UK before 1970 and had since returned. Audio recordings of the interviews were made and some interviewees supplied items of memorabilia for scanning and documentation. These items included photographs, remittance slips and receipts of payment for the journey on the ship to the UK.

By June 2006, there were three occasions in which the initial findings of the project were presented. The first two presentations were to members of the academic community at conferences held at the University of the West Indies.[4] The third was held in June 2006 and was made to the migrant community who had initiated this project. Perhaps the most important and sensitive of all presentations, the research team presented its initial findings according to each of the four areas of focus.[5] This chapter will also include the responses by those present at the June 2006 presentation.

THE MIGRANTS SPEAK OUT

Though the project looked at the migration experience as a whole, this chapter examines what these Barbadian migrants believed were some of the key socio-cultural issues that emerged whilst living and working in the

UK Emphasis will be placed on presenting *their voices* as they recount their memories of these experiences in the migrant space.

NEGOTIATING THE LIVING AND WORKING SPACE

In responding to the questions which addressed the issues of working and living conditions, all respondents recounted their memories of settlement and the ways in which they negotiated spaces of belonging within the UK environment. Note the narrative of this female respondent who was based in London:

> I used to work at Lyons Tea Shop for Four Pounds Ten a week … and have to pay One Pound Ten for rent, so [I] had to share with somebody. You there in one room, and the stove in there and you had to pay one pound ten because if you don't do that you got to pay bus fare, buy food, how you gine live?

Further in her interview she remembered that she changed jobs as she sought out better rates of pay. In one of them her task was to press thirty-six shirts a day. Seeing that she was sending one-fourth of her earnings 'home' to Barbados, she calculated that nine pressed shirts of the thirty-six shirts contributed to this exercise. Her concept of remittances was made tangible through her calculations. Note also that with approximately half of her meager earnings going to remittances and rent, it was necessary to tolerate living in cramped conditions in one room, an experience repeated by many others.

This is the voice of a male migrant who also lived in London. His narrative speaks to living in crowded conditions as migrants, desperate for a place to live, find themselves fitted into one room:

> North London No. 2 Eatons Road and we had a large room and it was seven of us in that room. Seven of us in that room - some of us had singles but some had one on top the other - that kind of thing - bunks. We all kind of got along pretty good. Pretty good - the seven of us - we got along pretty good. I was the first one to leave and I went a little further down the road - a Jamaican lady - she, her husband and her daughter and I used to live in the attic in her house.

Most migrants spoke to the rampant racist practices that characterized the experiences of acquiring accommodation. The well-known migrant narrative of seeing signs on doors in London which read 'no blacks, no dogs' was repeated by these Barbadian migrants in their interviews. However, this female respondent who lived in Reading, remembered that some Barbadians devised ways of acquiring accommodation through what some may call creative thinking. In this instance the Barbadian migrants had to satisfy the requirements of their Polish landlords:

> They would go at Poles to rent a room … The people that buy the houses, a lot of white people from Poland would get big houses, you know, big houses, and rent out rooms with things in them … But if you are a double, you got to marry … So you know when they first go up there the men can't married, they go and buy a ring and put on 'pon their hand and (fake it) … and then when after time they go and married.

With the practice of many English landlords of not providing accommodation for Barbadians and West Indians, migrants were forced to seek accommodation however and wherever they could. And with the discriminatory insistence of only renting rooms to married couples, many migrants were forced to play the game of being a couple, with the purchase of a ring from Woolworth. When circumstances had improved, many of these couples did get married.

Finally, many respondents spoke to the tensions that evolved from living with several individuals in one room and/or in one house. In particular, many respondents remembered the ways in which they negotiated simple tasks, such as cooking a meal. Note the somewhat amusing narrative of the female respondent based in London:

> As I said, everybody in a room so you used to put a shilling. You had a meter in the kitchen and you would drop a shilling in to give you gas to cook … So when you coming in from work and you have to cook something to eat so you drop this shilling and as soon as you hear ting-a-ling, people all in a hurry, man. You would see the people coming out their rooms and putting on the stove with the four burners and they would put their saucepans and thing on to

cook, so before your rice can boil up, the shilling would be gone. If you didn't have another shilling you had rice tea (laughter).

EXPERIENCES IN CHURCH

All interviewees made comments on their experiences with the local church. They emphasised the initial contact with the clergy and congregations which affected their interaction for the duration of their stay in the UK. Only a few of our respondents were warmly received in the church.

For example, this first respondent was a nurse based on the Isle of Wight and has fond memories of going to church:

> I think that going to church we were welcomed because there was one big church on the Isle of Wight. They knew we were Student Nurses. I think at the time there were only approximately half a dozen black students, but they tended to be African students who were at Private Boarding Schools on the Isle of Wight. Unfortunately, we never did mix. The church was certainly not an unpleasant experience

However, many respondents argued that this was unusual and stressed that the Isle of Wright experience was peculiar because of the isolated location.[6] Nurses based in London and other parts of the mainland recalled acts of racism and alienation which they experienced in the church. For example, the following female respondent was a nurse in Buckinghamshire and she has a different perspective of relations with the church. In her narrative she captures how she and her friends constantly had to negotiate the migrant space, even in the church. At every stage of this encounter there is a process of confrontation and accommodation as the nurses seek to enjoy a morning of worship:

> Well the church I been to when I was in Buckinghamshire that was the Church of England … The first time I been to church it was five of us. I said to the girls come let us go and sit to the front and they were 'oh now we can't go and do that' so I said, 'I am going and if you do not follow me that is it'. And we went and sit in the second seat in the front and the Reverend he was preaching and talking about different minorities and different this and that and the other and he said something and I did not like it very much and

I said to the girls 'come let's go' and they didn't because he might say to the Matron that we went in and we walked out and they would not come. So we waited until the service was finished and we came out. While he was there shaking everybody's hand, I would not let him shake my hands. I said we come to a church like anybody else and you should not joke about other different nationalities. So I said, I would not shake your hands and I won't come back to your church and that was it.

Having chosen to occupy the second pew from the front, an act clearly visible to the entire white congregation, the five Barbadian nurses became the subject of the sermon! The priest chose to talk about 'different minorities this and different this and that' in what can be read as an act to speak to their presence and make them feel unwelcome. Their desire to leave the church mid-service was tempered by the thought of upsetting their Matron and thus possibly jeopardising their jobs. As a result they stayed and endured the now unfriendly church atmosphere. The final refusal of the respondent to shake hands with the minister served to provide some reprieve and allowed the nurses to reclaim their dignity in the alien church space.

CULTURAL PRACTICES: A CHILD'S PERSPECTIVE

When the migrant was a child, the act of negotiating the space took on its own complexities. In this narrative the female respondent had migrated to Coventry in the 1960s as a child and remembers how her hair became a conduit for representing difference in the playground.

They always wanted to know, because West Indians have this habit of like plaiting the children's hair and they want to know, 'how did your hair get like that. Who did that?' and touching your hair all the time to see how it felt because our hair obviously is different to theirs and in those days my hair would be plaited, braids now, and they used to giggle and laugh and thought it was funny. And they used to say things like your hair is like cotton wool and this kind of thing. Why is it so curly and stuff like that'? But after a while, children to me, I find adapt and adjust quicker than older people and I just adjusted and adapted.

It has been stated that black hair is a tangible re/presentation of the discourse of racism. Mercer argues: 'Where 'race' structures social relations of power, hair — as visible as skin colour, but almost the most tangible sign of racial and social difference — takes on another forcefully symbolic dimension.'[7] This narrative clearly speaks to this. The mother of this respondent, now living in Coventry, had continued the cultural practice of plaiting and braiding the hair of her child as she had done in Barbados. This ritual spoke to the practice of styling African-Barbadian hair as well as to the ritual of African-Caribbean childhood. When interacting with other children of white English origin, the hair of this Barbadian child became a signifier of difference. Note the reference to the difference in texture and appearance of her hair to theirs and the racist stereotype of 'cotton wool' coupled with the actions of touching and giggling. In this way her African-Barbadian cultural practices regarding her hair became part of the discourse of racism and the child became the 'other'. For this migrant, her memories of childhood are entangled with the memories of finding ways of negotiating difference in the migrant space.

RACE RELATIONS

When designing the questionnaires, the migrants chose to concentrate on a range of questions that spoke to the issue of racism. They emphasised that these memories were integral to the retelling of the migrant narrative. In recording their narratives, several migrants reflected on the ways in which white British communities constructed images of them as migrants. The discourse was usually characterised by the use of stereotypes in the effort to demean and dehumanise the female and male migrant. It was also constructed to make them not feel welcome as citizens though they were British nationals of the British colony of Barbados.

This first respondent lived in London. He captures many of the elements of the racist discourse:

> I was black, I was a monkey, I was an African, I was a Jamaican never a Bajan, they never know to Barbados in those days because as I said we were living, literally the pioneers who went there in 54/55 from Barbados.

This narrative was provided by a female respondent who had been a nurse based in a London hospital. Note can be taken of the racist discourse as well as the response:

> I sat on this lady's bed and had put four spoonfuls of porridge into her mouth, all of a sudden she just spat this mouthful of porridge straight into my eyes, s-p-l-a-c-k and then she started screaming, help, help, murder, murder, get this black monkey from over me, she is going to eat me. I just knocked her straight out of the bed. I know that nobody in Barbados ever hit me but my parents, but to spit in my face that was unacceptable, so I reacted and she landed on the floor and I landed in the Matron's office.

Finally, this male respondent provides a narrative in which he remembers the experience of a Barbadian male conductor who worked with London Transport. Note how in the act of remembering he seeks to understand the thinking behind the racist comments:

> One chap . . . he was traumatized when for two days, a woman was saying to him, 'you remind me of someone, I can't place it', and he is trying to [say] who could I remind you of, and about the third day and she was genuinely searching, 'where did I see him before?' And then she said, 'oh you remind me of the gollywog on the jam jar', and you would understand how he felt then. But as I said, people might think that it is a joke, but it's this woman's impression … people would insult you like that with no emotions to it as if they didn't mean to insult you. It is just how it is.

These three narratives speak to the acts of racial discrimination experienced by Barbadian and other migrants. They speak particularly to migrant experiences in Britain where racial discourse served to make West Indian migrants very visible within the white British society. Having been among the early phase of migration these interviewees had to face the full onslaught of the racist discourse. The narrative of the male respondent in London who emphasises that they were 'literally the pioneers who went there in 1954/55 from Barbados referred to this. These early migrants had to find work and accommodation in predominantly white communities. In addition they had to quickly learn ways in which they could navigate and survive the hostile racist British environment.

Barbadian migrants found themselves embroiled in a discourse constructed to make them the Other in the society. The language that emerged to describe these individuals who were employed as nurses, conductors, bus drivers, for example, was entangled in stereotypes aimed at demeaning and questioning their humanity. The narratives of being called a 'monkey' as given here were repeated by many migrants in their interviews, some recalling vivid memories of these examples of racism some forty years later. Stereotypes also served the purpose of not allowing the viewer to see the individual. All migrants were summoned into convenient categories such as 'black', 'African', 'Jamaican' and 'golliwog on the jam jar'.

Negotiating this racist discourse became part of the everyday lived experience of the Barbadian migrant in the British society. Most of the time she/he was forced to endure the experience on the job, as did the conductor on the bus. The game of intrigue had continued for three days with the polite conductor doing his best to assist the passenger. When she recognised him as the 'golliwog on the jam jar', she had solved her mystery and with one phrase had attacked his individuality, his humanity and his sense of belonging within British society. However, there were also occasions when migrants did not accept the racist discourse as is the example of the nurse and the patient. In a fit of outrage at the verbal attack, 'help, help, murder, murder, get this black monkey from over me, she is going to eat me', which had been preceded by the actual spitting of the food, the Barbadian nurse ignored the training of her discipline and reacted accordingly, 'I know that nobody in Barbados ever hit me but my parents, but to spit in my face that was unacceptable'. Fortunately her matron understood the complexity of the circumstances and allowed her to continue in her job.

TEDDY BOYS

The memories of encounters with the *Teddy Boys*, a 1950s-60s British youth cult, remain fresh for many of the migrants interviewed. Indeed it was a hot topic of discussion in the June 2006 meeting as those present spoke of these gangs of white boys roving through the streets especially in search of migrants to torment. Many Barbadian migrants have a clear recollection of the incidents some forty years later. However, this was also an instance where geographic location played a role in the migrant experience. Those migrants who lived in the North of England were not as affected by the *Teddy Boys* and therefore the memories of this experience, as though who lived in the South, such as in London.

In this testimony the male respondent speaks to several issues: West Indian-Asian relations, Jamaican-Barbadian relations and the interaction with the *Teddy Boys*:

> The Asians in the early stages - they were not or did not consider themselves as being black. It was only after they were being attacked by the *Teddy Boys* that they sought refuge among us West Indians because the *Teddy Boys* had a fear of genuine black people because they thought that we were all Jamaicans and Jamaicans had knives and therefore they did not interfere with us. Incidentally they might interfere with a black person but they would not interfere on a one-to-one. They would be a six to one. That is how they would interfere with you.

It is interesting to note that in this case, the respondent uses the word 'interfere' to mean challenge and assault, as it is used in Barbadian dialect. The complexity of West Indian migrant relations is also noted. Note the stereotype which claimed 'we were all Jamaicans and Jamaicans had knives', a construct that is invalid under scrutiny, but which apparently became a useful perception/deception in their interaction with the *Teddy Boys*. Many interviewees did agree that Jamaican migrants came to their aid on some of these occasions and that being seen as 'genuine black people' became a suit of armour and a weapon of war. Again it can be noted that in negotiating the racist discourse, the migrants were forced to, or opted to use the very stereotypes created for them against their persecutors as they orchestrated tactics for their survival.

However, there were occasions where the gangs did single out the individual migrant. Such was the experience of a Barbadian nurse who lived in London in the 1960s. She had finished her shift at 8:00 pm and was on the train when she encountered the *Teddy Boys*:

While I was on the train there was four boys. The train was full and I had to be standing and these boys chanted up and down, up and down, towards me. The door was automatic open. I was standing by a door so I had a folding umbrella behind my back and my bag and I say to myself - the next step these come close to me they are going to mash me, what am I going to do - and I look up and roll my eyes, 'Lord you just tell me what to do right now'. So when they came chanting, chanting back to me, instead of they coming back to me for the last time I went forward and I took my little brolly and I was doing it like that (thrusting forward) but the words came out of my mouth, can't repeat ... I was nervous and in shock and as soon as the train stopped and the door opened they all gone. But if I had stayed there and kept quiet and didn't say a word they would mash me, beat me or something like that. And you know, all the white people, I was the only black one there. All the white people on the train and seeing those boys doing that not one of them never say nothing.

The lone Black Barbadian female migrant is isolated in this incident of a racist attack on the train. Dressed in her nurse's uniform she was very visible in the train filled with white passengers, all of whom chose to ignore what was happening. By verbally and physically defending herself, if only with an umbrella, she demonstrated that she was not the meek female — the ideal prey for the attackers. As she said, 'I was nervous and in shock ... if I had stayed there and kept quiet and didn't say a word they would mash me, beat me or something like that.'

In the June 2006 meeting with the migrant community, this respondent reflected further on her narrative. She commented that this was the general attitude that she had to adopt to survive in London in the 1960s. She found that she had to become more assertive as a female and what some might term aggressive in her daily activities. Such an outlook was necessary, or she would not have survived the experience of living in London as a female Barbadian West Indian migrant at that time.[8]

SPORTS

Participating in sports served to recreate the familiar within the alien space. For many male migrants, playing cricket and other sports allowed them to find ways of negotiating race, class and national boundaries in the alien

British environment. Known for their love of cricket, these Barbadian male migrants found, or made opportunities to live their passion within British society:

> The one thing that we survived on was cricket. We played cricket. Once the sun shone, we played cricket. The [bus] garages compete against themselves and was also darts competitions and snooker competitions and I was good at snooker and I played cricket, so that['s] socializing and there you meet — it was a joy beating a white person at their game like snooker, so you enjoyed getting your little pat on white people.

This narrative speaks foremost to the Barbadian passion for the game of cricket as well as games generally. With the ironic statement of 'Once the sun shone', an event that was unpredictable in a country known for its short summers and overcast weather, the respondent is emphasising the joy he experienced at playing cricket while living in England. The narrative also speaks to teams of workers playing against each other in several sports. Though the competition was based on ability and skill, this respondent clearly linked these games to the larger issue of race and race relations in which 'you enjoyed getting your little pat on white people.' Indeed, one interviewee spoke of how seating on the bus spoke to the race and class divide as the black worker/ cricketers were made to sit at the bottom of the bus while the white managers sat on the top deck. Though enjoying the social activities provided by sports, many migrants were also aware that they were still negotiating the exclusive migrant space.

Cricket also provided opportunities for other forms of interaction in the white English and British space/s that would not have normally been open to these African-Barbadian, working class males. With their skills as batsmen and bowlers they gained access to prominent social clubs, were hired to play for the clubs and became members. Note this narrative of a Barbadian migrant living in London:

> I was visiting a park called Peckham Rye Park in South-East London and watching this match and a gentleman got bowled and I said, just reactionary, 'well, that should have been a six', and then this English gentleman standing next to me very diminutive in stature said: 'do you play cricket?' so I modestly

said, 'well, a little' … he approached me to join the Club … he took me to a road off Lordship Road Lane, Mount Aden Park and he showed me a top three-bed flat and he said, 'that is your accommodation provided you play for the Club', so I did not hesitate … I became a semi-professional immediately and I lived in that accommodation for several years.

Finally, cricket and other sports also allowed the migrants to recreate West Indian cultural spaces in the middle of, for example, Paddington:

> I remembered in 1956 we formed a cricket club in Paddington, called the Paddington Overseas Club and that was West Indians of all denominations – Jamaicans, St. Lucians, Guyanese, Kittitians, the lot, and we were an unbeatable team in the '50s. We used to play at Ratons Park and I was the wicket keeper, not much of a batsman but I was a ball-stopper.

This 'ball-stopper' as he called himself went on to play with a cricket team for Lyons and other West Indian teams in London and Reading. Most interviewees emphasize that Barbadian males used cricket and other sports to recreate the familiar Barbadian and West Indian environment. Sports provided opportunities to create the familiar Saturday and Sunday afternoon activities usually spent at the cricket ground and in the rum shops when in Barbados, but now spent in West Indian communities in Britain.

Initial findings of the research indicate that to an extent sports created a gendered space within the migrant communities. Most female respondents do not speak of playing sports; and some explicitly stated that they were not interested in participating in games. They supported their boyfriend and husbands, cooked food for the games and organised the after-game activities, In this way, it can be argued that cricket provided the opportunity for Barbadian men to re-enact the cultural practice of 'spending time with the boys' though they were now living in, for example, London, Reading and Birmingham.

However, it must also be emphasized that not all male interviewees spoke to this delight of playing sports. One interviewee who had first migrated to Scotland stated that though he did fit the stereotype of being

Barbadian, Black and male, he disappointed many who thought he could play any sport at all. Another interviewee refused to participate in sports:

> I was very much involved in walking and things like that, but when it comes to other sports you didn't want to get involved because you were a black person getting involved in a career of white area and don't forget we were a generation that we didn't went there and came out of school, mixing with them. We went there specifically to work and do a job, so we actually kept ourselves mainly work, play, parties and whatever, and that was it.

In this case, the respondent was fully aware of the implications of entering the sporting arena in London where he was based. His narrative speaks to the issues of race, class and origin, which were key determinants in participating in British sporting activities. Unlike the other respondents quoted here, he concentrated on working and socializing within the West Indian community: 'We went there specifically to work and do a job, so we actually kept to ourselves, mainly work, play, parties and whatever, and that was it.' This and the example of the migrant who lived in Scotland indicted another way in which male migrant masculinity and identity was constructed. Such constructs are not dependent on participation in traditional West Indian pastimes such as cricket.

CREATING CULTURAL SPACES

Many narratives have spoken to occasions in which the interviewees recreated the Barbadian and West Indian lived experience while in Britain. Note, for example, the following:

> Everybody had their own group of friends. People would come to your house this weekend and the next weekend you would go to somebody else's house and the next weekend somebody else's and there was always pudding and souse, corned beef and biscuits, fish cakes and you do sweet bread and pudding and all the things that we missed from home and that was nice, and that kept us in touch with home and that was our way of keeping in touch with what we have left behind.

This narrative of spending time with friends and family on weekends was repeated by many interviewees. The familiar delicacies of fish cakes, corned beef and biscuits and sweet bread allowed them to actively identify with their Barbadian cultural roots. One respondent also remembered driving from London to Reading every Saturday to buy the Saturday delicacy of pudding and souse from another Barbadian migrant who was known for this dish. Such weekend treats allowed these Barbadian and West Indian migrants to retreat into the safety of the communities and away from the hostile environment in which they lived and worked. They created culturally familiar spaces in the migrant space.

'COMING FULL CIRCLE'

The analysis presented in this chapter speaks to the particular, that is, to the experience of the Barbadian migrants interviewed in the Oral History and Cultural Studies project. It has foregrounded *their voices* and is shaped by their memories, their stories of living and working in the migrant space. This study therefore has no intention of re/presenting the narrative of migration as a whole, but of understanding how, in these particular instances, memory has informed the historical narrative and how that historical narrative assists in the shaping of identity/ties.

In retelling the stories of their experiences these Barbadian migrants speak to Barbadians in the current debates of their right to claim space (both ideological and real) within Barbados. In constructing their identities these stories serve to provide an understanding of their lived experiences. As Linda Tuhwai-Smith argues, for marginalised groups, telling their stories in their own voice is critical in the process of constructing identity: 'It is not simply about giving an oral account ... but a very powerful need to give testimony to restore a spirit'.[9]

In designing the questionnaires for the project the migrants insisted that they wanted the research to do more than just focus on their experiences since they had returned to Barbados. They also wanted a range of questions that spoke to the reasons for their departure to the U.K. as well as their experiences whilst living and working there. According to Sylvester Jones, one of the key members of *The Journey*, the migrants 'had come full circle' by returning to Barbados. He thought that it was imperative that all who heard their narratives understood the importance of this.[10]

Such a perspective invites us to see the migration experience as part of a continuum. Migration becomes part of their life story, their ritual of maturity. It is indeed *The Journey* as it was aptly called by the individuals who created this project. This journey continued for many when they found themselves once again in Barbados:

> I am a Barbadian born here and grow up so I did all right. Some people say, 'I ent coming back to Barbados. I ent do this. You can't live 'bout here.' But I never do that. I is a Barbadian so I come back to Barbados and I 'ent regret it neither.

This female respondent had lived in Reading from the 1950s. Seeing herself as Barbadian she claimed a right to the island as her place of birth, as her home, real and imagined. She did continue the journey back to her native land and did ensure that she became part of the Barbadian community once again. She died in Barbados in 2004, a year after this interview was conducted. This is but one example of the many Barbadian migrants who endured the experiences of migration in the UK and who have returned to live and indeed, die in their native land.

NOTES

1. Special thanks to Barbadian/UK migrants Sylvester Jones, Erma Jones and Aubrey Deane for their comments on this paper and their dedication to the project.
2. 'A person of Barbadian ancestry, birth and culture as distinct from one of naturalized citizenship.' Richard Allsopp, 1996. *Dictionary of Caribbean English Usage* Oxford: Oxford University Press, p.71
3. Stuart Hall, 1996. 'Introduction: Who Needs Identity' In *Questions of Cultural Identity*, eds. Stuart Hall and Paul du Gay, London: Sage., p. 4.
4. The first presentation was to the Association of Caribbean Historians (ACH) at U.W.I., St. Augustine Campus in April 2006. Marcia Burrowes and Kenneth Walters presented papers on their findings. The second presentation was at the Migration conference at UWI Mona Campus in May 2006 where an earlier version of this paper was presented by the author.

5. The presentation was held on the Cave Hill Campus on 24th June 2006. Tony Philips presented his findings on colonial government policy on migration; Aviston Downes reviewed the reasons for migration, Marcia Burrowes looked at lived experiences while in Britain and Kenneth Walters looked at the narratives of return.
6. Meeting with migrant community at the Cave Hill Campus on June 24, 2006.
7. Kobena Mercer, 2000 'Black Hair/Style Politics'. In *Black British Culture and Society*, ed. Kwesi Owusu, 113. London: Routledge.
8. Conversation at the presentation to the migrant community on June 24, 2006.
9. Linda Tuhwai-Smith. 1999. *Decolonising Methodologies,* 28 London: Zed Books.
10. Discussion at South Bank University, London, July 25, 2006.

REFERENCES

Gmelch George. 1992. *Double Passage: The Lives of Caribbean Migrants Abroad and Back Home.* Ann Arbor: University of Michigan Press.

Hall, Stuart, 1995. Negotiating Caribbean Identities. *New Left Review*, 209, Jan - Feb: 3-14.

————. 1996. 'Introduction: Who Needs Identity'. In *Questions of Cultural Identity.* eds. Stuart Hall and Paul du Gay, 1-17. London: Sage.

Mercer, Kobena, 2000. 'Black Hair/Style Politics'. In *Black British Culture and Society.* ed. Kwesi Owusu, 111-121. London: Routledge.

Tuhwai-Smith, Linda. 1999. *Decolonising Methodologies.* London: Zed Books.

Western, John. 1992. A Passage to England: Barbadian Londoners Speak of Home. Minneapolis: University of Minnesota Press.

10

TRANSNATIONAL RETURN MIGRATION TO THE ENGLISH-SPEAKING CARIBBEAN

DWAINE PLAZA AND FRANCES HENRY

INTRODUCTION

The Caribbean has been incorporated into the global system of capitalism since the sixteenth century and the region has experienced successive waves of immigration, emigration and circulation. Most of the early flow was part of a system of coerced one-way immigration from Africa. Later movements included voluntary immigration from India, Syria, Portugal, China and various parts of Europe. Over time, migrations of all descriptions have been a fundamental force in the creation and maintenance of Caribbean societies (Conway 1988). Common to the migration traditions which have become entrenched in the culture of the Caribbean is the desire of Caribbean people to circulate, but ultimately to return to their place of birth as a result of either wealth or old age (Thomas-Hope 1985, 1992, 1999; Byron 1994, 1999, 2000; Marshall 1982, 1983, 1987; Gmelch 1980, 1987, 1992). This chapter examines the emergence of a transnational return migration tradition in the English-speaking Caribbean since 1834.

Until recently, migration was understood in terms of two opposing outcomes: permanent settlement or permanent return. Return migration especially was thought of as the final outcome of the migration process. This relatively static bipolar model is a simplistic and uni-linear depiction of migration and return migration which is not consistent with the realities of population movements in an increasingly transnational world. These complexities, which characterize migration and return migration, are more aptly analyzed in a model that emphases migration processes.

The transnational movement of people requires a more processual approach. Transnationalism refers to the multiple ties and interactions that link people and their institutions across the borders of nation-states. It is now understood to have many elements including 'social morphology, as a type of consciousness, as a mode of cultural reproduction, as an avenue of capital, as a site of political engagement, and as a reconstruction of place' (Vertovec 1999). As a descriptive category or social morphology, transnational groups are those that are globally dispersed but still identify in terms of their original ethnicity, and relate to both the host states in which they reside as well as the home countries from which they or their ancestors originated. They are tied together transglobally through a variety of social relationships or networks. Transnational diaspora communities therefore are characterized by combinations of ties and positions in networks and organizations that reach across the international borders to link people together. These communities are formed on the basis of dynamic social, cultural, political and economic processes, such as those in transnational social spaces which involve the accumulation, use and effects of various sorts of capital, their volume and convertibility. Migration and re-migration may not be definite, irrevocable and irreversible decisions; transnational lives in themselves may become a strategy of survival and betterment. Transnational webs may also include relatively immobile persons and collectives. Even those migrants and refugees who have settled for a considerable time outside their country of origin frequently maintain strong transnational links. These links can be of a more informal nature, such as intra-household or family ties, or they can be institutionalised, such as political parties entertaining branches in various countries, both of immigration and emigration.

Transnational diaspora communities can perhaps best be understood as part of processes of global integration and time-space compression. This is partly a technological issue: improved transport and accessible real-time electronic communication is the material basis of globalization. Social and cultural issues however, are equally important. Globalization is closely linked to changes in social structures and relationships, as well as shifts in cultural values concerned with place, mobility and belonging. This is likely to have important consequences, which we are only just beginning to understand (Bauman 1998; Castells 1996).

One of the most intriguing features of transnational communities is the role that personal identity plays in the consciousness of its members. Some identify more with one society or another while others assume multiple identities. Hall (1988) has noted that the condition of the transnational provides for ever-changing representations or identities. Robin Cohen observed that to a certain degree 'a diaspora can be held together or re-created through the mind, through cultural artifacts and through a shared imagination' (1987). Cultural products are important in maintaining identity — and such forms as music, religious practices, fashion, visual arts, films, language (accent and colloquial adages) and ways of cooking food are some of the most conspicuous areas in which such processes are observed.

ORIGINS OF THE TRANSNATIONAL CARIBBEAN DIASPORA

When slavery ended in the English-speaking Caribbean (following the legal proclamation of 1834), former slaves were eager to establish their own communities away from the plantations. Many moved to free lands on neighboring islands, or at least off the plantation property, but discovered that they could not survive without part-time or seasonal work on the plantations or at other places of employment. Circulation — a form of migration in which the migrant families live year-round in the home community while the migrant members of the family move away seasonally for work — became a part of the wider culture.

Gradually over time, local circulation expanded to include regional circulation and longer periods of migrant residence away from home. Circulation within the Caribbean region expanded further to include, for example, the longer distance movement to Panama in the late nineteenth century, the United States in the period of 1900 to 1930, Britain in the 1950s, and Canada and the United States again from the late 1960s to the present. The longer distance moves were associated with longer-term residence abroad and in some cases led to permanent settlement abroad. Over this long period up to the 1960s, the genesis of a Caribbean diaspora in some major cities in the eastern United States (New York, Boston and Baltimore), Canada (Toronto and Montreal), and in the United Kingdom (London, Manchester and Birmingham) can be observed. The formation of large Caribbean-origin migrant communities in these cities and the resources that such immigrant communities provided to new migrants strengthened and transformed the Caribbean culture of migration. Caribbean peoples began to see themselves as both 'here' and 'there' — with the 'here' being wherever they were living (in the Caribbean, Britain, Canada or the United States) and 'there' being any of the Caribbean communities in another country to which they were connected through family ties, friendships and community linkages. 'Home' began to be viewed not just as the place where one was born, or where one lived, but more generally everywhere that friends, relatives and members of the cultural community were to be found. In effect, what began as a Caribbean culture of migration expanded over time to become a diasporic Caribbean transnational cultural community.

Caribbean people in the international diaspora are quite diverse — they originate from different islands, ethnic groups, social classes and cultures within the Caribbean region, and many are now part of a second if not third generation in the metropolitan countries where they have settled. Despite this diversity, they form a cultural and social community based on their identification with the music, history, traditions and achievements of people from the Caribbean region and their participation in Caribbean community organizations, cultural events, churches and temples.

The Caribbean-origin communities in New York, Toronto or London are clearly transnational, drawing on strong links and support from family and friends in the Caribbean and other countries. Most Caribbean migrants who have legal immigrant status move about quite freely. Many make return trips to the Caribbean to vacation and to see friends and kin. They receive visits from relatives living in the Caribbean, Canada, the United Kingdom and the United States. Family members in the metropolitan countries send large amounts of cash (remittances) and gifts (often in the form of 'barrels' of clothing and household items) to support relatives in their respective home countries.

An impressive body of relevant research exists on diasporas (Clifford 1994), 'transnational social networks' (Fawcett 1989, Boyd 1989, Massey 1987), 'transnational communities' (Basch et al. 1994, Vertovec 2001) and global migration patterns (Castles and Miller 1993). Studies of Caribbean migrants and their communities in Britain, the United States and Canada have contributed in important ways to this large body of research (for example, Chamberlain 2006; Simmons and Plaza 2006; Henry: 1994; Waters 2001; Richmond 1993; Foner 1997; Goulbourne 2002) Previous studies have addressed such matters as the history of the Black diaspora in the North Atlantic (Gilroy 1993) and its cultural politics in Britain (Gilroy 1991, 2000). They have examined the evolution of the Caribbean culture and practice of migration from colonial times until the late twentieth century (Simmons and Guegant 1992). These and other studies draw attention to the role of political, cultural and social economic forces from colonial times to the present in the formation of the Caribbean diaspora and the development of Caribbean transnational communities.

The pioneering study of transnational process among various Caribbean communities in New York by Basch et al. (1994) provided important new insights on the role of transnational migrants 'who develop and maintain multiple relationships (familial, economic, social, organizational, religious and political) that span borders.' Various studies have examined how Caribbean transnational migrants forge a complex matrix of intense social relationships that connect localities — Kingston, Miami, London, New York, Toronto, Montreal — in different nation-states — Jamaica, the United States, the United Kingdom, Canada (for example, see Fog Olwig 1993; Portes 1996; Glick-Schiller 1998; Foner 1997; Ho 1999; Plaza 2000; Goulbourne 2002). Previous researchers also point to the importance of occupations and activities that require regular and sustained social contacts over time, and across national borders for their implementation (Guarnizo 1997).

These studies find that migrants do not forget their home communities, nor do they lose contact with families, community organizations and political movements in their countries of origin, as they become part of a new society (Ho 1993; Goldring 2001; Fog Olwig 2002). Rather, the migrants take advantage of new opportunities, through travel and inexpensive telecommunications, to be simultaneously part of their home society as well as the society to which they have moved (Glick-Schiller et al. 1992; Portes 1996; Vertovec 2001). Both the home and migrant new settlement societies are in turn simultaneously transformed by these transnational links.

Much of the research on transnational social networks and communities assumes that these societies are particularly strong when they arise as part of an effort to overcome oppression. Transnational social networks and communities among formerly colonized and still radicalized minorities are understood to be part of their effort to resist marginalization, discrimination, exploitation and segregation in the countries to which they have moved, in their home nations and in the international system generally. From this perspective, Caribbean carnival parades in New York, Miami and Toronto are perceived to be more than simply efforts by a cultural minority to feel 'at home' in a new place and to maintain cultural traditions. Such public displays of culture and other actions by the minority transnational community members serve to generate community solidarity, recognition and resources for social action and transformation (Ho and Nurse 2005).

Transnationalism plays a major part in the return migrants' reintegration and mobilization for social development. Faist (2000) highlights the bridging function of social capital. This function occurs not only when groups are formed at home and overseas, but also when there is an active transnational exchange between these groups; that is, between migrants who are abroad and their families, kin and advocates who are in the origin country. Such transnational exchanges help the development of the origin community, even as these exchanges allow migrants to prepare for their eventual return and retain contacts with their hometowns. On the other hand, as migrants abroad plan for their eventual return, they pool their economic and social resources to offer assistance to the origin community.

LITERATURE ON RETURN MIGRATION TO THE CARIBBEAN

Although return migration on a global scale has been the subject of considerable study in places like Italy, Greece, Mexico, Ireland and Turkey, only a handful of studies have been done on return migration to the English-speaking Caribbean (Bovenkerk 1974; King 1986). Most research on the phenomenon of return migration to the Caribbean region has focused on Puerto Rico and the Dominican Republic — primarily because these Spanish-speaking territories have sent larger numbers of their population to the United States — more than any other country in the region. As a result of their substantial numbers of migrants, these two locations have the largest number of individuals as potential returnee migrants (Pesser 1997; Muschkin 1993; Grasmuck and Pessar 1992; Guarnizo 1997).

Return migration to the English-speaking Caribbean only began to receive serious attention from research scholars in the early 1970s. Most of the early studies concentrated either on the returnee's adjustment problems (Patterson 1968; Davidson 1969; Taylor 1976; Nutter 1985) or the development implications of return migrants and retirees (Gmelch 1987; Stinner 1982; Thomas-Hope 1985; Byron 1994). There have also been a few studies of return migration from Britain to the Caribbean that indicate the significance of the social and economic aspects of the return phenomenon. Peach (1968) showed how each wave of returnees fluctuated depending on the booms and busts in the British economy. Davidson (1969) found that the returnees to Jamaica experienced a shock upon return due to the realization that the cost of living had risen alarmingly and there was neither work, nor housing. Philpott (1968) reported similar results of disillusionment for return migrants from Montserrat who ultimately went back to England after a short return period. Studying the social adjustment aspect of return to the region, Taylor (1976) noted that there were differences in happiness and success between retiring returnees to rural versus urban areas in Jamaica. Returnees to the rural areas indicated much higher levels of satisfaction than individuals returning to the urban areas.

Another limitation of the existing return migration literature to the English-speaking Caribbean is that it has been focused on the experiences of the returnees, who are typically around retirement age (Rubenstein 1982; Thomas-Hope 1985, 1999; Gmelch 1980, 1987, 1995; Byron 1994). In looking at the economic impact of returnees on the host society, Gmelch (1980) found that retirees brought with them innovations and investments which benefited the Barbadian economy and society. Thomas-Hope (1999) noted a similar phenomenon in Jamaica whereby retiring return migrants had a dramatic impact in jump-starting the poor economy through the influx of foreign currency and, by hiring builders and other trades people, they also aided the local labour market. Abenaty (2000) also pointed out a similar pattern among seniors returning to St. Lucia. Many continued to be economically active by starting small entrepreneurial enterprises, many of which employed locals. Abenaty also noted that senior returnees experienced problems in terms of disappointment on their return to St Lucia. Many had high expectations for being welcomed back to the island of their birth. Most however, found a great deal of resentment towards them for what the local population regarded as ostentatious displays of their wealth.

More recently, Thomas-Hope (2002) remarked on a similar disillusionment with the decision to return among a group of skilled returnees to Jamaica. During their stay abroad, the highly skilled group tended to develop livelihood expectations that could not easily be met in Jamaica, their country of origin. After living in their place of origin for more than a year many continued to maintain close economic and social links with their former country of residence. Many of the skilled returnees in the sample continued to maintain a foreign citizenship, thus suggesting that their return to Jamaica might not be the final move in the migration cycle.

Goulbourne's (2002) study of returning migrants to Jamaica in the 1990s further highlighted new issues and problems for families and governments in areas that both receive and send migrants. The return of men and women in old age has a number of negative effects, starting with the absence of grandparents in upbringing and development of the young who remain behind in Britain. The impact of the returnees on the local housing stock, the local communities and the medical facilities was seen as detrimental and resulted in a driving up of costs for local governments, particularly those hardest hit by structural adjustment policies over the last ten years. The added drain on the system by these newly returned local-foreigners resulted in disillusionment among both the returnees and the local population.

Nutter (1985), Byron (2000) and Plaza's (2002) work has captured the most recent phenomenon of second-generation return migration to the Caribbean. Nutter's sample of return migrants in Kingston, Jamaica represented significantly skilled minority with respect to the national workforce, and their success appeared to be related to their education and work experience obtained overseas. Byron's (2000) research finds that some young, economically active returnees to the region have tended to invest in small cluster business categories linked to the tourism industry. Others have sought jobs as employees within hotels. Most, however, have entered self-employment, providing accommodation, transportation, boutiques and bars to serve the tourism industry and, more generally, the service sector. More recently, Plaza (2002) identified a growing trend of 'return' migration to the Caribbean among second generation British Caribbean persons. Second generation 'returnees' from Britain did not fit the typical profile of elder retired migrants returning to their place of birth. These individuals typically had a university degree or a specialized professional qualification and a desire to work once they moved back to the Caribbean. The findings from Plaza's (2002) research suggested that a hoped for idyllic re-connection with the Caribbean had not manifested itself for second generation returnees because the issues of race, gender, skin colour and class politics prevent their smooth transition into their 'home' societies.

More recently there has been an increased interest in the return migration phenomena by government officials in the English-speaking Caribbean because the circulation of these individuals appears to have an impact on the local economy in terms of the growth of self-employed businesses, tourism and service sector industries (De Souza 1998; Thomas-Hope 1999;

Potter 2001). The future cohorts of returnees do represent a potential resource for local Caribbean governments since they often bring savings, skills and an entrepreneurial fervor that might be used to help kick start economies depleted by years of structural adjustment.

Despite the existence of some important research on return migration to the English-speaking Caribbean, much still needs to be done, especially with respect to new trends and developments.

FACTORS INVOLVED IN MAKING THE DECISION TO RETURN

The decision to return to one's place of birth is very complex and depends on a set of facts about a migrant's life, cultural references and values. It is also a strategic choice made at a particular time in an individual's life. The path leading from *intention* to return (professed by the majority of migrants) to *actual* return is difficult to predict. Economic theory offers two different perspectives on return migration. Neoclassical economic theory views return migration as a cost-benefit decision, with actors deciding to stay or return in order to maximize expected net lifetime earnings (Todaro 1976). In the neoclassical model, social attachments generally operate on the cost side of the equation. Attachments to people and institutions in the origin country lower the costs of going 'home', both psychologically and monetarily, and they raise the costs of remaining abroad. In contrast, attachments (to grandchildren, family or kin) at the place of destination operate in precisely the opposite direction, raising the costs of return migration while decreasing the costs of staying.

Migrant motives for return to the English-speaking Caribbean have included strong family ties in the home country, dissatisfaction with present social status or conditions (typically in Canada, the United States or Britain), obligation to relatives, feelings of loyalty, guilt for living abroad, patriotism, perception of better opportunities opening up in the Caribbean and nostalgia. Some intervening factors that influence return include the following: changes in the social or political conditions in either homeland or receiving context (such as recession or political opposition to migration); marriage while in the destination country; marriage or relationship breakdown while abroad; having children in the new country of residence and the need to socialize them in the Caribbean; the number of family members who have migrated; ownership of property in the receiving country; the distance between the source and destination country; the number of return visits over the period of migration; the form of government in the home country; inequality in the source country; the acquisition of citizenship in the host country; length of stay in the host country; and the age at the time of migration.

Among the most important factors that encourage return are lasting ties with family and local society, and the education of migrant children. Among the conditions that prompt return include the maintenance of affective ties with the home country through frequent trips home, close relations with fellow absent compatriots, listening to local music, participation in traditional cultural events, the maintenance of the local language (dialects) and reading both newspapers and internet web sites from home. But these factors are only determinant when they compound a low degree of host country satisfaction.

Reagan and Olsen (2000), using data from the National Longitudinal Survey of Youth, compared patterns of return migration among both male and female immigrants. They did not find a gender differential but they did uncover lower probabilities of return migration among those who had arrived at younger ages, those with higher potential wages, those with more years in the US and those participating in welfare programmes. Duleep and Regets (1999) characterize the emigration of foreigners either as 'mistaken migration', whereby disillusioned immigrants return home soon after arrival or 'retirement migration', where immigrants return home after withdrawal from the labour force at an older age.

An observation on length of stay in the country of immigration implies that the process of integration is an evolutionary one that transforms the aspiration, ways of thinking, and interests of the émigrés. This realization enables Cerase (1974) to refine his observations and to outline three types of returns: failure returnees (return before two years), innovative returnees (returning after six to ten years), and retirement returns (return after eleven to twenty years). Failure returns are frequently prompted by disappointment and often follow short stays overseas. Failure is not an abstract notion, and many empirical studies have sought to determine its characteristics. Difficulty in adjusting to the host country is found to be the primary cause of failure. There are many facets to adjustment including migrant age: the older a migrant is at the time of departure, the shorter the stay abroad. The manifestation of racism in host countries constrains or limits access and opportunity for migrants of colour and is a strong factor in lack of adjustment.

Others, while recognizing the impact of racism, are able to accommodate themselves in the new, yet discriminatory society. Returns are also promoted by cataclysmic events such as loss of employment or housing, illness, divorce, death, and so on. These difficulties play the role of catalyst, transforming a potential choice into a positive decision.

Most return migrants in the English-speaking Caribbean cannot be viewed as failures, but as 'successes'. That is, most returnees have met their income goals and are returning home to enjoy the fruits of their success. Therefore, unlike neoclassical economics, the new economics of labour migration predicts that return migrants will be negatively selected with respect to work effort — those migrants who work fewer hours per week will have to remain abroad longer to meet a given income target. Factors of attraction, although difficult to measure, are clearly determined and appear to be a stronger motivation than factors of dissuasion. This does not mean that dissuading factors are unimportant. On the contrary, they are often more mentioned in the literature and include racism, difficulty in integration, difficulty in finding work and difficulty in coping with climate.

The decision to return to one's country of origin is essentially an affective one, tempered by a strategy for a higher socio-professional status. At the two extremes, failure returns and structural returns (when chances and opportunities are either positively or negatively comparable in the two countries, emotional factors take precedence in the decision to return). Between failure and structural return, the decision to move back is the result of a strategy that has social ascension as its goal. The migrant negotiates between the affective nature of his or her decision for themselves, their family and the receiving society.

RETURN MIGRATION INTENTIONS

Many reasons motivate Caribbean migrants to think about returning to their place of birth. Immigrant's return intentions will be influenced by their demographic characteristics and labour market outcomes, as well as the macroeconomic environment. The fact that some Caribbean migrants plan to return while others do not, suggest to researchers that there must be some compelling differences within the population in terms of labour market behaviour, skill accumulation, consumption patterns, acculturation, feelings of belonging, nationalism, and exposures to the ugliness of racism. Added to these factors are, of course, the socio-economic and political stability of the 'home' country to which most would likely return.

In order to examine the factors which appear to motivate migrants of Caribbean origin in the international diaspora to consider returning back to their 'home' country a study undertaken by Simmons and Plaza (2005) on remittance practices of specific Caribbean-origin immigrant communities resident in Canada is instructive. Using survey methodology, migrants from Trinidad, Jamaica and Guyana living in Toronto (with a sample size of 307) were questioned on their migration experiences and transnational linkages There were significant differences in the remittance practice for each group. Results from the study also indicated that there were differences in return migration intention including such factors as place of birth, gender, age, ethnicity housing tenure, income, number of return visits, remittance practices, and membership in transnational social organizations. Each of these factors seemed to influence each ethnic cohort in terms of intention to return.

Some preliminary findings from this study also suggest that there is a significant number of both men and women who seem to desire to return to their place of birth in the future. There are however differences in terms of sex and country of origin. Guyanese migrants in Toronto are the least likely to indicate a desire to return in the future to their home country and this trend seems to be stronger among Guyanese women. Ethnicity and age also seem to be influential factors in terms of the desire to return but some are constrained by means and ability to return. Younger age people seek to return more strongly but this is greatly influenced by ethnic origin. Indo-Caribbean migrants seem to be less likely than Afro-Caribbean people to have a strong desire to return to a place of origin. Some of these differences might be explained by the history of ethnic divisions in the country of origin or the overt and covert racist practices that African-origin people in Canada experience compared to Indo-Caribbean people (Plaza 2004). The general results of this study suggest that members of Caribbean communities in Canada are not homogenous in terms of their attitudes or desire to return. What is most interesting about the differences in return intention is that each cohort in Canada experience different degrees of success, as well as having different experiences and reactions to racism and discrimination. Their connections to their place of origin also differ based on number of return visits or sustained transnational connections. Some of these factors help to explain why there are different return intentions based on place of origin, gender, age, ethnicity and connection to home county.[1]

FACTORS WHICH INCREASE SUCCESSFUL REINTEGRATION TO THE HOME COUNTRY

Once returnees from the international diaspora return to their place of birth many factors help to increase the success of their re-integration. One of the most critical factors which influences re-integration and the entire return migration process is the role of financial capital. If earning more abroad is a primary reason for emigration, then bringing home significant savings and investment from abroad is important to sustain a migrant's intention of return and successful reintegration. In addition, however, there are other factors that can make re-entry difficult or relatively easy: These include:

(a) Length of stay abroad, the returnee's stage in the lifecycle, their socio-economic status and their access to resources on return all affect re-entry. Those who have stayed abroad a long time without making return visits in between find it difficult to reintegrate;

(b) Socio-economic status and available resources — brought back, previously invested or mobilized on return — have a strong bearing on the degree and speed of reintegration to the home country;

(c) Reintegration hinges on the capacity of the society of return to accommodate the returnees. Much depends on that society's security and stability, the state of its economy and its capacity to mobilize resources to assist or facilitate reintegration of the sojourner;

(d) Return migrants who have not been significantly alienated from the culture and practices of their origin communities will have a greater chance to become reintegrated;

(e) Maintaining a transnational connection over the period they were away plays a major part in reintegration into a migrant's birthplace. Such transnational exchanges help in the development of the origin community, even as they allow migrants to retain contacts with their hometowns and prepare them for their eventual return;

(f) Re-integration often hinges on the presence of extended families, kin or co-ethnics in communities receiving returnees;

(g) Sojourners who have stayed abroad a long time without making return visits may find it difficult to reintegrate. This is especially true for the children of returnees or those born and raised abroad. This may raise issues of what constitutes 'home' for these so-called returnees.

CONCLUSION

Return migration and circulation has long been an integral part of the social and economic fabric of the English-speaking Caribbean region. Returnees in the past as well as the present play an extremely significant role in the region's development. Returnee groups, as a result of their lifetime of work overseas, are able to contribute to the region's experience and skill base. Many returnees are also parents and grandparents who add to the human and social capital of their 'home' nations in a myriad of ways, and they add to the transnational reciprocal linkages which serve to bind members of the diaspora together.

Several opportunities and problems are generated by the process of return and resettlement to the English-speaking Caribbean. These include both practical and psychological difficulties involved in the decision to move from one place to another, and these are often compounded by the returnees' memories and expectations of the idealized homeland that they departed from some ten or more years ago.

The long term future of return migration to the Caribbean is still very unpredictable. Demographically, there is a growing number of second- and third-generation Caribbean men and women living in the international diaspora. These are individuals who do not know the Caribbean as their place of birth or idealized paradise. Some of these men and women are the product of inter-ethnic non-Caribbean/Caribbean relationships. Most, however, know the Caribbean as a region where they can visit distant family and kin. Their connection to the Caribbean region may be primarily based on their parents' or grandparents' experiences and reminisce. It may also be based on their love of Caribbean food or music: both of which they have come to equate with being authentically Caribbean. As a consequence of the shifting demographic realities, the current phenomenon of return migration may diminish in the future because the pool of traditional 'returnees' will become fewer and fewer.

One factor that might continue to fuel the desire for return among the future third and fourth generations in the international diaspora is the continued existence of racism and alienation in metropolitan countries where Caribbean people have settled. Faced with these unfortunate realities, many people in the future may continue to hold onto the same dreams as their ancestors — to return to the 'source', where they will be accepted and feel at home regardless of skin colour or ethnicity. This naïve desire does not, of course, recognize the stratification patterns of Caribbean societies that are also based on 'race', gender, social class and sexual orientation. They are also societies which have had to weather the harsh problems created by structural adjustment economic policies which have helped to create a more individualistic society where it is 'everyone for him or her self'. Thus, we are left to question how long the return migration phenomenon will sustain itself among Caribbean-origin men and women now living in the international diaspora.

Table 10.1: Correlates of return migration intention among Caribbean immigrants in Toronto by place of nativity and controlling for gender

		Guyanese		Jamaican		Trinidadian	
		Male	*Female*	*Male*	*Female*	*Male*	*Female*
Age	18-34 years	76.9	33.3	60.9	50.0	58.6	52.9
	35-54 years	29.2	11.5	53.8	45.7	41.7	52.0
	55 over	14.3	18.3	20.0	71.4	14.3	0.0
Ethnic	African	36.4	0.0	57.1	44.6	48.3	29.6
	Indian	50.0	25.0	33.3	50.0	50.0	55.6
	Other	27.3	13.3	33.3	80.0	46.2	56.3
Marital Status	Single	46.2	0.0	61.1	45.8	48.0	42.9
	Married	39.3	16.7	47.4	58.3	58.8	45.5
	Divorced	33.3	36.4	50.0	42.9	16.7	33.3
Residence	Renter	50.0	38.1	56.0	52.3	54.8	44.1
	Owner	30.0	6.5	36.4	42.9	23.1	40.0
Education	High school	61.1	21.6	50.0	40.0	50.0	42.1
	College	35.7	7.1	55.0	61.3	33.3	40.9
	University	16.7	18.5	66.7	40.0	61.5	50.0
Household Income 2004	<19,999	57.1	40.0	50.0	42.1	58.8	44.4
	20-39,999	54.5	7.1	61.1	45.5	50.0	38.9
	40,000+	29.2	13.0	41.7	56.0	30.8	43.8
Return Visits Past 5 Years	0 Return	33.3	16.7	71.4	42.9	40.0	28.6
	1-2 Return	44.4	17.9	52.2	30.3	48.1	45.8
	3+ Return	50.0	21.4	45.5	75.0	50.0	42.9
Telephone Calls Back Each Month	Zero	0.0	0.0	0.0	0.0	0.0	0.0
	1-2 calls	13.3	11.1	73.3	31.8	37.5	27.8
	3-5 calls	64.7	29.4	66.7	48.0	54.5	40.9
	6 or more	60.0	28.6	66.7	72.7	72.7	70.0
Money Remitted to Home in past 18 months	Zero	0.0	0.0	0.0	0.0	0.0	0.0
	1-2 times	17.6	15.8	57.1	25.0	35.7	50.0
	3-5 times	63.6	6.7	52.2	58.3	56.3	31.6
	6 or more	54.5	33.3	55.6	56.7	50.0	52.6
Alumni-Transnational	Membership	50.0	29.4	27.3	68.2	64.3	64.3
Sample size =		44	54	41	68	48	52

NOTES

1. See table 10.1 for the correlates of return migration intentions among Caribbean immigrants in Toronto. This table provides the per cent of males and females from Guyana, Jamaica and Trinidad who indicate a return migration intention. The cross tabulations show the per cent from within each group that indicated a positive desire to return

REFERENCES

Abenaty, Frank. 2000. St. Lucians and Migration: Migrant Returnees, their Families and St. Lucian Society. PhD dissertation, South Bank University.

Basch, Linda et al. 1994. *Nations Unbounded: Transnational Projects Post-colonial Predicaments and Deterritorialized Nation-States.* Amsterdam: Gordon and Breach.

Bauman, Zygmunt. 1998. 'On Globalization: or Globalization for Some, Localization for Some Others', *Thesis Eleven,* 54: 37-49.

Boyd, Monica. 1989. 'Families and Personal Networks in International Migration: Recent Developments and New Agendas. *International Migration Review,* 23, 3: 606-30.

Bovenkerk, Frank. 1974. *The Sociology of Return Migration: A Bibliographic Essay.* The Hague: Martinus Nijoff.

Byron, Margaret. 1999. 'The Caribbean-Born Population in 1990s Britain: Who Will Return?' *Journal of Ethnic and Migration Studies* 25, 2: 285-301.

————. 2000. 'Return Migration to the Eastern Caribbean: Comparative Experiences and Policy Implications'. *Social and Economic Studies* 49, 4: 155-88.

————. 1994. *Post War Caribbean Migration to Britain: The Unfinished Cycle.* London: Avebury Press.

Castells, Manuel. 1996. *The Rise of the Network Society.* Oxford: Blackwell.

Castles, Stephen and Mark Miller. 1993. *The Age of Migration: International Population Movements in the Modern World.* New York: Guilford Press.

Cerase, F. 1974. 'Migration and Social Change: Expectations and Reality: a Study of Return Migration from the United States to Italy'. *International Migration Review,* 8, 2: 36-50.

Chamberlain, Mary. 2006. *Family Love in the Disapora: Migration and the Anglo-Caribbean Experience.* New Brunswick, New Jersey: Transaction Publishers.

Clifford, James. 1994. 'Diasporas'. *Cultural Anthropology* 9, 3: 302-38.

Cohen, Robin. 1987. *The New Helots: Migrants in the International Division of Labour.* Aldershot: Gower Publishing.

Conway, Dennis. 1998. 'Conceptualizing Contemporary Patterns of Caribbean International Mobility'. *Caribbean Geography* 2, 3: 145-63.

Davidson, B.1969. 'No Place Back Home: A Study of Jamaicans Returning to Kingston'. *Race* 9, 4: 499-509.

De Souza, Roger-Mark. 1998. The Spell of the Cascadura: West Indian Return Migration. In *Globalization and Neoliberalism: The Caribbean Context*, ed. Thomas Klak, 227-53. Maryland: Rowman and Littlefield Publishers.

Duleep, Harriett and Mark Regets. 1999. 'Immigrants and Human-Capital Investments'. *American Economic Review* 82: 186-91.

Faist, Thomas. 2000. 'Transnationalization in International Migration: Implications for the Study of Citizenship and Culture'. *Ethnic and Racial Studies* 23, 2: 189-222.

Fawcett, James. 'Networks, Linkages, and Migration Systems'. 1989. *International Migration Review* 23, 3: 671-80.

Olwig-Fog, Karen. 1993. *Global Culture, Island Identity Continuity and Change in the Afro-Caribbean Community of Nevis*. Reading: Harwood Academic Publishers.

———. 2002. 'A Wedding in the Family: Home Making in a Global Kin Network'. *Global Networks,* 2, 3: 205-18.

Foner, Nancy. 1997. 'The Immigrant Family: Cultural Legacies and Cultural Changes'. *International Migration Review* 31, 4: 961-74.

Gilroy, Paul. 1993. *The Black Atlantic: Modernity and Double Consciousness*. Cambridge, Mass: Harvard University Press.

———. 1991. *There Ain't No Black in the Union Jack: the Cultural Politics of Race and Nation*. Chicago: University of Chicago Press.

———. 2000. *Against Race: Imagining Political Culture Beyond the Color Line*. Cambridge, Mass: Belknap Press of Harvard University Press.

Glick-Schiller, Nina, 1998. 'The Situation of Transnational Studies'. *Global Studies in Culture and Power.* 4, 2: 155-66.

Glick-Schiller, Nina et al. 1992. *Towards a Transnational Perspective on Migration*. New York: New York Academy of Sciences.

Gmelch, George and Sharon Bohn Gmelch. 1995. 'Gender and Migration: The Readjustment of Women Migrants in Barbados, Ireland and Newfoundland'. *Human Organization* 54, 4: 470-73.

Gmelch, George. 1992. *Double Passage: The Lives of Caribbean Migrants Abroad and Back Home*. Ann Arbor: University of Michigan Press.

———. 1980. 'Return Migration'. *Anthropology,* 9, 1:135-59.

———. 1987. 'Work, Innovation and Investment: The Impact of Return Migrants in Barbados'. *Human Organization* 46, 2:131-40.

Goldring, Luin. 2001. 'The Gender and Geography of Citizenship in Mexico-U.S. Transnational Spaces'. *Identities: Global Studies in Culture and Power*, 7, 4: 501-37.

Goulbourne, Harry. 2002. *Caribbean Transnational Experience*. London: Pluto Press.

Grasmuck, Sherri and Patricia Pessar. 1992. *Between Two Islands: Dominican Migration*. Berkley: University of California Press.

Guarnizo, Luis Eduardo. 1997. 'The Emergence of a Transnational Social Formation and the Mirage of Return Migration among Dominican'. *Identities: Global Studies in Culture and Power*, 4, 2: 281-322.

Hall, Stuart. 1988. Migration from the English-Speaking Caribbean to the United Kingdom, 1950-1980. In Appleyard ed. Reginald, *International Migration Today*, Vol. 1, Paris: UNESCO.

Henry, Frances, 1994. *The Caribbean Diaspora in Toronto: Learning to Live with Racism*. Toronto: University of Toronto Press.

Ho, Christine and Keith Nurse. 2005. Globalization, Diaspora and Caribbean Popular Culture. Kingston: Ian Randle Publishers.

Ho, Christine. 1999. 'Caribbean Transnationalism as a Gendered Process'. *Latin American Perspectives* 26, 5: 34-54.

———. 1993. 'The Internationalization of Kinship and the Feminization of Caribbean Migration: The Case of Afro-Trinidadian Immigrants in Los Angeles'. *Human Organization*, 52,1: 32-40.

King, Russell, 1986. Return Migration and Regional Economic Development: An Overview. In *Return Migration and Regional Economic Problems*, ed. Russell King, 1-37. London: Croom Helm.

Marshall, Dawn. 1982. 'The History of Caribbean Migrations'. *Caribbean Review* 11, 1: 6-9.

———. 1983. Toward an Understanding of Caribbean Migration. In *U.S. Immigration and Refugee Policy: Global and Domestic Issues*, ed. Mary Kritz, 152-69. Lexington, Mass: Lexington Books.

———. 1987. The History of West Indian Migrations: Overseas Opportunities and Safety-Valve Policies. In *The Caribbean Exodus*, ed. Barry Levine, 155-176. New York: Praeger.

Massey, Douglas 1987. *Return to Aztlan: The Social Process of International Migration From Western Mexico*. Berkeley: University of California Press.

Muschkin, Clara. 1993. Consequences of Return Migrants Status for Employment in Puerto Rico. *International Migration Review* 27, 1:79-102.

Nutter, Richard. 1985. 'Implications of Return Migration for Economic Development in Kingston, Jamaica'. In *Return Migration and Economic Development*, ed. Russell King, 125-145. London: Croom Helm.

Patterson, H. 1968. 'West Indian migrants returning home'. *Race* 10, 1: 69-77.

Peach, Ceri. 1968. *West Indian Migration to Britain.* London: Oxford University Press.

Pessar, Patricia. 1997. *Caribbean Circuits: New Directions in the study of Caribbean Migration.* New York: Center for Migration Studies.

Philpott, S.B. 1968. 'Remittance Obligations, Social Networks and Choice Among Montserrat Migrants in Britain'. *Man* 3, 3: 465-76.

———. 2000. 'Transnational Grannies: The Changing Family Responsibilities of Elderly African Caribbean-Born Women Resident in Britain'. *Social Indicators Research,* 5, 1: 75-105.

———. 2002. 'In Pursuit of the Mobility Dream: Second Generation British/Caribbeans Returning to Jamaica and Barbados'. *Journal of Eastern Caribbean Studies,* 27, 4: 135-60.

Plaza, Dwaine. 2004. 'Disaggregating the Indo-and African-Caribbean Migration and Settlement Experience in Canada'. *Canadian Journal of Latin American and Caribbean Studies,* 57: 241-266.

Portes, Alejandro. 1996. Transnational Communities: Their Emergence and Significance in the Contemporary World-System. In *Latin America in the World Economy,* ed. R.P Korzeniewicz and W.C. Smith,120-43. West Port Connecticut: Greenwood Press.

Reagan, P.B. and R.J. Olsen. 2000. 'You can go home again: Evidence from longitudinal data'. *Demography,* 37: 339-50.

Rubenstein, Hymie. 1982. Return Migration to the English-Speaking Caribbean: Review and Commentary. In *Return Migration and Remittances: Developing a Caribbean Perspective,* ed. W. F. Stinner, K. de Albuquerque and R.S. Bryce-Laporte, 100-125. Washington: Smithsonian Institution.

Simmons, Alan and Jean-Pierre Guengant. 1992. Caribbean Exodus and the World System. In *International Migration Systems: A Global Approach,* ed. M. Kritz, L. Lim and H. Zlotnik, *210-45.* Oxford: Oxford University Press.

Simmons, Alan and Dwaine, Plaza. 2005. The Remittances and Sending Practices of Jamaicans and Haitians in Canada. Unpublished CIDA commissioned study. http://www.yorku.ca/cerlac/abstracts.htm#remittances.

———. 2006. *The Caribbean Community in Canada: Transnational Connections and Transformations.* In Transnational Identities and Practices in Canada, ed. Vic Satzewich and Lloyd Wong, 130-149. Vancouver: University of British Columbia Press.

Stinner, William. 1982. *Return Migration and Remittances: Developing a Caribbean Perspective.* Washington: Praeger Press.

Taylor, Edward 1976. The Social Adjustment of Returned Migrants to Jamaica. In *Ethnicity in the Americas,* ed. Frances Henry, 115-25. The Hague: Mouton.

Thomas-Hope, Elizabeth. 1985. 'Return Migration and its Implications for Caribbean Development: The Unexplored Connection'. In *Migration and Development in the Caribbean: The Unexplored Connection*, ed. Robert Pastor, 145-68. Boulder, Colorado: Westview.

———. 1992, *Explanation in Caribbean Migration*. London: Macmillan Press.

———. 1999. 'Return Migration to Jamaica and its Development Potential'. *International Migration* 37, 1:183-205.

———. 2002. 'Transnational Livelihoods and Identities in Return Migration to the Caribbean: The Case of Skilled Returnees to Jamaica'. In *Work and Migration: Life and Livelihoods in a Globalizing World*, ed. Ninna Nybergg Sorensen and Karen Fog Olwig, 187-201. London and New York: Routledge.

Todaro, Michael. 1976. *Internal Migration in Developing Countries*. Geneva: International Labor Office.

Vertovec, Steven. 1999. 'Conceiving and Researching Transnationalism'. *Racial and Ethnic Studies,* 22, 2: 447-62.

———. 2001. 'Transnationalism and Identity'. *Journal of Ethnic and Migration Studies* 27, 4: 573-82.

Waters, Mary. *2001. Black Identities: West Indian Immigrant Dreams and American Realities*. Cambridge: Harvard University Press.

SECTION II

◉

Paradoxes and Possibilities of Transnationalism

11

MIGRATION OF PARENTS FROM THE CARIBBEAN:
Implications for Counselling Children and Families in the Receiving and Sending Countries

AUDREY M. POTTINGER, ANGELA GORDON-STAIR,
SHARON WILLIAMS-BROWN

Since the 1960s, significant numbers of West Indian mothers began migrating to the United States to seek work as nurses and nannies, leaving their children behind (Thomas-Hope 2002). Attention needs to be directed at the population of children left behind by these parents as well as the emotional, social and psychological needs of the immigrants. How both populations adapt to the migration will determine the contribution each makes to the economic, educational, health status and cultural harmony of the society in which they reside.

Migration of parents from the Caribbean to North America can take four forms, some of which are unique to the Caribbean and will allow for immigrants to remain involved in the development of their country of origin:

(1) Commonly, parents will migrate for up to six months at a time to work in the host/receiving country (seasonal migration);

(2) Parents will migrate either singly or together with the intention of sending for the rest of their family at a later date (serial migration);

(3) Parents will migrate for a defined time or indefinitely but have no intention of having their children live in the overseas country (parental migration);

(4) Parents will migrate with their family (family migration). The type of migration selected is determined by economic reasons.

While, disruption to the parent-child bond from migration can occur across the differing socio-economic levels of society, the family migrating together tends to be more of a 'middle class' movement and the other three forms are more commonly done by low-income families (Crawford-Brown and Rattray 2002).

The Harvard Immigration Project (Suarez-Orozco, Todorova, and Louie 2002) has drawn international attention to the vast number of children, as many as 85 per cent from the Caribbean, Central America and Asia, who endure lengthy separation from their parents during the process of serial migration. This chapter focuses on both serial and parental migration patterns in the Caribbean as the clinical literature suggests that these children face issues of grief, loss and attachment during the separation (Glasgow and Ghouse-Shees 1995; Crawford-Brown and Rattray 2002). The parents also undergo a parallel experience with their grief manifested in sadness, guilt and anxiety over the separation (Suarez-Orozco, Todorova, and Louie 2002). Proponents of Attachment Theory may argue that the resulting disruption to the parent-child bond from these patterns of migration puts the child at risk not only in the short term, but also for poor long-term psychological adjustment (Rutter and Rutter 1992; Bowlby 1982).

OUTCOME OF MIGRATORY SEPARATION FOR CARIBBEAN CHILDREN

School community samples out of Trinidad and Jamaica have indicated prevalence rates of 10.5 per cent and 30–35 per cent respectively of children who have parents who have migrated (Jones, Sharpe, and Sogren 2004; Samms-Vaughan 2000; Pottinger 2003). Clinical studies have also indicated high rates (ten per cent) of migratory loss for children who attend Child Guidance Clinics in Trinidad (Jones, Sharpe, and Sogren 2004).

Most parents prior to migrating will attempt to put a surrogate parenting system in place to try and minimise the disruption to their child's life. However, despite this, anecdotal reports indicate that many children who are left behind report a sense of abandonment by their parents. Some receive little or no emotional nurturance from surrogate caregivers, while others are surrounded with love but the surrogate parent refrains from setting rules and boundaries for fear of disciplining another person's child. Additionally, some children may assume adult-like responsibilities prematurely including managing large amounts of money that their parents send, or looking after younger siblings. Further, despite parents' efforts to remain in touch via telephone, contact is often reported to be irregular and falls short of meaningful exchange between parent and child (Suarez-Orozco, Todorova, and Louie 2002). Some Caribbean researchers have also alluded to these children being under-protected or inadequately supervised, resulting in them being exposed to harmful consequences such as sexual abuse (Crawford-Brown and Rattray 2002) and child prostitution (Morrison 1993).

As the rate of migration is high from urban poor communities in Jamaica, local investigators have examined parental or serial migration from these communities and its effects on the children left behind. A case-control sample of 54 nine to ten year olds living in inner city communities in Kingston and St Andrew, Jamaica, showed that children's reactions to their parents migrating were directly related to poor school performance and psychological difficulties (Pottinger 2005a). Thus, the more unhappy or angry children were about the migration the lower their grades in mathematics, reading and literacy. These children's school performance may have been affected by their troubled feelings, but it has also been noted that children with parents residing overseas may lose focus on their school work as they adopt a 'waiting to migrate' mentality (Crawford Brown 1999). Negative feelings about the migration were also associated with increased reports of depressive symptoms and suicidal ideation. However there were no associations found with behavioural problems.

Pottinger's findings (2005a) were based on correlational relationships as ANOVA revealed no statistically significant differences in social and psychological outcomes between the groups of index cases and controls. Nonetheless, group differences indicating increased risk for depression associated with migratory separation are supported in a comparative study of 146 13–16 year old adolescents living in Trinidad.

Both these studies and others indicate that even when children are left in the care of relatives or friends, the separation from parent may cause psychological damage that is manifested in deviant, 'acting out' behaviour, poor self esteem, depression and poor school performance (Suarez-Orozco, Todorova, and Louie 2002; Glasgow and Ghouse-Shees 1995; Pottinger 2005a; Jones, Sharpe, and Sogren 2004). Further, when loss of parent through migration was compared with other parental loss, including death and parental divorce or 'break up', children whose parents had migrated reported a more pervasive negative impact on their well-being (Pottinger 2005b).

GRIEF EXPERIENCE FOR CHILDREN

Despite differences in the ethnic make-up and economic performance of Caribbean islands, similarities in psychological outcome and grief experiences of children whose parents have migrated have been noted. These children report a mixture of loneliness, anger, sadness, anxiety, feelings of abandonment and fears of rejection. This is despite the majority of them being in regular contact with their parents (87.5 per cent and 84 per cent from Trinidad and Jamaica respectively.) The mother was the migrant parent in most cases: 75 per cent and 41 per cent from Trinidad and Jamaica respectively. Stability of guardianship was more of an issue with the Jamaican child, as more of these children compared to those in Trinidad had experienced multiple child shifting as a result of the migration. Lengthy periods of separation from parents were identified with the range of separation for Jamaican children being seven months to nine years, and 2–15 years in Trinidad. Additionally, many of the children (> 50 per cent of the Trinidadians and 20 per cent of the Jamaicans) had not been informed about the migration and thus reported not being prepared for the separation.

In both samples of children in Trinidad and Jamaica a 'disconnect' between intellectually understanding the reason for migrating and emotionally accepting was also found. Most children reported that they understood that their parents migrated in order for them to have a better life and over 80 per cent of both groups reported financial benefits. However, the majority of children in Trinidad nonetheless described lingering doubts and only one-third of the Jamaican sample indicated feeling happy about the migration. Factors that have been identified as protecting these children from the negative consequences of migration include living in a supportive and nurturing family, having someone to talk to about the migration, and doing well academically (Pottinger, 2005a; Jones, Sharpe, and Sogren 2004).

MIGRATORY SEPARATION: THE EXPERIENCE OF PARENTS

The experience for parents has only recently begun to be studied so there are not many published scientific reports. However, parents who migrate without their children also seem to undergo a parallel experience of grief, anxiety and guilt (Crawford-Brown and Rattray 2004; Suarez-Orozco, Todorova, and Louie 2002). These grief feelings are compounded when parents are aware of the difficulties their child may be facing as a result of the separation. Some respond to this knowledge with depression or guilt born out of helplessness (Suarez-Orozco, Todorova, and Louie 2002), some display insensitivity to the importance of the surrogate caregiver to the child (Smith, Lalonde, and Johnson 2004) while some lack insight as to the magnitude of the psychological impact of separation on children (Smith, Lalonde, and Johnson 2004).

Parents may also experience conflicting emotions; on one hand wanting to stay in the host country for the economic gains, and on the other, return to be with their child and remain economically challenged. Parents who choose to remain despite the conflict, may try to compensate for their absence by sending excessive gifts and money for their child. Social work practitioners in Jamaica have coined the term 'barrel children' when referring to children who receive barrels of goods from their migrant parents (Crawford-Brown and Rattray 2002). When the child, parent and surrogate caregiver are comfortable with the care giving arrangement, the distress is likely to be reduced for both parent and child. However, even under those circumstances, parents will still worry excessively about their children and report experiencing an abiding sense of guilt with bouts of loneliness (Suarez-Orozco, Todorova, and Louie 2002).

PARENT-CHILD REUNION

The child and parent reunion is undoubtedly a time of excitement and joy for many. However for some this process is also fraught with challenges. For one, migrating and reuniting often occur in adolescence (Lashley 2000), when children are battling with developmental issues of identity and figuring out where they belong. Also, once again they are being called on to separate from a primary caregiver, in this case, their surrogate parent as well as from friends.

Further, upon arriving in the host or 'receiving' country some children face reconstituted families with step-parents and siblings they hardly know and have to figure out how to fit in with this new family (Crawford-Brown and Rattray 2002). Sometimes the parent is working more than one job or working and going to school (Lashley 2000) leaving little or no time to help them settle in their new environment, or to provide them with adequate supervision. Recent immigrant children may also have to struggle with differences in language, accent, social systems as well as race classification. In addition, many encounter selection procedures at school and a school environment that considers them to be at a disadvantage to their North American peers (Gopaul-McNichol 1993). When both parents and children's expectations about the reunion are not met, there can be disappointment resulting in depression in the parents and anger and rebellion in the children (Smith, Lalonde, and Johnson 2004).

IMPLICATIONS FOR COUNSELLING

The migration separation-reunion experience is reportedly one of the common problems bringing Caribbean families residing in North America in to counselling (Smith, Lalonde, and Johnson 2004). These researchers have identified common themes in counselling relating to issues of loyalty, identity development, discipline and authority, disillusionment, rejection and counter-rejection and bereavement (Smith, Lalonde, and Johnson 2004). They further state that these children will present with both internalizing and externalizing symptoms including anxiety, depression, poor school performance, and delinquency such as truanting and running away from home (Smith, Lalonde, and Johnson 2004).

When working with these families, mental health professionals, especially those who are not from the Caribbean, may need to understand how parents can willingly take a decision to separate from their children and in some cases their infant child. Caribbean people have always been a migrant population and historically have used migration as an economic tool for progressing in life. Their decision to migrate is based on the belief that a mother will do anything to let her children have a better life than she had. Thus, when a parent migrates and leaves her children behind this separation is not stigmatised by members of the community (Waters 1999) but instead may even be lauded. Caribbean communities also tend to have strong familial networks that allow mothers to migrate and leave children with relatives, friends or neighbours (Thomas-Hope 2002).

COUNSELLING CARIBBEAN FAMILIES IN RECEIVING COUNTRIES

Glasgow and Ghouse-Sheese (1995) have noted that mental health professionals in North America are often ignorant of West Indian cultural attitudes toward migration as well as family structures and child socialization practices that exist in the Caribbean. As insensitivity to the cultural traditions of clients can impede communication in counselling, it is important that counsellors educate themselves about these issues and about the challenges of migration and strategies used to deal with it. The danger of stereotyping however must be avoided as issues facing one family may differ markedly from those facing another.

Counsellors are likely to interact with Caribbean migrant family members in varying settings including school, health services and the justice system. The school counsellor, however, is likely to be the professional with whom Caribbean families will interact first and most often. Mitchell (2005) recommends that school counsellors who work with Caribbean students should act as advocates for culturally sensitive school environments. They can help to change biased attitudes toward immigrant students and work to improve academic planning and family empowerment. School counsellors will need to take a proactive, preventive approach as West Indians view counselling as indicative of pathology and use it as a last resort, after the child is in trouble. With the high value placed on education by Caribbean families however there is more receptivity to psycho-educational interventions. Hence, special orientation sessions at schools for new immigrant children and their parents may be better utilised by Caribbean immigrants. Migrant families who have dealt with transition issues could be used as resource persons for these sessions which would allow for positive role modelling, networking and support.

Working with the entire family and not just the child or adolescent is important in the counselling context. Often the 'acting out' behaviour of a child is reflecting the difficulty of the transition which is compounded by parental pressure and expectations. Helping parents modify their expectations therefore can be an important part of the counselling intervention, for example, when parents view their fourteen year old as 'little Johnnie', the child they left at age eight and so expect the adolescent to comply with their wishes as a younger child would.

The interview with a professional counsellor should begin with a full history that includes emotional, social, economic, educational and health factors that affected the client and family in their country of origin as well as factors currently affecting them in the host country. Simple instruments screening for anxiety and depression could be useful as these symptoms may be masked in both adults and children but their presence has obvious implications for treatment planning.

COUNSELLING CARIBBEAN FAMILIES IN THE SENDING COUNTRIES

Counselling intervention related to migration in the 'sending' countries needs to utilise both preventive and interventive methods. The focus should be on counselling families prior to the migration of the parent and offering support to those impacted once migration has occurred. At present in the Caribbean, counselling with this population usually occurs when children show emotional or behavioural difficulties which require intervention and pre-migration counselling is often overlooked.

Psycho-education is seen as a major tool for pre-migration interventions. The public needs to be educated about the psychological impact of migratory separation on the children who are left behind. This can be done through the media and through community groups such as churches and parent-teacher associations. These groups along with international embassies could develop and promote programmes aimed at informing potential immigrant parents of steps they can take to minimize the impact of migratory separation on children. These steps include: (1) making informed decisions based on awareness of consequences of migrating, (2) preparing children well in advance about the intent to migrate, (3) placing children in a family environment supportive of their needs, (4) and when overseas, establishing regular contact and meaningful communication with child and surrogate caregivers.

Children who have had a parent migrate are potentially 'at risk' and therefore their schools should be informed about this loss as they are informed about other major losses. Informing schools would allow the child to be monitored for signs of difficulty in adjustment. Teachers can play a critical role in early identification; hence their training needs to include information on the potential impact of parental migration on students' performance. To this end, the curriculum for teachers in training should include material on sensitising teachers about how children may manifest grief-related behaviours in the classroom. They should also be taught how to plan strategies for directing and sustaining such children's attention to school work.

The counsellor who is dealing with children whose parents have migrated should also work with their surrogate caregivers and the other parent who has remained with the child. These caregivers may need help in understanding their response to the migration as well as the emotional needs and reactions of the child and how they can respond appropriately to these needs. In addition, surrogate caregivers may need to be helped to develop an open style of communication with the migrant parent, so concerns are neither concealed nor magnified. They can also be taught how to help the child communicate meaningfully and regularly with the parent. These caregivers may benefit from community based support groups which can be organised through churches and schools.

CONCLUSION

While migration of parents from the Caribbean should not be assumed to have negative consequences, the potential trauma it poses for children has been generally overlooked. Health providers and caretakers of children need to recognise and acknowledge that the separation arising from migration and even the experience of later reuniting can negatively impact on the well-being of both child and parent. Caretakers of children therefore need to be more alert to identifying this population and assessing its needs to determine whether mental health intervention is necessary.

Although the focus of this chapter was on serial and parental migration from the Caribbean, future research could identify the needs of children separated (seasonally) by parents who travel to work on the farm work or more recent hospitality programmes. Continued investigation into the psychological implications for these varying groups of children would inform intervention. Counselling families facing migration-related challenges in both the 'sending and receiving' countries ought to be seen as an imperative. As counsellors learn more about issues relating to migration, counselling is expected to be done in a more effectively and timely manner.

REFERENCES

Bowlby, J. 1982. *Attachment and Loss: Vol 1. Attachment.* 2nd. ed. New York: Basic Books.

Crawford-Brown, C. 1999. *Who Will Save our Children? The Plight of the Jamaican Child in the 1990s.* Kingston, Jamaica: Canoe Press, University of the West Indies.

Crawford-Brown, C. and J.M. Rattray. 2002. 'Parent-child Relationships in Caribbean Families'. In *Culturally Diverse Parent-child and Family Relationships,* eds. N. Boyd Webb and D. Lum, 107-30. New York: Columbia University Press.

Glasgow, G. F., and J. Ghouse-Shees. 1995. 'Themes of rejection and abandonment in group work with Caribbean adolescents'. *Social Work With Groups,* 17:3-27.

Gopaul-McNichol, S. 1993. *Working with West Indian Families*. New York: Guilford Press.

Jones, A., J. Sharpe, and M. Sogren. 2004. 'Children's experiences of separation from parents as a consequence of migration'. *Caribbean Journal of Social Work,* 3:89–109.

Lashley, M. 2000. 'The unrecognized social stressors of migration and reunification in Caribbean families'. *Transcultural Psychiatry,* 37:203-17.

Mitchell. N. A. 2005. 'Academic achievement among Caribbean immigrant adolescents: The impact of generational status on academic self-concept'. *Professional School Counseling* 8:209-18.

Morrison, I. 1993. *Report of the task force on child abuse.* Kingston, Jamaica. UNICEF.

Pottinger A. M. 2003. *Report on pilot project on loss and violence in students in inner city communities and a school-based intervention programme.* Ministry of Education Youth and Culture, Kingston, Jamaica.

Pottinger A. M. 2005a. 'Children's experience of loss by parental migration in inner city Jamaica'. *American Journal of Orthopsychiatry,* 75:485-96.

Pottinger A. M. 2005b. 'Disrupted caregiving relationships and emotional well- being in school age children living in inner city communities'. *Caribbean Childhoods: From Research to Action,* 2: 38-57.

Rutter M., and M. Rutter. 1992. *Developing Minds: Challenge and Continuity Across the Life Span.* London: Penguin Books.

Samms-Vaughan, M. 2000. *Cognition, educational attainment and behaviour in a cohort of Jamaican children. Working Paper No. 5.* Policy Development Unit, Planning Institute of Jamaica.

Smith, A., R. Lalonde, and S. Johnson. 2004. 'Serial migration and its implications for the parent-child relationship: a retrospective analysis of the experiences of the children of Caribbean immigrants'. *Cultural Diversity and Ethnic Minority Psychology* 10:107- 22.

Suarez-Orozco, C., I. Todorova, and J. Louie. 2002. 'Making up for lost time: The experience of separation and reunification among immigrant families'. *Family Process* 41:625-43.

Thomas-Hope, Elizabeth. 2002. *Caribbean Migration.* Kingston, Jamaica: University of the West Indies Press.

Waters, M. 1999. *Black Identities: West Indian Dreams and American Realities.* Cambridge: Harvard University Press.

12

FROM IMMIGRATION TO DE-INTEGRATION TO RE-INTEGRATION IN THE CARIBBEAN:
Exploding the Deportee Phenomenon

CLIFFORD E. GRIFFIN

INTRODUCTION

A series of anti-crime and anti-terrorism bills passed by the US Congress during the early 1990s has led to the biggest dragnet in US history. Between 1995 and 2004, some 61,851 nationals of 20 Caribbean territories were deported from the US, 67.5 per cent for committing various criminal offences (See Table 1). During this same period, crime statistics compiled by Caribbean police departments reveal a monotonic increase in all cases, and a significant increase in many cases, in the reported incidence of most categories of crime. Also throughout this period, the region witnessed a proliferation of private security services and personnel; significant investments in guard dogs; the installation of expensive, high tech security apparatuses, and the burglar proofing of homes, businesses and motor vehicles - developments having taken place in direct response to a perceived sense of insecurity posed by criminals.

Government leaders, journalists, commentators and political pundits alike across the region have responded to these developments by asserting more than a correlation between the influx of deportees and rising crime. Many assert a direct causation by pointing to 'sophisticated' crimes, ranging from carjackings in Guyana, to gun slayings in the Dominican Republic, to kidnappings in Haiti, to bank robberies in Barbados. These assertions inform the general view that the USA (and other developed countries) should not be 'dumping' these individuals on Caribbean societies.

Table 12.1: US Deportees to the Caribbean 1995-2004

Country	Total US Deportees	US Deportees per 100,000	Total US Criminal Deportees	US Criminal Deportees per 100,000
Anguilla	8	62	0	0
Antigua and Barbuda	331	487	270	397
Bahamas	1,039	346	348	116
Barbados	527	188	389	140
Belize	1,535	569	1,047	385
Bermuda	93	143	52	80
British Virgin Islands	37	168	12	55
Cayman Islands	4	9	4	9
Cuba	675	6	577	5
Dominica	256	371	162	235
Dominican Republic	29,699	345	19,759	230
Grenada	222	249	159	179
Haiti	5,355	71	3,109	
Jamaica	18,252	676	13,050	483
Montserrat	25	278	10	111
St. Kitts and Nevis	204	523	115	294
St. Lucia	255	159	158	99
St. Vincent & Grenadines	227	189	148	123
Trinidad and Tobago	3,079	283	1,904	175
Turks and Caicos	30	158	13	68
Totals	61,851	5,280	41,773	3,225

Source: *Statistical Yearbooks of the INS*

This view contends that: deportees are implementing their criminal skills honed in major metropolitan cities of the USA and other developed countries in these far less sophisticated societies, thereby contributing to an increasing sense of insecurity; Caribbean countries do not have the capacity to handle this influx of criminal deportees; many deportees suffer from serious problems like drug addiction, HIV and AIDS, other communicable diseases requiring aggressive and expensive care; and given that these individuals had migrated at very young ages and had become fully integrated into the sending countries, they have little or no ties to the countries of their birth from which they have been culturally and otherwise divorced. Consequently, criminal deportees should be the sending countries' responsibility.

Paradoxically, while objecting to these deportation policies, Caribbean countries continue to deport undesirables from their societies. For example, the Cayman Islands new immigration policy entails a routine check with US and Jamaican counterparts to determine if Jamaicans living in the Cayman Islands have ever been convicted of a crime and/or deported from the US. Officials are authorized to deny entry to non-nationals, who have served more than 12 months in prison anywhere for a crime. Jamaicans, as of 2005, are required to secure visas in order to enter that territory (*Caribbean Net News* May 23, 2006).

Barbados, in 2002, deported 118 non-nationals for various offences, including fraud, drug trafficking, burglary, theft and prostitution (Alleyne 2000); in 2003, the government of Jamaica deported a total of 237 individuals, 115 of whom were deported to the UK (*Economic and Social Survey Jamaica* 2002). And in July 2000, Trinidad and Tobago and Nigeria, expressing concern about incarcerating each other's nationals for long periods of time, signed an agreement whereby nationals, who contravene either country's immigration laws, will have their cases speedily determined and will secure the offender's deportation with the minimum of delay following incarceration (*Nation*, August 1, 2000).

Meanwhile, for most of the decade of the 1990s, not only did Caribbean governments respond to the crime problem largely by using the deportees as the scapegoats, but they also remained unsuccessful in negotiating a relaxation of US deportee policy or, at the very least, securing a set of protocols that would enable Caribbean countries to better manage the flow of deportees. It was not until the 2002 CARICOM Heads of Government meeting in the Bahamas that a regional Crime and Security Study was commissioned. The report cites criminal deportees as 'a factor of increasing significance in the escalation of crime and violence' and one of the principal security threats to the region despite a number of studies that are reluctant to make such a claim (Headley 2005; Griffin 2002).

It is, therefore, against this backdrop that this chapter seeks to 1) put the deportee phenomenon into wider theoretical perspective by situating it within an international political economy (IPE) framework; 2) assess the impact of deportees on Caribbean societies; and 3) recommend and sketch a reintegration strategy for deportee management in the region.

INTERROGATING INTERNATIONAL MIGRATION

The past four decades have witnessed scholars researching international migration from a number of disciplinary perspectives, including anthropology (Brettell 1999; Barret 1997; Layton 1997; Buijs 1993; Durham 1989; Thomas-Hope 1985; Gmelch 1980; Cohen 1978; Bourdieu 1977); economics (Da Vanzo 1976; Becker 1964; Sjaastad 1962); sociology (Chiswick 2000); politics (Ghosh 2000; Hollifield 2000; Koslowski 1999; Tichenor 1994; Weiner 1993); demography (Keely 2000); international relations (Hollifield 2000; 1992a; 1992b); international political economy (Hollifield and Johnson 1999; Rosenblum 1998; Meyers 1995; and globalization (Christopher 1998). Despite this diversity of theoretical approaches, some scholars still claim that the theoretical base for understanding this phenomenon remains weak and lacks a single, coherent theory. What exists, instead, is 'only a fragmented set of theories that have developed largely in isolation from one another, sometimes but not always, segmented by disciplinary boundaries' (Massey, Arango, Hugo, Kouaouci, Pellegrino and Taylor 1994; 1993).

Asserting that a full understanding of contemporary migration will not be achieved by relying on the tools of one discipline alone, or by focusing on a single level of analysis, Massey et al. note also that not only does its complexity and multifaceted nature warrant a theory that incorporates a variety of perspectives, but that contemporary analyses fail to incorporate an international relations' contribution to the understanding of international migration. There is merit to this call for a more multi-level, interdisciplinary approach, precisely because of the complexity and multifaceted nature of human motivations and human behaviour, which are reflected in decisions to move from one geographical space to another. Indeed, the IPE perspective, which, by construct, is both multi-level and interdisciplinary, takes a giant step toward bridging the theoretical shortcomings of international migration studies alluded to by these authors. It is from this perspective, therefore, that de-integration — the central issue of concern in this analysis — will be analyzed.

IPE AND IMMIGRATION

All migration entails the relocation of people from one geographic locale to another, and for a variety of reasons. However, international migration is distinctive in that not only does it entail physical relocation but issues associated with a change of jurisdiction from one sovereign state to another. Where relocation is permanent, international migration also entails a change of membership from one political community to another (Zolberg 1981, 15-51). More important, the nature and scope of international migration are functions of and reflective of the state of the global political economy at a given point in time, which, in turn, influences the dispositions of individuals toward relocation, the migration policies of the states of origin, as well as those of the destination states. International migration, therefore, can be seen as an arena of contestation between and among the individuals who opt to remain at home and those who leave, on one level, and the states in which they live and those to which they seek admission, on another level (Zolberg 1991, 302). This analysis focuses on the latter.

In recent years, issues and consequences of international migration have included, but have not been limited to, law enforcement, economic life, and the conduct of foreign affairs. Standard explanations of immigration policy, which is generally understood to comprise two elements — immigration control and immigrant integration — tend to focus on domestic political factors such as the impact on classes and interest groups. However, given that the state in an interdependent world necessarily looks in two directions — inwardly toward the domestic polity and outwardly toward other international states — any meaningful explanation of the determinants, significance, and impacts of immigration policy must incorporate the view from both directions (Zolberg 1987, 42–69). This two-level perspective is consistent with the theory of complex interdependence, which acknowledges that domestic and international politics are regularly interrelated (Keohane and Nye, 1997).

While the globalization of trade, capital flows and production has long been a standard fare of IPE studies and reflective of this two-level approach, the international flow of people has not despite the obvious political economy dimensions. For many individuals, countries, and specific regions, including countries like Mexico, the Dominican Republic, Cuba, Jamaica, for example, where remittances account for a substantial portion of capital flows (Haus 1995, 285–313), the impacts and consequences of immigration are perhaps just as important as the impacts and consequences of trade or foreign investment. According to the Inter-American Development Bank (IADB), remittances to Latin America and the Caribbean from migrants in Asia, Europe, and North America totaled $62 billion in 2006, which could grow to $100 billion by 2010 (www.iadb.org/NEWS). The Pew Hispanic Center estimates that total remittance flow from the USA to Latin America and the Caribbean could approximate $30 billion in 2007, making it by far the largest single remittance channel in the world (Suro 2007; Díaz-Briquets and Pérez-López 1997, 411–437; Durand, Parrado and Massey 1996, 411–444).

Some scholars have begun to focus an IPE lens on this matter. Much of this work examines the decision of countries to variously liberalize and restrict immigration. States often initiate immigration by liberalizing rules of entry, which usually occurs under certain conditions. For example, receiving states are likely to restrict entry during difficult economic times or periods of global economic crisis (Zolberg 1991, 3012). Immigration policy is also considered to be a Janus-faced policy with both domestic and international consequences (Money 1997, 685–720). On the one hand, the domestic environment reflects a paradox whereby many politicians are forced to address a politically powerful backlash against foreign residents, documented and undocumented while, simultaneously, employers continue to petition for greater access to both skilled and unskilled migrant labour. On the other hand is the desire of developing countries to secure greater immigration opportunities for their citizens versus the preference of developed countries for limited access to immigration. Added to these concerns is the likelihood of international conflict resulting from one country's decision to implement immigration policies that transfer its control problems to other countries (Haus 1995).

But while much of this literature focuses on the liberalizing/restricting dichotomy of states' immigration policies, this analysis examines a third component of immigration policy: removal or deportation (de-integration), which I define here to reflect the decision of the sovereign state to withdraw the privilege of immigrant residence and integration by deporting a class of immigrants to their original countries. A digression into the legal basis of sovereignty and immigrant integration/de-integration follows in order to inform the current policy context.

IMMIGRATION AS INTEGRATION AND DEPORTATION AS DE-INTEGRATION

A key characteristic of US immigration law, which is used to inform US immigration policy, is that its application reflects the country's power to make unilateral decisions regarding who may be allowed entry into its territory, the conditions under which entry is granted, and the legal consequences of such entry (Schuck 1984). For example, US immigration policy requires that immigrants seeking membership in the country's moral and political communities remain non-members for a period of time while being vetted before being granted the privilege of full integration via permanent residency and eventual citizenship.

While undergoing this vetting process, significant (integrating) relationships are formed with other individuals. Some immigrants bring or are joined by their spouses while others marry members of the local community; immigrant children attend local schools and cultivate customs and habits; employment is found and taxes are paid; and churches and other civic organizations are joined and ties are cemented. By engaging in these processes and activities, the immigrant is becoming integrated into the society and is contributing to the stock of social capital.

Permission to enter and become integrated into a country constitutes a privilege and not a right and, therefore, may be rescinded should the authorities determine that the immigrant has violated or abused this privilege. This means, therefore, that a fundamental aspect of sovereignty is a country's right to terminate the integration process. Such action initiates de-integration, which may initially result in incarceration to be followed by deportation to the immigrant's country of origin or to a third country.

Classic US immigration law, argues Schuck (1984), tended to view deportation or de-integration as a civil, administrative proceeding rather than a criminal prosecution, because an immigrant's entry into the USA is considered a privilege as opposed to a right, and that the ability to continue to enjoy that privilege depends on compliance with the terms of entry. Deportation, therefore, was thought to be nothing more than a revocation of that privilege. In reality, however, deportation has little in common with civil sanctions in that it is often imposed for criminal conduct, serves as an important adjunct and supplement to criminal law enforcement, and reflects judgments that are largely indistinguishable from those routinely made by criminal law. Deportation, therefore, contains all of the characteristics of banishment, and may involve incarceration.

The non-attainment of US citizenship is a necessary condition for deportation and can produce a sense of statelessness. Some deportees, who will not be rendered stateless, may never be able to return to their country of nationality due to difficult economic and/or political circumstances. Those who are deported to a third country may have to live as a stranger in a strange land. But even those who can return to their country of origin may find themselves expelled from the only society to which they feel some attachment, and are obliged to reside in a place with which they have only the most tenuous link. Regardless, the reality of deportation is that the process wrenches and uproots the immigrant from what are often some of the most profound human attachments, many of which are valued by the larger community.

The argument here, then, is not that the USA has implemented a more restrictive immigration policy; rather, that the USA has begun to enforce its de-integration policy more assiduously as a result of its determination that a number of immigrants have abused the privileges granted to them. This policy, which strongly impacts immigrants hailing from more than

178 countries, is proving most contentious among 'third border' countries — polities with which the USA has and pursues a number of mutual issues.

THE PUSH TOWARDS DE-INTEGRATION

The early 1990s witnessed a number of US legislators wondering aloud about a possible connection between immigrants, crime and (domestic) terrorism. These sentiments reflected citizen concern that immigrants create numerous economic and social problems, including committing acts of criminality and various acts of terror. Usually articulated most strongly during economic slowdowns, these sentiments were expressed during the early 1990s while the USA was attempting to grow itself out of an economic recession. Newt Gingrich and the Republicans' 'Contract With America' promised to cut the crime rate and save hundreds of millions of dollars in detention costs by deporting more foreign criminals, notably immigrants who frequently evaded detection by the United States Citizenship and Immigration Services (USCIS) after serving jail sentences. Right Wing Presidential candidate and political commentator, Pat Buchanan, was among the most vocal of anti-immigration advocates in the USA.

While increases in immigration sometimes coincide with increases in economic and social problems, such as rising rates of crime, this coincidence does not necessarily establish a direct link between these phenomena. Despite the absence of empirical, causal support for this coincidence of factors, immigrants are regularly and increasingly blamed for social and economic difficulties, such as national unemployment, high rates of crime, drain on welfare, housing shortages and other problems (Chapin 1997).

National crime data from the early 1990s suggested that the USA was unsuccessfully managing its growing crime problem. The Federal Bureau of Investigation (FBI) data indicated the following: the rate of violent crime in the USA was worse than in any other Western developed country, with a murder occurring every 21 minutes, a rape every five minutes, a robbery every 46 seconds, and an aggravated assault every 29 seconds; violent crime victimizes one in four US households; nearly 5 million people are victims of violent crime, such as murder, rape, robbery, or assault, and 19 million

Americans are victims of property crimes, such as arson or burglary every year; juvenile crime between 1981 and 1990 registered a 68 per cent increase (compared with a five per cent increase among adults); and that the number of inmates convicted of drug offenses rose 14 per cent between 1983 and 1989 (*Congressional Quarterly*, November 19, 1994, 3367–3371).

Authorities became even more concerned over the fact that individuals on probation, parole, or bail commit at least 30 per cent of the murders in the USA, and that while the risk of punishment had declined over the past 40 years, the annual number of serious crimes had skyrocketed. However, of greatest concern to legislators was the fact that significant numbers of illegal, as well as legal, permanent residents (LPR) were among these perpetrators and recidivists. Searching for answers, attention became increasingly focused on immigrants. More recently, but especially since the terrorist attacks in the USA on September 11, 2001, the perceived linkage between crime and terrorism has drawn the most strident policy initiatives against immigrants in the USA. As a result, there appears to be a rising tide of sentiments against immigrants sweeping across the US and many other advanced industrial countries as well.

Conceived as essentially a domestic policy initiative, this deportation or de-integration programme is inherently intermestic in nature, and has to be factored into the long history of controversial policies that have characterized relations between the USA and the Caribbean. While, on the one hand, the USA focuses largely upon crime as well as terrorist attacks and potential threats to Americans and American property, the issue of concern for Caribbean countries is the impact of this anti-crime and anti-terror campaign that is rooted in the provisions of Public Law 103-322 (the Omnibus Crime Control Act (OCCA) of 1994; the Anti-terrorism and Effective Death Penalty Act (AEDPA), which was signed in the aftermath of the World Trade Center and Oklahoma City bombings; the Illegal Immigration Reform and Immigrant Responsibility Act (IIRAIRA) of 1996; and the Patriot Act of 2001. The AEDPA and the IIRAIRA of 1996 reflect US policy responses to the problem of crime and terrorism. Both pieces of legislation have had a profound effect on the immigrant communities in the USA. For example, USCIS deported more than 66,000 aliens in 1986, three per cent of whom were criminal aliens. A decade later, 69,680 criminal aliens were deported. And by 2004, some 202,842 aliens were formally removed, 88,897 of whom were determined to be criminals under US law (See table 12.2).

Table 12.2: Annual number of persons removed from the US 1986 and 1995-2004

Year	Formal Removals	Criminals Deported	% Criminal Deportees
2004	202,842	88,897	43.8
2003	189,368	81,108	42.8
2002	150,542	71,940	47.8
2001	178,026	72,679	40.8
2000	186,222	72,297	38.8
1999	181,072	70,590	39.1
1998	173,146	60,965	35.2
1997	114,432	51,141	44.7
1996	69,680	37,243	53.4
1995	50,924	32,665	64.1
1995-2004	**1,496,254**	**639,525**	42.7
Annual Average	**149,625**	**63,953**	**42.7**
1986	65,933	1,978	3.0

Source: *Statistical Yearbooks of the INS*

It turns out that the overwhelming majority of these individuals have been sent to Mexico, Central America and Caribbean countries, including Honduras, Guatemala, El Salvador, Brazil, the Dominican Republic, Jamaica and Haiti, principally for crimes associated with dangerous drugs, immigration violations, assault, burglary, robbery and larceny (See Table 3). Between 1995 and 2004, some 29,699 individuals were deported to the Dominican Republic at an average annual rate of 2,910; and 16,009 to Jamaica at an average annual rate of 1,779. Twenty Caribbean countries collectively received 61,851 deportees (average annual rate of 6,185), 41,773 (68 per cent) as criminal deportees. Between 1995 and 2003, therefore, these 20 countries received an average annual rate of 4,177 criminal deportees (See table 12.1).

It is this consistently increasing number of returnees that is at the core of the emotional charged debate that associates deportees with rising crime in the region. However, as the following analysis demonstrates, there is no statistically significant relationship between deportees and crime levels of deportees to Barbados. Beyond this conclusion, the analysis contends that, as a matter of public policy, governments in the region must begin to develop formal mechanisms to re-integrate these individuals into their societies.

IMPACT ON BARBADOS

Just over one decade ago, as table 12.3 indicates, a steady trickle of criminal deportees, largely from the United States, began arriving in Barbados. The view of many Barbadians, including a number of government officials, has been that along with the deportees arrived a type of crime with which Barbados was unfamiliar and with which it is unable to cope. In December 1998, for example, law enforcement officers in Barbados were confronted with what they considered a new approach to bank robbery. Instead of the daylight attempt in which gunmen grabbed all they could and make a dash for the door, the perpetrators struck by night. As a precautionary move, the bandits cut the telephone lines in the area, thereby making communications with the nearby police station impossible. The perpetrators then drilled through the thin wall of a neighbouring launderette into the bank, using padding to muffle the sound of crumbling concrete, and made off with approximately USD$200,000, one of the biggest heists in Barbados' history. Evidence in this case, which remains under investigation, points to some collusion between local players and members of a travelling show that spent no more than one week in the country. And although there have been a number of armed robberies of banks, supermarkets and an automobile dealership they have all taken place during daytime working hours. Individuals are also being robbed at gunpoint in their homes and on the streets.

Prior to, and even subsequent to, that spectacular bank robbery, the general view in law enforcement circles remains that, for the most part, criminal deportees tend to keep a low profile. Surveillance activities by the

Table 12.3: Distribution of annual reported crime and deportee crime in Barbados 1995-2004

Year	Annual Reported Crime	Deportees Crimes Annually	Deportee Crimes by Total Crime %	Cumulative # of Deportees	Deportees Charged Annually	% Deportees Charged With Crime
1995	10,541	29	0.27	165	15	10
1996	10,312	27	0.26	224	18	8
1997	10,203	34	0.33	279	17	7
1998	10,094	37	0.36	336	22	6
1999	10,199	36	0.35	404	23	5
2000	10,908	44	0.40	464	24	5
2001	11,588	89	0.76	517	32	6
2002	11,871	60	0.50	572	26	4
2003	9,823	34	0.34	626	20	3
2004	9,435	69	0.73	694	35	5
Total	104,974	469	0.44	694		

Source: *Barbados Criminal Intelligence Unit*

Criminal Investigation Division (CID) led Senior Superintendent Lionel Bill Johnson to conclude that these criminal deportees have not been extensively involved in criminal activities. According to Johnson's interview with the *Barbados Saturday Sun* June 28, 1997, by mid-June 1996, a total of 29 nationals had been deported to Barbados for that year for their involvement in drugs and firearms, and only one of them had been linked locally to any crime. And as of mid-June 1997, some 28 nationals had been deported for that year, none of whom had been linked to any crime in Barbados. Johnson also discounted the fear that the returning criminals might bring with them sophisticated methods of committing crime. In his view, most of them were busy adjusting to the Barbados way of life now that living in North America and Europe was no longer an option.

The data presented in tables 12.3 and 12.4 support this contention. A total of 694 nationals of Barbados were deported between 1995 and 2004 for a variety of criminal activities that ranged from traffic violations to murder; however, illicit drug activity, robbery and firearm possession were the primary offences. Of that number 77 per cent were deported from the USA; 17 per cent from Canada; 3 per cent from the UK, Sweden and Norway combined; and the remaining 5.7 per cent from various Caribbean countries. 94 per cent of all deportees were male.

Prior to their emigration from Barbados, 5.4 per cent of these individuals were known to the Royal Barbados Police Force. Since their return, 16 per cent, including two females, were arrested and charged by the police between January 1, 1995 and December 31, 2004 for committing a total of 469 acts of criminality. 32 per cent of these persons (including five known to the police prior to their emigration, have become recidivists. Approximately 48 per cent of the 113 individuals were arrested and charged for the same type of behaviour which led to their deportation, while another 18 per cent graduated from minor criminal activity to becoming major criminal offenders (from petty thievery and/or minor drug offences to major crimes such as robbery and burglary). Those factors notwithstanding, the data indicate that between 1998 and 2004, the number of deportees arrested and charged accounted for one per cent or less of the total number of persons arrested and charged for criminal activity during the same period.

Table 12.4: Deportees to Barbados by number charged with crime 1998-2004

Years	# of Persons Charged With Crime Annually	# of Deportees Charged With Crime Annually	Deportees as a Percentage of Persons Charged
1998	2,474	22	0.8
1999	2,259	23	1.0
2000	2,730	24	0.8
2001	3,130	32	1.0
2002	3.095	26	0.8
2003	2,973	20	0.6
2004	2,849	35	1.2
Total	19,510	113**	0.58

Some persons were arrested and charged for multiple offences during a single year
Source: *Barbados Criminal Intelligence Unit*

Speaking to the *Barbados Weekend Nation* in October 1998, Barbados Attorney General David Simmons stated that there was no evidence that deportees were involved in the latest rash of crimes, especially the armed robbery of businesses, in Barbados. Home grown criminals are just as capable of this type of activity as are criminals from other countries. For Simmons, it is the increasing use and abuse of illegal drugs, and not necessarily criminal deportees, that is largely responsible for the upsurge in crime Barbados and throughout the region.

Others called into question the notion that criminal deportees are largely responsible for the rise in criminal activity in the country. For example, Eric Sealy, writing in the *Barbados Daily Nation*, 18 October 1999, expressed a concern shared by many in law enforcement that many young Barbadians, who never went to the USA—or Europe, for that matter—are engaged in and executing their criminal craft with professional skill. These individuals, they contend, seem to believe that the only thing that matters is to get money at any cost. Thus, while criminal deportees bear the brunt of the blame, it is quite likely that many home-grown criminals attempt to implement techniques gleaned from watching various television shows or international news bulletins in the commission of crime. But given the FBI's own analysis, which concludes that a mere seven per cent of criminals commit two-thirds of all violent crimes, including three-fourths of rapes and robberies, it is not unreasonable to conclude that a small number of deportees could be responsible for a disproportionate amount of crime in the country.

Nevertheless, when one examines the rate at which criminal deportees are officially recognised as members of the crime fraternity in Barbados, one is left with three possible conclusions: 1) that the police service in Barbados is inefficient and ineffective in capturing criminals; 2) that the criminal deportee is highly skilful in eluding capture; and 3) that the criminal deportee has not resorted to criminal activity to the extent that most people claim. Regardless, the fact that there are no sentiments in the sending countries supporting an end to this policy of deportation, and the fact the numbers continue to grow annually, governments in the receiving countries have a responsibility to their citizens — including these deportees — to develop modalities for their reintegration.

THE CASE FOR RE-INTEGRATION

Adjusting to the way of life in the various Caribbean countries to which deportees are being returned can be difficult at best. For example, deportees to Haiti with criminal records are arrested upon their arrival in Port-au-Prince, thrown into crowded prisons, which are often without electricity, running water or basic sanitary facilities, where they remain incarcerated for days, weeks or months without charges. Deportees to Guyana have their names and addresses posted in the Government's Gazette as well as the local newspapers. Most deportees to Barbados must apply for a national identification card; and must find accommodation, employment and monetary resources to become self-sufficient once again. Some social services departments within government have assisted deportees in accessing various services provided from time to time, including temporary accommodation, financial assistance, health care, counseling, and acquiring proper documentation. However, formal systems are slow to be put in place.

Section 54 of Belize's Law Reform Act of 1998 authorizes the Ministry of National Security and Immigration to impose certain restrictions, including monitoring Belizeans deported from other countries, especially from the USA, for having committed serious offences. Each deportee may be required by the Commissioner of Police: 1) to report to the police daily or at specified locations and intervals; 2) not to change residence without giving prior notification to the Commissioner of Police; 3) not to associate with or become a member of any criminal gang; and 4) to comply with any other requirements specified by the Commissioner of Police. Each deportee is issued with a reporting sheet containing his full personal details, which he or she is required to carry on his/her person at all times, while a Deportees Register is maintained at the National Police Headquarters and at all District Police Stations. Any violation renders the deportee guilty of an offence and is liable upon summary conviction to a punishment of not exceeding $1,000 or imprisonment for a maximum period of up one year. Further, any deportee convicted of a crime in Belize will not be treated as a first offender and, therefore, becomes ineligible for community service of any other form of suspended sentence. That is, the criminal record that a deportee has in another country will be treated as a domestic criminal record once that deportee is convicted of a crime in Belize. Although this policy had been in place since October 1998 in Belize City, it took effect officially on March 12, 1999 (*Amandala* March 21, 1999).

The common reality is that many of these individuals return with little or no resources to assist with reintegration. In order to survive in relatively unfamiliar surroundings, many turn to the skills learned on the streets abroad — to drug dealing, stealing, extortion, sometimes even murder. Others try to stay out of trouble, but their path is not easy. Some sink into despair, foraging for food or living on handouts sent by family members left behind in the countries from which they were deported. What is needed, therefore, is formal national reintegration programmes, such as the one currently in place in St. Kitts and Nevis, the Dominican Republic, and that under consideration in Barbados, that eases the stress and any other emotional trauma these individuals might have experienced from being deported.

Specifically, the programme's activities should be geared toward equipping deportees with the necessary tools and skills to reintegrate into Caribbean society via a series of programme activities, including counselling and support sessions for deportees and relatives; skills training workshops; employment search/job placement; registration for securing national documentation; housing assignments; familiarization tours of the country; legal support (if needed, for example, appealing deportation; financial aid support (food, clothing, etc.); medical check-ups; and public education. The main goal of the programme, therefore, would be to assist deportees to a point where they are able to become self-sufficient and would no longer require constant use of the services offered. The programme would not be designed to become a permanent source of assistance for all deportees; instead, it would serve merely as a mechanism to ease and aid reintegration into these societies.

In addition to the establishment of a national reintegration programme, steps should also be taken by policy makers to create an agreement with deporting countries with respect to deportees, as some Caribbean governments have taken steps to create an agreement called a memorandum of understanding (MOU) between them and deporting countries regarding deportees. While recognizing and respecting the rights of deporting countries to set their own policies on deportation, it nevertheless structures and negotiates some policy space that better enables the receiving countries to cooperate and coordinate their responses in this regard.

ACKNOWLEDGEMENTS

The author wishes to acknowledge the assistance of S/Sgt. Timothy A. Springer, M.A. of the Royal Barbados Police Force Crime Intelligence Unit in securing the data on the statistical relationship between deportees and crime in Barbados.

REFERENCES

Alleyne, Barry. 2000. '33 Prostitutes Among Deportees,' *Weekend Nation* July 17.

Barret, Stanley R. 1997. *Anthropology: A Student's Guide to Theory and Method.* Toronto: University of Toronto Press.

Becker, Gary S. 1964. *Human Capital.* New York: NBER.

Blackstone, William. 1999. 'Commentaries on the Laws of England 94 (1769).' In *Black's Law Dictionary* 7th edition, St. Paul, MN: West Group.

Bourdieu, Pierre. 1977. *Outline of a Theory of Practice.* Cambridge: Cambridge University Press.

Brettell, Caroline B. 1999. 'New Immigrants to America: Contributions to Ethnography and Theory', *Identities,* 5:603-17.

Buijs, Gina, ed. 1993. *Migrant Women: Crossing Boundaries and Changing Identities.* Oxford: Berg.

Chapin, Wesley D. 1997. 'Ausländer raus? The Empirical Relationship Between Immigration and Crime in Germany.' *Social Science Quarterly,* 78, 2.

Chiswick, Barry R. 2000. 'Are Immigrants Favorably Self-Selected?' In *Migration Theory: Talking Across Disciplines*, eds. Caroline B. Brettell and James F. Hollifield. New York: Routledge.

Cohen, Ronald. 1978. 'Ethnicity: Problem and Focus in Anthropology.' *Annual Review of Anthropology,* 7:379-403.

Da Vanzo, Julie.1976. 'Difference between Return and Non-Return Migration: An Econometric Analysis.' *International Migration Review* 10:13-27.

Díaz-Briquets, Sergio and Jorge Pérez-López, 1997. 'Refugee Remittances: Conceptual Issues and the Cuban and Nicaraguan Experiences', *International Migration Review,* 31, 2.

Durand, Jorge, Parrado, Emilio A. and, Massey, Douglas S. 1996. "Migradollars and Development: A Reconsideration of the Mexican Case." *International Migration Review* 30, 2.

Durham, William H. 1989. 'Conflict, Migration, and Ethnicity: A Summary.' In *Conflict, Migration and the Expression of Ethnicity,* eds. Nancie Gonzalez and Carolyn S. McCommon. Boulder, COL: Westview Press.

Economic and Social Survey Jamaica. Kingston, Jamaica: Planning Institute of Jamaica, 2002.

Ghosh, Bimal, ed. 2000. *Managing Migration: The Need for a New International Regime.* Oxford: Oxford University Press.

Gmelch, George. 1980. 'Return Migration.' *Annual Review of Anthropology* 9:135-59.

Griffin, Clifford E. 'Deportees and Crime in Barbados.' *Caribbean Dialogue* 6, nos. 1 & 2, January-June 2000.

Haus, Leah. 1995. 'Openings in the Wall: Transnational Migrants, Labor Unions, and US Immigration Policy.' *International Organization,* 49, 2.

Headley, Bernard. 2005. *Deported: Entry and Exit Findings Jamaicans Returned Home from the US Between 1997 and 2003.* Kingston, Jamaica: Stephenson Litho Press, 2005.

Hollifield, James F. 2000. 'The Politics of International Migration.' In *Migration Theory: Talking Across Disciplines*, ed. Caroline B. Brettell and James F. Hollifield. New York: Routledge.

———. 2000. 'Migration and the 'New' International Order: The Missing Regime.' In *Managing Migration: The Need for a New International Regime,* ed. Bitmal Ghosh. Oxford: Oxford University Press.

Hollifield, James F. and C. Johnson, eds. 1999. *Pathways to Democracy: The Political Economy of Democratic Transitions.* New York: Routledge.

———. 'Migration, Trade, and the Nation-State: The Myth of Globalization.' *UCLA Journal of International Law and Foreign Affairs* 3, no. 2, 1998-9 (Fall/Winter).

———. 1992. *Immigrants, Markets, and States: The Political Economy of Postwar Europe.* Cambridge, MA: Harvard University Press.

———. 1992. 'Migration and International Relations: Cooperation and Control in the European Community.' *International Migration Review* 26/2:568-95.

Inter-American Development Bank. 2007. 'Remittances to Latin America and the Caribbean Could Top $100 billion by 2010, IDB Fund Says.' Press Release March 18, 2007, available at: *http://www.iadb.org/NEWS/articledetail.cfm?Language= En&parid=2&artType=PR&artid=3692*downloaded 18 October 2007.

Johnson, Dawn Marie. 1999. 'The AEDPA and the IIRIRA: Treating Misdemeanors as Felonies for Immigration Purposes'. *Journal of Legislation* 27:2.

Keely, Charles B. 2000. 'Demography and International Migration.' In *Migration Theory: Talking Across Disciplines*, eds. Caroline B. Brettell and James F. Hollifield. New York: Routledge.

Keohane, R.O. and J.S. Nye, 1977. *Power and Interdependence: World Politics in Transition.* Boston: Little Brown.

Koslowski, Rey. 1999. *Migration and Citizenship in World Politics: From Nation-States to European Polity.* Ithaca, NY: Cornell University Press.

Layton, Robert. 1997. *An Introduction to Theory in Anthropology.* Cambridge: Cambridge University Press.

Martin, Lisa L. 2000. *Democratic Commitments: Legislatures and International Cooperation.* New Jersey: Princeton University Press.

Massey, Douglas S. 1998. *World in Motion: Understanding International Migration at the End of the Millenium.* Oxford: Clarendon Press.

Massey, Douglas, et al, 1994. 'Theories of International Migration: The North American Case.' *Population and Development Review,* 20, 4.

———. 1993. 'Theories of International Migration: A Review and Appraisal', *Population and Development Review,* 19, 3.

Meyers, Eytan. 1995. 'The Political Economy of International Migration Policy.' Unpublished Ph.D. dissertation, University of Chicago.

Money. J. 1997. 'The Political Economy of Immigration Control.' *International Organization* 51, 4 (Autumn): 685-720

Portes, Alejandro. 1997. 'Immigration Theory for a New Century: Some Problems and Opportunities.' *International Migration Review,* 31: 799-825.

Putnam, Robert D. 1988. 'Diplomacy and Domestic Politics: The Logic of Two-Level Games', *International Organization,* 42, 3.

Rosenblum, Marc R. 1998. 'Abroad at Home: Foreign and Domestic Sources of US Migration Policy', Paper prepared for the American Political Science Association Meeting, Boston, Massachusetts.

Rudolph, Christopher W. 1998. 'Globalization, Sovereignty and Migration: A Conceptual Framework.' *UCLA Journal of International Law and Foreign Affairs* 3/2: 325-55.

Schuck, Peter H. 1984. 'The Transformation of Immigration Law,' *Columbia Law Review,* 84 Column. L. Rev.1 at http://web.lexis-nexis.com/universe/

Schuck, Peter H. 2006. 'The Transformation of Immigration Law.' *Columbia Law Review* 84, Column L. Rev.1, 1984. Available at *http://web.lexis-nexis.com/universe,* downloaded June 10, 2006.

Sjaastad, Larry A. 'The Costs and Returns of Human Migration.' *Journal of Political Economy* 70, no. 5, Part 2: Investment in Human Beings, October 1962.

Springer, Bevan. 'Cayman Jamaican Relations Are Fine Says Cabinet Minister.' *Cayman Net News* 2006. Available at: *http://www.caribbeannetnews.com/cgi script/csArticles/ articles/000016/001699.htm*, downloaded August 14, 2006.

Suro, Roberto. 2007. 'Remittance Senders and Receivers: Tracking the Transnational Channels.' *Pew Hispanic Center Reports and Factsheets.* Available at: *http:// pewhispanic.org/reports/report.php?ReportID=23* downloaded 18 October, 2007.

Thomas-Hope, Elizabeth. 1985. 'Return Migration and its Implications for Caribbean Development' In *Migration and Development in the Caribbean: The Unexplored Connection,* ed. Robert A. Pastor, 157-172. Boulder: Westview Press.

Tichenor, Daniel J. 1994. 'The Politics of Immigration Reform in the United States.' *Polity* 26/3: 333-62.

———. *Barbados Nation,* 'Trinidad and Nigeria Sign Treaty,' 1 August 2000.

Weiner, Myron. 1995. *The Global Migration Crisis: Challenge to States and to Human Rights,* New York: Harper Collins College Publishers.

———. ed. 1991. *International Migration and Security.* Boulder, COL: Westview Press, 1993.

Zolberg, Aristide R. 'Bounded States in a Global Market: The Uses of International Labor Migrations.' In *Social Theory for a Changing Society,* eds. Pierre Bourdieu and James S. Coleman. Boulder: Westview Press, 1991.

———. 1987. 'Beyond the Nation-State: Comparative Politics in Global Perspective.' In *Beyond Progress and Development,* eds., J. Berting, W. Blockmans, and U. Rosenthal, London: Bowker.

———. 1981. 'International Migrations in Political Perspective." In *Global Trends in Migration,* eds. M.C. Kritz, C. Keely, and S. Tomasi. New York: Center for Migration Studies.

13

INVOLUNTARY AND COERCED MIGRATION: 'DEPORTEES' COMING 'HOMEWARD'
NGOs as Actors in Reintegration Policy in Jamaica and the Dominican Republic
SUZETTE MARTIN-JOHNSON

INTRODUCTION

This chapter is set within the context of government policy responses to deportation from the United States to the Caribbean over the last decade, with a particular focus on Jamaica and the Dominican Republic. Enquiries soon revealed that government policy responses in both countries had been slow, with an overall attempt to absorb deportees into the normal system. It also became apparent that there were a number of gaps in the governmental approach, as noted by one Jamaican police officer's concerned admission that upon deportees' admission to the country, it was often left to the discretion of immigration officers or others to assist, literally out of their own pockets. This provoked another question: beyond such occasional assistance on a micro-level, and those government agencies for the indigent which were called upon to assist, who was providing assistance? Further, was there a coordinated policy on deportation in either the Dominican Republic or Jamaica in the period 1996-2006?

Deportation is 'the act of banishing a foreigner from a country, usually to the country of origin.' According to Act 2-1994 amending Jamaica's Criminal Justice (Administration) Act, a 'deportation order' means an order (however described) made by an authority of a foreign state which requires the person subject to the order to leave and remain out of that state and 'deportation' shall be construed accordingly. The term used to describe these 'banished' individuals however, is subject to some debate. In the course of the research, the researcher was rebuked by some representatives non-governmental organizations and one government official for referring to persons deported from abroad as 'deportees'. Instead, alternative terms like returnee, involuntary returning resident (IRV) and involuntary returned resident were suggested. Similarly, civil society entities and deportees in the Dominican Republic preferred the term *repatriado* to *deportado*.

The purpose of this chapter is to examine the contribution of civil society actors in both the Dominican Republic and Jamaica in policy responses to deportation from the United States between 1996 and 2006. The main methodologies used for this comparative study were interviews of government officials and NGO workers, as well as mini focus groups. Secondary data and legislative frameworks from both countries were also examined.

It was expected that the period selected would be sufficient and timely in demonstrating the policy responses of two Caribbean receiving countries. Interviews and mini focus groups,[1] part of the methodology selected for this study, have justified the selection of this time period, with participants opining that deportation became an issue in the Caribbean between the mid-1990s and 2000, and generally indicating that its growing importance continues today. Many indicated the phenomenon became particularly marked after the September 2001 attacks on the World Trade Center in New York, when a number of interviewees alluded to an almost indiscriminate rounding up and subsequent deportation of persons.

While the question of deportation is not a new one for Jamaica or the Dominican Republic, the passing of the 1996 US Illegal Immigration Reform and Immigrant Responsibility Act (IIRIRA) and its entry into force in 1997 authorised the US Government to immediately deport resident aliens convicted of a felony. While Jamaica receives a significant number of deportees from Canada and the United Kingdom, and both the Dominican Republic and Jamaica receive deportees from some Caribbean territories and European countries, it is fair to say that an overwhelming number of deportees are received from the United States of America.

Indeed, a six-month investigation by the Associated Press in 2003 posited that some 500,000 'criminal deportees' had been sent back to more than 160 countries around the world, and that eighty per cent of the deportees were being sent to seven Caribbean and Latin American countries: Jamaica, Honduras, El Salvador, Colombia, Mexico, Guatemala and the Dominican Republic. It was correctly pointed out that these countries have marked economic and social limitations and were thus severely restricted in the options available to address the challenges being posed by these deportations. [2]

In this context, Jamaica and the Dominican Republic were selected as Caribbean countries that received the largest numbers of deportees from the USA in 1996–2006 period on which this study focuses.

The case of the Dominican Republic has long been complicated by migration. An estimated one million Haitians live in the Dominican Republic, and regular mass deportations of Haitians take place, often under allegedly discriminatory conditions.[3] The moral crisis of deportation to the Caribbean is further complicated by the treatment of Haitians who are often forcibly repatriated from and/or mistreated in the Dominican Republic itself. Human Rights Watch (2002) and other organizations have spoken of the Dominican Government's forcible repatriation of hundreds of thousands of Haitians and the deportation of a number of Dominicans of Haitian descent to Haiti. These individuals are often arrested in the streets, at their homes or their places of work, often simply on the basis of their 'Haitian appearance'.[4]

Jamaica, in contrast, exercises relatively minor periodic deportations of Haitians, Hondurans, Dominicans, Chinese and others. While being featured in local news, they are hardly newsworthy elsewhere. However, Jamaica receives significant numbers of deportees from the United Kingdom and Canada, and the USA. Deportees received in the Dominican Republic are overwhelmingly from the USA. These marked differences have public policy implications.

CIVIL SOCIETY IN JAMAICA AND THE DOMINICAN REPUBLIC

Anecdotes provided by interviewees have made it clear that the emotional and practical aspects of welcoming deported individuals 'home' have been dealt with by individuals and informal structures, usually networks of family and friends. However, more formally organized civil society groups have begun to participate in the process. The main focus of this chapter will be on these formal groups in the countries of return and their interaction with government in those countries.

It is often argued that non-governmental organizations pick up where governments leave off. Casey (1998:21) describes NGOs as:

> Non-government, non-profit organizations that articulate a wide range of interests, but primarily those related to public goods. They can be part of social movements or other interest groups, formed specifically to intervene in the policy process; but, at the same time, all NGOs can potentially participate in lobby activities even though they have not been constituted directly for this purpose. The decision to restrict their activities specifically to service delivery, or, on the contrary, to play a more political role, depends on the internal tendencies of the organization.

Dauda (1992:2) defines public policy as 'what government does or does not do.' Policy failure is defined simply as 'inability of a policy to meet its stated objectives or goals.' Civil society entities such as NGOs may choose to intervene in this process through a variety of measures. Greater openness in the system of governance creates more channels for this intervention and may prevent the policy failure mentioned above. Alternatively, it is quite possible that some non-governmental entities believe that they can function quite effectively without interaction with or assistance from the government, and indeed in the course of this study it was noted that some do.

The Dominican Republic made a nominal transition to democracy in 1978. However, there were a number of steps to be taken in the development of civil society (Espinal 2001:102-103). It has been argued that meaningful democracy did not emerge until the end of the 1980s. Civil society has traditionally put pressure on government through labour union demands, street violence, attacks on businesses and national strikes. Recent methods have become more sophisticated.[5] Although the historical profile and culture of the Dominican Republic differs from Jamaica, the civil society has become more active in recent years, and counts a number of non-governmental organizations. Nevertheless, Espinal (2004:14) notes that:

> . . . Participatory economic policy-making has not been a part of Dominican democracy. Not only has the legislature been weak and torn apart by party and intra-party conflicts, but civil society organizations have not played a vital role in economic policy-making, with the exception of business groups that have had more resources to lobby legislators and other public officials to benefit their own constituencies.

While this statement focuses on economic policy, it is also true of other areas.

Jamaican civil society is perceived as quite vibrant and active, with a number of NGOs performing several functions. Assisting the indigent, providing spiritual guidance and offering skills training are examples. In terms of the legal system in Jamaica, the entry into force in 2005 of the Access to Information Act is expected to gradually raise Government accountability through encouraging civil society feedback. Only one of the NGOs studied in Jamaica, the Red Cross, has been referred to constitutionally as an auxiliary to the government. Another law applicable to non-profit organizations is the Companies Act, most recently revised in 2004, which stipulates how these organizations should be registered with the Office of the Registrar of Companies.[6]

The Jamaican system thus requires that persons forming NGOs register, as is the case in the Dominican Republic under the New Law 122-05. Despite a history of dictatorship, which is not shared with Jamaica, the Dominican Republic has made numerous official attempts to facilitate NGOs and their official recognition in the society, at least on paper. Legislation appears to see non-governmental organizations and non-profit organizations as one and the same.

Decree No. 407/01 of March 21, 2001 issued by then President Hipólito Mejia, sought to follow up in particular on those NGOs receiving subsidies from the Dominican Government, and to protect the image of those doing positive work in communities. However, the decree had little credibility with NGOs as they were not consulted in the process.

Law 122-05 was approved on April 8, 2005 under the Leonel Fernandez administration and articulates in greater depth the vision of NGOs and their role in relation to government. Some NGO participation was involved in this process, although many from grassroots organizations disagree. [7] Paragraph 4 of the preamble states that:

> ... non-profit organizations[7] translate citizens' initiatives coming from the desires of the citizenry to participate in society-building, facilitating democratising change processes in the culture and political practices which allow for greater societal control of political representative(s). [8]

They also recognise in paragraph 5 that the activities of non-profit organizations are increasingly moving beyond national boundaries, establishing links with similar organizations abroad, as well as foreign governments, public institutions, and international organizations. Paragraph 8 of the preamble speaks to the lack of a permanent government framework for these organizations. It also specifies in paragraph 10 that the existing legislation does not establish mechanisms for interacting with the state, nor for the development, promotion and support of activities being carried out by non-profit organizations, and makes reference to Decree No. 685-00 of September 1, 2000 whose stated objective was to decentralise public administration through civil society participation in assisting with national social issues. Paragraph 12 makes reference to legislation which facilitates the reform of the state, in which the state believes NGOs should have a role. The final paragraph of the preamble refers to inadequate, older legislation, particularly Executive Order no. 520 of July 26, 1920, which addressed and governed NGOs from that point to the present day.

Reading the 24-page document reveals the Dominican government's definition of non-profit association to be:

. . . The agreement between five or more physical or moral persons to develop or execute socially constructive activities or activities in the public interest for purposes which are legal and which have no purpose or objective of obtaining pecuniary or substantial profits in money to share between his or her associates.

Interestingly, the new Law under the Fernandez administration also creates a new monitoring organization, the National Centre for Development and Promotion of Non-Profit Organizations, with a wider mandate than the one declared under the 2001 Mejia decree. However, new initiatives such as these breed scepticism because of the lack of continuity between administrations.

The strong presidential system in the Dominican Republic and a correspondingly weak legislature have fed these continuity issues. Jamaica, while having political culture concerns of its own, has differed because of a British-style civil service, which remains largely in place regardless of changes in governing party and because of the inability of the Jamaica Labour Party (JLP) to wrest power from the ruling People's National Party (PNP) from its election in 1989 until the end of our period of study in 2006.

There are a number of international non-governmental organizations including the Red Cross and the Salvation Army, which are *la Cruz Roja* and the *Ejercito de Salvación* in the Dominican Republic respectively. In Jamaica, both of these organizations have assisted deportees as a part of their general work with indigent persons. They became policy actors in mid-2005, working in conjunction with both the Ministry of National Security and non-governmental organizations, to develop a coordinated national policy on deportation. Both organizations are aware of each other in Jamaica but seem to work less closely in the Dominican Republic. The Red Cross in the Dominican Republic seems preoccupied by deportation and migration as it relates to Haitians, rather than to deported Dominicans.

EXISTING DATA

A preliminary examination of the literature suggests that there is a dearth of statistical data and publications to explain deportation from the United

States and its relations with other phenomena. While the governments of Jamaica and the Dominican Republic carry out some data collection at airports when specific deportee flights land, it is alleged that a number of deportees slip through this net when they arrive on normal airline flights. It was also alleged by some civil society interviewees in the Dominican Republic that for a fee, one could avoid such unpleasant formalities altogether. The year 2006 found both governments in the process of entering these data electronically. In June 2006, the Dominican Republic Department of Deportees at the National Police Headquarters had already classified its deportee population by city and neighbourhood, and entered the information including photographs, and data collected at the time of re-entry into the country, into Microsoft Word.

NGOs in both receiving countries have been able to provide a great deal of anecdotal information, but much more statistical data are required, with more comprehensive studies on the returnee population and the informal networks reintegrating them into Caribbean societies. This, although not impossible, may prove challenging, given the stigma attached to deportation and the consequent 'disappearance' of many returnees upon their arrival in Jamaica, either into family networks or otherwise.

Spurred in part by media publicity, there has been an impetus to explore the link between criminality in the Caribbean and deportation. However, no link has been established between significant increases in crime and the spike in returnee arrivals. A study conducted in September 2004 of 8,228 of the persons deported to Jamaica from the US in the 1997-2003 period concluded that the public impression of deportees as small children leaving Jamaica and returning to Jamaica as adult, hardened criminals might not be a fair one.[9] The study used US government exit data. It was heavily critiqued in the Jamaican press[10] by the public and key figures in the Jamaican Government who either criticized other factors such as the validity of the data or its interpretation. However, these highly publicised criticisms were not substantiated by data.

In related literature, Griffin (2003) noted that there was no evidence of 'sophisticated' crime in Barbados following the re-introduction of deportees to the society and that there was not enough evidence to connect criminal deportees to any systematic pattern of criminal activity (pp. 79–80). In the course of interviews conducted for comparative study, the belief that deportees had initiated sophisticated or different categories of crime such as drive-by shootings, persisted amongst all except the majority of deportees interviewed. Media reports continue to be bold in tone. There has been much negative media speculation in the Caribbean region as to the results of receiving, often without notice, large numbers of these citizens, many of whom apparently have little connection to their country of birth.

GOVERNMENT POLICY AND PROCEDURES

Obtaining documentation of any policy towards deportees has proven difficult in the Dominican Republic. It is important to note that the government has produced largely internal documents focusing on the potential effect of deportees on public order. President Mejia commissioned a report in 2002 which expressed concern about the effect that deportation could have on tourism, both in terms of increased crime and reduced tourism receipts, and President Fernandez' new think-tank, FUNGLODE, held a seminar on deportation issues in March 2006 to unite stakeholders and suggest policy solutions.

Deportees are generally sent to the Dominican Republic on specialised flights every two weeks, on Wednesdays, with no viable plan from the government other than that of receiving them at the airport and processing them at the Department of Immigration. Some deportees arrive piecemeal on normal American Airlines commercial flights. Deportees are then categorised according to whether they committed a simple overstaying offence, in which case they are released, and those with a criminal record, who are sent to the national police headquarters for further processing in the police court and other departments. Preliminary enquiries and interviews with government officials in the Dominican Republic gave the impression that the process was a well-organized one, with deportees being collected in an air-conditioned bus and processed in an air-conditioned room at the National Migration Department. While the new migration department has a state of the art building near to the capital's seafront, a cursory glance at the cramped, low-ceilinged and generally insanitary surroundings at the National Police Headquarters, belied the account of a comfortable re-entry process.

Subsequent interviews with deportees and non-governmental organizations, and unofficial ones with government officers, revealed an even worse truth. While some deportees had been released on the same day, it emerged that prior to 2003, others had experienced a process lasting a number of days, during which they were detained in police lock-ups in Santo Domingo and many were exposed to extortion attempts from government officials at the airport, the migration department and the police station for between 5,000 to 50,000 Dominican pesos, with latter being approximately US$1,500 according to the highly variable exchange rate. No such situation was reported in Jamaica in the course of the research.

Jamaica's policy on deportation between 1996-2006 had three main foci:

(i)   Managing the flow of deportees, ensuring that only Jamaican citizens are admitted into the country;

(ii) Ensuring that those posing a serious risk are monitored by police; and

(iii) Engaging in dialogue with major deporting countries, the USA, UK and Canada at every possible opportunity.

In Jamaica, interviews with governmental officials, non-governmental organizations and deportees also revealed that conditions were not ideal, with government officials noting the Government's desire for reintegration policy but printing out its lack of financial and physical capacity.[11] It was explained that in the case of deportees from the United States, many had been travelling since 4:00 am without food or drink and were subsequently put through a long form of processing at immigration at the airport and at the Central Police Station downtown. Many officials interviewed were concerned about the difficulty of the process for deportees and that some had nowhere to go at the end of the processing. Often, police officers or other officials had to assist the returnees by giving them a prepaid phone card or some other item to allow them to resettle. In one case, an individual had been in the United States from the age of nine years and was deported at 45. He came home with only the name of an aunt in St. Ann. An airport employee took the returnee to an East Kingston address as he had nowhere to go. A week later, it was discovered that the aunt had died some three years previously. The man remained at the employee's home for a while but this could not continue indefinitely. The man was on the streets when workers from a non-governmental drug rehabilitation facility found him. Examples like these were proof of the importance of family networks in resettlement efforts and the need for liaison between different actors involved in the return of deported individuals.

INTERNATIONAL CONTEXT

Caribbean governments were not slow to react to the deportation phenomenon at the international level. At the Caribbean/United States Summit held on 10 May 1997 in Bridgetown, Barbados, Heads of Goverment signed off on the Bridgetown Declaration of Principles. Article 9 states, with regard to the *deportation of criminals* —

> *We recognise the right of each State to determine its policies on deportation subject to international law, and agree to:*
>
> *9.3. . .provide adequate advance notice to designated authorities prior to a criminal's deportation;*
>
> *9.4. . . provide appropriate information regarding the persons to be deported;*
>
> *9.5 . . .establish, prior to the deportation, that the deportee is a national of the receiving State;*
>
> *9.6. . . hold consultations on other issues associated with deportation; and work to improve arrangements by which the deportee has access to his or her assets located in the deporting State.*

It was noted that the United States intends to offer technical assistance in establishing parole and monitoring systems.

The substance of such legislation is debatable. Although individual states and alliances such as CARICOM continue to lobby for meaningful assistance to be given to the nations tackling the influx of deportees and moderate success has been achieved in this area (Jones-Correa, 2003, 316), attempts by the developing countries to confront the USA more directly on the issue have met with serious resistance. For instance, in October 2001, the

United States did not hesitate to place visa sanctions on Guyana when it charged that the nation was moving too slowly in issuing travel documents for 113 criminal deportees (Ishmael, 2001). Guyana had resisted the sending home of some of the deportees for several reasons, including the fact that a number of them would arrive without proper documentation, and that some would even be found to be non-Guyanese citizens once their identity had been properly verified.

Promised financial assistance and proper notification of the arrival of deportees are two goals for which the Caribbean nations and their supporters continue to advocate. Inquiries from both countries have revealed that police and immigration authorities in the Caribbean countries are furnished approximately one week in advance with a list of deportee names and their offences. They continue to request that there be a lead time of approximately three months to allow for preparations to be made in the receiving countries, and that a complete criminal record be provided. They complain that the current manifest shows only the current offence for which the returnee was jailed and not all past criminal history.

At the international level, lobbying efforts by Caribbean nationals, NGOs and sympathetic members of the US Congress concentrated on, *inter alia*, better support from the US government to receiving countries in their attempt to grapple with the influx of deportees and for a softening of some of the harsher deportation policies, including those which separate families. Lobbying in the USA for the passage of the last version of the Family Reunification Act in the 109th Congress, which sought cancellation of removal for certain long-term permanent resident aliens, stalled after its June 6, 2005 referral to the Subcommittee on Immigration, Border Security, and Claims.[12] The failure of President Bush's immigration bill in June 2007, outside of the decade of this study, seemed to justify pessimism over any short or medium-term reversal of the IIRIRA.[13] This failure was a reflection of growing anti-immigrant sentiment the US.[14]

In March 2006, in contrast, the United States was reportedly complaining about China's refusal to accept Chinese nationals slated for deportation from the USA, showing that size and influence truly have an impact on these issues and that Caribbean states have a deficit of those commodities by comparison with China.[15]

To exacerbate matters for Caribbean nations, increased global military activity and general militarization of development issues in the form of prioritising US security concerns, even in developing nations, indicate that any security threat from undesirable individuals within the US homeland will be met with a zero tolerance policy. Tightening immigration policy and the reduction of freedoms under the Patriot Act paint a bleak future both for deportees attempting to return to the United States and for resident aliens attempting to contest deportation orders, despite intermittent triumphs by immigrants in the USA.

POLICY OPTIONS: A JOINT GOVERNMENT AND CIVIL SOCIETY RESPONSE

The sheer numbers of persons deported to the Caribbean demands a policy response which integrates the deportation phenomenon with other aspects of migration, such as the brain drain and remittances. Existing strategies so far show that returnees are absorbed on an ad hoc basis into the general society and/or the existing social safety net. Comments of respondents in focus groups and interviews, and logic, suggest that there should be a specific policy response. Governments seem to agree and both claim to be formulating specific policies. This has not been without significant impetus from non-governmental organizations, which have served both as pressure groups and practical government auxiliaries.

With regard to migration and government, Morrison and Sinkin (1982, 819) note that 'the migration issue is not an area distinct from the various development focuses, but rather cuts across and is related to many of the programme areas in which the government is involved'. Nothing in studies so far has demonstrated that the governments being studied were proactive enough to have prepared a swift response to the new United States deportation policy which was passed in 1996, but both are showing signs of developing a coordinated response ten years later with significant assistance from NGOs in many areas and, indeed, leadership from said organizations in the social side of the reintegration process.

OBSERVATIONS

(i) **Lack of communication by the government with regard to its existing facilities and/ or policies.**

It was found that in the period of study beginning in 1996, there was no government policy beyond an immigration and security response in both countries, and an attempt to communicate with governments in sending countries to stem the flow of returnees and ensure that better information was received with regard to the returnees. Domestic reinsertion measures were absent in Jamaica. Nevertheless, government facilities did assist with problems experienced by returnees. One NGO interviewee mentioned, for example, the work of the government-sponsored Marie Atkins shelter on Hanover Street in Kingston, which has been of assistance to returnees. Other government programme have also helped returnees but treat them as ordinary citizens with difficulties. It seems unfortunate that many returnees accessed these agencies through desperation, chance and/or through the ad hoc help of concerned citizens, including police and customs officers acting in a private capacity. Many interviewees mentioned that people could learn of these facilities through the distribution of a simple leaflet to returnees upon their arrival at ports of entry.

(ii) **Lack of communication between governments and civil society.**

There is a lack of awareness among key civil society groups and individuals that the government is or may be developing a policy. The partnership approach comes more naturally to non-governmental organizations while government links with NGOs are less traditional. There is a need for greater two-way information sharing between the government and NGOs, between different government entities and between various civil society organizations. This was demonstrated when some mini focus groups became informational for the interviewees who asked the researcher for more information on the deportee situation in Jamaica and/or in the Dominican Republic.

Focus groups also brought together persons who had not necessarily met and provided a place for building networks and, in one case, obtaining funds for a cash-strapped organization.

(iii) Counselling services.

The Dominican Government has had a Department of Deportees since 2000. This includes a psychology arm with five psychologists employed to help deportees cope with reinsertion into Dominican society. This pioneering department has helped a number of deportees who are expected to report there at least twice during the first six months following their return to the country. There is no limitation on the number of times a returnee may go for counselling. However, the lead psychologist notes that more staff members are needed and that the two rooms in which they are all housed are too small. As such, there is no privacy. When the interviewer visited the office in question, she was suspicious of the very young age of some of the purported psychologists and had doubts as to their level of qualification for such a task. However, to the credit of the Dominican Republic's *Policia Nacional,* no parallel structure has been observed in the Jamaican government. It is worth mentioning, nevertheless, that various interviews with a thrice-deported activist in Jamaica revealed that she had been informally allocated office space within a Kingston police station to carry out activities to assist deportees in 2006. She had also been permitted to regularly meet deportee flights.

(iv) Lack of cohesion among NGOs.

On a positive note, NGOs are developing increasingly sophisticated negotiating capacity in inserting themselves into areas normally reserved for government. This is seen in ongoing development of deportation policy and indeed in arguably initiating the process. NGOs in both countries have shown a proactive role in developing policy and working independently to assist returnees in areas where government has failed to act.

Unfortunately, while NGOs have often asserted that they are left out of the policy process or are disempowered in a number of ways, there may even be a hierarchy amongst NGOs themselves. Some may be established and may have significant membership, while others may not. In one of the interviews conducted with an international NGO's office in the Dominican Republic, which is actively involved in resolving the challenges raised by deportation, it was suggested that NGOs form alliances, especially those which are strong only in one area, so that the strength of others could be used to form a better support system. An important outcome of the focus groups conducted is the ongoing linkages which have been formed.

Further to the theme of information-sharing, non-governmental organizations approached for the study have as yet failed to demonstrate international alliances, other than a few linkages with US-based immigrant rights groups as it relates to the deportation issue. Disappointingly, one of the international NGOs interviewed for this study, which was very active on this matter in Jamaica, was not in contact with its branch in the Dominican Republic, which had different priorities. This illustration does not augur well for organizations which purport to work for the wellbeing of deportees. While through the very process of this study, the Dominican Republic representative agreed to investigate the issue further, it demonstrates that much work needs to be done across national borders and across language barriers. With the same energy level as they have applied to pressuring their national governments to take action on deportation, NGOs could become more proactive in the sensitization of international bodies and approaching foreign governments to develop a more structured policy on deportation. One relief worker noted the solidarity of a number of NGOs in 2006 protests by immigrant rights campaigners in the United States. This solidarity should be extended to the issue of deportation, particularly in connection with universal human rights, including the principle of family unity.

(v) Government alliances.

Governments must also work harder on international alliances. While admirable and necessary, initiatives by government in the CARICOM arena as regards deportation are not sufficiently overwhelming in force because of the small populations involved. Another factor not examined in this context is that the crime patterns in Jamaica have tended to resemble those of its Latin American neighbours and not those of its CARICOM partners, since the 1970s. Whilst we have seen that most deportees have not been convicted of serious crimes, the English-speaking Caribbean should examine commonalities with its Spanish-speaking neighbours.

(vi) Need to reconcile civil society and government perceptions on data collection and other issues.

Most respondents in the focus groups of both countries did not perceive the collection of data and the development of a database on deportees to be a violation of the rights of IRVs, but had differences of opinion with regard to what data should be collected and in how they should be used. In complete contrast with the perspective of government officials, returnees and NGOs cited the unfairness of being given what is effectively a police record in the Dominican Republic upon returning as an IRV, as this affects employment possibilities and the ability to access financial services such as loans. However, police officials interviewed were at pains to say that this was not a police record, and that a clearance letter could be obtained after six months. They noted that everyone in the society at times needed a 'certificate of good behaviour' from the government to obtain work. NGOs, government and returnees need to have greater dialogue on this issue so that during the six months of surveillance, returnees can find work. One suggestion on the part of NGOs and returnees is that the six month monitoring programme be carried out by someone other than the police department, so that it would not affect their local police record.

(vii) Role of government and civil society in raising awareness.

Both governments and NGOs could be more proactive in terms of awareness-building. Neither group has mentioned raising the awareness of persons in the United States about deportation and the pitfalls of failing to seek citizenship. One respondent in the Dominican Republic mentioned the need for a manual to be developed for Dominicans migrating to the USA. The manual would explain cultural differences with everything from traffic offences to gender relations and, how these matters are seen legally in the USA. He believes that a number of Dominicans convicted in the USA are victims of their own lack of cultural understanding.

(viii) The private sector as a key part of civil society.

One interviewee in the Dominican Republic mentioned the need for strong private sector participation in the process to facilitate insertion of returnees into the labour force. Private sector voices have been notably absent from the deportee debate in Jamaica, save and except in relation to how deportees may have an impact on the crime rate in both countries and, in this vein, the investment climate.[16]

The undetermined number of deportees that have been re-absorbed into the labour market points toward the need for more meaningful public-private sector partnerships. Non-governmental organizations and some government officials are concerned that the number of those re-absorbed into the labour force may not be enough. In the Dominican Republic, various reports and the interviews conducted have shown that some returnees are absorbed into jobs in the hotel and tourism sector, and the call centre industry where there is a high demand for persons speaking English. This language asset is not one shared by Jamaican deportees, who already live in an English-speaking country.

CONCLUSION

Further government-civil society interaction in Jamaica and the Dominican Republic, and indeed in deporting countries, could lead to a 'best practice' model for returnee policy to be shared with other states.

Government-civil society interaction with regard to returnees, although innovative and progressive, is fraught with differences of opinion. Government agencies may feel bound by laws and procedures, whereas NGOs may have more fluid structures and be action-oriented. In short, NGOs may think that government bureaucracy moves too slowly and government entities may believe that there are procedures and legal structures to be adhered to before enacting working policies. This was an emerging factor in interviews conducted for the study with NGOs and indeed conceded (with explanation) in an interview with a government official.

Government-civil society cooperation is crucial given the fact that deportations to the Caribbean, mostly carried out against black males, are unlikely to stop. Recent militant activism on the part of the legally and illegally resident but largely law-abiding Mexican population in the USA only serves to emphasize just how low on the current pecking order an ex-convict may fall. This unpopular but pragmatic position advocates a more practical approach from governments which would match that of the NGOs. Government access to certain international fora and their stated role in general will clearly differentiate them from NGOs.

The year 2006 was a historic one for Caribbean Governments. It was hoped that the May 2006 victories by President Fernandez' PLD party in the Dominican Republic in legislative elections and the euphoria of Portia Simpson-Miller's March 2006 swearing-in in Jamaica would make it a year for new ideas and policies to be enacted. However, this has proved illusory. Organized and informal NGOs, as well as family networks, appear to have been the ones offering practical, short-term solutions for persons deported to the land of their birth.

It is hoped that the next decade will reflect a different reality, and that the governments' apparent sluggishness in promulgating a holistic deportation policy will appear to have been necessary in developing a sustainable, long-term solution.

REFERENCES

The Bridgetown Declaration of Principles - Caribbean/United States Summit - 10 May 1997 - Partnership for Prosperity and Security in the Caribbean. Copy available at *http://www.caricomlaw.org/docs/Bridgetown%20Declaration %20of%20Principles.pdf*

Casey, John P. 1998. Non-Government Organizations as Policy Actors: The Case of Immigration Policies in Spain, Universitat Autònoma de Barcelona. Available in Internet at: *http://blues.uab.es/mgp/papers/casey2.html*

Dauda, Bola. 2002. Toward a Reconstruction of Public Policy Theory and Practice, No P.92/12, Centre for the Study of Public Order, University of Leicester, October.

Espinal, Rosario. 2004. Limited engagement in policy-making: The Legislature and Civil Society in the Dominican Republic (Draft version).

Espinal, Rosario. 2001. '*La sociedad civil movilizada y las reformas demoacraticas en la República Dominicana*' in Espinal, *Estudios sobre Estado y Sociedad*, Vol VII No 21 May/ August, pp.101-132.

Espinal, Rosario. 2002. '*República Dominicana: El retorno del PRD al poder*' Nueva Sociedad No. 178, Conyuntura, Philadelphia, January 2002.

Griffin, Clifford E. 2003. 'Deportees and Crime in Barbados'; Caribbean Dialogue Vol 6 Nos. 1&2 January-June.

Ishmael, Odeen Ambassador of Guyana. 2001. The Impact of the September 11 Terrorist Attack against the United States on the Caribbean Political Economy (*Text of lecture at Spelman College, Atlanta, Georgia, on November 28, 2001) http://www.guyana.org/ Speeches/ishmael_112801.html*

Jackson-Miller, Dionne (November 27, 2003): Caribbean NGOs want real influence. *www.ipsnews.net*

Jones-Correa, Michael. 2003. 'Under Two-Flags: Dual Nationality in Latin America and its consequences for Naturalization in the United States' pp.303-333. In 'Rights and Duties of Dual Nationals: Evolution and Prospects' eds.Martin, David A. and Hailbronner, K. The Hague: Kluwer Law International.

Morrison, Thomas K. and Sinkin, R. 1982. 'International Migration in the Dominican Republic: Implications for Development Planning' no. 247 Offprint Series, International Migration Review, Vol. 16, No. 4, 1982, pp. 819-836. Center for Migration Studies, NY, USA.

Legal texts:

Act 2-1994 amending the Criminal Justice (Administration) Act (1994) (Jamaica). Electronic copy available at *http://www.caricomlaw.org/docs/The%20Criminal%20Justice%20(Administration)%20Act.pdf*

Decreto No. 401/01 (Decree No. 407/01) (Dominican Republic)

Ley No. 122-05 de 8 de abril de 2005 'Sobre Regulación y Fomento de las Asociaciones Sin Fines de Lucro en la República Dominicana' (Law No. 122-05 of April 8, 2005: On Regulating Non-Profit Organizations in the Dominican Republic).

NOTES

1. *http://www.caribbeannetnews.com*, 2003.
2. For the purposes of this article, Dominicans are from the Dominican Republic as opposed to sister island Dominica.
3. For example, President Leonel Fernandez, elected in 2004, established a think-tank, FUNGLODE, which held a seminar on deportation issues in March 2006. The conference provided a space for persons from the private sector, the government and civil society, including returnees, to meet and discuss the deportation issue and a way forward.
4. *http://www.hrw.org/spanish/informes/2002/r_dominicana.html*. Such an 'appearance' may simply mean dark skin and/ or non-Caucasian hair.
5. Interview with national Human Rights Commission representative, Dominican Republic, 4 June 2006.
6. Office of the Registrar of Companies, Jamaica, website and conversation with Mr. Gregory Spaulding from that office, May 26, 2006.
7. A representative from one non-governmental organization in the Dominican Republic noted that they prefer the term 'non-profit organization' as it defines what they are rather than what they are not.
8. Unofficial translation of Spanish text by researcher.
9. Headley, Bernard et al. 2005. Deported, Volume 1: Entry and Exit Findings Jamaicans Returned Home from the US between 1997 and 2003, Kingston, Stephenson Litho Press.
10. The *Sunday Gleaner,* October 3, 2004, Kingston, Jamaica.
11. Telephone interview with government official, June 12, 2006.
12. http://www.govtrack.us/congress/bill.xpd?bill=h109-2055.
13. http://www.washingtonpost.com/wp-dyn/content/article/2007/06/08/AR2007060802509.html.

14. For example, Steven Camarota of the Center for Immigration Studies was shown on a cnn.com video clip on June 12, 2007 bemoaning 'flawed immigration laws' 'weak enforcement mechanisms' and opining that absconders (illegal immigrants) may benefit from immigration laws in their current form.

15. 'US says China refuses deportees' 16 March 2006 http://news.bbc.co.uk/2/hi/americas/4811458.stm.

16. Telephone conversation with a Jamaica Banker's Association representative, May 19th 2006 at 10a.m. The representative noted that in Jamaica's current situation private sector organizations were not particularly interested in having particular programmes for deportees. She noted that the PSOJ has talked about deportees but in terms of their relation to crime. Others, for example a Jamaica Manufacturer's Association representative interviewed by phone that morning was not averse to assisting, but was not sure where deportees were.

14

MIGRATION AND REMITTANCES:
Typologies and Motivations

MARK FIGUEROA

INTRODUCTION

In seeking to understand remittance flows to the Caribbean and other global areas, economists have considered various motives including altruism, co-insurance and risk spreading. Analyses have proceeded at the macro and the micro levels but the underlying migratory patterns that connect to different motives have not always been clearly identified. This article explores a set of typologies that distinguish various migrant relationships corresponding to different stages in the migration cycle. The distinctions identified are linked to the motives posited in economic models for remittance flows with a view to fostering the inclusion of a more sophisticated understanding of migration within economic analyses of remittances. The aim is to provide a firmer foundation to guide data collection, sharpen analysis and improve model building. This should contribute to better explanations for past increases in remittance flows and improved forecasts of growth and sustainability.

This article is part of a larger study on the characteristics and significance of the diaspora for Caribbean economies currently being undertaken by the Caribbean Diaspora Research Group of the Department of Economics, University of the West Indies, Mona. So far, our primary focus has been on remittances.[1] In seeking to model remittance flows, economists have made explicit and/or implicit assumptions concerning the motives of those who remit cash and kind to their home country while living abroad. Underlying the assumptions about motivation are assumptions about the nature of migration. Yet these assumptions are not always specified. In addition, it is not clear that models embody a good grasp of the migration experience. This article delves more deeply into the nature of migration, particularly as it relates to the Caribbean experience. In this way, it is hoped that we will be able to develop improved economic models that are able to explain the patterns of remittance flows that we have observed in the past and to improve forecasts of their future growth and sustainability.

In the migration literature, there have been many studies that either develop or utilize typologies. For example, the distinction between migrations: forced and free has produced a set of typologies and much debate as to the nature of migrations and the extent to which persons have chosen to, or been forced to migrate.[2] To contextualize my discussion, I give examples of typologies developed by other authors and show how typologies are derived from the perspective that drives them. I then discuss the factors that help to determine a disposition to remit, the motives that have been ascribed to remitters and a typology of migrant remitters. While not seeking to be exhaustive, I provide examples of how my categories relate to economic models that are applied to data on remittance flows.

The development of an appropriate set of typologies with reference to the migrant relationships that drive remittances must be seen as an iterative process. As we have sought to model remittance flows, we have found it necessary to understand the migration process. But typologies are important both for analysis and data collection. Thus, in designing a national survey to capture data on remittances it was necessary to develop typologies as a foundation for question formulation.[3] As we collect and analyze more data, this will help us to refine our typologies leading to further improvements in data collection, analysis and modelling. In what follows, I identify some of the issues on which model builders can focus if they have adequately disaggregated data. These are preliminary steps; other areas are left to be pursued. These include the refinement of definitions and the creation of data collection strategies that can support the theoretical distinctions we may wish to make.

MIGRATION TYPOLOGIES

There is no generic migration typology that covers all cases of interest. The characteristics of a typology are derived from the perspective that created it. I provide three examples. The first comes from an article by Meissner (1992, 67) on 'Managing Migration'. Starting from the perspective of 'managing migration pressures' she declares that 'migrants fall into five basic categories' as follows: 1) Legally admitted immigrants and non-immigrants; 2) Contract labour migrants; 3) Illegal immigrants; 4) Asylum-seekers; and 5) Refugees. This listing provides us with a relatively simple typology. In contrast, my second example allows us to develop a multi-dimensional typology. In an article focusing on 'Types and Patterns of Later-Life Migration', Walters (2000) analyses the characteristics of the destinations to which persons migrate in later life. He relates these to the migrant's union status, income level and disability status. He presents a four way classification of later life migrants and suggests, for example, that high income migrants who do not have a disability will tend to gravitate to places with good leisure facilities whether their spouse is present or not. Low income persons in the same situation seek a lower cost of living. Persons with moderate disabilities are more concerned with being close to adult children or locations where they are able to secure informal health care, and those with severe disabilities gravitate towards sites with access to formal health care.

My third example relates much more closely to the issue of remittances. In her article on 'Transients and Settlers: Varieties of Caribbean Migrants and the Socio-Economic Implications of Their Return', Elizabeth Thomas-Hope relates the type of migrant to the objective of migration, the impact of migration on the skills set of the migrant and the quantities and types of remittances that they return to the home country (table 14.1). In advancing her typology she rejects a distinction that has been made in the literature. 'There has been a tendency to create an unnecessary distinction between long-term "migration and return" on one hand and short-term "circulation" on the other (1986, 559).

As we will see below (see also tables 14.1 and 14.2) there is an overlap between her typology and mine but there are groups in her typology that I exclude. This is because the flow of funds that are associated with these groups have not been included within the concept of remittances with which I have been working. In particular, she refers to 'International Vendors' whom I have up to now not considered as being engaged in remitting in as far as the value that they bring home is more or less equivalent to the value that they take abroad. This would also be true for those 'Business Commuters' who do not have a business abroad. The contrast between the two typologies derives in part from the difference in the starting point from which they are developed. In her case, she is interested in the impact of circulation/migration and return. In my case, I am interested in what is sent home primarily in the sense of a net return.

These three examples illustrate how different migration typologies can be. The first comes from the perspective of the state managing migration and focuses on the migrants' legal status with respect to national and international law. The second is concerned with identifying factors that motivate late life migration and focuses on the needs of the older migrant, which depend on the degrees of freedom that they derive from their economic, social and health status. The third example seeks to demonstrate the pervasiveness of migration as part of the Caribbean life cycle and the degree to which circulation brings benefits to the home country. It, therefore, encompasses all groups who could be seen as circulators and considers all that they send/bring back home as a result of their migration.

CREATING A REMITTANCE TYPOLOGY

To develop an appropriate typology for remitters, I take into consideration the factors that may help to determine a willingness to remit. In doing so, a very large number of factors need to be taken into account. Initially, I classify these as follows: 1) Outlook of remitter; 2) Personal circumstances of the remitter; 3) Nature of family/household/network relations; and 4) Relative socio-economic situation in home and/or host country. I subsequently discuss the motives of individual remitters and the patterns of migration into which they might fall. Throughout the discussion it is important to note that migrants travel abroad for multiple reasons and with various objectives; expecting a short, medium or long-term stay. Once they get there they can, and do, change their minds. They may also experience changes in their socio-economic circumstances. As such, the categories used are not always intended to be mutually exclusive.

OUTLOOK OF THE REMITTERS

There are four sub-categories within which we need to consider the outlook of the remitter. These are: 1) Goal orientedness in migration; 2) Attitudes to matters in the home and host countries; 3) Reason(s) for migration; and 4) Intensity of desire to, and planned timing of return to the home country. Goal orientedness refers to the extent to which the migrant left with a specific objective or set of objectives in mind as opposed to a generalized or even unclear aim. Clear objectives might include: savings to purchase a home; acquiring university qualifications; or earning enough to pay for the education of children left at home. Generalized aims could include: improved quality of life, new opportunities and/or experiences. Where the migrant has very clear objectives that relate to financing activities at home and where these objectives relate to family rather than self, there is a greater disposition to remit. Where goals relate to the individual migrant and not other family members, or to achievements in the host country, or do not relate to financing activities in the home country, we would expect lower levels of remittances. A lack of clarity on goals could lead to an intermediate position. More positive attitudes towards the home country in general or towards persons, places and things left behind should lead to higher levels of remittances, while more positive attitudes towards the host country may have the opposite effect.

Reasons for migration are many and can be classified as economic, social and other. They also involve pull and push factors and may relate to the individual who is migrating or to the migrant's family/household or other types of socio-economic networks. Where push factors are sufficiently negative, they may cause migrants to turn their back on the home country and hence not send remittances. At the same time negative economic circumstances that push persons to migrate may be the reason why they send large remittances to family members left behind. This, like many other examples, illustrates that the complex nature of migration does not facilitate the use of simple dichotomous variables to predict remitting behaviour.

Economic reasons on the pull side relate to three (sometimes overlapping) objectives: 1) an increased income stream for household consumption purposes including day-to-day expenditures, the acquisition of consumer durables and/ or the purchase or upgrading of one's home; 2) an increased income stream with a view to accumulate financial and/or other assets to be utilized in new or ongoing business enterprises; 3) the acquisition of education, skills and/or experience. In each case the migrant may or may not intend to return. In working towards a particular goal, the migrant may be striving as an individual or as a member of a family or other network whether at home or abroad. Thus objective 3) above could involve the migrants going to school abroad, going abroad with children and working to pay for their children's education abroad or going abroad and sending money home to pay for the education of their children at home. In addition to the three objectives noted, a migrant may seek new business opportunities abroad; this is done either by moving an existing business abroad or starting a new one. In the latter case, it could be to return to set up the same kind of business at home while, in the former case, it does not preclude the simultaneous operation of a business in both the home and the host country. This further illustrates that economic goals can be oriented to either the home or host country with consequences for the flows of remittances.

I include four objectives under social reasons. The first three are general while the fourth may be more relevant to countries like Jamaica: 1) access to quality amenities and or opportunities in areas such as health, recreation, education and personal development (I would include here the advantage of acquiring a new citizenship or residence status for self or family members); 2) enjoyment of a pleasant social and/or natural environment; 3) reconnection with family and/or other social networks and 4) personal safety and/or peace of mind. The latter suggests strong push factors such as crime, violence and unresolved social conflicts. This may lead to a negative attitude towards the home country and or an early return home. The greater the push factor and the fewer the home connections, the less likely it is that these social reasons for migration will be accompanied by a high remittance rate. It is also possible that those who migrate for reasons 1) and 2) may be better off, leaving relatively secure family members at home. Those who join families abroad may also have fewer realtives at home. Overall we may hypothesize that social migrants may be sending fewer remittances than economic migrants.

I consider four objectives under general reasons: 1) general improvement/ better opportunities; 2) new/broader opportunities/experiences; 3) follow the trend; 4) comply with decision to migrate taken by someone else. Given the very amorphous character of these objectives it is not possible to indicate the impact on the remitter. We may speculate that, as with those discussed above who have unclear economic reasons; migrants with general objectives may fall into an intermediate position regarding their remittance behaviour The issue of clarity on objectives relates also to the last element of the migrants' outlook which I discuss; this is the intensity of desire to and planned timing of return to the home country. Persons who are unclear would fall into the intermediate position above. Those who definitely intend to return may remit considerable sums if they fall into the appropriate sub-category under economic reasons. Similarly those who do not intend to return may remit regularly, for example, if they are supporting family members whom they intend to send for in due course.

CIRCUMSTANCES OF THE REMITTER

The personal circumstances that I consider relevant are: 1) level of security/immigration status; 2) demographic characteristics of the migrant and more generally 3) socio-economic status of the migrant. Immigration status alone is not the only factor I take into consideration as persons who are outside of the official system may have widely varying levels of security depending on the types of networks to which they belong. The impact of this variable on remittances is not unidirectional. There are some persons who are so insecure that they do not wish to access official remittance transfer mechanisms and are therefore handicapped in what they send. In contrast, the fact that one has become a citizen or a permanent resident may signal that one has given up one's connection with the home country. The absence of a unilinear relationship between immigration status and remitting behaviour points, once more, to the difficulty in modelling, as economists have to use available data. Attitude data is harder to obtain so proxies may be used. For example, the acceptance of citizenship could be used as a proxy for a disconnection from the home country. If this or any other proxy is not a good one, inappropriate inferences may be drawn.

Socio-economic status needs to be considered in absolute as well as relative terms. In order to remit, migrants must secure what they consider to be a minimum level of subsistence. This may lead us to believe that better-off migrants are more likely to remit, but this is not necessarily true. Persons who are better-off may have better-off relatives so that the relative gap between the remitters and those receiving remittances may be a more important issue.[4] In addition, better-off persons may have a more elevated notion as to what subsistence involves and may use up a much larger proportion of their income on subsistence, leaving less money for remittances.[5] Demographic factors including age (a proxy for stage of life cycle); union status and relationship to household headship (proxies for family connections); and sex are all expected to be significant predictors of remitting behaviour.

FAMILY AND OTHER NETWORKS

The nature of family, household and other networks introduces another complex set of issues. Economic models have often tended to treat remittances as intra-household transfers. Such a relationship exists when a family member (often a male) goes abroad as a migrant (guest or contract) worker and sends home money for the rest of the family. This is common for the Arab world where workers leave poorer Arab states or other Islamic nations and go to work in the wealthy Arab countries. Such relationships also exist where Caribbean migrants go to Britain and North America but these are not the only types of arrangements. Persons who leave a household in the Caribbean may establish a new household abroad. Persons may also leave from one household and send remittances to persons living in another household. Given the prevalence of family ties that are extended, based on visiting (rather than co-habiting) unions and which involve a range of other practices such as child shifting and serial polygamy, it is not surprising that remittances to the Caribbean would involve inter-household transfers. Economists need to take these relationships into account in their models.

For migrants who leave a household and remit, there are two considerations to which economists have drawn attention. The first contemplates whether the decision to migrate involved consultation with others. Did the migrant make a personal decision; receive help in making the decision; come to a joint decision or even strike a deal regarding the choice of person to migrate and expected conduct while abroad? In addition to joint decision making, there is the possibility that the migrant received assistance to finance the migration and/or in the identification of a job abroad. It could be that a decision was taken to support the migration of the family member who was seen as having the best income earning possibilities abroad. In such situations, an arrangement could have been made concerning remittances especially if there were obligations at home that someone else had agreed to undertake. What is true of household decision making and consequential remittances as intra-household transfers may also have its parallels with relationships within communities and other social networks.

Where there is strong joint decision making and even planned migration, economists have applied models of co-insurance, risk sharing and income smoothing. Where the migration has been facilitated, economists have sometimes taken remittances as a loan repayment. The possibility that families are actually positioning different members globally to maximize family welfare has been raised. This leads to the concept of transnational families and transnational communities, which I discuss later in greater detail. The former concept is relevant even for those who have reservations concerning a household model based on an optimizing calculus. What is true for the family can also apply for communities and other social networks. The stronger the role of the family/network in the migration process, the more we would expect in terms of remittances (so long as family/network members remain in the home country). Once we introduce transnational arrangements, it is not clear how remittances will flow. Significant two way flows become a possibility and the direction of net flows may depend on the demographics involved as well as the point that various persons have reached in the migration cycle.

MACROECONOMIC FACTORS

The last category that I consider consists of those factors that economists seek to capture as macroeconomic variables in models of remittances. These include the prospects for employment; price levels and inflation; interest rates and investment opportunities; foreign exchange rate movements and the presence or absence of unofficial foreign exchange market premiums; income levels/per capita GDP; as well as the general stability/socio-economic climate in both the home and host country. For each of these variables, we can distinguish how economists might include them in a model as opposed to how an individual may experience them. For some of these variables, the absolute values in the home and host country may not be as important as the relative gap between the values in each country. In addition, we need to be aware of the distinction between what motivates the remitter and the variable that the economist might use as a proxy. For example, changes in relative per capita GDP may be used as a proxy for capturing an element of the willingness to remit but the person who actually sends the money would be more concerned with their own personal circumstances and those of the persons to whom they were sending the money. Thus the home economy could be experiencing a general boom while the migrant's family member may be employed in the one economic sector that is contracting.

In general, the socio-economic variables, especially as they relate to the host country, are not as relevant to a typology of remitters as they tend to operate across the board rather than assist us in distinguishing between different types of remitters. An improvement in employment and/or the prospect of employment in the host country may make remitters more willing to send money, but this should have an impact on all remitters. The impact of a similar improvement in employment and/or the prospect of employment at home is not as clear. If remittances are primarily sent to support the day-to-day needs of the family, then this may cause a decrease but, if remittances are in the form of investments, growth in the home economy may lead to growing confidence and hence increased flows for this purpose. The devaluation of the local currency is another example where a change in a macroeconomic variable would impact, in different ways, on remittances depending on the reason behind the transfer. Remitters who are supporting family consumption may send less as they expect that the value of foreign currency previously sent would now purchase more (locally produced goods) as a result of the devaluation. At the same time, it may represent an opportunity to purchase property relatively more cheaply and result in increase investment flows. Yet this may not happen where devaluations lead to a feeling of insecurity that reduces confidence in the economy and weakens investment flows.

MOTIVES OF THE REMITTER

In economic models of remittance flows it is common to distinguish two types of motives: the altruistic and the self-interested. There is also the possibility that remitters may have a combination of motives or motives that might be seen as mixed or lying between the two extremes of pure altruism and pure self-interest. With pure altruism, the remitters send money for no other reason than to assist family, friends, community members or favourite causes in the home country. This does not rule other motives. Remitters could send home money to assist those in need, while also sending funds to meet their current and or future personal needs. In this case, the remitter has a combination of motives. With pure self-interest, remitters send money for no other reason than to satisfy their current and future needs. Many actions are obviously self-interested, but others can be less clear. For example, one may appear to be altruistic in providing assistance to those in need, but one could actually be making contributions with a view to maintaining reputation or status. In this type of situation the motive would be self-interested.

Self interested motives can thus involve direct or indirect benefit. Direct benefits would include light and durable consumer goods purchased and contributions towards housing. They may also include savings and investments and purchase of goods for business purposes. Some remittances are used to cover personal or business transactions that benefit the remitter, but others may cover obligations that are not mediated through the market. For example, a family member at home may be supported with cash and kind so long as they live in the family home and take care of an aged relative or young child. Such relationships involve reciprocity but not necessarily market type transactions.

Economic models, which are based on the assumption that the remitter is acting as part of a household, place emphasis on indirect benefits that might accrue to the remitter. Two self-interested motives that are included in such models are co-insurance and risk sharing. These can be differentiated from the case of the pure self-interested motive in that there is an element of mutuality between the remitter and the recipient. Under the assumption that co-insurance is in operation, we posit that should the remitter fall into need the recipient would most likely be ready, willing and able to assist. Thus, risks such as that of loss of income are shared.

We can therefore think of a range of motives; starting with pure self-interest. Closely related to this is what we might term enlightened self-interest. A remitter may send home funds in order to maintain reputation, gain favour with their family, secure an inheritance or ensure that there is a home to return to in the event that things do not work out abroad (an option value) or the remitter may actually be planning to return home. I have already given examples of possible cases of mutual interest between remitters and their families. Shifting further we can refer to tempered altruism (table 14.3).

The remitter may not have an intention to return, but maintains the family home. The main beneficiaries are those that live there but the remitter may derive an existence value. That is the remitter may gain satisfaction from knowing that the family home is still there, the way it always was. This is different from an option value discussed above where the remitter is seeking to ensure that if a return home becomes necessary there is somewhere to live. The remitter may also send money due to an affinity value. The remitter may gain satisfaction from feeling part of the family or community group to which money is sent. The remitter may also gain satisfaction from the creation of a behest in the form of the family property that will be passed on to the next generation. A somewhat more transactional motive relates to a sense of obligation or repayment of a debt. In as far as family or other networks assisted the remitter to migrate, the remitter may feel some obligation to send money in return. This obligation may also relate to other forms of assistance and the expectations associated with them, and extend beyond the actual sum of money advanced to support the original migration.

From the above, it is easy to see that remitters may have a mixture of motives. There are a few others that are worth mentioning. These are inertia, indecision and uncertainty. Economists tend to assume away decision costs but remitters who have been sending money for an extended period may continue to do so because of a failure to take a decision to stop (that is, due to inertia). Having got into the habit of sending money, the remitter does so without reassessing if this is the most appropriate action to take. The remitter may also be indecisive, in that consideration is given as to whether to stop but no decision is taken. This may be fuelled by the uncertainties faced by the remitters on questions such as whether they will or will not be able to stay in the host country and hence, what is the best course of action to follow.

Having discussed motives and decision making, we need to distinguish between the motives that guide the remitters and the ends served by the remittances. Remitters may be motivated to different degrees by altruism, self interest, family, community or other affinities/obligations. There could also be cases of indecision and inertia. The ends being served include: immediate and longer term consumption, repayment of loans or other obligations, long or short term savings, insurance, the preservation/accumulation of physical, financial, human, social and other forms of capital, creation of behests and status values, the preservation of reputation and the conservation of option or existence values. Remittances, as I have considered them, are not simply transfers; they may include market transactions. Remitters may, for example, send money to look after business on their own account. Quite apart from such transactions, remittances may have a quid pro quo element. These include gifts or transfers of market values that are tied to the fulfilment of obligations but which are not conducted within a strict market framework for example: the completion of tasks at home, the pay back for services previously or currently rendered or indeed for the financing of the original migration. It should also be noted that the flow of funds may be mediated through formal, informal, legal or illegal mechanisms.

A TYPOLOGY OF MIGRANT REMITTERS

In developing a typology of migrants (table 14.2), my concern is not primarily with individual migrants or the original intention of the migrant. I recognize that migration is a fluid process and that there are various cycles of migration. Over their life time remitters will move from one category to another. A migrant may leave home with one intention and subsequently change. I am concerned with the conduct of migrants as a group. Thus, at any given time there will be migrants who fall into all the categories that I identify. In presenting the types of migrants, I discuss how the circumstances faced by each group relate to the issues or willingness to remit and the motives of remitters discussed above. Given the complexity of these issues, it is not possible to provide a discussion that relates each group to each of the issues. In the paragraphs that follow, I consider ten different types of migrants.

The contract workers. These are persons who travel to the host country to carry out a specific job with a specified employer. Here I am referring to cases such as the United States and Canadian farm work programmes where the worker has very few degrees of freedom. For many of these workers from the Caribbean, remittances are part of the contract and accommodation is often provided. Other than these restrictions the contract workers can be seen, in essence, as a subset of the migrant workers discussed below. They have been singled out because they are such a well known group within some Caribbean countries.

The migrant workers. These persons leave home to seek temporary residence in the host country, with a view to seeking employment and then return home. Like contract workers, migrant workers may be employed on a fixed term or to a particular project. The distinction I make (regardless of the terminology used in different countries) is between migrant workers who have greater flexibility over their length of stay and expenditure in the host country and contract workers who have much less flexibility. Although not under contract to remit, migrant workers who are oriented to the home country will tend to send home or return with a large portion of their earned income. The main limit on this is the need for subsistence. Such workers may live very frugally in order to maximize what is sent or taken home. Alternatively, they may be frugal and not immediately remit as much as we would expect, in cases where they adopt the strategy of bringing home goods (consumption, intermediate and capital) as opposed to cash. The timing of their remittances could also vary. If, for example, the interest rates are higher at home or the prices lower they may be inclined to send remittances quickly. If the opposite is true, they may be inclined to save in the host country or spend the money in the host country with a view to bringing home everything in a lump sum or in kind. In remitting it should be remembered that they may be remitting income as well as savings which are to be accumulated or invested.

To illustrate the complexity of the relationships that may be involved in migration and remittances we can consider migrant workers who are at two ends of a spectrum. The first, we would expect to remit a larger proportion of income. They would be very goal oriented; having left for economic reasons, they would be members of a strong family unit with strong ties at home; highly motivated to return within a specified time period, they would be in possession of a secure migration status. Such workers may have gone abroad with the support and assistance of family and are motivated by mutual interest to send remittances home. In contrast, other workers may have general motives; with fewer ties at home, they may have left home with a view to the possibility of overstaying their visa status. They may have taken an individual decision to migrate and may primarily be motivated by self interest in sending home remittances. Some of the latter group of migrants may, over time, shade into the next group.

The permanent migrants. These persons leave their home country with no intention of returning to live. They may still have ties and remit to meet obligations left behind. They may, for example, remit to cover the needs of an aged parent. They would not be remitting primarily to save or invest. They may remit more if those at home become more distressed. Thus higher rates of poverty or higher prices at home would tend to impact on their remittances. Initially, they may feel strong ties of obligation but ultimately there must be a trade off between needs in the home country and needs in the host country. As such, we would expect that the variables in the host country would affect this type of remitter. The remitting pattern of these persons could be affected by whether they visit for vacation regularly. Regular visits might cause them to maintain the upkeep of the family household so as to ensure greater comfort on return visits. Other than such special circumstances, it is expected that remittances would decline over time as the ties of the permanent migrant to the home country diminish.

Never to return migrants. These are persons who have decided that they will never return to their home country. This could be due to some very negative experience, for example, a case of criminal victimization. The never to return migrant may completely cut ties with the home country. This may involve a complete family migration. Alternatively, some ties may remain but these are unlikely to be significant if the migrant has decided not to ever 'set foot' in their home country again. In relation to some global migrations, these migrants abandon their home language, teach their children nothing of their antecedents' heritage and seek to fully integrate into the dominant cultural forms in the host country. We would expect the lowest level of remittances from this group.

The family migrants. For each family there would be one or more person who migrates as a pioneer with the intention to send for the entire family. This phased type of migration could be due to factors such as limited resources, the need for a pioneering or more qualified member to go first, a preference for education of children in the home country, or the presence of aged relatives who wish to remain at home. Remittances, in this case, are likely to flow for an initial period and diminish thereafter as it becomes less and less important to maintain assets in the home country as there are fewer and fewer family members there. The home country variables would be very important especially at the start, but it would be expected that variables such as interest rates would not be very important unless the migrant was very sophisticated in calculating relative returns on savings in the two countries.

The part life migrants. Persons in this group migrated for a limited number of years. At one extreme, this includes the migrant who intends to stay an entire working life but wishes to return home to retire. Alternatively, these are persons who aim to stay just long enough to meet some felt need. This need could relate to acquiring an education, accumulating capital to start a business, building or furnishing a home. An objective could be the education of self or children or the raising of children to an age when they can manage on their own. This category shades over into the migrant worker if the period is very short and into the return migrant if the period is very long. In addition, the category may shade into the part time migrant. An example would be women who migrate to give birth with a view to providing the child with the nationality of the host country. If the migration takes place for the birth of one child or during the period of child bearing this is a part life migration. If there are multiple births involving separate trips abroad, we are getting close to the case below.

The part time migrants. These are persons who spend regular periods often a part of each year in the host country. Within this category are persons who take regular seasonal, for example, summer work in the host country; workers who spend part of the year as the visa permits, those who seek to bolster family income by working part of the year abroad but come home regularly to their family. Nurses are involved in this type of migration, as are persons who work in the domestic sphere. In extreme cases, persons could be described as commuting. This group shades over into the migrant worker.

The return migrants. These persons had at one point in time migrated and either did not have a definite plan to return or may not have intended to return at all. For the latter group something may have changed and a process of remigration took place. For example, during the Thatcher years, many West Indian migrants to Britain became alienated from the system and decided to return home. The variables that may influence a return home may be economic as well as socio-political and cultural. Return migrants are being thought of as persons who spent a long time in the host country. While abroad they may or may not have sent home remittances but on return there is a considerable flow which continues until death if a pension is involved. They are identified as a separate group because their remittances are often in the form of capital assets that are repatriated and, if retired or receiving disability compensation, income in the form of pensions and other benefits. For countries like Jamaica, flows from the latter have been on par with earnings from some traditional exports. The return migrant shades into the part life migrant.

The transnational family members. Arguably there are now transnational families which are in effect taking the decision to build a base in different countries. In economic terms, these families are taking a set of resource allocation discussions that relate to the location of the family and its various members. Based on these decisions, individual family members are able to take advantage of opportunities in different places at different points in their life cycle. This can, for example, facilitate the education of the young and the health care of the old. It is also a good arrangement for families involved in businesses that are engaged in international trade. Within these families we would expect a complex flow of remittances. It is often forgotten that remittances flow both into and out from the Caribbean. Families pay for children to study abroad or assist young persons to migrate. Families 'fall on hard times' while abroad as well, so it is not always the case that the most prosperous members of the family are the ones living outside of the Caribbean. In the past we had the 'town' and 'country' cousins now we have the local and foreign cousins.

The transnational community members. Just as we now have transnational families, we also have transnational communities. There are persons whose social networks now extend beyond national boundaries allowing them to feel at home in two or more countries. Their connections need not be based on kinship and may be due to a range of other affiliations. Like the members of the transnational families, we would expect that their behaviour regarding remittances would be quite complex.

CONCLUSION

Unravelling the complex migrant relationships that underlie the flows of remittances to the Caribbean is not a simple task. Some insight can be gained by considering the factors that dispose migrants to remit, their motives and objectives as well as the categories of migrant into which different types of remitters fall. Table 14.4 illustrates two examples of migrant profiles and related remittance expectations. By clarifying our understanding of the remitter, we improve our ability to identify those variables that are likely to impact most on each type of remitter. Based on this we can then choose variables, build models and predict which coefficients are likely to be the largest and/or most significant. We will also be able to evaluate our data sources and design new surveys for the collection of new data that can assist us in better understanding remittances.

To carry out effective analysis and design policies it is important to know the relative share of the different kind of remitters in the population. If we do not know the share of each type, we are unlikely to have an idea as to which variables will impact most heavily on remittances. Classifying the various types of remitters is thus an important step in developing our analysis and the creation of relevant policies. In the context of social analysis, the typologies are of interest in themselves. They can also play an important role in the fashioning of economic models that seek to make sense of past and future trends in remittances. By exposing the complexities of the migration processes that drive remittance flows these typologies help us to create models that are structured to take on the full range of relevant considerations. Our models are likely to be much less helpful in the absence of a thorough-going analysis of the complex patterns of migration as they relate to the Caribbean region.

Table 14.1: Caribbean international circulation

1) Transient or Shuttle Migrants			
	Type of Migrant	**Skills Transformation and Occupational Changes**	**Principal Remittance**
(a)	**International Vendors**	Upgrading of entrepreneurial activity	Consumer goods for retail
(b)	**Contract Workers**	Trades or small farming entrepreneurial activity	Cash and personal consumer goods
(c)	**Other Itinerant Labour Migrants**	No significant changes	Cash
(d)	**Business Commuters**	White collar employment to self-employment	Cash and personal consumer goods and commercial goods for manufacturing and retail
2) Settlers for Long Stay Migrants			
	Type of Migrant	**Skills Transformation and Occupational Changes**	**Principal Remittance**
(a)	**Long-term Workers**	Agriculture and trade to blue collar to White collar	Cash and personal consumer goods
(b)	**Dependents**	Blue collar to white collar (managerial)	None
(c)	**Students**	White collar to white collar (professional or para professional)	None
(d)	**Long-term Circulators**	Blue collar to domestic service	Cash and personal consumer goods

Source: *Elizabeth Thomas-Hope (1986)*

Table 14.2: A typology of migrant remitters

Type of Migrant Relationship	Illustration of Type of Migrant Relationship
1. Contract worker	Employed on Farm-worker scheme in US
2. Migrant worker	Goes to Toronto to seek Domestic work
3. Permanent migrant	Migrates after receiving permanent visa
4. Never return migrant	Crime victim with very bad memories
5. Family migrant	Parent goes and then sends for children
6. Part life migrant	Nurse saving to return and buy a home
7. Part time migrant	Teacher who works every summer in US
8. Returning migrant	Retired pensioner back home from London
9. Transnational family	Members located to maximize advantage
10. Transnational community	Brooklyn-Kingston network

Table 14.3: A typology of migrant remitters

Motivation	Example of Remitter's Objective
Pure self interest	Exchange, build up own material values, status values
Enlightened self interest	Secure inheritance, reputation, intends to return home
Mutual interest	Risk sharing, co-insurance
Tempered altruism	Maintain family house, create behest, existence values
Altruism	Help those at home who are poorer
Affinity	Family and community support
Obligation	Loan repayment, give back to those who helped
Indecision/uncertainty	Not sure whether to return home
Inertia	Have always remitted

Table 14.4 Example: migrant profiles and remittance expectations

Migrant Type	Family	Permanent
Intention to Return	No	No
Migration Status	Secure	Secure
Family Status	Spouse Children At Home	Family Well Off
Family Role	Joint Decision to Migrate	No Family Support for Migration
Motivation Type	Mutual Interest	Enlightened Self Interest
Remittance Type	Regular Family Support	Special Occasion Gifts

NOTES

1. For examples of results produced, see works in References by Dillon Alleyne, Mark Figueroa, Claremont Kirton and Georgia McLeod. The effective definition that one uses for remittances depends to a great extent on one's data source. Save for instances when we have been constrained by our data sources, we have tended to include in our discussions of remittances nearly all flows of cash and kind regardless of the purpose for which they are being sent home.
2. For a discussion of this kind of typology see Elisa Mason, 'Forced Migration Studies: Surveying the Reference Landscape,' *Libri*, 50 (2000): 241–251.
3. The Caribbean Diaspora Economy Research Group has cooperated with the Statistical Institute of Jamaica (STATIN) and the Planning Institute of Jamaica (PIOJ) to develop a remittance module that is being administered with the 2006 Jamaican Survey of Living Conditions.
4. Dillon Alleyne, in 'Impact of International Remittances' (2006), shows that, in the Jamaican case, all income quintiles receive remittances and these are not skewed to the lower quintiles.
5. This leaves open the question as to whether remittances are a residual for many migrants or the first call on their income.

REFERENCES

Alleyne, Dillon. 2006. 'Impact of international remittances on poverty and inequality in Jamaica'. Paper presented at *Caribbean Migration: Forced & Free*, University of the West Indies, Mona, June 12th-14th, 2006.

Alleyne, Dillion, Claremont Kirton and Mark Figueroa. 'Macroeconomic determinants of migrant remittances to Caribbean countries: Panel unit roots and co-integration'. *Journal of Developing Areas 41 (2): 137-53.*

Alleyne, Dillon, Georgia McLeod, Claremont Kirton and Mark Figueroa. Forthcoming. 'Short-run macroeconomic determinants of remittance flows to Jamaica 1983.1-2001.4'. *Applied Economics Letters.*

Kirton, Claremont. 2005. 'Remittances: The experiences of the English-speaking Caribbean'. In *Beyond small change: Making migrant remittances count*, eds. Donald F. Terry and Steven. IAOB, Washington D.C.

R.Wilson, 261-94. Washington D.C. Inter-American Development Bank (IADB).

Kirton, C., Dillon Alleyne and Mark Figueroa. Forthcoming. 'The determinants of migrant remittances: The Caricom experience'. In *Migration, Diaspora and the Global Caribbean Economy*, eds. Keith Nurse and Michele Reis. In preparation, 2008.

Mason, Elisa. 2000. 'Forced migration studies: Surveying the reference landscape'. *Libri* 50, 4: 241–51.

Meissner, Doris. 1992. 'Managing migrations'. *Foreign Policy* 86: 66-83.

Thomas Hope, Elizabeth M. 1986. 'Transients and settlers: Varieties of Caribbean migrants and the socio-economic implications of their return'. *International Migration* 24, 3: 559-71.

Walters, William H. 2000. 'Types and patterns of later-life migration'. *Geografiska Annaler. Series B, Human Geography* 82, 3: 129-47.

15

THE REMITTANCE PROFILE OF JAMAICAN IMMIGRANTS

RANSFORD W. PALMER

INTRODUCTION

The flow of remittances from immigrants abroad is an important source of foreign exchange for Jamaica. Each year this flow reflects the cumulative impact of past migration. The chapter develops a profile of the remittances of those who migrated over the previous ten years, using data for the period 1975 to 2000. It also attempts to assess how economic conditions in the United States and changing interest and exchange rates in Jamaica may affect the profile. Finally, the chapter examines the impact of the flow of remittances on economic growth. The results show that immigrants begin to have a significant net positive impact on the flow of remittances around the fifth year of migration; that rising interest rates and falling exchange rates have had a positive and negative impact on remittance flows, respectively; and that the annual flow of remittances had little or no impact on aggregate capital formation and the rate of real economic growth.

Remittances[1] from immigrants[2] abroad account for a significant share of foreign exchange for Caribbean countries. This chapter focuses on Jamaica, a country with a high dependence on the inflow of remittances from its nationals abroad. In recent years, there has been a plethora of studies examining the impact of remittances on the economies of origin countries but none so far has examined the remittance profile of the immigrants. This profile is important because it indicates how long it takes an immigrant cohort to begin to have a positive impact on the annual flow of remittances to its home country.

~ 258 ~

The migration process is driven largely by the desire to maximize household[3] income. In Jamaica where average household income is one tenth of that in the United States, this desire has produced one of the highest emigration rates in the world. The migration process is circular in character with the flow of remittances operating as a vital link between the migrant and the members of his household left behind. Remittances finance the consumption of these household members as well as their ultimate reunification abroad. Remittances not only enhance the welfare of family members left behind; they provide confirmation of a better life abroad and therefore a strong incentive to migrate. When the household is reunited abroad, the circle is closed and remittances cease. Thus the flow of remittances is an indicator of the existence incomplete migration circles.

By 2000 the flow of remittances had become the second largest share of Jamaica's foreign exchange earnings, behind receipts from tourism (See figure 15.1). The size of this inflow influences the national exchange rate and its dependability improves the credit rating of the government in international capital markets.

Figure 15.1: Shares of tourist receipts (TR), migrant remittances (MR) and bauxite and alumina exports (BA) in GDP, 1970-2000.

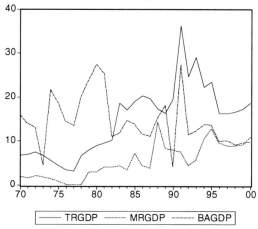

Exports (BA) in GDP, 1970-2000.

The source for figure 15.1 is as follows: Based on data from Statistical Abstracts of the Statistical Institute of Jamaica; International Monetary Fund Country Reports; and the Bureau of Labor Statistics of the U.S. Department of Labor.

PROFIT OUTFLOW VERSUS IMMIGRANT REMITTANCES

In the broader context of the movement of capital and labour, Jamaica, like most Caribbean countries, is a net exporter of labour and a net importer of capital.

Table 15.1: Jamaica: remittances from migrants, foreign direct investment and outflow of investment income, 1992-1999 (US$ millions)

Years	Foreign Direct Investment	Remittances from Migrants	Outflow of Investment Income
1992	142.4	157.7	365.3
1993	77.9	187.2	305.3
1994	129.7	457.9	448.8
1995	147.4	582.3	507.0
1996	183.7	635.5	359.0
1997	203.3	642.3	424.1
1998	369.1	659.2	443.7
1999	523.7	679.4	474.6

Source: *International Monetary Fund, Balance of Payments Statistics Yearbook, 2000.*

Just as remittances flow back from migrating labour, investment income flows from foreign investments in the Caribbean to the United States and other countries. Table 15.1 shows that throughout the 1990s, much of the inflow of remittances from Jamaican migrants was offset by the repatriation of profits from capital. Capital flows to the Caribbean for higher rates of return and labor flows to the United States for higher wages. Theoretically, equilibrium is reached when the rate of return on both imported capital and exported labor is equal. Because in reality capital is much more mobile than labor, the adjustment process that is consistent with economic growth would require a larger inflow of foreign direct investment.

THE REMITTANCE PROFILE

While numerous studies have examined the flow of remittances over time (Lucas 2006, Özden and Schiff 2006, Ratha 2003), no study has looked at the contribution of previous migration to current remittance flows. This chapter develops a remittance profile by looking at the impact of past migration of one to ten years on the flow of remittances. Table 15.3 contains the data for migration for the years 1965 to 2000 and remittances for the years 1975 to 2000. An attempt is also made to estimate the impact of domestic interest and exchange rates on the flow of remittances and the impact of these remittances on economic growth.

Table 15.2: Data for regression

Year	Migration	Remittances US$ million	Year	Migration	Remittances US$ million
1965	1,837		1984	19,822	80.4
1966	2,743		1985	18,924	153.2
1967	10,483		1986	19,595	111.6
1968	17,470		1987	23,148	117.2
1969	16,947		1988	20,966	436.5
1970	15,033		1989	24,523	299.5
1971	14,571		1990	25,013	299.5
1972	13,427		1991	23,828	159.0
1973	9,538		1992	18,915	157.7
1974	12,692	33.7	1993	17,241	187.2
1975	11,076	22.7	1994	14,349	457.9
1976	9,026	2.0	1995	16,398	582.3
1977	11,501	15.1	1996	19,089	635.5
1978	19,265	15.2	1997	17,840	642.3
1979	19,714	70.0	1998	15,146	659.2
1980	18,920	81.7	1999	14,733	679.4
1981	24,746	123.3	2000	16,000	814.0
1982	17,662	134.5			
1983	19,497	94.7			

Source: *U.S. Department of Homeland Security; I.M.F. Balance of Payments Yearbook; Statistical Institute of Jamaica, Statistical Abstracts.*

The following distributed lag equation is chosen as the model for the impact of past migration on the flow of remittances:

(1) $R = a + bM + \lambda b_1 M_{-1} + \lambda^2 b_2 M_{-2} \ldots\ldots\ldots + \lambda^{10} b_{10} M_{-10} + u$

where R is the annual flow of remittances, M annual migration to the United States, λ the weighted impact of migration on remittances, and u the error term.[4] The Koyck transformation of this equation reduces the parameters to be estimated to two:

(2) $R_t = a(1-\lambda) + \beta M_t + \lambda R_{t-1} + u$

where   is assumed to be the diminishing weight of the impact of the independent variable, $0 \, d'' \, \lambda < 1$. The parameter β is the impact multiplier which measures the instantaneous impact of a change in migration (M) on remittances (R) and the equilibrium or long run multiplier $(\beta/1-\lambda)$ measures the change in the equilibrium value of R due to a marginal change in M. The results of the OLS estimate of equation 2 are as follows:

$R_t = -.92777 - 0.004811 \, M_t + 1.007975 \, R_{t-1}.$ Adj. $R^2 = 0.84$

(-0.99)   (11.53)   [t statistics are in parentheses]

Contrary to the assumption of diminishing weight for λ, these results show that λ is greater than one (1.007975), indicating that the farther back in time we go the larger the impact of past migration on the current flow of remittances. Although the instantaneous impact (β) of migration is negative, the long run multiplier $(\beta/1-\lambda)$ is positive.

Since the purpose of this chapter is to develop a profile of the impact of migration over the previous ten years on the flow of remittances for the 26-year period from 1975 to 2000, the regression analysis necessarily includes migration data going back to 1965. (See Appendix Table B). The profile that emerges from the impact of past migration on remittances over the 26-year period is depicted by the value of λb, as shown in table 15.3 and graphed in figure 15.2. The results show that the impact of migration on the flow of remittances fluctuated around an upward trend, starting negatively in the first four years and rising to higher peaks in subsequent years. This suggests that it takes four to five years for an immigrant group to establish itself in the United States before it begins.

But the longer they stay in the United States the higher their household incomes will be to make a net positive impact on the flow of remittances. This does not mean, however, that money is not sent home by some immigrants in the first few years; it may simply reflect that fact that the amount sent back by some may be more than offset by the drawing down of Jamaican assets by others to cover migration and settlement costs. It may also reflect the fact that during the early years, many immigrants allocate a large share of their income to improving their human capital to acquire job security and to enhance their income. Consequently, they may have little left over to remit back home. and the greater their ability to remit money to close relatives left behind, hence the rising trend depicted in the graph. This is consistent with the findings of Barry Chiswick (1980) who described a U-shaped occupational path for new immigrants. On the left hand side of the U there is occupational downgrading and on the right a restoration or improvement in occupational status after a period of investment in education and training.

Table 15.3: Regression results

Independent Variables	Coefficients b	t-Statistics	Λ	λb
M	-0.013539	-0.95		-0.013539
M1	-0.004209	-0.24	1.007975	-0.004242
M2	-0.000351	-0.02	1.016013	-0.000356
M3	-0.004679	-0.29	1.024116	-0.004791
M4	0.003674	0.23	1.032283	0.003792
M5	0.008598	0.56	1.040516	0.008946
M6	-0.005220	-0.31	1.048814	-0.005474
M7	0.015414	0.95	1.057178	0.016295
M8	-0.004086	-0.24	1.065609	-0.004354
M9	0.011636	0.76	1.074107	0.012498
M10	0.021778	1.73	1.082673	0.023578

Adj. R^2 = .53

The remittance profile of the immigrant may also be influenced by economic conditions in the United States. To test this, actual migration is adjusted for the unemployment rate in the United States by dividing the actual migration data for each year by the corresponding index of unemployment for that year. The year 1963 is used as the base year with an unemployment index of 100. Thus as the unemployment rate falls, the index falls and the adjusted migration gets larger than the actual. The opposite is true when the unemployment rate rises. A lower unemployment rate is interpreted to mean that a given volume of actual migration will have a larger impact on remittances because of greater opportunities for employment at higher wages. (See data for regression in Appendix Table B).

Figure 15.2: Remittance profile

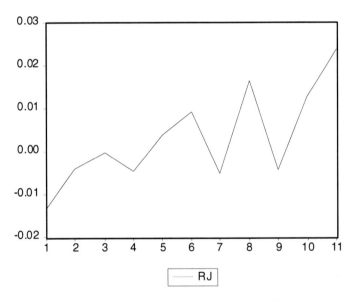

The following is the OLS estimate of equation 2 with migration adjusted for the unemployment rate in the United States:

$$R_t = .0748 + 0.001439M + 0.9910R_{t-1}$$

    (0.27)   (9.21)   Adj. R^2 = 0.83

                  t statistics are in parentheses

Because $\lambda < 1$, the remittance impact will diminish marginally as we go further into the past but the long run multiplier $(\beta/1-\lambda)$ will be positive since â is positive. The regression results for the unemployment adjusted migration data for equation 1 are shown in table 15.4 and figure 15.3.

With unemployment-adjusted migration, the remittance profile is generally above the profile for actual migration as shown in figure 15.3. Both measures roughly parallel each other except that the slope of the trend line for the adjusted profile is flatter and adjusted migration is depicted to have a positive impact on remittances from year 1.

Table 15.4: Regression results for unemployment adjusted migration.

Independent Variables	Coefficients b	t-Statistics	λ	λb
M	0.018278	1.22		0.018278
M1	0.007374	0.39	0.9910	0.007307
M2	0.004252	0.24	0.9820	0.004175
M3	0.007380	0.42	0.9732	0.007182
M4	0.013260	0.79	0.9644	0.012787
M5	0.006481	0.38	0.9558	0.006194
M6	-0.001049	-0.06	0.9472	-0.000993
M7	0.021636	1.28	0.9386	0.020307
M8	0.001722	0.10	0.9302	0.001601
M9	0.003139	0.18	0.9218	0.002893
M10	0.013517	1.09	0.9135	0.012347

Adj. R-squared = 0.40

In both graphs, the impact of migration of remittances rises sharply in the eighth year. The fact that migrants who leave today will have their greatest impact on the flow of remittances eight years later suggests one of two things: either that the close relatives left behind may not begin to receive significant support until the eighth year or that the funds remitted at this time may be used to finance the reunification of the household abroad.[5] Although the data used in this study do not allow us to look beyond year 10, logic suggests that as the number of close relatives left

Figure 15.3: Remittance profile with actual (RJ) and unemployment-adjusted (RJA) migration.

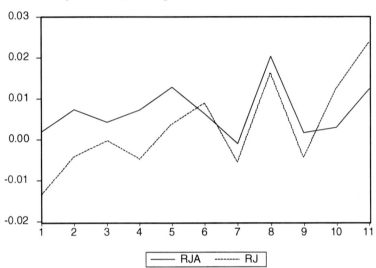

behind declines either through death or reunification of the family abroad, the flow of remittances from each immigrant cohort will decline. In this regard, the adjusted migration impact is a little more realistic since its rise in year 10 is lower than in year 8. But in order for the flow of remittances to be sustained, there needs to be a continuous outflow of migrants. But this can not be guaranteed. A tighter US immigration policy together with rising unemployment rates could reduce the number of immigrants and lower the flow of remittances. If US immigration policy continues to embody the principle of family re-unification which allows close relatives of immigrants to receive visas, some migration would continue. But in the unusual event of a termination of such policy the effect on the flow of remittances would be delayed since the flow is disproportionately influenced by past migration.

THE REMITTANCE IMPACT OF DOMESTIC VARIABLES

The flow of remittances may also be influenced by the reaction of immigrants abroad to changes interest and exchange rates in their country of origin.

INTEREST RATES

Immigrants by their very nature are forward looking people. It is therefore reasonable to assume that they will be sensitive to anything that might change the present value of the future stream of their remittances. In this regard, they may view a rise in the interest rate in their country of origin above that which prevailed in the year of their migration as reducing the present value of future remittances. As a result, they are likely to respond by countering that reduction with an increase in their current remittances. Thus although all immigrant groups face the same current interest rate in any given year, each group reacts to it differently, depending upon the relationship of that interest rate to the interest rate in the year of migration. It follows therefore that if the current interest rate is the same as that in the year of migration, its impact on the flow of remittances is expected to be small or zero. Since interest rates have risen steadily over the 25-year period (See Table C in the Appendix), for most immigrants, current interest rates have generally exceeded the interest rates in the year of their migration. Interest rates are therefore expected to have a positive relationship to the flow of remittances as the following regression estimate of the model in equation 2 indicates:

$$R = -21.85 + 3.55IR + 0.932R_1$$
$$(-.052)\ (1.59)\ (9.62)\ \text{Adj. } R^2 = .85\ \text{t stats in parentheses.}$$

Since $\hat{a}$ is positive and $\lambda < 1$, the long term multiplier impact $(\beta/1-\lambda)$ of interest rates on remittances is positive but diminishing. The diminishing character of this impact may be observed in the results from the distributed lag model of equation 1 in table 15.5 and figure 15.4 where the peak of each subsequent remittance impact (λb) is lower than the previous one. This suggests that the longer the immigrant resides abroad the less important will be the need to preserve the present value of the future flow of traditional remittances. For these earlier immigrants, the transformation of their remittance flows into profitable investments will become their main objective.

Table 15.5: Regression results

Independent Variables	Coefficients b	T stats	λ	λb
IR	-8.246	-1.56		-8.246
IR1	-6.718	-1.51	0.932	-6.261
IR2	15.332	1.89	0.868	13.308
IR3	3.253	0.30	0.809	2.631
IR4	-4.965	-0.48	0.754	-3.743
IR5	17.616	1.49	0.703	12.384
IR6	-1.293	0.71	0.569	5.291
IR7	-12.394	-1.58	0.610	-13.050
IR8	9.30	0.71	0.569	5.291
IR9	21.952	1.53	0.530	11.634
IR10	3.765	0.25	0.494	1.859

Adj. R^2 = 0.92

EXCHANGE RATES

The analysis of the impact of exchange rates on remittances follows the same path as the analysis of interest rates. Again the assumption is that the immigrant is interested in preserving the present value of a future stream of remittances. Over the period between 1970 and 2000, the exchange rate of the Jamaican dollar fell sharply, meaning that a given US dollar amount of remittances generated a larger amount of Jamaican dollars. At the same time the inflation rate rose sharply, reducing the purchasing power of the Jamaican currency (See table C in Appendix). To the extent that the immigrants suffer from money illusion, that is to say that they see only that larger amount of Jamaican currency resulting from depreciation and not the declining purchasing power resulting from inflation, they may to reduce the amount of their remittances. If this is true, the depreciation of the currency will have had a negative impact on the flow of remittances. The following results of the estimate of the impact of the real exchange rate (ER) on remittance, using the model of equation 2, suggest that this may be the case:

R = 239.55 − 22.19 ER + 0.870 R$_1$
    (2.41) (-2.21) (8.52)   Adj R^2 = 0.86 [t stats in parentheses]

Because the instantaneous multiplier β is negative and λ <1, the long run multiplier β/1-λ is negative. An estimate of the exchange rate impact using the distributed lag model in equation 1 produces the results in table 15.6 and figure 15.6.

From figure 15.6, it is clear that remittances were negatively impacted by the declining real exchange rate in the first four years after migration. Despite the modest positive impact for the earlier immigrants, the overall the impact was negative. The fact that the remittances of recent immigrants were far more negatively impacted than those of earlier immigrants suggests that the earlier immigrants were better able to assess the role of inflation and adjusted their remittances accordingly. Over the years, the overall negative impact of real exchange rates may well have been neutralized by the positive impact of interest rates, allowing flow of remittances continued to grow.

Figure 15.4

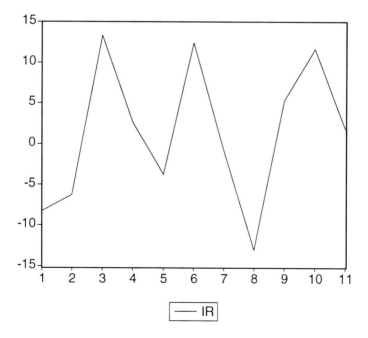

Table 15.6: Regression results

Independent Variables	Coefficients b	T – stat	λ	λb
ER	-50.43	-3.10		-50.43
ER1	-21.83	-1..22	.870	-18.99
ER2	-11.33	-0.61	.756	-8.56
ER3	-5.62	-0.30	.658	-3.69
ER4	10.27	0.56	.572	5.87
ER5	10.77	0.58	.498	5.36
ER6	2.00	0.11	.433	0.86
ER7	4.50	0.25	.377	1.69
ER8	-13.44	-0.80	.328	-4.40
ER9	7.28	0.73	.285	2.07
ER10	-28.60	-2.39	.248	-7.09

Adj. R^2 = 0.65

Figure 15.5: The Remittance impact of exchange rates (ER).

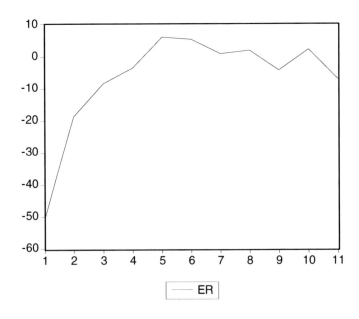

THE IMPACT OF REMITTANCES ON ECONOMIC GROWTH

The long term transformation of remittances from a source of consumption financing for family members left behind into a source of financing for capital projects that benefit a larger number of people is critical for economic development. When remittances become capital flows both the immigrants abroad and their country of origin benefit. The return on such capital flows will augment the income of the immigrants and the capital projects financed will enhance domestic economic growth.

The schema in figure 15.7 illustrates what could happen to economic growth if a larger share of remittances were allocated to financing capital investment. A reduction in the share of remittances financing consumption (C) from **a** to **a** increases the rate of economic growth (G) from *d* to *d* because a reduction in C is assumed to increase the share of remittances financing investment.

Over the three decades between 1970 and 1999 remittances from Jamaican immigrants grew twenty-five fold, from US$26.9 million to US$ 679.4 million, while GDP in constant (1990) prices grew by only 28 per cent, from J$ 25.9 billion to J$ 31.2 billion. When GDP in constant prices is converted from Jamaican dollars into U.S. dollars there is a sharp decline from US$ 31.0 billion to US$ 798 million due to the precipitous decline in the exchange rate of the Jamaican dollar. That the small portion of remittances that financed the construction of homes and the establishment of small retail businesses had little impact on capital formation in the country as a whole is illustrated in the following results of the regression of remittances (REM) on real GDP and on the share of gross capital formation (GCF) in GDP:

(i) Real GDP = 26151.64 + 9.43 REM
             (46.23)   (5.12)   Adj. R-squared = 0.46

(ii) GCF/GDP = 20.61 + 0.0159 REM
             (16.17) (3.83)   Adj. R-squared = 0.32

             t statistics are in parentheses

In both equations the impact of remittances is statistically significant but very small. In equation (ii), a US$ 1 million of remittances added only .01 to the share of gross capital formation in GDP.

While the sending country has no control over U.S. immigration policy and U.S. unemployment rate, it could influence capital flows from its nationals abroad by borrowing money from them with special bond issues. The success of such borrowing will depend upon the confidence of the immigrants in the ability of the government to meet its debt obligations. At the same time, the ability of the government to meet these obligations is enhanced by the stability of the flow of traditional remittances. The earmarking of borrowed money for socially desirable projects may arouse in potential lenders a desire to participate in the development of their homeland, a desire that is not effectively expressed in their traditional remittances.

The remittance profile suggests that there is potential for every immigrant who has been away for seven or more years to be a supplier of capital to his home country. However, the transformation of migrant remittances into a flow of capital will not be driven by patriotism alone. First and foremost, the investment must be safe and the rate of return at least as high as that available elsewhere. In other words, the cost of borrowing from the Diaspora is not likely to be any cheaper than the cost of other foreign borrowing.

CONCLUSION

The remittance profile of Jamaican immigrants shows that the first major impact of migration on the flow of remittances occurs somewhere between the fourth and fifth year after migration with an even larger impact in the eighth year. This suggests that it takes each year's immigrant group that long to establish itself and to raise its income to a level that allows it to send large amounts of money back home either to finance consumption or to assist with the reunification of the household abroad. It is reasonable to expect that when the number of close family members left behind is reduced either by reunification abroad or by death, the flow of remittances will decline.

Based upon the assumption that immigrants wish to maintain the present value of the future flow of remittances, changes in domestic interest rate and the exchange rate are shown to have had a positive and negative impact, respectively over the period studied. These two influences may well have cancelled each other out, leaving other powerful forces to determine the long run equilibrium of the flow of remittances. As families are reunited abroad the flow of remittances will inevitably decline. But it is in this post-family-reunification period that the potential for transforming these remittances into capital flows appears to be greatest. If immigrants can identify attractive opportunities for investing their savings, they would enhance the rate of growth of the Jamaican economy.

Figure 15.6: Schema of the relationship between remittances and economic growth.

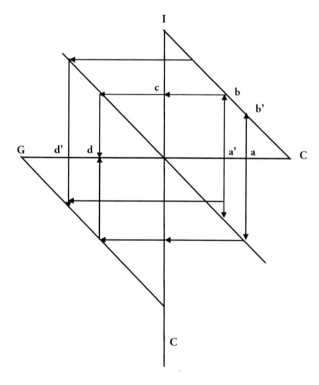

I = Share of total remittances financing investment; C = Share of total remittances financing consumption; G = Rate of economic growth.

NOTES

1. Remittances are defined as private current transfers for the purpose of this chapter. Dilip Ratha has pointed out that current transfers as presented in the balance of payments underestimate the total flow of remittances because it excludes food, clothing, and other supplies sent home by immigrants and the wages and salaries of non-resident workers. Since this study focuses on permanent residents, remittances are regarded as a portion of their wages and salaries. 'Workers' Remittances: An Important and Stable Source of External Development Finance,' *Global Development Finance 2003*, pp. 157-175.

2. For the purpose of this study, immigrants are permanent residents. They are regarded as migrating upon receipt of their immigrant visa. This means that many may have physically left their home country years before having received their visa. During this time many will have been able to work with a special work visa. These include students and workers with special skills.

3. See Ransford W. Palmer, *Pilgrim from the Sun: West Indian Migration to America*. New York: Twayne Publishers, 1995, pp. 59-63 for a discussion of this view.

4. See M. Dutta, Econometeric Methods. Cincinnati; South-Western Publishing Co., 1975 for a discussion of distributed lags.

5. Between 1998 and 2003, immediate relatives of U.S. citizens accounted for 54 per cent of Jamaican immigrants and 47 per cent of immigrants from the Dominican Republic, (Immigration Statistics, U.S. Department of Homeland Security). It usually take five to seven years for an immigrant to gain citizenship.

REFERENCES

Dutta, M. *Econometric Methods*. Cincinnati: South-Western Publishing Co.

Chiswick, Barry R., 1980. 'Immigrant Earnings Pattern by Sex, Race, and Ethnic Groupings,' *Monthly Labor Review 103*.

Lucas, Robert E. B., 2006. *International Migration and Economic Development*. Cheltenham, U.K. Edward Elgar.

Özden, Çaglar and Maurice Schiff. 2006. *International Migration, Remittances & The Brain Drain*. Washington, D.C. The World Bank.

Palmer, Ransford W., 1995. *Pilgrims from the Sun: West Indian Migration to America*. New York: Twayne Publishers.

APPENDIX

Table A: *Jamaica: tourist receipts; migrant remittances; bauxite and alumina exports, 1970-2000. (US$ million)*

Year	Tourist Receipts	Migrant Remittances	Bauxite and Alumina Exports
1970	95.5	26.9	223.5
1971	115.8	27.0	229.8
1972	126.6	35.5	220.9
1973	127.4	34.7	87.5
1974	133.3	33.9	515.9
1975	128.5	22.7	536.1
1976	105.6	2.0	427.5
1977	104.5	15.1	438.2
1978	148.2	15.2	446.5
1979	194.3	70.0	577.0
1980	241.7	81.7	735.9
1981	284.3	123.3	760.3
1982	337.8	134.5	363.2
1983	399.2	94.7	251.8
1984	406.6	80.4	350.4
1985	406.8	153.2	292.9
1986	516.0	111.6	294.5
1987	595.0	117.2	334.0
1988	525.0	436.5	465.8
1989	593.0	299.5	653.7
1990	740.0	299.5	653.7
1991	764.0	159.0	357.5
1992	858.0	157.7	575.5
1993	942.0	187.2	400.4
1994	973.0	457.9	605.3
1995	1,068.5	582.3	620.0
1996	1,092.2	635.5	665.0
1997	1,168.0	642.3	729.1
1998	1,220.0	659.2	671.0
1999	1,276.0	679.4	709.0
2000	1,395.0	814.0	734.0

Source: *Bureau of Labour Statistics, U.S. Department of Labour; Statistical Institute of Jamaica, Statistical Abstracts; International Monetary Fund, Country Reports.*

Table B: Jamaica: remittance (1975-2000) and migration(1965-2000) adjusted for US unemployment rates

	R	M	M-1	M-2	M-3	M-4	M-5	M-6	M-7	M-8	M-9	M-10
1965		2,138										
1966		3,913	2,138									
1967		15,326	3,913	2,138								
1968		26,918	15,326	3,913	2,138							
1969		28,434	26,918	15,326	3,913	2,138						
1970		21,978	28,434	26,918	15,326	3,913	2,138					
1971		14,078	21,978	28,434	26,918	15,326	3,913	2,138				
1972		13,202	14,078	21,978	28,434	26,918	15,326	3,913	2,138			
1973		11,103	13,202	14,078	21,978	28,434	26,918	15,326	3,913	2,138		
1974		14,196	11,103	13,202	14,078	21,978	28,434	26,918	15,326	3,913	2,138	
1975	22.7	7,794	14,196	11,103	13,202	14,078	21,978	28,434	26,918	15,236	3,913	2,138
1976	2.0	6,517	7,794	14,196	11,103	13,202	14,078	21,978	28,434	26,918	15,236	3,913
1977	15.1	8,746	6,517	7,794	14,196	11,103	13,202	14,078	21,978	28,434	26,918	15,236
1978	15.2	17,170	8,746	6,517	7,794	14,196	11,103	13,202	14,078	21,978	28,434	26,918
1979	70.0	19,047	17,170	8,746	6,517	7,794	14,196	11,103	13,202	14,078	21,978	28,434
1980	81.7	17,167	19,047	17,170	8,746	6,517	7,794	14,196	11,103	13,202	14,078	21,978
1981	123.3	18,818	17,167	19,047	17,170	8,746	6,517	7,794	14,196	11,103	13,202	14,078
1982	134.5	11,712	18,818	17,167	19,047	17,170	8,746	6,517	7,794	14,196	11,103	13,202
1983	94.7	10,689	11,712	18,818	17,167	19,047	17,170	8,746	6,517	7,794	14,196	11,103
1984	80.4	14,128	10,689	11,712	18,818	17,167	19,047	17,170	8,746	6,517	7,794	14,196
1985	153.2	14,784	14,128	10,689	11,712	18,818	17,167	19,047	17,170	8,746	6,517	7,794

	R	M	M-1	M-2	M-3	M-4	M-5	M-6	M-7	M-8	M-9	M-10
1986	111.6	16,676	14,784	14,128	10,689	11,712	18,818	17,167	19,047	17,170	8,746	6,517
1987	117.2	20,006	16,676	14,784	14,128	10,689	11,712	18,818	17,167	19,047	17,170	8,746
1988	436.5	20,966	20,006	16,676	14,784	14,128	10,689	11,712	18,818	17,167	19,047	17,170
1989	299.5	25,895	20,966	20,006	16,676	14,784	14,128	10,689	11,712	18,818	17,167	19,047
1990	299.5	22,293	25,895	20,966	20,006	16,676	14,784	14,128	10,689	11,712	18,818	17,167
1991	159.0	18,615	22,293	25,895	20,966	20,006	16,676	14,784	14,128	10,689	11,712	18,818
1992	157.7	14,777	18,615	22,293	25,895	20,966	20,006	16,676	14,784	14,128	10,689	11,712
1993	187.2	14,901	14,777	18,615	22,293	25,895	20,966	20,006	16,676	14,784	14,128	10,689
1994	457.9	13,639	14,901	14,777	18,615	22,293	25,895	20,966	20,006	16,676	14,784	14,128
1995	582.3	16,698	13,639	14,901	14,777	18,615	22,293	25,895	20,966	20,006	16,676	14,784
1996	635.5	19,438	16,698	13,639	14,901	14,777	18,615	22,293	25,895	20,966	20,006	16,676
1997	642.3	19,203	19,438	16,698	13,639	14,901	14,777	18,615	22,293	25,895	20,966	20,006
1998	659.2	18,768	19,203	19,438	16,698	13,639	14,901	14,777	18,615	22,293	25,985	20,966
1999	679.4	19,539	18,768	19,203	19,438	16,698	13,639	14,901	14,777	18,615	22,293	25,985
2000	814.0	22,824	19,539	18,768	19,203	19,438	16,698	13,639	14,901	14,777	18,615	22,293

Table C: Jamaica treasury bill rate; exchange rate; consumer price index; and real exchange rate, 1965–2000

Years	Treasury Bill Rate	Nominal Exchange Rate (J$ per US$)	Consumer Price Index (1990 Prices)	Real Exchange Rate
1965	4.46	.710	3.3	21.5
1966	4.46	.710	3.5	20.2
1967	4.68	.831	3.7	22.4
1968	4.47	.839	3.9	21.5
1969	3.52	.833	4.1	20.3
1970	4.03	.836	4.7	17.7
1971	3.81	.784	5.0	15.6
1972	4.32	.852	5.3	16.0
1973	5.54	.909	6.2	14.6
1974	7.19	.909	7.9	11.5
1975	6.94	.909	9.3	9.7
1976	7.23	.909	10.2	8.91
1977	7.21	.909	11.3	8.0
1978	8.26	1.695	15.3	11.0
1979	9.25	1.781	19.7	9.0
1980	9.97	1.781	25.1	7.0
1981	9.83	1.781	28.3	6.2
1982	8.61	1.781	30.1	5.9
1983	12.38	3.278	33.6	9.7
1984	13.29	4.930	42.9	11.5
1985	19.03	5.480	54.0	10.1
1986	20.88	5.480	62.1	8.8
1987	18.16	5.500	66.2	8.3
1988	18.50	5.480	71.7	7.6
1989	19.10	6.480	82.0	7.9
1990	26.21	8.038	100.0	8.0
1991	25.56	21.493	151.1	14.2
1992	34.36	22.185	267.0	8.3
1993	28.85	32.475	327.0	9.9
1994	42.98	33.202	441.6	7.5
1995	27.65	39.616	529.5	7.5

Years	Treasury Bill Rate	Nominal Exchange Rate (J$ per US$)	Consumer Price Index (1990 Prices)	Real Exchange Rate
1996	37.95	34.865	669.3	5.2
1997	18.10	35.400	733.9	4.8
1998	28.00	36.580	797.2	4.6
1999	21.70	39.14	844.9	4.6
2000	18.00	43.14	913.7	4.7

Source: *IMF International Financial Statistics; Statistics Institute of Jamaica.*

16

MIGRATION AND THE SMALL FARMING EXPERIENCE:
The Rio Grande Valley, Jamaica
AMANI ISHEMO

INTRODUCTION

The relationship between population mobility and farming activity is complex and has been the focus of numerous studies. This chapter examines this relationship from a small area perspective using the Rio Grande Valley as a case study. The Rio Grande Valley is an environmentally sensitive area of Jamaica, characterized by landslides, flooding and heavy rainfall, which occur regularly during the year. Despite population decline in many communities and frequently experienced environmental hazards, farming has survived and continued to expand. Several studies have alluded to various soil conservation strategies of farmers, small scale farmers' ability to adapt to environmental hazards and changing external market demands for agricultural commodities, as important reasons for the persistence of small farming in the area. However, a frequently overlooked factor is the rate of population mobility in sustaining small scale farming in the area. This study examines the ways in which the process of migration operates in the Rio Grande Valley and the influence of externally derived cash in small farming system.

THE IMPACT OF MIGRATION AND REMITTANCES ON DEVELOPMENT AND AGRICULTURE: A GENERAL PERSPECTIVE

There is increasing consensus among scholars of migration that there is a close relationship between migration and socio-economic development, and in recent years a number of scholars have sought to explain this connection. The work of Thomas-Hope (1999; 2002), Freeman (2000) and Conway (2000) are notable in that respect. The significance of migration to development is also emphasized in the work of Jennings and Clarke (2005) who notes that Latin America and the Caribbean is the largest remittance-receiving region. With 9 per cent of the world's population, the region receives approximately 32 per cent of the world's remittances. According to Lapper (2007), migrant workers sent back more than $62.3 billion to their families in Latin America and the Caribbean region in 2006, a rise of 14 per cent on 2005. He notes that for the fourth successive year, remittances will exceed the combined flows of foreign direct investments and overseas aid into the region.

Many scholars provide an explanation of both the positive and negative impacts of international migration and remittances. Some, like Connell and Conway (2000), note that the development of islands in the Caribbean region cannot be divorced from the influence of international migration. There are two perspectives on the impact of migration and remittances. The first focuses on the negative aspects, such as the unproductive nature of expenditures, the adjustment difficulties encountered by returning migrants and the various problems that return migration and remittances cause. This approach is evident in the work of Shankman (1976), Connell (1980), Brana-Shutes (1982), Rubenstein (1982), Momsen (1986), McKee and Tisdell (1988), Mandle (1996) and Duany (2001).

The general negative implications point to the fact that migration and remittances reinforce the unequal relations between 'satellites' and the 'metropolis' by keeping poor rural families at low levels of productive capacity, through the perpetuation of small and economically marginal farm plots (Shankman 1976; Connell 1980). The consequences of this negative implication for Caribbean agriculture, as identified by Brana-Shute (1982), are a decline in agricultural activity and productivity; the removal of land for cultivation; decreased interest in farming and the resultant half-hearted efforts of those left behind as labourers or overseers; the encouragement of land speculation for housing rather than agricultural production; and the shift from a demand for local produce to preferences for purchases of imported canned goods. This position is also supported by Brierley (1988). Similar research findings on remittance utilization in the Pacific and Caribbean regions suggest that despite a considerable diversity in the use of remittances, their primary use has been for consumption purposes (Connell and Conway 2000).

The work of Conway and Glesne (1986), Gmelch (1987), Thomas-Hope (1993), Brown and Connell (1993), de Souza (1998), and Poirine (1998) offer a more balanced interpretation of the impact of international migration and remittances on development. They question the exaggerated negative analyses and insist on the need for a continued reassessment of the relationship between migration and development in island microstates. Indeed, when viewed in terms of the two different perspectives, migration and remittances should be seen as a double-edged sword. It serves to safeguard, yet also erode, the vitality of the home region. It sustains and improves welfare while at the same time undermines production (Connell and Conway 2000). Other scholars, for example, Petras (1988) and Chaney (1985), view migration as a historically established component of many Caribbean household survival strategies. Rubenstein (1982) acknowledges migration to be a survival strategy without which some households would 'slip over the edge'. For Wood (1981) migration is an integral part of the sustenance strategies the household adopts.

The works of Thomas-Hope (1985, 2002) and Conway (2000) have provided excellent analyses of the implications of migration in the Caribbean. These studies take into consideration the effects of historical factors on the development of these small island states, within the context of the global economic system of which they are a part. In her work, Thomas-Hope has consistently argued that the capital transfers that form part of the migration circuit are essential for the economic viability of a significant number of Caribbean households and communities. This capital makes a major positive contribution to development since, without it, economically viable household populations could not exist above the minimum survival level (Thomas-Hope 1985). On the other hand, she cautiously acknowledges that a negative impact can be realised in situations where there is persistent dependency on externally sourced funds, which, in the long run exacerbates the process of underdevelopment. She further notes that Caribbean development hinges on the extent of this dependence. Conway (2000) further maintains that extra-regional migration and circulation perpetuate hemispheric dependency, but that this is neither new nor is it a debilitating tendency given today's increasingly interdependent, globalizing world.

According to Thomas-Hope (1993), remittances make a major contribution to the rural household economy and, despite common assumptions to the contrary, some remittances do go towards the expansion and upgrading of farms. In this regard, she identifies types of migrants who concentrate on investing in agriculture (Thomas-Hope 1985). She is also of the view that the nature of investments associated with international migration is consistent with both the diverse nature and economic objectives of migration. Migration is also consistent with the character of rural communities, their tradition of multiple household occupations which incorporate agriculture, and with the aims and objectives of migrants, which allow for individual and household achievement.

Another aspect of the study deals with types of migrants and the impact that long-term and short-term emigrants have on their return home. It is felt that migrants, particularly long-term migrants, represent people endowed with human capital. Thus, remittances and return migrants contribute to social and cultural capital accumulation, which in turn strengthens family and communal networks and ties. They not only help to maintain these institutions but also enlarge their social fields of interaction, incorporating them into transnational multi-local networks of support and experiment (Connell and Conway 2000).

On one hand, Griffith (1988) acknowledges that the absence of key individuals (male household heads) from the farming system is usually met by cutting back on farming production during years of prolonged seasonal migration. On the other hand, he notes that seasonal migration loosely coincides with the accumulation of productive assets that can be used for agricultural and non–agricultural activity. Contrary to that view, Rubenstein (1982) and Griffith (1986) have shown that Caribbean migrant earnings do not significantly contribute to development in the home country. McCoy (1985) expands on this by observing that these earnings are mostly spent in the host country on consumer durable goods, on the immediate consumption needs of the migrant and on sending remittances home rather than on investments. According to Chaney (1985), these earnings may increase individual standards of living with no appreciable gain in the national economy. Such paradox of remittances was also pointed out by Momsen (1986) who cautioned that migration may lower agricultural production if remittances were sufficiently large to permit households to divorce themselves from an agricultural livelihood.

THE SUSTAINABILITY OF SMALL FARMING IN THE RIO GRANDE VALLEY

Research on farming sustainability has for several years maintained that sustainability of farming hinges on the adaptive strategies demonstrated in the diversification or application of a variety of types of farming, particularly in terms of diversification of crop species and spatial diversity within the context of a traditional system, a complex agro-ecosystem (Netting 1986, Altieri 1987, Hills 1988, Blarel *et al* 1992).

Several studies on the sustainability of farming in the Rio Grande Valley exist and their findings are consistent with the views of the scholars noted above. For example the work of Meikle (1998), Davis-Morrison and Barker (1997), Thomas-Hope, Spence and Semple (1999 and Reid (1999), have greatly contributed to the understanding of the area's farming system. Questions remain as to how small farming in the Rio Grande Valley has managed to survive and expand, despite various environmental hazards frequently experienced and out migration, which has resulted in population decline in some communities. Davis-Morrison and Barker (1997) and Davis-Morrison (1998) have alluded to the ability of small-scale farmers to adapt to environmental hazards and changing external market demands, as the primary reason for the persistence of small farming in this area. However, a frequently overlooked factor is the rate of population mobility in sustaining small-scale farming in the area. The Rio Grande Valley thus presents a relevant background for examining the relationship between population mobility and agriculture at the micro-level.

LOCATION AND PHYSICAL ASPECTS OF THE RIO GRANDE VALLEY

The Rio Grande Valley covers an area of approximately 286 square kilometres, or 71,600 acres, which is approximately one third the size of the parish of Portland (figure 16.1). More than three-quarters of the Valley is 1500 metres or more above sea level and more than one half of the land has slopes of over 20 per cent. The terrain of this area is generally hilly with steep hillside slopes and moderate to normal gullies and valleys. The Rio Grande Valley is the wettest part of Portland, which is the wettest parish in Jamaica. The average annual rainfall of the valley is approximately 2,250 millimetres (Harris 2002). In addition, a network of perennial or intermittent streams traverses the Rio Grande Valley.

The heavy rainfall in the valley also carries large quantities of sediment into streams and gullies and contributes to frequent flooding. A dominant geological feature is the Richmond Formation, which consists of grey to yellow calcareous sandstones, siltstones and mudstones. The combination of the area's

Figure 16.1: The Rio Grande Valley, Portland, Jamaica

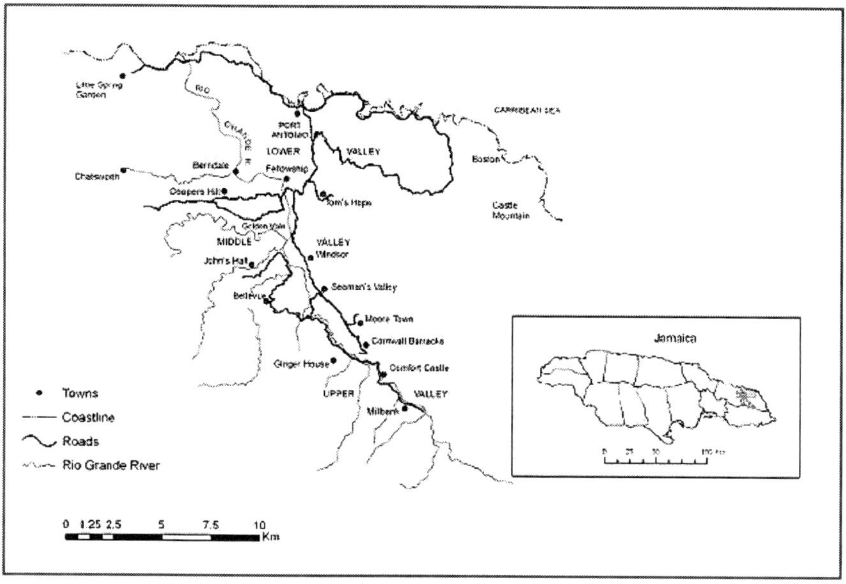

fragile geological formation, steep slopes and heavy rainfall pattern contributes to the prevalence of landslides. Most of the communities in the valley are located on flood plains or on unstable hillside slopes, and are therefore vulnerable to flooding and landslides. The high level of hazard susceptibility suggests that there may have been a link between these environmental conditions and population migration to different areas within the valley, as well as emigration from the valley.

AGRICULTURAL LAND UTILIZATION IN THE RIO GRANDE VALLEY

In the Rio Grande Valley, small farms are traditionally located on the hill slopes, while large farms, except for coffee farms, are located in the alluvial flood plains. Edwards (1961), Beckford (1972) and Spence (1996) have documented this pattern of small and large farm location. They all make reference to the dual nature of Jamaica's agro-economy, where large export-oriented farms account for the largest portion of and best quality farmlands. In this regard, Spence notes that the structure of Jamaica's agro-economy shows that small farms are clustered in the hilly interior of the island, while larger farms occupy coastal lowlands and interior valleys. Weis (2006) refers to the contemporary biophysical constraints as reminiscent of an incomplete process of emancipation as ex-slaves were left to either move into dependent relationship with estates, as wage labourers or tenant farmers, or to pursue gruelling freedom in Jamaica's rugged interior or carving out small plots from largely underdeveloped hillside forests.

In light of the above, the work of Momsen (1987) is significant in that she critically analyses the role of the state in the pattern of land allocation in the pre-independence and post-independence periods. Her discussion is centered on the premise that the government land settlement schemes in the Caribbean region have always been the main source of land ownership for the peasants. This has resulted in the maintenance of the status quo, with ownership of the prime farm lands lying mainly in the hands of large farmers while, to a larger extent, marginal lands (mainly sloping lands which are highly susceptible to erosion) are occupied by peasants (Momsen, 1987).

A general trend noted by Critchlow (1988) in tracing the Jamaican agricultural sector data since the early 1940s, shows that small farmers' share by acreage has remained small while large plantations have maintained a disproportionately large share of land. The study also shows that, in addition to the disparity of land ownership, some small farmers clustered on the periphery of large farms. Thus, the resource base of small farmers, in terms of land, has diminished substantially while their numbers have steadily increased.

Critchlow also notes that while the small holder's acreage decreased in Jamaica, the actual number of farms that they owned or operated increased, particularly after 1961. Based on her tabulation of agricultural census survey data, the average acreage of the holdings that they cultivated consistently fell from 1.79 acres in 1954, to 1.59 acres in 1968, to 0.13 acres in 1978. Similarly, Meikle (1994) and FAO (1997) have noted that the shrinkage of farm lots in the Rio Grande Valley is consistent with the national agricultural censuses of Jamaica for the years 1968, 1978 and 1996.

According to Ishemo (2005) and Ishemo *et al* (2006), despite per capita decline in the size of small farm holdings in the Rio Grande Valley, cumulatively small farm size increased from 348 hectares to 1222 hectares form 1968 to 1998. That is an increase of 28 per cent in a thirty-year period. The increase of land cultivated suggests that although there was a general trend of decline in household farm size, there was an increase in the number of people engaged in farming.

The decline in the size of farm holdings is attributed to residential shifts within the valley, towards accessible areas, especially in the lower and middle parts of the valley. As a result of this almost unidirectional internal population shift, over the years these areas experienced increased population density (majority of whom engaged in farming operations), thus incrementally declining farm sizes from an average of 5 acres down to 2 acres per household. However, the average of 2 acres has been a gradual improvement scenario of the magnitude of household farm holding given the circumstance of clustered population in accessible areas of the valley. Consequently households have tended to increase in the size of these farms through multiple farm holdings. Majority (80 per cent) of small farmers cultivate two farm lots while 5 per cent and 15 per cent of small farmers

Table 16.1:   Farming Involvement by Household for the Period 1994 - 1999

Extent of Farming	Frequency	Percentage
Abandoned Farming	16	4
Reduced Priority	69	19
Renting Portions of Farmland	10	3
Expanded Farming	214	58
Same extent of Farming	31	8
Farming Closer to Residence	29	8
Total	**369**	**100**

Source: *Ishemo 2005*

cultivate three and one farm lots respectively. The number of lots farmed suggests a prevalence of a diverse land tenure status of small farmers in the area.

Historically, the pattern of multiple holdings as part of the farming system is important. It is usually argued that this pattern is maintained by farmers as it allows them to hedge their bets against crop failure or theft in any one plot. Further, it provides for year round harvest as well as takes advantage of the micro-environmental differences in choice of crops (Comitas 1973; Mintz 1974; Mitchell 1985). While these factors play a part in influencing the tenure pattern, internal migration is a significant additional factor.

Based on a sample of 369 small farmers, most of them (58 per cent) reported that during the period they expanded farming operations while just a small percentage reported that they had abandoned their farms or had maintained the same level of operations (table 16.1). These statistics reflect a situation of small farm persistence and viability despite the problems of environmental hazards and population migration.

MIGRATION IN THE RIO GRANDE VALLEY

Internal and external migrations are the dominant forms of population mobility in the Rio Grande Valley and they both reinforce each other. Overall, the valley has experienced population decline over the decades. For example, from 1970-1991 the population declined by 10.05 per cent

Table 16.2: Percentage of population change in the Rio Grande Valley between the periods 1970-1982, 1982-1991 and 1970-1991

Area	Population 1970	Population 1982	Population 1991	% Change 1970-1982	% Change 1982-1991	% Change 1970-1991
Lower Valley	7,005	6,072	5,975	-13.30%	-1.59%	-14.70%
Middle Valley	3,730	3,810	3,708	2.14%	-2.67%	-0.58%
Upper Valley	974	819	849	-15.91%	3.66%	-12.83%
Total Population	11,709	10,701	10,532			
Total % Change				-8.60%	-1.50%	-10.05%

Source: *Calculated from the Jamaica Demographic Statistics of 1984 and 1998, Statistical Institute of Jamaica.*

(table 16.2). Although the population declined in some enumeration districts, in others it increased. Actually, 43 per cent of the 28 enumeration districts (EDs) of the valley recorded population increase between 1970 and 1991. This pattern suggests that the area is characterized by internal migration within the valley and outward migration, with population decline minimized by a higher level of internal migration.

It is important to establish the places of origin of households in the valley. The findings of Ishemo (2005) shows that of the 431 sample households 56 per cent originated from other localities within the valley. This situation suggests that the majority of the residents went through the process of residential shifts within the valley. As noted earlier, areas of the valley which had attracted most of the internal migrant population has been the lower and the middle valley but with many of the in-migrants, particularly returning residents, being attracted to the lower valley, closer to Port Antonio.

The returning residents and the absentee farmers' investments in large commercial farming in the lower and middle valley had been a source of attraction for residential moves of small farmers in the pursuit of wage labour employment. To a large extent, large farms for a number of years had also promoted circular agro-labour mobility within the valley and the seasonal migrants from Port Antonio and other areas of Portland and St. Mary in search of agro wage labour. Most importantly, this dynamic relationship between residential moves within the valley and external migration has enhanced agro-labour retention in the area and, by implication, maintained the viability of farming.

In addition to 17 per cent of the farmers in the Valley who fell into the category of returning residents and absentee farmers, 12 per cent of farmers had previously been temporary overseas migrants. The latter category of migrant is mainly comprised of persons who have engaged in overseas farm work programmes and those employed in cruise ship activities. Although 29 per cent of the farmers in the area had been migrants, nevertheless it was from this group that remittances and money transfers from abroad became a major source of financial capital among the farming population.

MIGRATION AND FARMING SUSTAINABILITY

This study identifies two types of factors for household relocation. First, there are household-specific factors including marriage, children's accompaniment of parents and search for employment opportunities. These factors influence decisions to migrate over a long period of time, depending on the magnitude of stress they cause at the individual level. The second type of explanatory factor includes adverse environmental conditions such as hurricanes, landslides and flooding causing community dislocation and transportation breakdown. Under these conditions, a large segment or an entire community migrates. Population mobility affects small farming in complex ways in the Rio Grande Valley. One way of analyzing the relationship between migration and farming is to use a life cycle approach and examine farming patterns before and after migration. In this way hitherto unaccounted factors are brought to light. Table 3 shows some of the implications of migration on farming practices.

The most important asset of farming practice before migration was that farmers had between 5 and 10 acres of farmland for each household. In addition, most farmers had secure land ownership based on the status of family land. The abundance of farmland allowed for farming practices that included fallowing and crop rotation, and the secure land tenure

Table 16.3: Summary of farming experiences: before and after internal migration

The Period Before Migration	The Period After Migration
• Abundant farmland/large lots	• Diminishing Farmland
• Very limited farm fragmentation	• Shrinkage of farm size
• Land tenure mainly family lands	• Farm fragmentation
• Mainly traditional labour organization	• Land tenure diversity
• Minimal capital input in the farming process	• Hired labour replacing traditional labour organization
• Mainly mixed cropping	• Increased agro-chemical application
• Primarily household farming	• Increased emphasis on specialized crops
• Farming as main occupation – less diversification of activities	• Increased engagement on off-household farming (agro-wage labour employment)
	• Increased diversification of activities (income)
	• Declining dominance of farming as main occupation

Source: *Ishemo 2005*

fostered the cultivation of a wide mix of annual and perennial crops. Most farm holdings were regarded by farmers to be large enough for them to cope with environmental problems such as land slides and flooding as land would always be available to farm while affected portions were damaged and left to regenerate. Hence, abundance of farmland was the factor, which chiefly conditioned the popularity of the traditional farming system.

It was found that 71 per cent of the total households in the study area was based upon farming as the main occupation, with little diversification of activities and very limited farm fragmentation. In other words, land was adequate to relieve the pressure on farmers of the task of acquiring multiple farm holdings as a means of increasing farm acreage and productivity. Farm labour among households was readily available and adequate and was accessed through the principle of reciprocal arrangements of 'day for day' and 'morning sport'. In addition, there was a reliable supply of in-house labour. The factors highlighted above constituted a farming system, which was less costly, and more appropriate in terms of its application by most farmers. Essentially, the 'traditional' system made it possible for households to cultivate farms that were relatively large given the small number of farmers.

On the other hand, the period after migration was characterised by a number of stressful farming practices. As households relocated to more favourable locations, the population density increased in those areas resulting in diminishing amounts of farmland and thus to the shrinkage of farm size. In order to increase farm acreage farmers resorted to acquiring more land holdings at greater distances from the main farm plot. This process increased both farm fragmentation and land tenure diversity. Small farmers also became increasingly reliant on agro-chemicals to improve crop yield. This increased the cost of the farming systems thus necessitating greater capital input. As farming operations became increasingly dependent on the availability of cash, households were of necessity, stimulated to engage more in various income generating activities. Overall, the diversification of household labour created a shortage of in-house labour for farming activities. Consequently, hired labour became the dominant form of farm labour coupled with a decline in farming as a main activity. The stressful nature of farming for those farmers that re-located within the valley and as land for farming became increasingly scarce in the preferred lower sections of the valley, opportunities for migration from the area was sought by many households. For most persons who were left behind, livelihoods became dependent upon receipt of remittances.

There are two observations to be made in respect of the second and first phases of migration. The second phase of migration (outward migration) from the valley supports the views of Boserup (1965) and Netting (1993) who regarded migration in the rural areas as an outcome of population growth and decreasing farm productivity. In their view, migration was considered an alternative to agricultural intensification. On the other hand, the first phase of migration which was characterised by residential moves from one place to another within the Rio Grande Valley was an outcome of environmental problems and factors associated with remoteness of some communities rather than scarcity of land resources as a consequence of increased population density. Prior to migration, agricultural land was abundant enough to support agricultural operations than was the case in the post-migration period. This serves to reinforce the significance of household relocations for the nature of farming operations.

It is possible to make a distinction between farmers moving within the Rio Grande Valley and those migrating from the valley. Whereas the migrants from elsewhere in the valley moved with the intention of re-establishing themselves with finance gained from labouring on large farms, or elsewhere, the majority of those migrating to the Valley, particularly from overseas, relocated with a strong cash resource base. For most of these people, farming in the valley was a continuation of capital accumulation rather than the initiation of a new capital venture. Their strong capital base allowed them to acquire large portions of land and to be further along in the farm establishment process in a short period of time.

Migration in the valley of these two categories of farmers demonstrated the convergence of labour and capital in the context of how their operations depend on each other. The difficulties experienced by small farm operations were gradually reduced by the existence of large farm operations as they provided alternative income in the form of agro-wage labour. As farming now depends more on capital input and hiring of labour, employment in large farms provided a 'kick-start' for small farm undertakings and a source of extra income for the maintenance of household livelihood. In other words, the investment of externally earned capital into large commercial farming, incrementally improved the capacity to afford a greater amount of land for farming among small farmers. Consequently provision of wage employment became a source of capital for hiring agricultural labour and procurement of agro-chemical input on the part of small farmers. Such sustainable agro-wage employment promoted the retention of agricultural labour in the valley.

As stated earlier in this study, historically large commercial farms had occupied large and prime agricultural lands in the Caribbean. The disadvantaged nature of small farming particularly in terms of their limited access to land and unfavourable locations is well documented by several researchers. However, given the socio-economic and environmental circumstances, commercial farming has a net beneficial impact on the survival and the viability of small farming in the Rio Grande Valley, because of the opportunities it provides for part-time employment of small farmers. The supportive role of commercial farming for small farming is also experienced elsewhere. For example Morton (1999) noted that richer farmers in the Machakos district of Kenya were the generators of agricultural labour demand for labour-intensive crops and that they were also responsible for creating a lifeline for poorer households in the area, enabling them to cling to their stake in the rural economy. The complementarity of large and small farms was also observed earlier by Dumont (1967) in his review of Tanzania's *Ujamaa* policy. He noted that there could be no meaningful progress in agriculture without the help of a class of 'progressive farmers'. Similarly, in the Caribbean region, Griffith (1988) noted the complementarity of large and small farming operations in Jamaica in terms of the agro-wage labour provided by large farms, which served to support peasant agriculture.

REMITTANCES AND FARMING SYSTEMS

One of the ways of understanding the relationship between external capital and the extent of farming involvement and cropping practices of households is to examine whether there are differential impacts between farmers who receive and those who do not receive remittances.

With reference to table 16.4, a strong correlation between farm size and a households' receipt of remittances is seen. Farmers without remittances have less acreage in farm holdings. Conversely, there is a tendency for those receiving remittances to have relatively larger farms regardless of the cropping system, as compared with those who do not receive remittances. However, with remittances, farms that produce export crops appeared to be larger than those that produce other crops. It should also be noted that regardless of age, all household heads have a tendency towards farm expansion for both cash (export) crops and other (mixed) crops. In addition, due to adverse environmental impacts there is a notable increase in the utilization of cash remittances in the rehabilitation of small farms.

The consideration of age is important in order to understand the impact of remittances on major players in small farming. Remittance recipients have been differentiated into three age cohorts; under 45, 45 to 64 and 65 years and over. Those between 45 and 64 years of age, on average, have a larger farm size, particularly for cash crops, even without remittances. This is probably because this is the age group with the most farming expertise and for whom farming is the primary occupation. Therefore, with or without remittances, farm expansion occurs. On the other hand, remittances have a great influence on young farmers in the under 45 year age group and elderly farmers in the 65 years and over age group. Multiple-occupations characterise the livelihood of young farmers, who eventually adopted farming as their primary occupation. For them, remittances led to greater involvement in farming.

It also appeared that regardless of remittances, non-export crop farm holdings had expanded between 1994 and 1999, but the sizes of the farms were still smaller than those of non-export crop holdings that were aided by remittances. Therefore, regardless of cropping system, remittances were a factor in farm expansion and significantly influenced export crop holdings.

As shown in Table 4, it can be seen that cash remittances enabled farmers, regardless of the age group, to undertake the cropping system of their choice. It is generally expected that elderly farmers, due to their reduced physical ability, would opt for more manageable mixed cropping on smaller sized farm holdings within the confines of, or in close proximity to, his/her residence. With cash remittance support, elderly farmers could expand farms for cash cropping like farmers in the younger age categories. By receiving consistent and adequate remittances, older farmers could afford to hire agricultural labour and enhance their purchasing of other farm inputs.

The distinction is that while most farmers in the young age category had a higher rate of non-cash crop expansions without the influence of remittances, elderly farmers had mostly relied on remittances for expansion of non-cash crop holdings. In this case, it is assumed that young farmers had the advantage of diversifying their labour to other income-generating activities that would support their farming activities, while for the elderly

Table 16.4: Remittance recipients based on farmers' age and extent of farm expansion, 1994-1999

Age Group	Export Crops				Other Crops			
	Non - Remittance		Remittance		Non Remittance		Remittance	
	Avg. farm size (acres)	Freq. Farm exp.	Avg. farm size (acres)	Freq. Farm exp.	Avg. farm size (acres)	Freq. Farm exp.	Avg. farm size (acres)	Freq. Farm exp.
< 45	2.7	7	4.3	29	2.1	59	2.4	2
45 – 64	4.2	13	4.8	15	2.0	56	2.9	4
> 65	3.1	4	4.3	10	0.7	4	2.3	7

Note: Exp = expansion

Source: Ishemo 2005

it was remittances that allowed them to expand their farms. In other words, it can be suggested that the elderly population reduced farm expansion was caused by a decline in capital as they aged. With the availability of capital, mainly through remittances, it is seen that aging was not a significant factor in the choice of farming system.

Hills (1988) suggests that remittances caused the elderly to reduce farm size and shift to subsistence cropping while Barrow's (1993) findings on small farm operations in Barbados, suggests that older farmers were more oriented towards the economic maintenance of their households and less oriented towards commercial expansion. However, this study contradicts these findings by revealing that in the Rio Grande Valley remittances neutralised cropping specialization related to age and that regardless of the farmer's age, remittances enhanced increased agricultural production.

CONCLUSION

The relationship that exists between migration and sustainability of farming is complex — mutually supportive at times and contradictory at others. This chapter has supported this position by establishing that migration has the potential to enhance farming livelihood resilience through the effect of externally derived capital on household income. It also has the ability to diminish resilience by weakening the long established and adequately applicable traditional relations of production and hampering access to adequate farmland. Although the impact of internal and external migration on farming appears contradictory, farming activity in the Rio Grande Valley hinges on this complex relationship.

The findings of this study reveal that the relationship between population mobility and the viability of farming activity ought not to be examined simply from the viewpoint of external migration. Rather, it should be viewed from a holistic perspective, which examines the interplay among various forms of mobility and their resulting impact on farming activity, based on the specific socio-economic and environmental conditions of the area. In this context, the linkage between internal migration and external migration in influencing farming livelihoods is extremely significant. It has been argued that the complexity of such a relationship can be investigated best at a micro, rather than a macro-level. Using this approach, the Rio Grande Valley in Jamaica was chosen as the locality for exploring such linkages.

REFERENCES

Altieri, Miguel A. 1987. *Agroecology: The Scientific Basic of Alternative Agriculture.* Second edition, Boulder, COL: Westview Press.

Barrow, Christine. 1993. Small Farm Food Production and Gender in Barbados. In Janet Momsen (ed.), *Women and Change in the Caribbean, a Pan-Caribbean Perspective.* pp. 181-193. Bloomington: Indiana University Press.

Beckford, George L. 1972. *Persistent Poverty: Underdevelopment in Plantation Economies of the Third World.* New York: Oxford University Press.

Blarel, Benot *et al.* 1992. The Economics of Farm Fragmentation: Evidence from Ghana and Rwanda. *World Bank Economic Review*, Volume 6, Number 2, pp. 233-254.

Boserup, Esther. 1965. *The Conditions of Agricultural Growth.* Chicago: Aldine.

Brana-Shute, Rose mary and G. Brana-Shute. 1992. The Magnitude and Impact of Remittances in the Eastern Caribbean: A Research Note in W. W. Stinner, K. de Albuquerque and R. S. Bryce-Laporte (eds.), *Return Migration and Remittances: Developing a Caribbean Perspective.* pp. 267-290. Occasional Paper Number 3, Research Institute on Immigration and Ethnic Studies, Washington, D.C: Smithsonian Institute. 1982.

Brown, Richard. P. C. and J. Connell. 1993. The Global Free Market: Migration, Remittances and the Informal Economy in Tonga. *Development and Change*, Volume 24, Number 4, pp. 611-47. 1993.

Chaney, Elsa. 1985. *Migration from the Caribbean Region: Determinants and Effects of Current Movements.* Center for Immigration Policy and Refugee Assistance, Washington D.C. Georgetown University.

Comitas, Lambros. 1973. Occupational Multiplicity in Rural Jamaica. In *Work and Family Life: A West Indian Perspective.* L. Comitas and D. Lowenthal (eds.), pp. 157-174. New York: Anchor Books.

Connell, John. 1980. *Remittances and Rural Development: Migration, Dependency, and Inequality in the South Pacific.* National Centre for Development Studies. Occasional Paper Number 22, Canberra: Australian National University.

Connell, John. and D. Conway. 2000. Migration and Remittances in Island Microstates: A Comparative Perspective on the South Pacific and the Caribbean, *International Journal of Urban and Regional Research.* Volume 24, Number 1, pp. 53-77.

Conway, Dennis. 2000. The Importance of Migration for Caribbean Development. *Global Development*, Volume 2, Numbers 1-2, pp. 73–105. 2000.

Conway, Dennis and C. Glesne: 1986. Rural Livelihood, Return Migration, and Remittances in St. Vincent. In *CLAG 1986 Year Book,* Muncie ed., pp. 3-11. Volume 12, Conference of Latin Americanist Geographers, Ball State University.

Critchlow, Michaeline A. 1988. *Agricultural Policy and the Development of Small-Holding Stratum in Jamaica, 1930–1980.* Unpublished Ph.D. dissertation, State University of New York, Binghampton, New York.

Davis-Morrison, Vileitha D. 1998. The Sustainability of Small-Scale Agricultural Systems in the Millbank Area of the Rio Grande Valley, Portland, Jamaica. In *Resource Sustainability and Caribbean Development.* Duncan McGregor, David Barker and Sally Evans. eds., pp. 296-316. Kingston, Jamaica: The University Press of the West Indies.

Davis-Morrison, D. Vileitha and D. Barker. 1997. Resource Management, Environment Knowledge and Decision-Making in Small Farming Systems in the Rio Grande Valley, Jamaica. *Caribbean Geography.* Volume 8, Number 2, pp. 96-106.

De Souza, Roger M. 1998. The Spell of the Cascadura: West Indian Return Migration as Local Response. In *Globalization and Neoliberalism: the Caribbean Context,* T. Klak ed., pp. 227-253. London: Rowman and Littlefield.

Duany, Jorge. 2001. Beyond Safety Valve: Recent Trends in Caribbean Migration. In *Caribbean Sociology: Introductory Readings,* Christine Barrow and Rhoda Reddock eds., pp. 861-876 Kingston, Jamaica: Ian Randle Publishers.

Dumont. René. 1967. Tanzanian Agriculture after the Arusha Declaration. Discussion Paper, University of Dar Es Salaam, Tanzania.

Edwards, David. 1961. *Report on an Economic Study of Small Farming in Jamaica.* Kingston: Institute of Social and Economic Research, University College of the West Indies.

FAO. 1997. Findings of the Socio-Economic and Agro-Forestry Surveys Conducted in the Spanish River, Swift River and Rio Grande Watersheds, Portland. Baseline Report Agro-forestry Development in North Eastern Jamaica. Project (GCP/JAM/017/NET).

Freeman, Carla. 2002. Mobility, Rootedness, and the Caribbean Higgler. Production, Consumption and Transnational Livelihoods. In *Work and Migration, Life and Livelihoods in a Globalizing World,* N. Sorensen and K. Olwig eds., pp. 61- 77. London: Routledge.

Gmelch, George. 1987. Work Innovation and Investment: the Impact of Return Migrants in Barbados. *Human Organization,* Volume 46, Number 2, pp. 131-40.

Griffith, David. 1986. Social Organizational Obstacles to Capital Accumulation Among Returning Migrants: The British West Indian Temporary Aliens Programme. *Human Organization,* Volume 45, Number 1, pp. 34-42.

————. 1988. Labour Migration and Changing Peasant Agriculture in Jamaica'. In *Small Farming and Peasant Resources in the Caribbean,* John S. Brierly and Hymie Rubenstein eds., 101-118. Winnipeg: University of Manitoba Department of Geography.

Harris, Norman. 2002. Rain Induced Slope Failures and Damage Assessment in Portland, Jamaica: The Flood Event of January 3-4, 1998. In *Caribbean Geology into the Third Millennium. Transactions of the Fifteenth Caribbean Geological Conference,* Trevor Jackson ed., pp. 235- 254. Kingston, Jamaica: University of the West Indies Press.

Hills, Theo L. 1988. The Caribbean Peasant Food Forest, Ecological Artistry or Random Chaos. In *Small Farming and Peasant Resources in the Caribbean,* John S. Brierly and Hymie Rubenstein eds., pp. 1-28. Winnipeg: University of Manitoba Department of Geography.

Ishemo, Amani. 2005. *Population Mobility and the Sustainability of Farming Households: The Rio Grande Valley, Jamaica.* Unpublished PhD. dissertation, University of the West Indies, Mona.

Ishemo, Amani, H. Semple and E. Thomas-Hope. 2006. 'Population Mobility and the Survival of Small Farming in the Rio Grande Valley, Jamaica'. *The Geographical Journal,* Vol. 172, No. 4, pp. 318-330.

Jennings, Allen and M. Clarke. 2005. 'The Development Impact of Remittances to Nicaragua'. *Development in Practice.* Volume 15, Number 5, pp. 685-691, 2005.

Lapper, Richard. 2007. *US migrant workers send home $62.3 bn.* The *Financial Times* (London). 15 March.

McKee, David L and C. Tisdell. 1988. 'The Development Implications of Migration from and between Small Island Nations'. *International Migration,* Volume 26, Number 4, pp. 417-425.

McCoy, Terry L. 1985. 'The Impact of US Temporary Worker Programs on Caribbean Development: Evidence from H-2 Workers in Florida'. In *Migration and Development in the Caribbean,* Robert Pastor ed., pp. 178-206. Boulder: Westview Press.

Mandle, Jay R. 1996. *Persistent Underdevelopment, Change and Economic Modernization in the West Indies.* Amsterdam: Gordon and Breach.

Meikle, Paulette. 1994. *Farming in the Rio Grande Valley: Farming Systems and Project Impacts.* Monitoring and Evaluation Unit. Fellowship Report, Port Antonio: Rio Grande Valley Project.

———. 1998. 'Rural Change and Agricultural Sustainability: the Rio Grande Valley Project, Portland, Jamaica'. In *Resource Sustainability and Caribbean Development,* Duncan McGregor, David Barker and Sally Lloyd Evans eds., Kingston, Jamaica: The University of the West Indies Press.

Mintz, Sidney W. 1974. *Caribbean Transformations.* Chicago: Aldine.

Mitchel, Rutty. 1985. *Social Forces Affecting Farmers' Decisions. Assessment of Hillside Agriculture in Two Watersheds of Jamaica.* Report submitted to USAID-Jamaica by the Fragile Lands Rapid Assessment Team. Institute for Development Anthropology, Binghamton, New York.

Momsen, Janet H. 1986. 'Migration and Rural Development in the Caribbean'. *Tijdschrift Voor Economische en Sociale Geografie 77:50-58.*

———. 1987. Land settlement as an imposed solution. In *Land and Development in the Caribbean,* Jean Besson and Janet Momsen eds., pp.46-69. Warwick University Caribbean studies. London: Macmillan Publishers. 1987.

Morton, John. 1999. 'Population Growth and Poverty in Machakos District, Kenya'. *The Geographical Journal,* No. 1. 165, Part 1, pp.37-46.

Netting, Robert M. 1986. *Cultural Ecology.* Illinois: Waveland Press.

———. 1993. *Small holders, Householders: Farm Families and the Ecology of Intensive, Sustainable Agriculture.* Stanford, CA: Stanford University Press.

Petras, Elizabeth M. 1988. *Jamaican Labor Migration: White Capital and Black Labor 1850 – 1930.* Boulder: Westview Press.

Poirine, Bernard. 1998. 'Should We Hate or Love MIRAB?' *The Contemporary Pacific,* Volume 10, 65-106.

Reid, Michelle. 1999. *Agro-biodiversity and food security among farming households in the Rio Grande Valley, Jamaica.* MSc. Thesis, University of West Indies, Mona.

Rubenstein, Hymie. 1982. The Impact of Remittances in the Rural English speaking Caribbean: Notes on Literature. In *Return Migration and Remittances: Developing a*

Caribbean Perspective, W. F. Stinner, K. de Albuquerque and R. S. Bryce-Laporte eds., Washington, D. C. Research Institute on Immigration and Ethnic Studies, the Smithsonian Institute. Occasional Paper Number 3, pp. 3- 34.

Shankman, Paul. 1976. *Migration and Underdevelopment: the Case of Western Samoa.* Boulder, COL: Westview Press.

Spence, Balfour. 1996. 'The Influence of Small Farmers' Land Use Decisions on the Status of Domestic Food Security in Jamaica'. *Caribbean Geography.* Volume 7, Number 2, pp. 132-142.

Thomas-Hope, Elizabeth M. 1985. 'Return Migration and its Implications for Caribbean Development'. In *Migration and Development in the Caribbean: The Unexplored Connection,* Robert A. Pastor ed., pp. 157-172. Boulder, COL: Westview Press.

———. 1993 'Population Mobility and Land Assets in Hill Farming Areas of Jamaica'. In *Caribbean Geography*. Volume 4, Number 1, pp. 49-63.

———. 1999. 'Return Migration to Jamaica and its Development Potential'. In R. Appleyard ed., *International Migration Quarterly Review*, Vol. 37, Number 1, pp. 183-205.

———. 2002. 'Transnational Livelihoods and Identities in Return Migration to the Caribbean: The Case of Skilled Returnees to Jamaica'. In *Work and Migration: Life and Livelihoods in a Globalizing World*, N. Sorensen and K. Olwig eds., pp.187-197. London: Routledge.

Thomas-Hope, Elizabeth M., B. Spence and H. Semple 2006. 'Biodiversity within the Agricultural Diversity of Small Farming in the Rio Grande River Watershed, Jamaica'. *Memorias del Seminario Internacional Sobre Agrodiversidad Campesina*, pp. 140-155 Toluca, Mexico:Universidad Autonoma del Estado de Mexico.

Weis, Tony. 2006. 'The Rise, Fall and Future of the Jamaican Peasantry'. *The Journal of Peasant Studies.* Volume 33, Number 1, pp. 61-88.

Wood, Charles H. 1981. 'Structural Change and Household Strategies: A Conceptual Framework for the Study of Rural Migration'. *Human Organization.* Volume 40, pp. 338-344.

17

AN ASSESSMENT OF THE EMIGRATION OF HIGHLY SKILLED WORKERS FROM JAMAICA

PAULINE KNIGHT, EASTON WILLIAMS AND STEVEN KERR

INTRODUCTION

The emigration of educated/trained workers has traditionally been considered a loss for the source country because of several factors. These include: the 'drain' from the country of the needed human capital; the foregone returns on the resources invested in these workers; the net welfare reduction for the workers left behind due to changes in labour supply and wages; and the lost positive externality effects which highly-skilled workers usually contribute to a society.

Recently, however, much attention is being paid to other considerations which may mitigate or even outweigh the emigration losses which source countries bear. Chief among these are the remittances which have grown considerably within the last decade and now constitute a large proportion of the Gross Domestic Product of many Third World countries. Additionally, it is argued that because of migration prospects, human capital formation is heightened in source countries thus contributing positively to economic performance.[1] Finally, beneficial feedback effects can be pinpointed, return migration after the acquisition of experience and knowledge abroad, and migrants' creation of business-related networks between recipient and source countries that serve to enhance trade and investment levels. Note has also been taken of the phenomenon of social remittances, which has both negative and positive connotations as it includes ideas, values, beliefs, practices, identities and social capital transmitted through the migration circuit from one country to another.[2]

Since the migrant flow is primarily from the lesser to the more highly developed countries, the impact of migration has the added dimension of aggravating differences in economic prosperity, between poorer and wealthier countries. The policy implications are therefore varied and far reaching. For example, there is need to consider questions such as: Where in the education system should source countries invest most heavily? Should they make strategic choices so as to target educational subsidies to those skill areas and levels that are most likely to remain at home? Should they simply train for export in view of the possible benefits to accrue in the future? Within this context, should they seek to develop partnership agreements with recipient countries? These are only some of the issues with which countries must grapple if they are to try to ensure that they are not total losers due to workers' international migration patterns.

In order to facilitate the development of appropriate policies, an evidenced-based approach is essential. In this regard, investigations have focused on: quantifying the true size of the 'brain drain' which has been defined as the 'proportion of working age individuals (age 25 and over) with at least tertiary educational attainment, born in a given country but living in another, ….'[3] The countries and regions most affected, the profile of migrant workers and the effects of migration on source countries — taking into account both the positives and the negatives have also been issues of concern. Prominent among the relevant studies are those by Carrington and Detragiache (1998, 1999), Docquier and Marfouk (2005) and Mishra (2006), which have all been conducted using internationally available data. Among the conclusions from these studies is that migration rates are generally higher for highly educated individuals and, compared with other regions, the Caribbean has the highest emigration rate in the world. With regard to Jamaica, the overall emigration rate for persons with tertiary education was estimated at 84.1 per cent in 1990,[4] and to the United States only it was an average of 78 per cent over the period 1965 to 2000,[5] and 77 per cent in 1990.[6]

The methodology of these studies utilizes information on foreign-born individuals, 25 years of age and over, available from the censuses of the destination countries, supplementing this with information on the characteristics of the working age population in the countries of origin. It is acknowledged by the authors that there are constraints due to the nature of the data used, and these undermine the precision of the results. A primary concern, for example, is that it is '... impossible to distinguish between immigrants who were educated at the time of their arrival and those who acquired education after they settled in the receiving country ....'[7]

The issue of where migrants obtain their schooling may or may not be of importance depending on the use to which the migration estimates will be put. As pointed out by Carrington and Detragiache (1998) if the intent is to assess the loss of monetary investment in human capital by the source country, then it is critical that this distinction is made. If such a distinction is not made, it must be recognized that the so-called 'drain' merely quantifies the pool of highly skilled nationals who are expatriates, and not the outflow of skilled persons from the source country as it is usually taken to connote.

An attempt is made in the paper by Mishra to adjust for the country of education, this is done by restricting the sample to those who emigrated at 16 years of age or more as it is less likely that these persons would have obtained their schooling in the USA. On this basis, the adjusted emigration rate from Jamaica to the US *increases* for those with secondary education (from 29 per cent to 58 per cent) and *decreases* for those at the tertiary level (from 78 per cent to 53 per cent).

METHODOLOGY

This chapter quantifies the outflow of high skilled emigrants from Jamaica, the main difference from the above studies being the use of detailed information from local sources, and the refinement of information on education levels to differentiate between persons trained locally vis-à-vis those trained overseas. Three approaches are employed, namely:

1. Computation of the emigration stock of tertiary level individuals as a proportion of the relevant population originating from the source country in 2000 (i.e. a replication of the above discussed approaches but with refinement);

2. Computation of emigrants as those that have left the labour force given the stock and inflow of trained tertiary personnel over the period 1990–2000.

3. Comparison of the output of persons from training institutions with the number of tertiary trained personnel that migrated to the main recipient countries, over the period 1990–2000.

METHOD I: EMIGRATION STOCK OF HIGHLY EDUCATED PERSONNEL

Three pieces of information are required for this calculation.

i. The stock of Jamaican migrants with tertiary skills living overseas (O).

ii. The stock of Jamaicans with tertiary skills living at home (H).

iii. The proportion of Jamaicans with tertiary skills that are trained overseas (P).

The proportion trained overseas (P) is $F/(F+L)$, where F is the number trained overseas and L is the number trained locally.

The overall migration rate (R) is $O/(H+O)$. The adjusted migration rate or the outflow of trained persons (W) is $[O- P(H+O)] / (O+L)$. That is, those living overseas (O) less those trained overseas $[P(H+O)]$, as a proportion of the total pool of tertiary trained workers (O+L).

I. TERTIARY LEVEL JAMAICANS LIVING OVERSEAS

Information on the stock of migrants in all Organization for Economic Co-operation and Development (OECD) member countries is the source of the requisite data. This database was developed by Docquier and Marfouk in relation to the foreign born population 25 years and over, based on the censuses or registers in these countries. Educational attainment is categorized into three levels: low skilled; medium skilled and high skilled. Low skilled workers are those with primary education (or with 0–8 years of schooling); medium skilled workers are those with secondary education (9–12 years of schooling); and high skilled workers are those with tertiary

Table 17.1: Stock of Jamaican migrants 25 years and over in OECD countries by educational attainment, 2000

Years of Schooling	Educational Attainment	America	Europe	Asia and Oceana	Total
0-8 years	Primary	62,786	69,860	98	132,744
9-12 years	Secondary	222,045	34,845	249	257,139
13+ years	Tertiary	268, 312	22,326	528	291,166

Source: *Docquier and Marfouk, 2005*
From the table, the total number of tertiary level Jamaicans overseas (O) is 291,166.

education (13 years and over). The information for Jamaica is summarised in table 17.1.

II. TERTIARY LEVEL JAMAICANS LIVING AT HOME

The 2001 Population Census provides information on the number of years of schooling as shown in Table 2 and Figure 17.1. The data on migrants define tertiary level as 13+ years of schooling, based on the fact that secondary education is completed in the OECD countries (especially the USA) in 12 years. However, given the Jamaican education system and norms, the break between secondary and tertiary education is not as clear-cut. In the Jamaican context, in the 13th year of schooling persons are normally in their final year of secondary education (Fifth Form), and in the 14th and 15th year are most likely to be still seeking to get some secondary level certification (e.g. in Community Colleges or private institutions); or are at the upper tier of the secondary system (Sixth Form); and a few would be in tertiary institutions such as Teachers' Colleges. Many persons are thus still completing their secondary education at 14 and 15 years and the majority would begin tertiary education at 16 years.

Figure 17.1: Population 25 years old and over by years of schooling

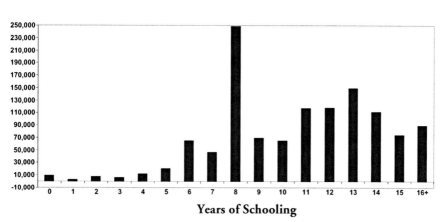

Tertiary level was, therefore, defined as 16+ years of schooling and the local stock of such persons (H) amounted to 89,060 in 2001. This total is in keeping with data on the labour force which shows that in 2001 (year average) it contained 82,200 persons with tertiary training.[8]

III. PROPORTION OF PERSONS TRAINED OVERSEAS

Data on Jamaicans enrolled in tertiary institutions locally and in the U.S. are the sources of information for this variable. Similar information on other destination countries are not available but given the preponderance of the migrants to the U.S. this is not considered a serious gap. The average annual enrollment of Jamaicans in local tertiary institutions (L) was 20,399 for the period 1990–2000,[9] while average annual enrollment of Jamaicans in these institutions in the US (F) amounted to 4,200 over the period 2001–2005 [10](data for the comparable period was not readily available). The proportion trained overseas (P) is F/(F+L), and on this basis P is calculated at 0.171; figure 17.2 shows the share of persons trained locally and in the US.

Table 17.2: Population 25 years and over by years of schooling

Yrs. of Schooling	Male	Female	Total
0	5,051	4,116	9,167
1	1,411	1,145	2,556
2	4,231	3,712	7,943
3	3,211	2,773	5,984
4	6,679	5,323	12,002
5	10,250	9,826	20,076
6	32,850	32,009	64,859
7	23,128	23,031	46,159
8	124,560	123,647	248,207
9	36,405	32,934	69,339
10	31,932	32,557	64,489
11	56,916	60,093	117,009
12	55,744	62,107	117,851
13	68,969	79,785	148,754
14	49,707	61,530	111,237
15	30,269	43,484	73,753
16+	34,525	54,535	89,060
Total Valid	575,838	632,607	1,208,445
Non-response	42,809	36,889	79,698
Total Population	618,647	669,496	1,288,143

Figure 17.2: Country of training of tertiary personnel

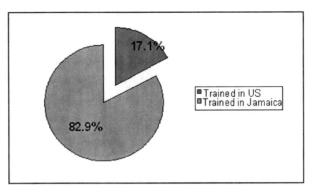

FINDINGS

The overall migration rate (R) amounts to 76.6 per cent. The adjusted migrate or outflow of trained persons (W) amounts to 59.5 per cent (see table 17.3).

Table 17.3: The outflow of high-skilled personnel

Tertiary Stock at Home (H)	Tertiary Stock Overseas (O)	Total Tertiary Stock (H+O)	Overseas Tertiary Stock trained in Jamaica (T)	Rate of Outflow of Tertiary personnel [T/(H+O)]
89,060	291,166	380,226	226,147	59.5%

Source: *Calculated by Authors*

These findings must be compared with those from the international studies. Using the Docquier and Marfouk study, some of the findings are summarized in table 17.4. In the calculations of that study, the UN population estimates were used, to which Barro and Lee's education structure for Jamaica was applied in relation to the population 25 years and older.

Table 17.4: Population 25 years and over by years of schooling residing in Jamaica and in OECD countries, 2000

Years of Schooling	Educational Attainment	Working age Residents in Jamaica	Emigrants in OECD	Emigration Rate (%)
0-8 Years	Primary	723,000	132,744	15.50%
9-12 Years	Secondary	474,000	257,139	35.20%
13+ Years	Tertiary	51,000	291,166	85.10%
Total		1,248,000	681,049	35.30%

Source: *Docquier and Marfouk, 2005*
Emigration Rate=col 4 divided by col 3+ col 4.

A marked difference between the data used in Table 4 and that in the present investigation is the estimated stock of Jamaicans at home with tertiary education, 51,000 vs. 89,060. Docquier and Marfouk estimated the stock of tertiary personnel in Jamaica using an education structure devised by Barro and Lee.[11] This has been found to underestimate the percentage of the working age with tertiary schooling. In Barro and Lee, 4 per cent of the cohort is attributed with tertiary level education or the assumed equivalent of 13+ years of schooling. In the Jamaican Census, however, the proportion with tertiary schooling is 6.9 per cent using 16+ years of schooling as the tertiary equivalent (as is advocated here). Notably, if the tertiary equivalent is set at 13+ years of schooling the persons at tertiary level would amount to 422, 384 or 32.8 per cent of the cohort.

It should also be noted that the larger the local pool of tertiary working age persons, the lower the migration rate would be. Hence if tertiary level persons are equated with 14+ years of schooling, the overall migration rate would be 51.5 per cent, and if equated with 15+ years it would be 64.1 per cent.

METHOD II: STOCK AND INFLOW OF TRAINED TERTIARY PERSONNEL

This analysis examines migration in relation to more precise measures of tertiary level education as it uses information on persons that have completed tertiary courses of study. Data from the Population Censuses are used to ascertain the number of persons with degrees and other professional qualifications in 1991 and 2001 and these are then compared with the number of professionals trained during the inter-censal period. In 1991, the total number of persons with tertiary qualifications stood at 83,963. During the period 1991–2000, 59,570 persons graduated from tertiary institutions.[12] At the end of the period, in 2001, the estimated number of persons with tertiary qualifications was 123,074. In light of the numbers trained, the total number of professionals in 2001 should have been 143,533.[13] This shows that the loss to the labour force due to migration/attrition was approximately 20,459 persons or 34.3 per cent of those trained (see table 17.5).[14]

Table 17.5: Loss of population with tertiary qualification, 1991-2001

Category	Number
Number of Tertiary Persons in 1991	83,963
Output of Tertiary Persons (1991-2000)	59,570
Expected Total in 2001(1991+ output)	143,533
Actual Number of Tertiary Persons in 2001	123,074
Loss (Expected less Actual)	20,459
Percentage Loss	34.3%

Source: *Population Census 1991, 2001*
Economic and Social Survey of Jamaica 1991-2001

METHOD III: PROPORTION OF TERTIARY PERSONNEL MIGRATING

This methodology takes into consideration the output of Professionals, Senior Officials and Technicians from tertiary institutions in relation to the migration of this occupational grouping as reported by the host countries over the period 1990–2000. As shown in table 17.6, the total number of Jamaicans graduating with tertiary certification during the period 1990-2000 numbered 63,045.[14] Information garnered from the US and Canadian embassies over this period revealed that 13,722 Jamaicans were immigrants with professional qualifications. The rate of migration as a percentage of the persons trained therefore, averaged 21.8 per cent, with a peak of 40.3 per cent in 1990 (see figure 17.3). It is recognized that one limitation of this methodology is that the main migrant may have had one or more dependents with tertiary qualifications. If one estimates that three-quarters of the main migrants had such a dependent, a multiplier of 1.75 can be used to estimate the number of tertiary level persons that would have migrated over the period. On this basis, approximately 38.1 per cent of the tertiary cohort would have migrated over the period.

Figure 17.3: Output of professionals from tertiary institutions and migration to North America

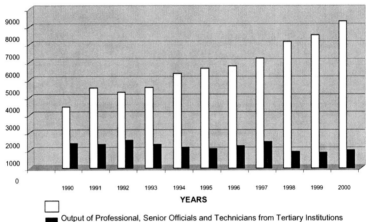

☐ Output of Professional, Senior Officials and Technicians from Tertiary Institutions

■ Migration of Professional, Administrative & Managerial Personnel (USA & Canada)

Table 17.6: Output from tertiary institutions and migration of professionals, etc. to North America (1990-2000)

Years	Output of Professional, Senior Officials and Technicians from Tertiary Institutions	Migration of Professionals, Administrative & Management Personnel (US & Canada)	Migrants as a Proportion of Professionals Trained during the Period
1990	3475	1401	40.3
1991	4,559	1,354	29.7
1992	4,320	1,606	37.2
1993	4,572	1,364	29.8
1994	5,356	1,204	22.5
1995	5,669	1,124	19.8
1996	5,805	1,267	21.8
1997	6,237	1,525	24.5
1998	7,172	944	13.2
1999	7,555	901	11.9
2000	8,325	1,032	12.4
Total	63,045	13,722	21.8

Source: *Economic and Social Survey of Jamaica, 1991-2000.*

SUMMARY AND CONCLUSION

The investigations in this study give an estimate for the overall migration rate for tertiary level Jamaicans in 2000 of approximately 76.6 per cent. Since this includes persons trained overseas it is necessary to adjust for this group, in order to obtain estimates of the outflow of tertiary personnel. These estimates are as follows:

- 34.3 per cent (stock and flow calculation)
- 38.1 per cent (migrants vs. training output calculation)
- 59.3 per cent (migrant stock vs. local stock calculation).

While the estimate of 59.3 per cent is close to that obtained by Mishra of 53 per cent, the other two estimates are much lower but are also similar to each other. Given that the latter two use reliable micro-level data, one may conclude that they provide more precise estimates than the former, however, they are still in need of further refinement.

With regard to the estimates made by the international studies, it is evident that there is a basic flaw in the data used to obtain the education structure of the Jamaican population. This has resulted in over-estimate of the overall migration rate by approximately 10 percentage points, which may be considered relatively small. For Jamaican policy makers, however, the concern that over 80 per cent of the tertiary output of the training system is migrating is much alleviated as the true outflow is in the range of 34–59 per cent. This is still fairly large and represents a sizeable drain on the economy and society.

NOTES

1. Frederic Docquier and Abdeslam Marfouk. 2004. 'Measuring the international mobility of skilled workers (1990-2000)', World Bank Group, Policy Research Working Paper Series; No. WPS 3381.
2. Peggy Levitt. 1996. 'Social Remittances: A conceptual Tool for Understanding Migration and Development', Harvard Center for Population and Development Studies, Working Paper Series; No. 96_04.
3. Docquier and Marfouk, Op cit, p.6.
4. Docquier and Marfouk, Op cit.

5. Prachi Mishra. 2006. 'Emigration and the Brain Drain: Evidence from the Caribbean', IMF Working Paper WP/06/25.
6. William J. Carrington and Enrica Detragiache. 1998. *'How Big is the Brain Drain?'* IMF Working Paper WP/98/102.
7. Docquier and Marfouk, Op cit, p. 9.
8. Statistical Institute of Jamaica. 2001 and 2002. *The Labour Force.*
9. Planning Institute of Jamaica. Editions 1990 to 2000. Economic and Social Survey of Jamaica.
10. International Institute of Education, Open Doors online database.
11. Barro, R. J. and J. –W. Lee. 1993. 'International Comparisons of Educational Attainment.' *Journal of Monetary Economics*, 32 (3): pp. 363-94.
12. Planning Institute of Jamaica. 1991 to 2000. *Economic and Social Survey of Jamaica.*
13. An average of 1767 work permits was issued annually for this occupational grouping during the period, however, it is not known how many would have been counted in the census.
14. Preliminary investigations revealed that the estimated attrition rate ranged from 2.8 per cent to 6.8 per cent
15. Planning Institute of Jamaica. 1990 to 2000. *'Economic and Social Survey of Jamaica* editions.

REFERENCES

Docquier, Frederic and Abdeslam Marfouk 2004. *Measuring the International Mobility of Skilled Workers (1990-2000).* World Bank Group, Policy Research Working Paper Series; No. WPS 3381.

Barro, R. J. and J.-W. Lee 1993. 'International Comparisons of Educational Attainment', Journal of Monetary Economics, 32 (3), pp. 363-94, December.

Carrington, William J. and Enrica Detragiache. 'How Extensive is the Brain Drain?'. *Finance and Development.* IMF Quarterly Publication, Vol. 36, No. 2, June 1999.

———. *How Big is the Brain Drain?* IMF Working Paper, WP/98/102, 1998. International Institute of Education, Open Doors online database. Accessed May 2006.

Levitt, Perry. *Social Remittances: A conceptual Tool for Understanding Migration and Development,.* Harvard Center for Population and Development Studies, Working Paper Series; No. 96_04, 1996.

Mishra, Prachi. *Emigration and the Brain Drain: Evidence from the Caribbean.* IMF Working Paper, WP/06/25, 2006.

Planning Institute of Jamaica. *Economic and Social Survey of Jamaica.* Editions 1990 to 2000.

Statistical Institute of Jamaica. *The Labour Force.* Editions 2001 and 2002.

———. Population Census, 1991 and 2001.

18

NURSE MIGRATION AND THE IMPACT ON HEALTH SYSTEMS IN THE CARIBBEAN:
The Case of St. Lucia and Jamaica

NATASHA KAY MORTLEY

INTRODUCTION

In his message to the world on the occasion of World Health Day 2006, Kofi Annan, the UN Secretary-General, stressed the significant role that health care workers play today:

> Health workers save lives. They strive to ensure that advances in health care reach those most in need. They contribute to the social and economic well-being of their countries. And they are essential to their countries' security, by being the first to identify a new disease or a new threat to public health. (The *Gleaner* April 7, 2006)

Nurses account for up to 70 per cent of health care staffing and they provide the majority of direct patient care, in addition to being the back bone of the public health system in the Caribbean region.[1] Shortages of nurses inevitably lead to a loss in capacity of Caribbean health systems to deliver effective and quality care. Caribbean governments, academics, professional and public groups are today expressing growing concern over the issues surrounding nurse migration and the attendant shortages of nurses in the region.

Caribbean nurses are moving out of the region at unprecedented rates. With global shortages of nursing staff becoming more acute and the active and aggressive recruiting within the region by developed countries, the nurse exodus is only expected to accelerate. Developing countries are affected by limited resources and an array of health problems, not the least of which is the growing HIV and AIDS epidemic. The loss of even a handful of health professionals can have major impacts, leading to further deterioration in the system and Caribbean governments' inability to meet the Millennium Development Goals. This has left CARICOM governments urgently seeking solutions and grappling with ideas such as *managed migration* and *training for export*. Many academics and professionals have suggested cooperation between sending and receiving countries in order to convert the *brain drain* into a *brain gain* for both. However, implementation of these ideas has not been forthcoming; in the meantime the problems have multiplied.

The departure from the region of nurses in considerable numbers is a social phenomenon likely to worsen in light of moves towards greater liberalization of world trade in all services, including health. There has been considerable debate as to whether the health sector, by the very nature of what it does, providing public goods and basic services, should be liberalized and fully commercialized. However, under the influence of the WTO-GATT there is likely to be growing support for expansion of international trade in health services.

The growth process in developed countries tends to be characterized by economies that are skill-biased. With skill-biased technological change, there is likely to be growing demand for skilled workers, including nurses in the health sector. Within the health sectors in particular, there is growing demand for such skilled (and also cheap) labour in light of an ageing population in developed countries. The population structure indicates that this demand will continue for many more years, thus leading to greater threat to the trained workforce in developing countries. It has been estimated that a 6 per cent shortfall (110,000) out of a registered nurses' workforce of 1.89 million in 2000, could increase to a shortage of 800,000 registered nurses by 2020 in the USA.[1] For the UK, it is estimated that demand will increase to 250,000 more than its 1997 levels by 2008.[2] Governments in both developed and developing countries have an obligation to their population to provide sufficient quantity and quality of public health and health care facilities.

According to Jong-Wook, Director-General of the World Health Organization (2000), improvements in health are essential if progress is to be made with the other Millennium Development Goals. Three out of the eight Millennium Development Goals, eight of the sixteen targets and eighteen of the 48 indicators relate directly to health. Health is also an important contributor to several other goals, thus bringing to the fore the significance of health and health care at an international scale.

Also important to current debates are ethical considerations on the extent to which recruiting agencies or governments of developed countries should be taking skilled workers from developing countries which are also suffering from shortages. On the other hand, there are several organizations that support and argue for individual nurses' rights to travel and work overseas to develop their practice and further their experiences.

What therefore does this mean for small island states such as Jamaica? This is the more general question that this chapter examines through an analysis of in-depth interviews conducted with some key players in the health sector. The insights gained throw fresh light on the nature of the problem plaguing Caribbean health systems, the effects on health care delivery of nurse migration and the possible, sustainable solutions for the future.

CARIBBEAN BACKGROUND

The Caribbean region is important for the study of the effects of emigration because it has the highest emigration rates in the world, most of which is labour migration (Mishra 2006). About 12 per cent of the labour force in the Caribbean has migrated to OECD countries (Docquier and Marfouk 2005). In Jamaica for example, the labour force was reduced by 10 per cent due to emigration to the USA alone between 1970 and 2000 (Mishra 2006). Further, the percentage reduction of the labour force in the Caribbean is much greater among the secondary and tertiary levels of schooling (see table 18.1). In fact, almost all the Caribbean countries are among the top twenty countries in the world with the highest tertiary educated migration rates (Docquier and Marfouk 2005). According to Nurse (2004) the problem with the Caribbean is that it is the highly skilled and educated that form the main group of migrants. In Guyana for

Table 18.1: 1990 skilled labour migration from selected caribbean countries

Countries	Tertiary educated share of total migrants	Migration rates of tertiary Educated
Jamaica	41.7	67.3
Trinidad & Tobago	46.7	57.2
Guyana	40.7	77.3

Source: *Carrington and Detragiache 1998*

instance, 60 per cent of university graduates have emigrated (Stubbs and Reyes 2004).

The magnitude and consistency of these emigration rates, especially within the skilled labour force brings to the fore issues of impacts on local labour markets and the welfare of those who remain behind, as well as raising the issue of *brain drain*. The departure of skilled emigrants affects development plans through a loss of investment money, expertise and talent that could help implement a shift towards service and high technology economies. In the case of the emigration of nurses, an important aspect of the 'brain drain' consideration is the loss conferred to Caribbean governments which finance the education of these migrants through their education budgets. Governments like Barbados, Trinidad and Tobago and Jamaica spend much more per capita on tertiary education than they do on primary and secondary education. For example more than 12 per cent of GDP is spent by the governments of Jamaica and Barbados on the education of their migrants.[3] This phenomenon termed *reverse subsidization*, means that developed countries absorb the skills and knowledge of critical workers, whose education was provided largely at government costs by developing countries, especially at the tertiary level. The issue has been receiving much attention in recent years and is a critical aspect of the current *brain drain* debate.

Nurse migration today is typically representative of Caribbean migration. Nurses qualify as highly skilled workers by virtue of three or four years of tertiary education. Further, nurses are mostly female. In the Caribbean, they are often the economic or physical heads of their households responsible for dependent children and elders. This means that home and familial obligations are usually high, fostering strong ties with home countries after migration. These ties can translate into a high propensity for return and circulation. The nursing shortage in the Caribbean is a major challenge to the delivery of safe, efficient and effective health care services. In a joint letter by the Chairman of the British Medical Association and the General Secretary of the Royal College of Nursing in the UK, they warned that efforts to deal with HIV and other health crises in developing countries were being hampered by nursing shortages (2005). An example of this can be found in the outbreak of malaria in Jamaica at the end of 2006 and the lack of sufficient resources and nursing staff to deal with this crisis. Many argued that the outbreak was worsened due to these shortages.

Nursing shortages are likely to be intensified by the continuing and aggressive recruitment of highly trained, competent Caribbean nurses by developed countries including the UK, USA and Canada. The Report of the Caribbean Commission on Health and Development (2005) indicated for selected CARICOM countries, a total of 2,810 nursing vacancies or 42.4 per cent of the total complement (see table 18.2). From the table also, it can be seen that four countries had vacancy rates exceeding twenty per cent: Barbados (20.6 per cent), Jamaica (58.4 per cent), St. Kitts (26 per cent) and Trinidad and Tobago (53.3 per cent). Ironically, the report found that the two countries with the highest vacancy rates (Jamaica and Trinidad and Tobago) were the ones with the highest number of nursing training institutions.

Table 18.2: Nurse vacancy rates for selected CARICOM countries

Number of Registered Nurse, Vacancies and Vacancy Rates by Country			
Country	Number of Registered Nurses	Number of Vacancies	Vacancy Rates (%)
Antigua	320	56	17.5
Barbados	930	192	20.6
Dominica	177	11	6
Grenada	432	16	4
Jamaica	2,256	1,317	58.3
St. Kitts	192	50	26
St. Lucia	409	18	4
St. Vincent	216	34	15.7
Trinidad	2,125	1,132	53.2
Total	**6,625**	**2,810**	**42.4**

Source: *Caribbean Commission on Health and Development*
Report of July 2005

President of the Nurses Association in Jamaica, Edith Allwood-Anderson, disclosed in a report to the *Sunday Gleaner* that currently 2000 nurses are employed in the public health sector while the system needed about 4,000 to 5,000 nurses in order for it to begin to cope effectively.[4] This scenario, she went on leads to nurses being burnt out, reduction in quality care and increased nursing and medical errors.

During my own interview with the President of the Nurses Association in St. Lucia, she revealed that while by international health standards the ratio of nurses to ambulant patients should be about 1:6; in St. Lucia that ratio is never reached. At the Victoria Hospital in Castries the ratio is about 1:20, especially on night shifts when there is a greater shortage of nursing staff. In Jamaica the ratios are even worse: at the Bustamante Hospital for children in St. Andrew for example, the ratio is one registered nurse to 30 and sometimes 40 patients.[5]

UK BACKGROUND

Figures from the UK are also very revealing, especially with regards to future trends in migration. In order to work in the UK all nurses, midwives and specialist community public health nurses must register with the Nursing and Midwifery Council (NMC). Applications to the register are made from home countries and once all the necessary criteria are met, a pin card and statement of entry are issued. Registration therefore, is a prerequisite to work in the UK and applications to the register indicate persons who want to work.

Table 18.3 shows registration data for nurses and midwives from the West Indies from 1998 to 2005. The table shows fluctuations in the figures with a marked increase in registration from 1999 to 2000, to a marked decrease the following year. However, these figures only indicate persons who wish to work, but do not tell us how many actually do work in the UK.

Table 18.3: Initial overseas admissions to the UK of registered nurses and midwives being admitted to register

Region	1998/99	1999/00	2000/01	2001/02	2002/02	2003/04	2004/05
West Indies	221	425	261	248	208	397	352

Source: *NMC Statistical Analysis of the Register August, 2005.*

UK work permit data for 2003 are more revealing (See Appendix 1). By providing different categories of work permits granted: work permits (22 per cent of total permits), first permissions (26 per cent), extensions (23 per cent) and changes in work permits (29 per cent), they tell us how many nurses and midwives actually do work in the UK, the turnover from one job to another and further they tell how many nurses are extending their stay in the UK, that is, nurses who are not returning to home countries. Figures for individual countries are too small to warrant individual analyses, so only total numbers or percentages will be discussed. Also because the number of midwives is such a minute figure, for discussion purposes figures for nurses and midwives will also be merged and treated as one.

Work permits approved are those permits issued to nurses who apply to work in the UK but are still in their home countries. Appendix I, table A shows 164 permits approved in 2003 for Caribbean nurses. For this category of nurses, although permits have been granted, the fact that they are still in their home countries means it cannot be stated with certainty that they in fact will migrate to work in the UK. Hence, while this figure tells us of nurses' intentions to migrate for work, it does not tell us of actual migration taking place.

First permissions, which are those permits issued to nurses while in the UK are more telling. Appendix I, table B shows that 199 first permissions were granted to West Indian nurses and midwives to start work in the UK in 2003. With this figure we can begin to speak of nurse migration as these nurses have actually already migrated and are ready to start work. The table shows that there are 35 more nurses applying for permits in the UK rather than from home countries, probably meaning that more nurses are taking their chances and migrating first, then hoping to get permits upon arrival. This shows an eagerness on the part of this group to migrate. Alternatively the data can also mean that this stock of Caribbean nurses may have not intended initially to work in the UK, but came for other reasons. Once in the UK, they may have made a decision to remain to work.

Changes in work permits (Appendix I, table C), represent those nurses who change employer while in the UK. It can mean changes from private to public institutions or vice versa or a change of employer within the private sector. However studies have found that most job changes occur from private to public sector or the National Health Service (NHS). For most nurses, working in the NHS is preferred to working in private health institutions since there is greater opportunity for career development and advancement. A further incentive is that in recent times salaries and benefits have improved within the NHS.

Appendix I, table C indicates 221 changes in work permits for 2003, which represents the highest number for all the categories of permits. This shows a high turnover rate among West Indian nurses once in the UK, implying a high level of mobility either among these nurses or within health institutions. This may be positive for West Indian nurses in the long run, for, as they move around from one institution to another, they gain more skills and experience and are more valuable to their health institutions, if and when they return home.

Finally, Appendix I, table D shows in-country extensions, that is, nurses who are extending their permits for longer than the initial term. The table indicates 173 West Indian nurses applied for permit extensions in 2003. This figure is higher than work permits approved and almost as high as first permissions, which means that more (or just as many) nurses are extending their stay in the UK than those applying for permits and first permissions. This figure tells us that a relatively high number of West Indian nurses are extending their stay in the UK and thus opting to remain in the UK to work. A high percentage of West Indian nurses in the UK are thus not returning home, and when this figure is added to newly arrived migrants, it means greater shortages in health institutions in the Caribbean for any one year.

In linking available data to this chapter's research questions and policy issues of West Indian nurse migration, each category of work permit is used to generate a set of questions about nurse migration to explore the question further. For instance, the category of work permit extensions raises questions as to why West Indian nurses are remaining longer in the UK, whether they intend to return home and under what conditions they would decide to return home. Similarly, the changes in work permit category brings to the fore issues of the high turn over rate within health institutions in the UK, the extent to which West Indian nurses' expectations of the job are met when they do start work in the UK and, generally, the rate of mobility among West Indian nurses in the UK.

THE PROBLEM OF NURSE MIGRATION

This chapter uses St. Lucia, Jamaica and the UK as a basis of analysis. In Jamaica and St. Lucia in-depth interviews were conducted with senior registered nurses, hospital managers, policy makers and officials at the Ministry of Health and other related institutions to determine the extent to which nurse migration is symptomatic of deeper systemic conditions in the health systems in the Caribbean. The impact of this movement on the quality of health care was also considered. The interviews were conducted in the UK, one of the major receivers of West Indian nurses, and showed why West Indian nurses do not and have not returned home as yet, and under what conditions they would consider returning. The experiences of those interviewed, as well as their answers to these questions, provide a base from which policy makers can begin framing concrete strategies in managing the movement in such a way that all the stakeholders, especially individual nurses, stand to benefit.

In light of statistical data, this chapter analyses fifteen in-depth interviews conducted with key players within the health systems in St. Lucia, Jamaica and the UK. A longitudinal approach is adopted through the interview, such that one person's views and experiences are traced through different times and places. This has provided valuable insights into participants' experiences of nurse migration, its impacts and possible solutions for the Caribbean. Throughout this chapter, some of the views and experiences of the participants are used to enhance the analysis and thus make suggestions for future solutions to managing the movement.

The interviews revealed that the main reasons why nurses migrate to work overseas are:

- Poor conditions of work
- No opportunities for professional development
- Low pay
- Limited opportunities for continued training and educational advancement

Ironically, analyses revealed that while improved salary was one of the reasons why nurses migrate, it was not the main reason. There is a general awareness that although the salary that nurses obtain abroad may be higher than that at home, nurses also have to deal with higher living expenses abroad in the form of housing, transportation, taxes and so forth. In one of the very first studies conducted in the Caribbean by Mary Seivwright on nurses migrating to New York, it was found that the educational development and promotional opportunities were key factors in the decision to migrate. Even when salary was featured, it was related to the fact that the nurses needed the improved salary for their educational development.

In the Caribbean conditions of work include poor facilities and very little resources to work with. Nurses in St. Lucia have indicated a lack of adequate medical supplies, offices not being properly equipped and insufficient beds for patients. In Jamaica, apart from inadequate tools and medications to work with, conditions of work are worsened by the staff shortages. A registered nurse (RN) at the Kingston Public Hospital (KPH) for more than 20 years, stated during an interview that she was fed up with the conditions that nurses at that institution have to work under'.

'Sometimes there is nothing to work with. No syringe, no needles, no gauze or drugs for the patient.' (The *Gleaner* April 30, 2006)

'Our offices are not even properly equipped; insufficient desks and chairs and no computer. We have no technology to work with.' (Interview with a senior registered nurse in St Lucia 4/11/05)

The Impact

> 'If we were to talk about impacts on the health system, I would say depletion of human resources, a crisis of confidence by the citizenry of the country…on the service there is the impact of the standard and quality of care being compromised.' (Interview with St. Lucia's Minister of Health 12/07/05)

While there is a plethora of empirical evidence and studies conducted suggesting negative impacts of nurse migration on the health system, my own interviews have revealed some positive impacts on the system. The extent to which these positive effects are sufficient to assuage the negative impacts, is yet to be decided through further research. The interview with the Minister of Health in St. Lucia, for instance, revealed positive effects in the form of better planning in the health system and thus greater efficiency in some areas. In terms of impacts on human resources, shortages in staff and resources create a challenge to the nurses which leads to greater performance management.

Further, when nurses return home there are the positive effects of experience, new skills and technologies being filtered back to the system. In Jamaica, the Head of the School of Advanced Nursing, revealed that there are positive effects when nurses go to enrich themselves and then return home. Persons like Dr. Mary Seivwright, Dame Nita Barrow and others, are examples of nurses who migrated in the early days and educated themselves and returned to make valuable contributions to the health system in the Caribbean. Their contributions have come in the form of research and information to inform policy and in public health education, all of which have added knowledge and value to the health system.

Nevertheless, the negative effects on the system have been numerous and are the main concern here, because these are the issues that policy-makers and professionals are currently grappling with and to which they are seeking solutions:

- Massive shortages of staff
- Overworked and over burdened staff
- Low staff morale

- Deteriorating quality of care
- Lack of confidence of the citizenry in the health care system

FUTURE STRATEGY AND CONCLUSIONS

Managed migration is a regional strategy for retaining adequate numbers of competent nursing personnel to deliver health programmes and services to the Caribbean nationals at the highest levels and while doing that, making sure that you have surplus, so that you manage it in such a way that we are comfortably covered...'(Head of the School of Advanced Nursing – UWI, Jamaica, 2005).

Policies to address nurse migration must take into account the interests and expectations of all the stakeholders, including the nurses themselves. Further, they must take into account ethical issues and the rights and freedoms of person to move. The key stakeholders are those who live and experience the problem of nurse migration. Among key stakeholders are nurses, hospital managers, administrators and persons who train and recruit nurses both at home and abroad.

Any framework for regulating or managing the movement of Caribbean nurses must draw on the views and experiences as expressed by these key stakeholders. For instance, interviews revealed that it was the nurses themselves, through the nursing association, who met at a region level and recognized the inevitability of nurse migration and therefore came with strategies for retaining and managing this movement. The concept of *managed migration* was borne out of this very initiative on the part of nurses and included six critical areas:

- Terms and conditions of work
- Recruitment
- Education and training
- Valuing of nurses and nursing
- Utilization and deployment of nurses
- Shared governance
- Policy and health sector reform

Other views expressed by interviewees for future improvements in the health system include:

- Continuing education
- Narrowing the gap between nurses and nurse managers e.g ward sisters
- Frequent appraisals and promotional opportunities
- Employer inputs and support
- Better packages for nurses

These views and experiences of the major stakeholders are the key to finding sustainable solutions to Caribbean nurse migration. Any strategy for future management of the movement must draw on and build on the experiences of those most affected by the problem.

NOTES

1. Report of the Caribbean Commission on Health and Development. July 2005.
2. Bach, S. 2003. 'International migration of health workers: Labour and social issues'.
3. United Nations Educational Scientific and Cultural Organization figures cited in Mishra, 2006.
4. The *Gleaner*. Jamaica. 30th April 2006.
5. Ibid.

REFERENCES

Bach, S. 2003. 'International migration of health workers: Labour and social issues'. Working Papers. Geneva: International Labour Office.

Buchan, J. 2001. 'Nurse migration and international recruitment'. *Nursing Inquiry,* 8,4: 203-204.

CARICOM, 2005. Report of the Regional Commission on Health and Development, Caribbean Commission on Health and Development, 2005.

Carrington, W.J. and E. Detragiache, 1998. 'How big is the brain drain?' IMF Working Paper 98/102, Washington DC. IMF.

Docquier, F. and A. Marfouk, 2005. "International migration by educational attainment (1990-2000)," Release 1.1, World Bank.

The *Gleaner*, April 7, 2006.

The *Gleaner*. April 30,2006.

Mishra, P. 2006. 'Emigration and brain drain: Evidence from the Caribbean', International Monetary Fund (IMF) Working Paper (WP/06/25).

Muula, A.S. et al. 2003. 'The ethics of developed nations recruiting nurses from developing countries: The case of Malawi', *Nursing Ethics,* 10, 4: 432-438.

Nursing and Midwifery Council Annual Statistics 2004-2005. Accessed: http://www.nmc-uk.org/aArticle.aspx?ArticleID=1689

Nullis-Kapp, C. [2005] 'Health worker shortage could derail development goals', *Bulletin of the World Health Organization,* 83(1).

Nurse, K. 2004. 'Diaspora, migration and development in the Caribbean', *Focal: Policy Paper* (September). 3-10.

Report of the Special Committee on the Migration and Training of Nurses, St. Lucia Ministry of Health. August 2004.

Singh, J.A. et al. 2003. 'The Ethics of Nurse Poaching from the Developing World'. *Nursing Ethics,* 10, 6: 666.

Stubbs, J. and H. Reyes. 2004. 'Migration in the Caribbean: A path to development?' *En Breve,* no.48 (May).

UK Work Permit Data. Retrieved Migration Research Unit Database, University College London.

APPENDIX I

Table A: Work Permits Approved, Excluding Groups and SBS Applications (2003 and 2004)

Occupation 2003	Total	Antigua	B'dos	Dominica	Grenada	Guyana	Jamaica	St. Kitts	St. Lucia	St. Vin.	T&T
Nurses	163	0	8	1	1	81	23	2	8	4	35
Midwives	1	0	0	0	0	0	0	0	0	0	1
Total	164										

Table B: First Permissions Approved, Excluding Groups and SBS Applications (2003 and 2004)

Occupation 2003	Total	Antigua	B'dos	Dominica	Grenada	Guyana	Jamaica	St. Kitts	St. Lucia	St. Vin.	T&T
Nurses	197	0	6	0	5	10	61	0	6	4	105
Midwives	2	0	0	0	0	0	0	0	0	0	2
Total	199										

Table C: Change in Work Permits, Excluding Groups and SBS Applications (2003 and 2004)

Occupation 2003	Total	Antigua	B'dos	Dominica	Grenada	Guyana	Jamaica	St. Kitts	St. Lucia	St. Vin.	T&T
Nurses	213	1	12	2	0	46	64	0	3	6	79
Midwives	8	0	1	0	0	0	5	0	0	0	2
Total	221										

Table D: In Country Extensions, Excluding Groups and SBS Applications (2003 and 2004)

Occupation 2003	Total	Antigua	B'dos	Dominica	Grenada	Guyana	Jamaica	St. Kitts	St. Lucia	St. Vin.	T&T
Nurses	169	0	9	0	2	24	38	0	2	11	83
Midwives	4	0	0	0	0	0	0	0	0	0	4
Total	173										

Source: Data Sets from Migration Research Unit at University College, London

19

IN SEARCH OF THE DIASPORA EFFECT:
Lessons From the Asian 'Brain Gain' For the Caribbean 'Brain Drain'

JASON JACKSON

INTRODUCTION

The cross-border movement of persons has been one of the key features of the current wave of globalization. However, the much-lauded liberalization of factors of production associated with globalization has been one-sided, with capital moving with increased freedom between North and South and skilled (but critically less so, unskilled) labour from developing countries being selectively welcomed in the North. Much of the recent influx of highly skilled migrants has been directed towards high technology poles in the advanced industrialised countries, such as Silicon Valley and Route 128 in the United States. However, an increasingly important trend currently being observed sees skilled migrants from developing countries returning home after participating in high technology sectors overseas. Many of these returning migrants — scientists, engineers and technology managers — play important roles in technology-intensive ventures back home, both as employees recruited by existing firms as well as entrepreneurs, leading traditional discussions of 'brain drain' to include reference to 'brain gain' and 'brain circulation'. Most policymakers in developing countries, and increasingly in OECD countries such as the UK, recognise the value of their highly-skilled diasporas but few have enjoyed success in enticing them home. Taiwan and India stand as exceptions to this rule.

This chapter examines the 'brain gain' or 'brain circulation' dynamic that has been observed between India and Taiwan and the United States. It seeks to understand the role of the Taiwanese and Indian diasporas in the development of their burgeoning domestic technology- and knowledge-intensive sectors to identify lessons for technology and innovation policy in the Caribbean given its large skilled Diaspora. For example, Jamaica has one of the largest diasporas in the world — including both skilled and unskilled persons — and so their *potential* contribution to domestic development is great. However, this chapter argues that market forces cannot be relied upon: there is a clear role for innovative policymaking to tap overseas-based skills.

HOW BIG IS THE BRAIN DRAIN? BACKGROUND AND SOME EMPIRICAL EVIDENCE

The majority of economic literature on South-North migration tends to focus on the effects on the advanced countries and the ensuing policy responses, which usually entail restrictive immigration policies aimed at stemming the influx of migrants (often at the behest of domestic interest groups). However there has been increasing research interest in the effect of migration on the sending countries, most of which are located in the developing world. This reflects a growing recognition of the influence of the cross-border movement of highly-skilled people in dynamic technology-intensive development.

For more than three decades US immigration policy has made a discernable shift towards skills-based selectivity, with policies favouring the highly skilled while maintaining more stringent restrictions on entry of unskilled migrants. This policy shift has been driven by two main factors: (i) a growing gap between the domestic demand and supply of skilled labour, which has been made urgent by increasing global competition and (ii), more recently, concerns about the sustainability of the social security system due to America's ageing population.

Boosting the influx of highly skilled migrants has become an increasingly important aspect of industrial policy in most advanced industrialized countries (AICs). Intense global competition in high value-added goods and services amongst the AICs — and increasingly from advanced developing countries such as South Korea, Taiwan, China, India and Brazil — is leading the AICs to bolster the share of skilled labour in their populations via migration.[1] The threat that ageing populations in North America and Western Europe pose to the viability of national social security systems adds further impetus to this trend. Increasing migration flows — particularly amongst the highly skilled who command high incomes and pay the most taxes — is seen as a means to averting an impending crisis in the welfare state.[2] For example, Kapur (2001:282) cites recent research that places the net present value of highly skilled migrants in the 40-44 year age bracket at $96,000 as compared to negative $88,000 for a new born American.

While the industrialized countries of North America and Western Europe are the main receiving countries for highly skilled labour flows, developing countries in Africa, Asia and Latin America and the Caribbean are the principle source.[3] Most observers argue that developing countries suffer a double-blow as a result of the structure of Northern immigration policies. Increased barriers to unskilled migration constrain developing countries' ability to vent surplus unskilled labour and ease population growth, unemployment and accompanying social pressure.[4] Further, the high demand for skilled labour in the USA and Western Europe has raised concerns in developing countries of a brain drain that 'could well deprive such countries [of] their most skilled and talented people' and thus curtail their short- and long-term growth prospects. (Faini, 2003:1) Certainly the data justifies these concerns. Table 1 shows that the brain drain is a real and important phenomenon, in both relative and absolute terms. For example, Mexico and the Philippines each have almost a million highly-skilled migrants in the USA. While this figure is somewhat balanced by the high flow of unskilled migrants (which is almost certainly higher than this data suggests due to the large number of undocumented unskilled migrants), the highly-skilled comprise the overwhelming majority of Filipino migrants. The same is true for migrants from India, Morocco, Jamaica and El Salvador. Indeed, Adams (2003) notes that over 80 per cent of Jamaicans residing overseas are tertiary educated .

THEORETICAL APPROACHES TO THE BRAIN DRAIN

Traditional economic approaches to the effects of highly skilled emigration from developing countries have focused on the negative developmental effect of the brain drain. More recently there has been increased focus on potential positives or 'mitigating factors' that, it is argued, might alleviate traditional concerns about the brain drain. These include remittances, increased domestic investment in education as a response to the potential to migrate and earn higher wages, and temporary or permanent return migration.[5] The first two are further examined below while the third is addressed in the next section.

EARLY APPROACH: TAXATION OF LABOUR FLOWS

One of the earliest and best-known analyses of the impact of the brain drain on developing countries is associated with Jagdish Bhagwati (e.g. Bhagwati and Rodriguez, 1976; Bhagwati and Wilson, 1989; and Bhagwati, 1998). Contrary to previously held assumptions of perfectly competitive markets and unsubsidised public education, Bhagwati in his various contributions argued that migration of skilled labour from developing countries to the AICs resulted in a welfare loss in the sending countries if the individual welfare gain of the migrant was outweighed by the social welfare loss of his/her skills' contribution to society. Operating within a neoclassical general equilibrium framework, Bhagwati suggested that receiving countries should compensate the sending countries in the form of a 'brain drain tax'. This tax would compensate developing countries for the loss of tax revenue which would have accrued from these skilled workers, as well as for the lost fiscal investment in education[6] and taxes that would have been earned on their labour. Though there continued to be academic contributions through the late 1980s, this line of thought received less attention following Bhagwati's early works, at least in part due to concerns about the low likelihood of the implementation of a tax on advanced countries given asymmetric power differentials between the AICs and developing countries.

Academic work in the tradition of Bhagwati's 'brain drain tax' has however been recently revisited by others, most notably Desai, et al (2002; 2003). In this research the authors build on Bhagwati's earlier theoretical proposition through emphasis on specific tax instruments and 'the actual experience of alternative tax regimes and their potential impact on source countries.' (Desai et al, 2002:3) There are four means through which such a tax could be captured: an exit tax, a flat tax, a variant of the 'American model' of taxing overseas nationals, and through a multilateral cooperative model (Kapur, 2001). However, the authors admit problems with all four, namely avoidance, administrative weaknesses, weak incentives for cooperation based on migrants not planning to return and again, asymmetric power relations between industrialised and developing states, which would make it difficult for developing countries to elicit support for a multilateral approach from the industrialised world.[7]

REVISIONIST APPROACH: (I) REMITTANCES

The next major round of interest in migration and developing countries arose in the late 1990s and focussed on remittances. While the importance of remittances had long been recognised, financial liberalization conducted under neoliberal reforms led to flows of remittances being captured in national statistics. A remittances-focussed approach to skilled migration and brain drain might suggest positive benefits in the form of increased financial flows to the home country, which can serve a number of important functions including poverty reduction, easing the foreign exchange constraint, and potentially providing a pool of investment income for the home country recipients. (Faini, 2003) The World Bank has been the principal source of research on this issue, which is unsurprising given the nature of remittances and the Banks new explicit focus on poverty reduction.

There is no question that remittances are an important source of external finance, and that they are playing a critical role in most developing countries at the macro, mezo and micro/household levels.[8] First, the volume of remittances is significant in both relative and absolute terms, and flows appear to be growing at double digit rates.[9] Second, it has been argued that remittances have been filling the void of decreased private capital flows since the mid-1990s as well as declining international aid flows. (Nurse, 2003) This has been critical in maintaining macroeconomic stability in many developing countries, particularly small open economies like Jamaica and the Dominican Republic, where remittances are over 10 per cent of GDP, and further, in Jamaica remittances are now the second most important source of foreign exchange, after tourism and before bauxite receipts.[10] Third, it is clear from anecdotal evidence as well as statistical analysis that remittances have an important effect on poverty alleviation, if not poverty reduction.[11] Remittances in this view are an informal means of social insurance (Kapur, 2003). For example, a World Bank cross-country empirical study finds that international migration generally has a strong statistical impact on reducing poverty, with a 10 per cent increase in migration leading to a 1.9 per cent decline in poverty and specifically, a 10 per cent increase in the ratio of remittances to GDP leads to a 1.6 per cent decline in poverty (Adams and Page, 2003).

However, in spite of these, the effect of remittances on structural poverty and productive investment needed for long-term development appears to be weak. Kapur (2003) argues that it is important to dispel the myth that remittances compensate for the brain drain. That is, the argument that while countries lose one scarce factor of production (human capital) they gain another scarce factor (financial resources in the form of remittances). In fact, these are not substitutes (Ibid). A closer analysis of remittances provides some insights as to why this may be so, and why developing countries should find little consolation in remittances as a mitigating factor to brain drain.

There are at least two problems with this latter proposition concerning the use of remittances and the source: First, remitted funds tend to be consumed rather than invested in productive economic activity, with the important exception of remittances that go towards paying for education of dependents within the household.[12] Thus remittances do not appear to contribute significantly to domestic savings and investment. Second, highly-skilled migrants tend not to be big remitters. A simple view of remittances may consider migrants as a largely undifferentiated group. However, when one begins to disaggregate the behaviour of skilled and unskilled migrants in the context of remittances a more nuanced picture emerges. Despite hypotheses suggesting that higher-educated migrants remit more due to their higher earnings, Faini (2003:2) finds that in fact 'a higher skilled content of migration is found to be associated with a lower flow of remittances.' He interprets this observation 'as indicating that skilled migrants tend to loosen their links with their home country, are more likely to bring their family to the host country and, therefore, have a lower propensity to remit' (Faini, 2003:2). A more powerful hypothesis suggested by this chapter relates to class. That is, almost by definition, highly-educated migrants are drawn disproportionately from the middle and upper middle classes, and as such are less likely to remit because the family back home is not in great need of their financial support. In fact, net financial flows may well go the opposite way from South to North as families pay for their children's tertiary education abroad, as has become institutionalized amongst the middle class in the Caribbean. This group is differentiated from those migrants drawn from the lower middle and underclass who do not have a tertiary education and who remit heavily to support dependent households in the sending country.[13] Further, some have argued that remittances provide a disincentive to participate in gainful employment, particularly amongst young men.[14] Thus not only is there little to suggest that remittances reduce structural poverty, there may be some direct negative social effects associated with remittances as well. Even though remittances have some positive effects at the macroeconomic and household levels, remittances cannot be said to be mitigating the brain drain since for the most part those who make up the brain drain do not remit. Remittances mitigate migration generally but not for the highly skilled.

REVISIONIST APPROACH: (II) INCREASED INCENTIVE FOR INVESTMENT IN EDUCATION

There is a relatively new strand of 'brain gain' literature based on partial equilibrium analysis that argues for the existence of a 'brain-drain induced 'brain gain." (Schiff, 2005:2) In this view brain drain may raise growth levels in the sending country by raising the perceived return to education, which then leads to higher investments in education as persons pursue further schooling in the hope of migrating and taking advantage of higher wages overseas. The argument follows that this increased investment in education ultimately boosts growth in the home country. In sum, this new line of thinking posits that:

(i) 'the brain drain raises the expected return on education [since it implies that a share of skilled persons will migrate and earn higher wages overseas];

(ii) this induces additional investment in education (a brain gain);

(iii) this may result in a 'beneficial brain drain' or *net* brain gain, i.e. in a brain gain that is larger than the brain drain; and

(iv) a *net* brain gain raises welfare and growth' (Schiff, 2005:2-3).

While there is some intuitive appeal to this line of reasoning, the theoretical underpinnings of the approach have been challenged and the limited empirical evidence reported in the literature remains ambiguous. Faini (2003:2) finds 'little evidence suggesting that raising the skill composition of migration has a positive effect on educational achievements in the home country.' He finds a negative correlation between the tertiary enrolment ratio in sending countries and the share of skilled labour in migration. Schiff's (2005:6) theoretical critique suggests that a "beneficial brain drain' cannot occur in the steady state [and further] a net brain *loss* is likely to hold during the transition.' He concludes that the concerns of the early contributors to the brain drain literature that skilled migration hurt the developmental prospects of sending countries 'were probably close to the mark'[15] (Ibid).

KNOWLEDGE, TECHNOLOGY AND DEVELOPMENT

TACIT KNOWLEDGE FLOWS AND TECHNOLOGY TRANSFER

The importance of tacit knowledge and experience embodied in skilled persons is central to the rationale for reverse brain drain and brain gain, and in turn the distinction between tacit and explicit knowledge is the key factor underpinning the importance of cross-border movement of persons in facilitating technology transfer. While information is comprised of facts, knowledge is best regarded as a system of information, which has both tacit and explicit dimensions. Explicit knowledge in the context of industrial development can be defined as information and understanding that can readily be transmitted between individuals through use of formal, systematic language. Thus, by observing a process or by following codified instructions, one can successfully replicate a process characterized by explicit knowledge. Tacit knowledge or 'know-how' on the other hand cannot be easily codified, copied or formally defined. It is difficult to formalize and hence to be communicated or shared with others.[16] Thus the more tacit a technology the more difficult it is for a technology follower to adapt and effectively use it to catch up. Acquisition of tacit knowledge often requires direct exchanges between experts who possess this knowledge and those who are learning, hence the importance of cross-border movement of people within whom this knowledge is embodied to facilitate physically interaction with those who seek to learn.

Development economists and other social scientists have long stressed the importance of knowledge and learning in industrialization and development. Neoclassical economics, however, had been less inclined to include these factors before the introduction of endogenous or 'new' growth theory.[17] With this development in mainstream economic thought, recognition of learning effects, externalities, scale economies, asymmetric information and human capital became central to most economic models. In the technology policy literature, the debate centred on the constraints to technological upgrading in developing countries.

'SUCCESSFUL CASES OF CATCH-UP HAVE [ALWAYS] INVOLVED CONSIDERABLE CROSS-BORDER FLOW OF PEOPLE.' (NELSON, 2005)

Historically, the cross-border movement of people has played a critical role in the transfer of knowledge and technology necessary for successful industrial development. Following the first industrial revolution, British technical experts were invaluable to North America attempting to replicate English industrial growth. Demand for these talents in the fledgling United States grew dramatically as the country shifted from primary agricultural and mineral production to early stage industrialization. This cross-border influx of persons was critical as the transfer of knowledge and skills from Britain helped to fuel nineteenth century industrialization in the northeast United States. The case of Japan similarly illustrates the persistent role of knowledge flows. Central to Japan's astonishingly successful Meiji-era transformation from a feudal to a modern state was the influx of over 3,000 foreign experts (particularly engineers and scientists, but also military and other experts) coupled with the policy of sending thousands of Japanese students to Europe and the USA. The mantra from the Meiji Charter Oath 'Knowledge shall be sought throughout the world to strengthen the power of Imperial rule' was vigorously pursued. Meiji rule lasted less than fifty years (1868–1912), but Japan was already a major industrial power by the end of WW I due to Western expertise and critically, returning Japanese overseas students.

In the present period we see an increasingly competitive global economy where recruiting and retaining talent is critical for all countries in developing — or maintaining — the ability to compete. The desire to entice the return of highly-educated, highly-skilled migrants is not solely a developing country preoccupation. A recent OECD report from the Directorate for Science, Technology and Industry noted that 'In 2000 the British government... launched a five-year ... £20 million scheme to attract the return of Britain's leading expatriate scientists and the migration of top young researchers to the United Kingdom' (Cervantes and Guillec, 2002:1). They go on to note that this occurred in the same year that, 'under greater media coverage, the US Congress announced it was raising the annual cap on the number of temporary work visas granted to highly skilled professionals under its H1B visa programme, from 115,000 to 195,000 per year until 2003.'[18] (Ibid). Indeed, the chart illustrating on the tenfold growth of H1B visas in IT since 1990 demonstrates the importance of this policy tool and of overseas scientists and engineers to the continued technological leadership of the AICs.[19] The OECD report concludes that this effort on the part of the British government 'dispels a myth: that the problem only affects developing and transition economies'[20] (Cervantes and Guillec, 2002:1).

The diaspora represents a powerful option for developing country policymakers striving to develop technology-intensive industrial sectors. There are at least two viable policy approaches to tapping the potential of the Diaspora: reverse brain drain, which is the return option, and brain circulation, which entails the remote mobilization of skilled migrants through temporary or cyclical migration, including short-term visits, use of ICTs and utilization of sectoral networks and contacts that migrants have established in the industrialised countries. In this view the recovery of highly qualified professionals in the Diaspora is part of a comprehensive development strategy, with particular focus on (but certainly not limited to) technology- and knowledge-intensive sectors (Meyer, et al, 1997).

The existence of technological know-how, skills and experience in the Diaspora presents an opportunity for creative policymaking aimed at designing institutional mechanisms to develop the technological capabilities needed to boost dynamism in the productive sector. Similarly, just as immigration policy has become an explicit industrial policy tool in the North, so too do policies aimed at utilising the Diaspora need to become explicit elements of industrial policy in the South.

BRAIN GAIN IN TAIWAN AND INDIA

The data in the previous sections have illustrated that the brain drain is a real phenomenon in many developing countries. The cases of Taiwan and India below illustrate successful attempts at engaging the Diaspora in the development of high-technology sectors and should be a challenge and a source of optimism to other developing countries.[21] These cases were chosen because they illustrate two different types of high-technology sector (manufacturing and services), different sequencing of policies and hence evolution of approaches and ultimately different degrees of success. However, the common thread is that in both cases the value of the Diaspora was recognised from the outset, and strategies to engage and involve the

Diaspora were included in the formulation of industrial policy and were pursued throughout the various stages of implementation and sectoral development.

BACKGROUND: TAIWAN

The Taiwanese electronics sector is one of the most advanced in the world. It is the leader in manufacturing of high-tech components including silicon chips and, along with South Korea, is rapidly approaching the technological frontier in a number of other key areas, trailing only the United States and Japan in technological superiority.[22] Many accounts of the Taiwan success story point to government intervention via extensive industrial policies (Wade, 1989).[23] However, a less well-known aspect of the Taiwanese 'miracle' is the influence and impact of overseas Taiwanese on the country's rapid growth, particularly in the semiconductor industry. Saxenian summarises the factors underlying the initial emergence of Taiwan's dynamic electronics manufacturing sector in the early 1980s as: 'FDI and public investments in education and research capabilities initially, and later, policies to develop and transfer technology to the private sector and to support new industrial entrants, combined with growing ties to the Overseas Chinese community in Silicon Valley. (Saxenian, 2001:4-5).

TAPPING THE DIASPORA

Well before the electronics revolution, Taiwanese officials (motivated as they were by political imperatives that made rapid development a must) sought industrial policy advice from the Taiwanese Diaspora. 'Taiwanese officials began traveling to Silicon Valley in the 1960s and 1970s, long before most of the world was aware of its existence. Senior economic ministers studied the Silicon Valley experience and institutionalized mechanisms for eliciting advice on technology and industrial policy from the region's community of US-educated Taiwanese engineers' (Ibid). Indeed, under the advice of their Silicon Valley based diaspora, Taiwanese policymakers attempted to mimic many other aspects of the Silicon Valley model, including links between industry and public research institutions and the creation of venture capital industry to provide the financial support necessary for an inherently high-risk industry. Matthews (1997:27) cites the 'close relations with the California business and educational system' that ultimately led to the development of the Hsinchu Science Park — now known as the 'Silicon Valley of the East' — in the 1980s. Hsinchu was designed to provide world-class technological infrastructure for the growing industry, as well as to bring together the various players, including research institutes and venture capitalists, to take advantage of the clustering effects that are often cited as one of the critical elements of Silicon Valley's success.

REVERSE BRAIN DRAIN

The impact of the diaspora became apparent with the 'reversal' of the brain drain in the early 1990s, when thousands of Taiwanese engineers who had studied and worked in the USA returned to Taiwan either to work for start-ups or established companies, or to become entrepreneurs themselves . The role of Hsinchu was especially important. While the park attracted less than ten returnees a year in the early 1980s, more than 2,500 returnees began working in the Park during the 1990s, or some 350 per year' (Saxenian, 2001:9). By the 1990s 40 per cent of these returnees were in the managerial ranks where they were able to leverage their technical skill, organizational and managerial knowledge, entrepreneurial experience, and international connections, all of which were critical elements of Taiwan's successful catch-up strategy. (Ibid) Lowell and Gerova (2004) cite evidence claiming that a government policy initiative in Hsinchu to attract overseas Taiwanese R&D professionals led to 2,536 returnees by 1996, a figure which doubled to 5,025 by 2000. In fact, Saxenian (2001:10) goes as far as to suggest that returnees may have been even more important to the success of the Taiwanese high-tech sector than the Science Park itself, though of course the Park has been a key incentive for return. Today Taiwan is well known for its high capacity to absorb highly educated returnees, with some analysts claiming that postgraduate returnees in Hsinchu account for as much as 78 per cent of its total labour force.[24] (Stalker, 2000; Iredale and Guo, 2001:7) Their contribution to Taiwan's industrial development makes them a highly valued group and the Government of Taiwan continues to make significant efforts to attract them home and provide support through a series of policies and programmes.[25] Engagement with the diaspora has thus become an essential element of Taiwan's long-term industrial development strategy.

This experience has not gone unnoticed by policymakers outside of Taiwan, and amongst follower nations the government of mainland China has perhaps been the most aggressive in recruiting scientists and engineers from the USA. The same is true of other countries including Israel, Ireland and, as we shall see below, India. There is little reason why Caribbean countries, with their large, highly educated Diasporas, should not do the same.

BRAIN CIRCULATION

The Taiwanese case also illustrates the significant scope for 'brain circulation':, which over the last 10 years has emerged as a critical new dynamic, particularly for top engineers and entrepreneurs. This refers to émigrés involvement in economic activities in the home country, while still residing overseas, through frequent travel to the home country, 'astronauts' in Saxenian's parlance, or remotely through creative use of information and communication technologies (ICTs).[26] This option has been made increasingly feasible by the decreased time and cost of international travel and developments in ICTs. It is especially feasible for Caibbean countries given their geographic proximity to North America. It is a lower risk (for the émigré) and lower cost (for the home country) approach to utilising talent that exists in the Diaspora, and it is one that has become increasingly important in India and Taiwan. It also carries some potential benefits for the home country. Having engineers or scientists who remain based in AICs helps to ensure that their technical knowledge remains at the cutting edge. They also remain excellent sources of information on existing and new markets, thus helping the home country in addressing critical market risks.

THE CASE OF INDIA

The growth of the Indian information technology (IT) sector is one of today's most discussed issues in academia, business circles and the media.[27] In particular, the role of Indian IT through outsourcing is well-know, as is the influx of highly-skilled Indian migrants under H1B visas primarily to work in Silicon Valley's software sector. Much less, however, is known about the complexities of these migrant flows and, critically for this chapter, the impact on the domestic IT sector in India.

TAPPING THE DIASPORA

The flow of skilled Indian migrants to the United States dates back at least a generation to the 1970s, when there was a heavy influx of doctors and engineers. While this brain drain was a very visible dynamic in both countries, a less well-known process taking place involved the Indian Government. India's attempts to connect with its Diaspora can be traced back to at least the 1950s, with the first national effort to identify and trace overseas skills.[28] The government established an 'Indians abroad' section in the National Register of Scientific and Technical Personnel in order to collect information about qualified Indians overseas (Meyer, et al 1997:4). However, this was used as a method of locating potential appointees to government or university posts in India, rather than for influencing industrial policy and creating entrepreneurs as in Taiwan.[29] (Ibid).

As with electronics in Taiwan, overseas Indians have had a central role in the development of India's software industry from the outset. Chadhuri (2003) cites evidence linking the origins of the IT sector to Indian computer programmers who worked for early California-based computer firms like Sperry Rand (now Unisys) in the 1970s. Similarly Saxenian (2002b:7) notes that in the 1980s when investing in India was seen as quite high risk, it was senior Indian engineers in large US firms who convinced their US managers to invest in India, and these engineers were among the first to outsource software services to India thus helping to establish the credibility and reputation of Indian producers. Kapur (2001) also stresses the importance of Indian Diasporic networks in establishing credibility and signaling quality of India-based firms. These effects are most apparent in investments in IT R&D by multinationals such as IBM, Intel, Sun Microsystems, Oracle and the recently announced $3 billion AMD chip fabrication plant. To the extent that these MNC investments lead to the creation of high-skilled jobs that might in turn stem the outward flow of skilled labour, they may be of more long term development significance than direct investments by the Diaspora (Lowell and Gerova, 2004). This is particularly so if, as Lowell and Gerova (2004) suggest, the growing success of the Indian IT sector forms the basis of a new entrepreneurial model with spillovers across other sectors, including business services and various types of R&D.

More recently there has been much greater interaction between government and the Diaspora in determining policy to support the IT sector. Members of the Indian Diaspora have been critical contributors to the formulation of IT policies, and venture capital and in the services sector, especially IT-enabled services. A high profile example is the Chandrasekhar Report on Venture Capital to the Indian Securities and Exchange Board.[30] Thus Kapur (2001:275) argues that India's success in the software industry 'can at least in part be explained by the strategic role played by [the] Diaspora.' He cites the importance of the 'informational role' given the position of many of its members in global IT production networks.

REVERSE BRAIN DRAIN

Overseas Indians certainly are well placed to play a critical role in the development of the domestic IT sector. In 1998 Silicon Valley based Indian engineers were running more than 775 technology companies accounting for 16,600 jobs and $3.6 billion in sales. By 2000 these figures had grown to 972 firms, 25,811 jobs and $5 billion in sales. (Saxenian 1999a; 2002b) While India has had some success in encouraging return migration much more can be done. Cervantes and Guillec (2002:3) note that:

'While there are often media reports of successful Indian entrepreneurs in the United States who establish branches or even firms in India only a small number actually return; in 2000, it was estimated that some 1,500 highly qualified Indians returned from the United States.'

While this is certainly a large number in absolute terms, it is contextualised by the fact that 'more than 30 times that number depart each year' as well as by the sheer size of India with over a billion people.

But while India may not have benefitted from a strong numerical flow of returnees, the software industry is certainly characterised by a relative few high profile return émigrés, whose firms have had a tremendous impact on the IT industry.[31] This suggests that while it is certainly desirable it is not necessary to have a majority of émigrés return in order to reap significant benefits from the Diaspora. Even in the case of Taiwan, it is estimated that most migrants do not return, yet the developmental impact of those who have is unquestionable.

BRAIN CIRCULATION

As in the case of Taiwan, brain circulation is an increasingly important dimension of the engagement of the Indian Diaspora in the domestic IT sector. Kapur (2001) cites an interesting example of this phenomenon in India, an institutionalized networking group of Indian entrepreneurs and IT professionals, known as the IndUS Entrepreneur (TiE). The group is based around a number of angel investors and venture capitalists, who seek to identify and fund various start-up companies in the USA and India. While core members of the group seem to be based in the USA, membership in the group spans several other countries where Indian IT professionals operate. The group facilitates knowledge diffusion through mentoring, thus facilitating the development of new enterprises via a new Diaspora-centric business model. However, a strong dynamic of brain circulation, as exists in Taiwan, does not seem to be at work in India.[32]

CONCLUSION

This chapter presented empirical evidence of the brain drain as well as the developmental impact of the Taiwanese and Indian diasporas on high-technology sectors in their home country. What though are the implications for the Caribbean? A common feature of the Taiwanese and Indian experiences was the engagement with relevant members of the diaspora in the early stages of formulating technology and industrial policy. The value of identifying and connecting with skilled persons in areas where regional governments are trying to direct investment was critical, and Caribbean countries should do the same. In a rapidly changing and increasingly competitive global economy overseas nationals will generally have greater technical knowledge of their sector as well as better information about current and future trends. Efforts in Jamaica to create research institutes and technology parks between the University of the West Indies and the University of Technology are steps in the right direction, and would certainly benefit from the involvement of appropriate members of the diaspora. Resource constrained developing countries like Jamaica have to be careful in ensuring that efforts towards creating the conditions for innovation and high-technology entrepreneurship reflect an understanding of global production and markets. Engagement with the diaspora along with other overseas experts is an important approach to ensuring this outcome.

A strategic approach to attracting high-skilled nationals is crucial. It might be prudent for policymakers to take advantage of the close geographic proximity to the USA by encouraging 'circulation' (along with return) from the outset, as this might serve to reduce the risk of return for many aspiring émigrés as they can 'test the waters', so to speak, before making a more permanent decision to return. Cross-border University collaborations such as Singapore National University's links with the Wharton School at the University of Pennsylvania can be of immense value, particularly for developing capabilities in science and engineering. This can allow scientists in the diaspora to continue to work in top facilities in the USA while facilitating working relationships with colleagues in the home country. In the Caribbean case, facilitating research on regional issues by the increasing number of Caribbean graduate students not only creates a professional link between young émigrés (before their focus is fully diverted to the host country), it also links regional issues with established professionals as students' advisors oversee their work.[33] Finally, a regional approach to engaging with members of the diaspora would not only avoid limiting the pool of skills to country nationals but could facilitate development initiatives by utilizing the structures in place for regional integration under the CARICOM Single Market and Economy and taking advantage of the broader range of skills, experience and opportunities across the region.

NOTES

1. An OECD report noted that during the 1990s migration flows from Asia to the USA, Canada, the UK and Australia increased due to 'strong demand in the OECD countries for IT and other skills in science and technology as well as the selective immigration policies that favour skilled workers.'[1] (Cervantes and Guillec, 2002:1)

2. The other principal policy option to address the weakness of the social security system is increased taxes. However, there is little support for this option within the current US administration.

3. Please note that there is also significant migration within the Western industrialized countries (as well as from South Asia to the Gulf States). For example, the USA attracts significant amounts of highly-skilled migrants from Canada and the UK. However, developing countries remain the principle source of highly-skilled migrant flows.

4. This escape valve of sorts has played an important historical role for a number of developing regions, such as with high Caribbean and South Asian migrant flows to the UK in the 1950s and 1960s in response to low-skilled labour shortages during Britain's post WW II reconstruction period. (Nurse, 2003)

5. It is important to note, however, that of these three elements of the 'revisionist approach,' two are in fact not so new: both the potential for return and the issue of remittances were discussed in the early brain drain literature in the 1960s and 1970s. However, the lack of data at the time proved to be a serious constraint, particularly for analysis of remittances. In fact, it is improvements in data on remittances in the 1990s, particularly through the IMF's Balance of Payments statistics, that has facilitated this renewed focus.

6. This loss was included since it was assumed that developing countries bore the cost of education. In today's brain drain debate an interesting issue raised concerns the criteria for a migrant to be considered to be contributing to the brain drain. For

example, if the migrant receives their tertiary education overseas, how much of a loss is this to the sending country since they were technically unskilled before departure and further, their education was provided by the receiving country? Rosensweig (2005) is a proponent of a similar argument and argues that the World Bank's Jamaican brain drain figures, for example, should be revised downward. The view of this author, not pursued in any detail in this chapter, is predicated on class and suggests that most migrants who pursue tertiary education overseas bear this cost privately and also would likely also have done so at home had emigration not been a factor. Thus their departure remains a loss to the home country and not a cost to the receiving country.

7. It should be said however that current negotiations under Mode IV of the General Agreement on Trade in Services (GATS) could provide the forum and institutional framework within which such an approach could be made feasible. However, this would likely be limited to temporary migration (which may carry some positive 'brain circulation' attributes discussed later) and might do little for the most damaging permanent flows. They are also likely to have less direct employment spillovers, a critical concern of this chapter.

8. Other important sources of finance associated with the diaspora include foreign exchange accounts and various bond offerings, including remittance-backed bonds. (See Lowell and Gerova 2004).

9. Data on remittances is likely to significantly underestimate the true size of the phenomenon as it only captures funds sent through official sources. Actual flows could easily be over twice the officially reported size. Particular caution is advised in interpreting growth of remittances as flows in the 1980s are likely to be significantly underreported due to poor data collection during that period.

10. While the macroeconomic benefits are extremely important, on the other hand one could argue that flows of remittances, have allowed countries to sustain higher fiscal deficits than might otherwise have been possible. Kapur (2003) notes this caveat in the case of India (a large, not-very-open economy), where he argues that a consistently high fiscal deficit of around 10 per cent of GDP has been facilitated by a positive current account buoyed by the inflow of remittances amounting to 2.5 per cent of GDP.

11. The distinction being made here views poverty alleviation as a short-term effect and poverty reduction as a long-term effect, akin to structural poverty.

12. A second potential exception is investment of remitted funds into micro-business. However, the concern here from an industrial policy standpoint is that while micro-businesses are critical for supporting livelihoods, particularly for women-headed households, they tend to be the result of 'push factor' entrepreneurship resulting from under- or unemployment (as opposed to the 'pull factor' of

potentially dynamic growth and high profit associated with skill-intensive enterprises), they tend to employ few people outside of the family and they tend to be predominantly in low-technology, non-dynamic sectors, and so do little to promote industrialization and structural transformation, particularly since many are commercial rather than productive ventures. I should stress that this is a generalization: anecdotal evidence suggests that there may be important exceptions to this assertion.

13. This argument can be taken a step further through appeal to a counterfactual hypothesis. That is, even if highly-skilled persons were not to have migrated and remained in the home country they would likely still command high wages relative to the rest of the workforce, and so could still provide financial support to dependent relatives as needs be. This is particularly so in middle-income developing country where there is a market for their skills. It is the less-skilled who are more likely to be unemployed and unable to support dependent households, and thus it is their contribution that would be lost. Thus there is little net gain from migration of the highly skilled due to remittances.

14. Many observers argue that remittances have led to a culture of dependence in receiving countries, where some household members — young men in particular — opt to remain unemployed and wait for remitted funds and gifts from overseas relatives rather than enter the labour market at the reservation wage. (See Kapur, 2003, amongst others) Remittances in this view facilitate a (unsustainable) culture of high consumption (especially of luxury goods) that cannot be supported by unskilled local wages. One often hears this view in the Caribbean, particularly in the context of declining production and rising crime.

15. For an elaboration of this argument see Mountford (1997), Beine et al. (2001), Commander et al (2003), Stark (2004), and Docquier and Rapoport (2004). Faini (2003) and Schiff (2005) provide empirical and theoretical critiques.

16. The definitions of tacit and explicit knowledge presented in this subsection were partially informed by definitions at *http://www.thecore.nus.edu.sg/cpace/ht/thonglipfei/ tacit_explicit.html*. Polanyi (1966) is widely credited with the intellectual work behind this distinction.

17. Romer (1986) and Lucas (1988) are perhaps the most often-cited articles in this new literature, with Arrow's (1962) formulation being the classic work). Gary Becker's work on human capital in the 1960s also provides a useful antecedent to the mainstream approach.

18. Up to 1990 there was no numerical quota for H1B visas but in that year a 65,000 cap was imposed and with increasing employer petitions this quota rose steadily through 2001. At the peak of the programme most H1B visas were issued to Indian IT workers. (Lowell and Gerundi, 2004)

19. This figure is taken from Lowell (2004), figure 2.

20. As an interesting aside, they go on to state that 'In fact, the British Royal Society first coined the expression 'brain drain' to describe the outflow of scientists and technologists to the United States and Canada in the 1950s and early 1960s.' (Cervantes and Guillec, 2002:1).

21. Israel, Ireland, Singapore and Korea are other frequently cited examples of successful 'brain gain' strategies. China is increasingly likely to join this group.

22. It is worth noting that while there were similarities in the developmental state approach taken by Korea and Taiwan (both modelled on Japanese success a generation before), there were important differences in their development strategies, such as the focus on large, vertically integrated, oligopolistic *chaebol* in Korea and small, highly competitive firms in Taiwan (many of which developed from subsidiaries of Japanese and American multinational firms). Use of the Diaspora in catching up to the technological frontier was, however, a strategy employed by both. See Yoon (1992) for an elaboration of successful South Korean polices to reverse the brain drain.

23. World Bank (1993) presents a different point of view.

24. What is interesting to note, however, is that while highly-skilled migrants comprised a slight majority of returnees, 46 per cent had only a secondary education or lower. (Iredale and Guo, 2001:7) This is an important fact for developing country policymakers to note i.e. even in a high-flying economy like Taiwan, not all returnees who contributed were highly-educated. However, as managers and technological leaders the local firms benefited significantly from their knowledge and experience.

25. Policy efforts included travel subsidies for returnees and their family, job search assistance, business investment assistance, facilitation of academic visits and expert consultations, recruitment programmes which included competitive salaries (though many returnees seemed happy to take pay cuts of up to 30 per cent) and generally improved working conditions. (See Ireland and Guo)

26. The UN Digital Diaspora Network initiative provides a useful example. For examples in Africa and the Caribbean see *http://www.unicttaskforce.org/ddnc/* and *http://www.ddn-africa.org/*.

27. The emerging pharmaceutical and biotechnology sectors which receive less attention are perhaps even more interesting in terms of their rapid growth, emphasis on R&D, and hence closer proximity to the technological frontier than the IT industry that still focuses primarily on low value-added activities.

28. This coincided with the emergence of India's investment in training in science and technology and the development of domestic R&D capabilities. (Cervantes and Guillec, 2002:3) The timing of these efforts in the immediate decolonization period should not be surprising given the intense focus on national development.

29. This approach was repeated in the 1970s when the Council of Scientific and Industrial Research instituted a scheme for offering short-term research associates or visiting scientists appointments to Indians abroad. (Meyer et al, 1997:5)

30. See *www.sebi.gov.in*

31. The Indian BPO (Business Process Outsourcing) giant Wipro provides a good example even though its modern founder, Azim Premji, took over the then fledgling hydrogenated cooking oil firm as a 21 year old Stanford graduate. At least one of the co-founders of the other Indian BPO giant Infosys was also educated in the USA.

32. Saxenian (2002b) offers a very interesting explanation where high rents in low value-added activities in the software sector have proved to be a disincentive to moving up the value chain or spanning dynamic entrepreneurship. As such the industry remains dominated by a few large players focused on export markets and serving as an important node in global production chains. She concludes that unlike in the Taiwanese case there are few US-based Indian engineers that operate in both locales and might drive the technological upgrading necessary to transform the Indian IT sector.

33. A current example is research on ackee and prostate cancer being conducted by a Jamaican medical student at the University of Chicago. (See *http://www.jamaica-gleaner.com/gleaner/20051124/eye/* for the newspaper story and *http://www.ucurology.org/pdfs/5.RESCUE%20nl_03.pdf* for the research paper.

REFERENCES

Adams, Richard. 2003. International Migration, Remittances and the Brain Drain.' World Bank Policy Research Working Paper 3069, June 2003. *www.world bank.org*

Adams, Richard, and John Page 2003. International Migration, Remittances and the Brain Drain.' World Bank Policy Research Working Paper 3179, December 2003. *www.world bank.org*

Arrow, Kenneth. 1962. 'The Economic Implications of Learning By Doing.' *American Economic Review.*

Beine, M., F. Docquier and H. Rapoport. 2001. 'Brain Drain and Economic Growth: Theory and Evidence'. *Journal of Development Economics* 64, 1: 275-89.

Bhagwati, Jagdish. 1998. 'International Migration and Income Taxation', in *Jagdish Bhagwati: Political Economy and International Economics,* D. Irwin, ed. Cambridge: MIT Press.

Bhagwati, Jagdish and John Wilson, eds. 1989. *Income Taxation and International Mobility.* Cambridge, Mass.: MIT Press.

Bhagwati, Jagdish and Martin Partington. 1976. *Taxing the Brain Drain: A Proposal* Amsterdam: North Holland.

Bhagwati, Jagdish and Carlos Rodriguez. 1976. 'Welfare Theoretical Analyses of the Brain Drain'. In *The Brain Drain and Taxation: Theory and Empirical Evidence*, J. Bhagwati, ed. Cambridge, Mass.: MIT Press

Cervantes, Mario and Dominique Guellec. 2002. 'The Brain Drain: Old myths, new realities', Directorate for Science, Technology and Industry, OECD. *www.oecd.org/migration*

Commander, Simon, Mari Kangasniemi and Alan Winters. 2003. 'The Brain Drain: Curse or Boon?' IZA Discussion Paper No. 809. *www.iza.org*

Desai, Mihir, Devesh Kapur and John McHale. 2003. 'The Fiscal Impact of High Skilled Emigration: Flows of Indians to the US,' Paper No. 03-01. Cambridge, Mass.: Weatherhead Center for International Affairs, Harvard University.

————. 2002. 'Sharing the Spoils: Taxing International Human Capital Flows,' Paper No. 02-06, Cambridge, Mass.: Weatherhead Center for International Affairs, Harvard University.

Docquier, F. and H. Rapoport. 2004. 'Skilled Migration: The Perspective of Developing Countries.' *World Bank Policy Research Working Paper* No. 3382, Washington DC: World Bank. *www.worldbank.org*

Faini, Ricardo. 2003. 'Is the Brain Drain an Unmitigated Blessing?' WIDER Discussion Paper No. 2003/64, September 2003. *www.wider.unu.edu*

Iredale, Robyn and Fei Guo. 2001. 'The Transforming Role of Skilled and Business Returnees: Taiwan, China and Bangladesh,' Centre for Asian Pacific Social Transformational Studies (CAPSTRAN), University of Wollongong, Australia. *http://www.iussp.org/Brazil2001/s30/S39_04_Iredale.pdf.*

Kapur, Devesh. 2001. 'Diasporas and Technology Transfer" *Journal of Human Development*, 2, 2.

Lowell, Lindsay and Stefka Gerundi . 2004. 'Diasporas and Economic Development: State of Knowledge' Paper prepared for the World Bank, Institute for the Study of International Migration, Georgetown University.

Lucas, R. 1988. 'On the Mechanics of Economic Development," *Journal of Monetary Economics,* 22: 3-42.

Matthew, J.A. 1997. 'A Silicon Valley of the east: creating Taiwan's semi-conductor industry', *California Management Review*, Vol. 39 No 4, pp. 26–54.

Meyer, Jean-Baptiste. 2003. Policy Implications of the Brain Drain's Changing Face, Science and Development Network, May 2003. *http://www.scidev.net/dossiers/index.cfm?fuseaction=policybrief&dossier=10&policy=24*

Meyer, Jean-Baptiste *et al.* 1997. Turning Brain Drain Into Brain Gain: The Colombian Experience of the Diaspora Option. *http://sansa.nrf.ac.za/documents/stsjbm.pdf*

Mountford, A.1997. 'Can a brain drain be good for growth in the source economy?' *Journal of Development Economics* 53, 2: 287-303.

Nelson, Richard. 2005. 'Economic Development as a Catch-Up Process: What's different about the current environment'. Leontief Prize Lecture, Tufts University, October 2005.

Nurse, Keith. 2004. 'Diasporas, Migration and Development in the Americas', *Internationale Politik and Gessellschaft* (IPG), February 2004. *http://library.fes.de/pdf-files/id/ipg/200402nurse.pdf.* Last accessed August 2, 2008

Polanyi, Michel. 1966. *The Tacit Dimension,* London: Routledge.

Portes, Alejandro. 1996. 'Global Villagers: The Rise of Transnational Communities' *The American Prospect* (March-April) 74-77.

Romer, Paul. 1986. 'Increasing Returns and Long-run Growth,' *Journal of Political Economy,* 94:1002-37.

Rosenzweig, Mark. 2005. 'Consequences of Migration for Developing Countries,' UN Expert Group Meeting on International Migration and Development, New York, July 6-8, 2005.

Saxenian, Anna Lee. 2001. 'Taiwan's Hsinchu Region: Imitator and Partner for Silicon Valley', Revised Draft, SIEPR Discussion Paper No. 00-44, Stanford Institute for Economic Policy Research, June 2001.

Saxenian, AnnaLee. 2002. 'Transnational Communities and the Evolution of Global Production Networks: The Cases of Taiwan, India and China,' East-West Center Working Papers, No. 37, December 2001. *www.eastwestcenter.org*

Schiff, Maurice. 2005. 'Brain Gain: Claims about its Size and Impact on Welfare and Growth are Greatly Exaggerated,' Washington DC: World Bank and IZA, World Bank Policy Research Working Paper 3708, September 2005. *www.world bank.org*

Stalker, P. 2000. *Workers without Frontiers: The Impact of Globalization on International Migration,* Boulder: CO: Lynne Rienner Publishers.

Stark, O. 2004. 'Rethinking the Brain Drain.' 2004. *World Development* 32, 1: 15-22.

Wade, Robert.1989. *Governing the Market,* Princeton University Press, Princeton, NJ.

Yoon, Bang-Soon. 1992. 'Reverse Brain Drain in Korea: State-led Model' *Studies in Comparative International Development,* 27, 1: 4-26.

20

FREE MOVEMENT OF PERSONS IN THE CARICOM SINGLE MARKET AND ECONOMY:
Issues of National and Regional Security Policy

SOPHIA WHYTE-GIVANS

INTRODUCTION

The CARICOM Single Market and Economy (CSME) is now in existence with thirteen of the fifteen CARICOM states having acceded to the CARICOM Single Market (CSM). These thirteen states: Antigua and Barbuda, Barbados, Belize, Dominica, Grenada, Guyana, Jamaica, St. Lucia, St. Vincent and the Grenadines, Suriname, and Trinidad and Tobago acceded in 2006 and Montserrat in 2007. One of the many questions that have arisen recently is the extent to which 'free' movement is actually 'free'.

This chapter explores the issue of 'free' movement of persons by referring to the specific articles of the Revised Treaty of Chaguaramas which address the issue. It then explains in layman's terms what 'free' movement constitutes currently within the scope of the CSME, and how the interpretation could change over time. It goes a step further by arguing that 'free' movement of labour must be safeguarded by the Caribbean Court of Justice (CCJ). In addition, the case is made that the articles do not speak to 'free' movement of people within the context of national security vis-à-vis the exportation of crime from one country to another or whether or not known criminals should be exempted from this provision.

As such, the CCJ becomes even more critical in dealing with issues of crimes perpetuated by one national against another, within CARICOM's jurisdiction. Therefore, if the language of the statutes that govern the authority of the CCJ is not clear in extolling the extent to which criminals should be afforded the protection of the CCJ as opposed to the protection of the State, the whole issue of 'freedom' of movement will become a source of contention for other than the obvious reasons.

Granger (2004) makes the important point that the CARICOM Single Market and Economy (CSME) and the Caribbean Court of Justice (CCJ) will, inadvertently, create security implications. In its state of full implementation, 'the CSME will allow any Caribbean national to undertake economic activities in any jurisdiction without restrictions' (Arthur 2004:23). Therefore, national and regional security will not be fully impacted by the security considerations in the present. The future, when a state of full implementation has been reached, will reap the consequences. However, given the frustration of Owen Arthur (Prime Minister of Barbados) that we in CARICOM, 'seek merely a CSM, per se' (Arthur 2004:15), it may be premature to envision scenarios which may occur only with full implementation.

In addition, is Arthur's statement regarding movement without restrictions a true reflection of what freedom of movement means? When we examine Articles of the Revised Treaty, we see that 'free' does not mean 'without restrictions'. 'Free' means that one is able to move about as long as certain civil liberties and human rights are not compromised with respect to national sovereignty. To safeguard these aforementioned rights, caveats such as Articles 225, 226 and 237 of the Revised Treaty of Chaguaramas are in place.

THE REVISED TREATY OF CHAGUARAMAS AND FREEDOM OF MOVEMENT

The Revised Treaty of Chaguaramas (2001) allows for the creation of a Single Market through the removal of barriers to trade in goods, services, capital flows, technology, skilled labour and the prerogative to establish enterprises anywhere in the region.[1] The CCJ is also a necessary creation to interpret the Revised Treaty so as to mediate in disputes concerning the interpretation of rights pertinent to the CSME.

As regards the free movement of skilled persons (Chapter 3 of the Revised Treaty), restrictions will be phased out over an agreed time frame; this time frame, however, is not articulated within the Treaty. Accreditation and Certifying Bodies facilitate the provision at both the national and the regional levels, for example the Human Employment and Resources Training (H.E.A.R.T.) Trust and the National Training Agency (N.T.A.) in Jamaica, had to be created to prepare for such contingencies. In addition, a Treaty had to be devised to avoid the double taxation of the incomes of citizens who move from country to country. An agreement also had to be devised to permit the portability of their social security benefits.[2]

Articles governing free movement are delineated in chapter 3 of the Revised Treaty. The first is Article 35 which is related to the acceptance of skilled persons for labour opportunities.

Skilled community nationals, according to the Revised Treaty, are university graduates; media workers; sportspersons; artistes; and musicians. These nationals in the active labour force, are empowered to seek employment in any CARICOM country once they have proof of qualifications and are recognized by the receiving Member State as falling into one of the five approved categories. The five categories are not mutually exclusive and university graduates is the broadest of the five as such graduates may be from the University of the West Indies, the University of Guyana, the University of Belize or any accredited university worldwide, and may engage in any profession.

In November 2004, a Special Meeting was convened by CARICOM Heads of Government at which a decision was taken, pursuant on Article 46(4) a and b of the Revised Treaty, to add another category of skilled workers. The sixth approved category included: 'managers, technical and supervisory staff attached to a company or a self-employed person'.[3] Any CARICOM national who does not fall into any of the six categories has to obtain a work permit to work in another Member State. Anyone who falls into any of the six aforementioned categories has to go through a process to be recognized in another Member State. The first step is to obtain a Certificate of Recognition of CARICOM Skills Qualification (CARICOM Skills Certificate) from the portfolio ministry in the home country.[4] There is no harmonization here. The Ministry responsible in Grenada, Guyana, Saint Lucia and Trinidad and Tobago is the Ministry responsible for Caribbean Community Affairs. In Dominica and St. Vincent and the Grenadines, it is the Ministry responsible for Immigration. In Jamaica and Suriname, it is the Ministry of Labour. In Belize, this falls under the mandate of the Ministry responsible for immigration (Immigration Department) whereas in St. Kitts-Nevis, it is the Ministry responsible for National Security and Immigration.[5]

Each country has domestic legislation which relates to the procedures for obtaining the CARICOM Skills Certificate. This legislation is known as the Caribbean Community Skilled Nationals Act. Without the Certificate, the Community National will not be considered as one of the six currently permissible categories of wage earners. There are a number of documents that are needed by graduates to support their applications. These include: a university degree (at least a Bachelor's); birth certificate; a photocopy of the biodata, date of issue and expiry pages of the passport; marriage certificate, if applicable; passport-sized photographs; police certificate.[6]

Artistes, musicians, media workers and sports persons also need supporting documents. These include: a letter of registration from the national association or body which is responsible for either art, music, sports or the media; copies of relevant industry-specific qualifications; letters from former employees which speak to job duties and responsibilities; birth certificate; a photocopy of the bio-data, date of issue and expiry pages of the passport; marriage certificate, if applicable; passport-sized photographs; police certificate.[7] These categories of skilled workers require more supporting documents than university graduates.

Article 46 (2) refers to the need to consolidate this liberty legislatively, administratively and procedurally such that no skilled community national feels unwelcome or is harassed, in particular by immigration authorities at each receiving member's port of entry. However, when issues of national and regional security such as drug trafficking is involved, it may be necessary for immigration authorities to do their job.

Ultimately, CARICOM nationals will be able to travel without passports; not require work permits in community jurisdictions; have mechanisms in place to certify and establish equivalency of degrees, in addition to accreditation of institutions; and harmonise such that social security benefits are transferable, as indicated by Article 46 (2) bi-iv.

It is Article 46 (3) that is most important in terms of the security implications of free movement of labour. This caveat allows member states the discretion to refuse entry to any individual deemed to be undesirable. However, this is on a case-by-case or country-by-country basis. There is no blanket provision to state that: in the case of a person who has been convicted of any violent crime or drug trafficking, his/her right to travel to any other Member State to seek employment would be null and void. The caveat contained in Article 46 (3) states: 'Nothing in this Treaty shall be construed as inhibiting Member States from according community nationals unrestricted access to, and movement within their jurisdictions subject to such conditions as the public interest may require.[7] The phrase 'the public interest' is highly subjective and may mean different things in different Member states.

Article 46(4) provides scope for amending Article 46(3). For that reason, the matters concerning these Articles will be reviewed occasionally. This review process will allow CARICOM to: enlarge as appropriate, the classes of persons entitled to move and work freely in the Community; and monitor and secure compliance therewith. Article 46(4)a, therefore, allows for the five categories of skilled nationals in Article 46(1) to be expanded once it has been construed that other groups are also entitled to move freely, for example artisans such as masons, plumbers, etc. Article 46(4)b provides for monitoring the transition process to ensure that Member States are conversant with changes and are adhering to the stipulations of these amendments.

The main point to note here is that the regime governing the Movement of Skilled Community Nationals will evolve just as the CSME is expected to evolve. Gradually, Article 46 will be liberalized/expanded to make it compatible with Article 45. As the Revised Treaty currently exists, 'free' movement is "free' only for the segment of the collective CARICOM population which includes the current six permissible groups. Over time, more groups will be added to the list.

The Revised Treaty of Chaguaramas has both tacit and explicit security considerations. The subtle ones have already been introduced; the more direct ones are now explored. Chapter Ten of the Revised Treaty sets out both security exceptions and general exceptions which can serve as binding constraints on both the goal of free movement and deeper integration.

Article 226 also provides Member States with discretionary power. Articles 226(a) and 226(b), in particular reflect the concerns of this chapter. It is stated that nothing shall be construed as preventing the adoption or enforcement by any Member State of measures: (a) to protect public morals or to maintain public order and safety; and (b) to protect human, animal or plant life or health.[8]

Articles 225 and 226 clearly empower states. Article 237, which deals with reservations, also seeks to empower states with regard to matters that may be contentious and require fine-tuning. The Caribbean Court of Justice also empowers states and is the medium by which fairness in the process of integration — in this case with regard to free movement — will be achieved.

THE CARIBBEAN COURT OF JUSTICE (CCJ)

The CCJ has two main responsibilities. The first relates to the CSME while the second relates to civil and criminal matters. With respect to the CSME, the CCJ has three core functions which comprise its Original Function. The three functions are:

a) To apply rules of international law regarding the interpretation and application of the Revised Treaty of Chaguaramas;

b) To give judgements that will reinforce the rights and obligations of CARICOM citizens participating in the emerging common economic space and investment area called the CARICOM Single Market and Economy;

c) To give legal opinions, on request, on what the Single Market and Economy provisions permit, prohibit and oblige governments and citizens to do.[8]

On criminal matters, the CCJ is mandated to serve as the final court of appeal. This is the CCJ's Appellate Function, which means that the CCJ will replace the UK-based Privy Council.[9]

There are a number of checks and balances, on which the CCJ is premised, to allow it to carry out its job effectively, impartially and apolitically. They are outlined below.

1. It is the Regional Judicial and Legal Services Commission and not any political directorate that chooses/selects the judges.

2. It is the Bar Associations, Law Schools and Judicial and Public Services Commissions in the region that nominate the members of the Legal services Commission. The Chairman of the Regional Commission, who is also President of the Court, is chosen by CARICOM Heads of Government, on the advice/recommendation of the said Commission.

3. The members of the Regional Judicial and Legal Services Commission act only upon the instructions of persons or organizations within the Commission.[26]

4. The payment of staff of the CCJ is independent of political ties. A Trust Fund of US$100 million, which was provided by the Ministers of Finance across the region, has been created to fund the CCJ's operations. The Trust Fund will be administered by a Board of Trustees selected from regional entities. The first two years will cost US$12 million. The remaining US$88 million will be invested wisely for future operating costs.[27]

5.   The Judges who preside over cases and appeals are of the highest calibre in terms of both experience (not less than five years in civil and criminal law or teacher of law with fifteen or more years' experience)[28] and qualifications.[29]

The CCJ operates according to one of three mechanisms in civil and criminal matters. It is important to note here that there is no overlap of the three mechanisms; they are mutually exclusive. The first mechanism is one in which cases automatically qualify for appeal to the CCJ without a formal application to the local court. There are six categories of cases that qualify as such:

a)   Judgements in civil cases amounting to not less than EC[30] $25 000 or where the matter relates to a property or a right of similar value (EC$25 000).

b)   Judgements in divorce or marriage annulment cases.

c)   Judgements in civil or criminal cases which require interpretation of the Constitution of a Member State.

d)   Judgements relating to redress for breaching constitutional rights.

e)   Judgements relating to right of access to a superior court of your country.

f)   Other judgements that are specifically written into the law of a Member State.[31]

The second mechanism requires a formal application for 'Leave to Appeal' to the national court. This occurs in either of two types of cases:

a)   Judgements in civil cases considered to be of great general or public importance.

b)   Judgements in cases that are specifically written into the law of a Member State.[32]

'Leave to Appeal' must be applied for within 30 days of the date of judgement.[33] The third mechanism is called 'Special Leave to Appeal.' This is required for cases that require special permission from the CCJ. Through a lawyer, the Appellant must appeal directly to the CCJ within 42 days of the date of judgement.[34]

With the three mechanisms, once the Appeal has been granted by the local court or the CCJ, the 'Notice to Appeal' must be filed with the CCJ in Trinidad and Tobago.[35] An important point to note is that even though the CCJ is based in Trinidad and Tobago, it is a travelling court so the judges who will sit on each case are selected and travel to the country where the case originated. In other words, it is an 'itinerant court.'[36] All judgements delivered by the CCJ are enforceable by the local courts.

How Granger's (2004) comment regarding the security implications of the CSME could apply is raised with reference to the following example. Such a situation relates to Article 211[37] in particular, since it addresses the Jurisdiction of the Court in Contentious Proceedings.

> Kidnapping has become much more prevalent in recent years in Trinidad and Tobago, Guyana and Jamaica. Such criminal activity could become a national and regional security matter. If victims are moved not only within countries but also across borders by criminal networks operating in different countries that are liaising with each other, then trafficking in persons (TIP) also becomes intertwined with kidnapping. This demonstrates just one of the secondary implications of certain crimes. Although the Caribbean Court of Justice (CCJ) functions with respect to all CSME Member States, it has no stated authority to prosecute for a crime that has been committed if the victim is no longer in the country where the crime was initiated. Furthermore, if the victim of the crime, in this case kidnapping, is found in another country, there is no procedure in place for the CCJ to prosecute the person with whom the victim was found, even though that person is suspected of the crime. These situations are likely to occur given the close proximity and ease of crossing national borders, whether documented or undetected, between both CSME mainland and island Member States as well as non-CSME or CARICOM nations. For example, Guyana shares borders with Suriname as well as Brazil and Venezuela; Belize borders Guatemala and Mexico. The Eastern Caribbean islands of Antigua and Barbuda, St. Kitts and Nevis, Dominica, and St. Vincent and the Grenadines, are close to each other and also to the non-CSME and CARICOM states that are French Departments, Netherlands Antilles and British dependencies, all of which provide relatively easy undocumented access from the sea.

There are many challenges to regional security other than those that are already evident. The CSME, therefore, needs to be proactive and recognize that criminals are likely to intensify their activities, and these activities could also include terrorist and other activities that would be a security risk in any one or combination of the Member States.

CONCLUSION

The example cited emphasizes the importance of sharing information within CARICOM and the importance of statutes within treaties being made explicit. Critics will point out that a suspected criminal who has not been charged should not be denied his/her rights to migrate to another state. While this is true, the lack of the CCJ's jurisdiction over the persons once they have left the state in which a crime was allegedly committed, provides a significant weakness in the current justice system as it applies to the CSME.

If the Articles establishing the CSME do not speak explicitly to different types of criminal activities, there is a risk of undermining both national and regional security, and of facilitating the perpetuation of trans-national crimes. The discretion to amend and revise the Treaty needs to be acted on. Outlining these anomalies will make it easier for the CCJ to preside over contentious cases. Certain categories of crimes must be exempted within Article 45/46 and not left to the discretion of individual states at the time that the situation arises. These must also exist within the framework of a Regional Security Policy which integrates all national security policies. The lack of a coordinated security strategy may be to the detriment of regional sustainable development. Therefore, 'free' movement must exist within a context of national and regional security, especially protecting the most vulnerable groups and vulnerable states. A balance must be struck between freedom of movement for citizens vis-à-vis human security, national security and regional security.

NOTES

1. See CARICOM. 2001. The Revised Treaty of Chaguaramas Establishing the Caribbean Community Including The CARICOM Single Market and Economy. Signed by Heads of Government of the Caribbean Community on July 5, 2001 at their Twenty-Second Meeting of the Conference in Nassau, The Bahamas: 22-31 and Arthur 2004: 19 and 20.
2. See The Revised Treaty and Arthur 2004: 21.
3. See The Revised Treaty 2001: 10. COHSOD is the acronym for the Council for Human and Social Development as named in paragraph 2 of Article 10 of the Revised Treaty.
4. The Revised Treaty 2001: 30.
5. The Revised Treaty 2001: 30-31.
6. CSME Unit 2005: 10.
7. The Revised Treaty 2001: 31. The emphasis is the author's.
8. The Revised Treaty 2001: 132.
9. CARICOM Secretariat 2005 (a):12.

REFERENCES

Arthur, Owen. 2004. 'The Caribbean Single Market and Economy: The Way Forward' In *The Integrationist*, Volume 2 No. 1 (June 2004). Kingston: Ian Randle Publishers for UWI-CARICOM Project.

CARICOM. 2001. The Revised Treaty of Chaguaramas Establishing the Caribbean Community Including The CARICOM Single Market and Economy. Signed by Heads of Government of the Caribbean Community on July 5, 2001 at their Twenty-Second Meeting of the Conference in Nassau, The Bahamas.

CARICOM Secretariat. 1997. CARICOM's Charter of Civil Society for the Caribbean Community.

CARICOM Secretariat. 2005 (a). Caribbean Court of Justice: How Does it Work for Me? In 3 Steps.

CARICOM Secretariat. 2005(b). Caribbean Court of Justice: How the Original Court Works – The Original Jurisdiction.

CARICOM Single Market and Economy: Free Movement – Travel and Work.

CSME Unit. 2005. CARICOM Single Market and Economy: Free Movement, Travel and Work. Bridgetown: CARICOM Secretariat.

Granger, David A. 2004. 'Caribbean Security Cooperation: A Conceptual Framework' In *The Integrationist*, Volume 2 No. 1 (June 2004). Kingston: Ian Randle Publishers for the UWI-CARICOM Project.

21

CARIBBEAN MIGRATION IN THE NEOLIBERAL ERA:
Critical Policy Considerations

PETER JORDENS

INTRODUCTION

International migration has always been a central factor in the development of the Caribbean region. From the times of the Ciboneys, Arawaks and Caribs, people in every part of the Caribbean, from all ethnic, class, gender and age groups, have been 'on the move' into, within and out of the region. For good reasons the modern, post-1492 Caribbean has been called an 'internationalized' region, literally created by political, economic and demographic forces of an international nature (Edmondson 1974). Combinations of economic, political, ideological and cultural factors have historically conditioned transnational migration in the Caribbean context;[1] free, encouraged, strongly persuaded and forced forms of migration could be distinguished.

In the 1990s and the first decade of the twenty-first century, Caribbean migration is predominantly directed out of the region toward North America and Western Europe, although intra-regional migration is also a significant and growing phenomenon. The current waves of emigration may be attributed in large part to the economic stagnation, income inequality and poverty resulting from the economic policies implemented in the region since the 1980s, initially referred to as structural adjustment and now known as neoliberalism. Neoliberal policies, promoted by the major capitalist economies and the multilateral institutions (International Monetary Fund (IMF), World Bank, World Trade Organization), are basically aimed at reducing the role of the state in the economy and opening the way for markets and private enterprise. The regional record shows that these policies by and large have failed miserably at producing economic growth and social development.[2] Instead they have increased the pressure on emigration as an adaptive strategy for those adversely affected (Portes 2003; Bohórquez and Spronk 2004).

The flow of Caribbean nationals out of the region has been aided by aggressive transnational recruiting strategies on the part of employers in the countries of the North, targeted in particular at Caribbean nurses, teachers and information-technology experts, to answer economic expansion combined with low population growth and aging populations in the North.

Transnational labour recruitment and migration have been more beneficial to the economies of the North than to those of the South. Caribbean source countries are confronted with significant brain drain, growing local skills gaps, unbalanced labour markets, and reduced competitiveness. Meanwhile, the emigration of people of working age and the feminization of Caribbean emigration (Cortés Castellanos 2005) are also having an adverse effect on the social fabric of Caribbean societies.[3] Overall, transnational emigration in the current period has tended to reinforce the traditional global hierarchy of nation-states and the historical dependence of Caribbean countries on the North.

PURPOSE

This chapter situates Caribbean migration since the 1990s explicitly in the era of neoliberalism and globalization. While the countries and institutions of the North continue to proclaim the presumed virtues of economic neoliberalism and capitalist globalization, there is a simultaneous attempt on the part of these countries to problematise the free international movement of people and to control and contain migration. This chapter critically examines, from a Caribbean perspective, the tensions between these two tendencies, following upon an analysis of the dominant trends in migration policies. Using the insights obtained, the final section offers recommendations toward alternative, Caribbean-focused migration policies.

The term 'migration' in this chapter always refers to inter/transnational migration. Furthermore, 'migration policy' is understood as encompassing policies on immigration, emigration, immigrants and the diaspora. The 'neoliberal era' is defined as the current period in which neoliberal economic policies and capitalist globalization constitute the dominant paradigm of the international development discourse, as promoted in particular by the Northern countries and multilateral institutions. This era can be taken to coincide roughly with the last two decades: the 1990s and the 2000s; the particular emphasis of the chapter is on the period after the terrorist attacks on New York City and Washington DC of September 11, 2001 ('9/11').

TRENDS IN MIGRATION POLICY IN THE NEOLIBERAL ERA

Over the years migration has become recognised as touching almost every area of domestic and foreign policy, such as: population policy; economic and labour policy (including issues of brain gain and brain drain and labour market dynamics); poverty, welfare and development (including remittances); health (including transferable diseases such as HIV/AIDS); human rights; culture, national identity, citizenship and sovereignty (including transnationalism); and crime, law enforcement and security (including such issues as illegal migration, criminal deportees, human trafficking, the international drug trade and terrorism).

However, since the 1990s, and especially after 9/11, the USA and other countries of the North have redefined and effectively narrowed the international discourse and policy agenda on migration. Since 9/11, migration has virtually become a one-dimensional issue defined almost exclusively in relation to perceived threats to national security.

The immediate reaction in the USA to the events of September 11, 2001, was to connect international terrorism to migration because of the presumed association between terrorism and Islamic fundamentalism, international travel, illegal migration, narco trafficking and money laundering. In October 2001, US President George W. Bush issued the

Homeland Security Presidential Directive-2, significantly titled 'Combating Terrorism through Immigration Policies'. It created a Task Force for tracking foreign terrorists, enhanced the enforcement capabilities of the Immigration & Naturalization Service (INS) and US Customs, and sought to improve coordination with Canada and Mexico on immigration, customs and visa policies. Ever since, migration and security have been locked together in what is sometimes called the 'migration-security nexus'.

The policy response in the USA and other countries of the North has been an authoritarian, law-and-order, security-driven approach to immigration with strong state regulation and intervention in an attempt to bring international migration under control. Measures have focused on the reorganization of state agencies responsible for immigration and security, modernization of immigration controls using the latest technology such as biometrics, tighter border controls and security checks, sanctions for uncooperative air and sea carriers, increased visa requirements and screening, racial and ethnic profiling, increased frequency of police raids in search of undocumented working aliens, accelerated return procedures, and intensified deportation of criminal aliens.

Countries of the South are requested or persuaded to implement similar measures. In Fiscal Year 2005 the USA provided US$6 million for its so-called Third Border Initiative to help establish more secure border measures in the Caribbean through such programmes as border management assessments, aviation safety oversight and security training, and training and assistance to local customs and border officials. The USA is also funding the development of a Regional Information and Intelligence Sharing System (US Department of State 2006a; 2006b). The government of the Netherlands is presently directing significant investments into the upgrading and reorganization of the immigration service on the five islands of the Netherlands Antilles under the umbrella of a Security Plan.

Meanwhile the International Organization for Migration (IOM), sponsored by the US and Canadian governments, other bilateral sources and the European Union, provides support to Caribbean governments and non-governmental organizations to strengthen migration management. Programmes include technical assistance and capacity building in the areas of preventing and combating human trafficking, facilitating the return and reintegration of Caribbean nationals, and preventing the spread of HIV/AIDS via mobile populations (IOM 2002). The IOM, which operates in the Caribbean out of Washington, DC, helps to disseminate state-of-the-art immigration policies and technologies developed in the North.

The offer of such bilateral and multilateral aid for migration management is always packaged with a strong element of persuasion. The Caribbean nations are invited to join the ranks of the compliant defenders of Western values and policies and to collaborate in an honourable joint effort to promote security in the region. Rather than run the risk of being blacklisted as uncooperative — in the not so subtle language of US President George W. Bush, nation states in the post-9/11 world 'are either with us (the USA) or against us' — Caribbean nation-states are slowly but surely adopting migration policies, legislation and measures that are based upon a one-dimensional, state-centred view of migration and motivated by the particular security interests of the North (Girvan 2004).

It is interesting to note that the securitized approach to migration policy is in many ways similar to the North's strategy in the so-called war on drugs. The North's anti-drug policies focus on supply reduction through drug interdiction in or near the countries of the South that produce, distribute and tranship drugs. The North pays less attention to attacking the real problem, that is, the demand for drugs in the North itself, through demand reduction. When it comes to the currently dominant securitized migration policies, the North's focus is similarly on the supply side. It labels the immigrant coming in from the South as a potential security threat and expects the nation-states of the South to take collaborative measures against undesired migrants. Here too, the North hardly tackles the demand side, such as legal and illegal employment opportunities that attract immigrants to the North. The 'easy' approach is rather to stigmatise and criminalise the immigrant — all immigrants, but especially Third World immigrants.

The North's focus on the supply side of immigration has intensified over the years. Its securitized, immigration-hostile policies increasingly employ what might be called 'overseas pre-emptive deterrence strategies'.

The present author is applying this term, which is based on similar terminology used by the USA in its war on terrorism,[4] to a variety of emerging strategies aimed at screening and stopping undesired immigrants as close as possible to their place of origin, that is, in their source country or in a transit country, well before they can reach their country of destination. The North will generally seek the collaboration of countries of origin and transit in implementing these pre-emptive deterrence strategies, but does not consider such collaboration absolutely necessary.

A first instance of an overseas pre-emptive anti-immigration strategy may be recognised in the surveillance and interdiction by the US Coast Guard of Cuban, Dominican and especially Haitian 'boat people' in the Caribbean Sea. Interdiction has at times taken place in the territorial waters of Caribbean nation states without proper coordination with these nation states.

A second example is the establishment of some 40 overseas offices of the INS since 1997 under Operation Global Reach to provide a permanent presence of US immigration officers overseas, to help local authorities detect document fraud, and to deter migrant smuggling in selected source and transit countries. INS offices in the Caribbean region are located in Aruba, Cuba, the Dominican Republic, Haiti and Jamaica.

A third example of overseas pre-emptive deterrence is provided by the operation of US border pre-clearance facilities at airports in Bermuda, the Bahamas and Aruba. At these facilities, located within the jurisdiction of the Caribbean host nation but operated by the US Customs and Border Protection service, travellers pass through US Immigration, Customs and Department of Agriculture inspections before boarding their aircraft. Having cleared the inspections, the traveller receives an entry stamp from US Immigration even though he/she is still at an airport outside the USA. The process is intended to streamline border procedures and reduce congestion at airport inspection points inside the USA. It is said to facilitate the low-risk or 'legitimate' traveller, but serves the additional purpose of pre-emptive deterrence, at the source, beyond the geographical borders of the USA, of undesired visitors, migrants, refugees, smugglers and traffickers (Bryan and Flynn 2001).

A fourth instance of a pre-emptive immigration-deterrence strategy is the overseas 'basic integration exam' introduced by the Netherlands in March 2006. The Netherlands now require prospective immigrants from certain countries to pass this exam before they can apply for a temporary residence permit. The prospective immigrant can take the basic integration exam only at the Dutch embassy or consulate general in his/her home country, that is, the new requirement is to be satisfied while still abroad. The name of the exam suggests that the prospective immigrant is expected to already start 'integrating' into the Netherlands society while still a resident in his/her home nation.

The exam tests for basic knowledge of the Dutch language and Dutch society. The official philosophy behind the exam is that someone who wishes to settle in the Netherlands should be proficient in the Dutch language, be conscious of Dutch values and observe Dutch norms. The new requirement is intended especially for people who want to form a family with someone in the Netherlands (for example, through marriage) or want to reunite with relatives who already live there. All religious workers intending to work in the Netherlands are also required to pass the exam. Nationals of most European countries and other rich countries such as the USA, Canada, Australia, New Zealand and Japan are exempt from the new requirement.

The new requirement is suspect for a number of reasons. First, the cost of taking the exam is 350 or approximately US$445, which by itself can be a formidable barrier to entering the residency application process for many foreigners. Second, the exam is oral and based on speech recognition by telephone, but it is not yet clear whether the technology is sufficiently advanced to handle the heavy accents that some foreigners are likely to have. Finally, the specific targeting of religious workers in combination with the exemptions for nationals from European and other rich countries suggests that the requirement is particularly intended at restricting immigration of people from, poor, non-white and non-Christian backgrounds and from countries without a Western-type, liberal democratic tradition. Rather than an integration exam, the new requirement is in effect a masked anti-immigration measure.

The above policy examples — US interception of boat people in Caribbean waters, INS offices in the Caribbean, US border pre-clearance facilities at Caribbean airports, and the Dutch overseas basic integration exam — all implicate a 'border shift outward' (Lahav 2003) or re-territorialization of the nation state. These securitized migration policies push out and extend, as it were, the frontier of the nation states of the North into the territories of other, mostly Third World nation states. The particular case of the re-territorialization of the US nation state into Caribbean jurisdictions is even embodied in the name 'Third Border' now applied by the USA to the Caribbean region.[5] The re-territorialization of the US nation-state, through collaborative point-of-origin and transit controls within Caribbean territories, enables the US state to defend its 'Third Border' against perceived migration-related security threats and strategically complements its more traditional approaches to border protection and management along its first and second borders with Canada and Mexico.

In an attempt to further situate this notable phenomenon, one may again point to a similarity with the war on drugs, such as the Forward Operating Locations (FOLs) established by the US Air Force's Southern Command in Aruba and Curaçao since the year 2000. The FOLs are literally 'forward operating' in that they allow the US Air Force to run counter-drug operations well beyond its own geographical borders, much closer to the sources of drug production, distribution and transhipment. From the FOLs, US Air Guard units fly over open waters following and observing suspicious planes and ships as they make their drug delivery and return to their point of origin. The units then notify the relevant local law-enforcement agencies that will go in to make an arrest. So for reasons of both drug and migration-related security interests, the US state has a 'geopolitical need to promote extra-territoriality and infiltrate the sovereignty of other nation-states' (Flint 2002).

The phenomenon of re-territorialization of Northern nation states has an interesting parallel in the fact that the Dominican Republic, Jamaica, Cuba and Haiti have of late extended voting rights to nationals in their diasporas and have introduced the possibility of dual or even multiple nationality or citizenship, or are considering doing so (Graham 1997; Duany 2002; Bohórquez and Spronk 2004). These Caribbean states are including their diaspora in their conceptualization of the nation-state and are thereby extending their borders (as it were) into the countries of the North. The Haitian government even refers to its diaspora as an administrative district called the Tenth Department and its Cabinet includes a Minister for Haitians Living Abroad.[6] In sum, under the dynamics of migration in the neoliberal era, a re-territorialization of the Northern as well as the Caribbean nation-state is taking place.

While capitalist globalization is generally associated mostly with a de-territorialization of the nation state because of the growing prominence of transnational markets and actors, a simultaneous re-territorialization of the nation state is becoming more recognisable (Duany 2002) through the dynamics of migration-related policies in the neoliberal era. Globalization, then, is clearly not a one-way or irreversible process (Flint 2002, 3, 25) but 'should be analyzed as a process entailing, often simultaneously, both de-territorialization and re-territorialization as each generates differing political dynamics in terms of the governance of territory and economic activity' (Hazbun 2004). Significantly, the re-territorialization of the nation-state implicates not only a spatially extended but also a politically, legally, institutionally and culturally expanded role of the state in the neoliberal era.

CRITIQUING SECURITY-FOCUSED MIGRATION POLICIES

'The growing tendency to view international migration-related questions through a national security heuristic has also coincided with the re-emergence of anti-immigrant policies on the extreme right' (Lahav 2003, 90). The post-9/11 period has seen the ascendancy of several right-wing regimes in the North and the resurgence of a xenophobic, Eurocentric and racist climate in which the immigrant is perceived, feared and discriminated as a less civilised other and potential security threat. A case in point is current Dutch immigration policy which is clearly motivated by discriminatory religious, ethnic and other cultural considerations, as exemplified by such measures as the above-discussed basic integration exam.[7]

The perception of an 'immigrant threat' has enabled the state in North America and Europe to tie the immigration debate to security concerns and law enforcement (Lahav 2003). Conservative politicians have come to believe that a tough stance on immigration enhances their electoral prospects. An illustration is the case of the US immigration bill submitted by Republican F. James Sensenbrenner that was passed in the House of Representatives in December 2005. The bill focuses on security and enforcement and enables the justice system to treat an illegal alien's mere presence in the USA (currently a civil violation) as a felony, that is, a serious, punishable crime.

A peculiar case of anti-immigration policy is currently marking the relationship between the Netherlands and its two Caribbean territories: the Netherlands Antilles and Aruba.[8] The Dutch government has prepared a bill to enable it under certain circumstances to send Antillean and Aruban youths who have come to the Netherlands back to the Caribbean. The possibility of extradition would apply to Antillean and Aruban youths between the ages of 18 and 24 who have no prospects of employment or education within three months of their arrival in the Netherlands as well as to single Antillean and Aruban minors without a guardian in the Netherlands. In addition, the bill would facilitate the extradition from the Netherlands of Antillean and Aruban youths who have been convicted of a criminal offence in the Netherlands.

The announced legislation has been received with much astonishment and indignation in the Netherlands Antilles and Aruba and their diasporic communities in the Netherlands and is a source of severe friction between the Antillean and Aruban governments and the Dutch government. Antilleans and Arubans have the Dutch nationality and are equal to Dutch citizens under the Dutch Constitution. The proposed legislation would effectively introduce two types of Dutch citizenship, based on geographic origin, in order to enable the extradition of 'problematic' Antillean and Aruban youths from the Netherlands.[9] Bob Wit, a judge of Dutch origin at the Caribbean Court of Justice in Trinidad and Tobago, has commented that the Dutch bill is disproportional in relation to the crime problem or nuisance that Antilleans and Arubans in the Netherlands represent, is degrading and discriminatory, appears to be motivated by xenophobia, and typifies the narrow-mindedness of Dutch politicians in matters relating to the Netherlands Antilles and Aruba (*Amigoe* 2005b; 2006b).[10]

It is questionable whether restrictive immigration policies, driven by security concerns, really promote security in the long run. It can be argued that by reducing the possibilities for legal migration, one may force people to explore more risky avenues including illegal migration. In some countries this could result in the rise of an undocumented, marginalised, immigrant underclass that has no formal rights and consequently feels no civic obligations vis-à-vis mainstream society. The upshot can be a situation of reduced security, with outbursts such as the violent social unrest that took place in certain poor, immigrant neighbourhoods of French cities in November 2005.

A law-and-order approach to migration also does not necessarily translate into social justice; it may even have the opposite effect. This becomes apparent especially when one considers the profoundly contradictory impact that border security and migration control measures have on women. The increasing (para-) militarization of border controls worldwide can subject women to verbal, emotional and physical forms of gender-based intimidation, humiliation, coercion and (cultural) violence. Police and immigration authorities are often too concerned with upholding laws that are not sensitive to differences of gender and race and tend to ignore the dignity and personal security of individual travellers and migrants. Racial and ethnic profiling at border controls also produces anxiety and insecurity, while women can experience multiple forms of discrimination because of poverty, race and gender (Mushakoji 2003).

The traditional, state-focused, authoritarian concepts of security and law enforcement are to a large extent androcentric (they tend to posit men's lived experiences as universal) and masculinist (they privilege traditionally male-oriented values of security and authority). There needs to be greater recognition of the fact that the state's migration-related security policies can actually cause insecurity. It must also be realised that migration can be a response to forms of insecurity — such as poverty, inadequate health services and political persecution — for which the state is at fault. It can be argued that 'the major sources of insecurity for [women] are internal — within the [nation-]state and within the family.... [S]tructural insecurity for many women ... results from poverty, underdevelopment and the gendered division of labour' (Byron and Thorburn 1998, 217). Unfortunately, in the neoliberal era the patriarchal state has little concern for these areas of insecurity.

A critique of the global trend toward increased securitization of migration policies in the neoliberal era would be incomplete if it did not dissect and expose the tensions and contradictions between this trend and neoliberalism itself. Both securitized migration policies and neoliberalism are promoted by the powerful, liberal democratic, capitalist nation-states of the North, but they clearly contradict one another. In fact, the great paradox of dominant migration policy in the neoliberal era is that it is anything but liberal.

This paradox consists of several interrelated tensions or contradictions, to wit:

b e t w e e n		a n d	
	neoliberal economic globalization which presupposes and promotes the free, unrestricted flow of financial capital, labour, goods, services and information		state-imposed restrictions on the free international movement of people motivated by security concerns (Lahav 2003, 90; Aja Díaz 2006, 4, 15);
	private enterprise's economic need for foreign labour to supplement the domestic labour force in order to produce increased profits		the desire to place restrictions on immigration because of ethnic nationalism, religious chauvinism, and xenophobism;
	private enterprise's willingness to foster illegal immigration as a source of cheap and docile labour		the liberal democratic state's need to respect legality and liberal human rights including labour rights (Lahav 2003, 89);
	the official rhetoric of the nations and institutions of the North in support of (neo)liberalism		the actual policy practice of the nations of the North and their willingness to forego liberalism to serve nationalist, territorial and other interests.[11]

The above tensions reflect the contradictory nature of capitalist globalization in its present neoliberal phase: characterised by both globalising and nationalist moods, by tendencies toward both freer trade and tighter restrictions on human movement, with a state that is both withdrawing from the economy and intervening in migration, and a nation state that is drifting toward both de-territorialization and re-territorialization.

TOWARD ALTERNATIVE, CARIBBEAN MIGRATION POLICIES

This chapter has examined the global trend toward increased securitization of migration policy in the neoliberal era, showing that by way of this trend, the role of the state in relation to migration has become redefined as highly interventionist. Processes of re-territorialization and nationalist reassertion of the nation state were identified. The chapter has pointed to the problematic nature of the dominant, securitised migration policies as authoritarian, masculinist and xenophobic and as serving primarily the national security interests of the rich and powerful countries. It has also highlighted the contradictions between security-focused migration policies and neoliberal economic policies.

This final section offers four recommendations for the development of alternative migration policies that may be deemed more relevant to the Caribbean people and to social justice in the region.

First, Caribbean migration policies should be pertinent to the concerns of the region and should therefore be based on consultation with and active participation of local, immigrant and diasporic Caribbean communities. Inclusion of the views of progressive segments of Caribbean societies (for example, feminists and human rights activists) may help shift the discourse away from the nearly exclusive security focus advanced by the countries of the North. Migration policy should be predicated on a conceptual framework that does not focus primarily on migrants as a supposedly homogenous group but rather views migration as a complexity of processes with a variety of socio-structural and behavioural causal factors. Caribbean migration policies should be situated within a multidimensional, integrated development context and should be grounded in a keen awareness of the region's long legacy of migration, a critical understanding of the role of the Caribbean state, and sensitivity to matters of gender, race, ethnicity, religion, age, disability and health.

Second, Caribbean countries need to employ a regional approach to the development of migration policies and should seek to align and coordinate their policies regionally. This includes due attention to the nature and impact of intra-regional migration, which phenomenon may be expected to grow in the coming years in response to the tighter anti-immigration policies in the North. The available research on intra-regional migration is meagre compared to that on the Caribbean diaspora in North America and Europe[12] and should be expanded with a view toward appropriate policy formulation.

A third recommendation is that an acute awareness of the internal contradictions of securitized migration, liberalism and capitalist globalization is crucial for strengthening the region's negotiation position vis-à-vis the North and enhancing its chances of striking a more optimal, practical balance between these contradictions in the form of alternative, relevant and just migration and development policies.

Fourth and finally, Caribbean migration policies should ultimately seek to transcend the confines of (neo)liberal economics, xenophobic nationalism, and the traditional state-centred, authoritarian and patriarchal paradigm of security. Migration policy should not be driven by fear, but be based on compassion, respect and justice.

NOTES

1. In chapter 3, 'Migration and Geopolitics in the Greater Antilles,' Grosfoguel (2003, 103–127) provides a useful framework for conceptualizing Caribbean migration in terms of a 'capital accumulation [economic] logic, military/security geopolitical logic and ideological/symbolical geopolitical logic' (107).
2. Chang and Grabel (2005, 16–23) show that neoliberal economic policies in Third World countries have failed to generate greater economic growth during 1980–2000 as did the interventionist policies of the previous period and have contributed to greater income inequality both within and between nations.

3. An interesting but troubling demographic statistic from the Netherlands Antilles may serve as an example. Between 1998 and 2001 this Dutch territory experienced a massive human exodus to the Netherlands in response to the severe austerity that accompanied the implementation of an IMF-guided structural adjustment programme. Data from the Central Bureau of Statistics (Maduro-Jeandor et al 2003, 15) show that in 1997 households in the poorest population quintile were, as might be expected, larger on average than the remaining households in the Netherlands Antilles: 4.4 versus 2.9 persons per household. However, in 2001 — after the exodus — the average size of the poorer households was smaller than that of the remaining households: 2.5 versus 3.1 persons per household! One can imagine the far-reaching sociological implications of this acute reduction in the average size of poor households in terms of their gender and age composition, income level and overall vulnerability.

4. The Bush Administration announced the use of pre-emptive force as part of its national security strategy in late 2002 and used it to justify the 2003 military invasion of Iraq. The notion of 'pre-emptive' refers to forestalling, preventing or reducing the impact of an anticipated danger by acting before the danger can occur.

5. The name 'Third Border' seems to have been introduced by the Bush Administration in April 2001 (before 9/11) when the earlier-mentioned Third Border Initiative was announced at the Third Summit of the Americas held in Quebec City.

6. One may also draw a comparison between the reterritorialization of the nation state and the transnationalization of communities, households and identities as discussed in the contemporary scholarship on transnationalism.

7. The current government of the Netherlands consists of a coalition of centrist and right-wing parties. The Minister of Alien Affairs and Integration (including Immigration and Naturalization), who was responsible for the introduction of the basic integration exam, is a member of the People's Party for Freedom and Democracy (VVD) — a conservative, pro-business, pro-USA, a-religious party that bases itself explicitly on liberal principles. Its Liberal Manifesto of September 2005 takes as its point of departure the themes of democracy, security, freedom and citizenship.

8. Residents of other non-independent Caribbean territories who have migrated to their respective 'motherland' in Europe or the USA have also found that their nationality does not protect them from racial discrimination and anti-immigrant sentiments in the metropolitan centres (Brown 2004, 129–132; Grosfoguel 2004).

9. According to legal advice obtained by the Government of the Netherlands Antilles, the Dutch bill conflicts with the principle of equality contained in the Dutch Constitution, with the Kingdom Law on Dutch nationality, as well as with international law, including the European Covenant for the Protection of Human Rights, the International Covenant on Civil and Political Rights, the International

Covenant on the Elimination of All Forms of Racial Discrimination, and the European Covenant on Nationality (*Amigoe* 2005a; 2006a).

10. The Parliament of the Netherlands Antilles has recently gained the express support of the European Parliament and the Parlatino (Parliament of Latin America and the Caribbean) for its efforts to oppose the Dutch bill and to guarantee the principle of free movement of persons on the basis of the European Covenant on Human Rights.

11. Chang (2002) has argued that the North's economic development is the historical result of entirely different policies (mercantilism, protectionism, state subsidization of industrialization) than the neoliberal, 'good governance' policies that the North has been pushing the South to implement as the supposedly certain road to growth and development.

12. For some recent publications, see Brown (2002), Byron (2000), Mills (2002), Silié (2002) and especially the explicit attempts by UNECLAC (2001) and Puri (2003) to address the imbalance between the scholarship on intra-regional migration and that on migration to the metropolitan centres.

REFERENCES

Aja Díaz, Antonio. 2006. Migraciones y Políticas Migratorias en el Caribe [Migrations and Migration Policies in the Caribbean]. Paper delivered at the Meeting of the Latin American Studies Association, San Juan, Puerto Rico, March 15–18, 2006.

Amigoe. 2006a. Hoogleraar Laat Geen Spaan Heel van Wet-Verdonk [Professor Demolishes Verdonk Bill]. May 30, p. 5.

———. 2006b. Rechter Bob Wit Fel Gekant tegen 'Verdonkwet' [Judge Bob Wit Highly Critical of Verdonk Bill]. April 20, p. 3.

———. 2005a. Toelatingsregeling Antilliaanse Jongeren Juridisch Niet Haalbaar [Antillean Youths Admission Legislation Not Feasible Juridically]. October 22, p. 5.

———. 2005b. Rechter Bob Wit over Toelatingsregeling: 'Verdonk Speelt in op Vreemdelingenhaat [Judge Bob Wit on Admission Legislation: 'Verdonk Utilises Xenophobia']. June 18, pp. 1–2.

Bohórquez, Paola and Susan Spronk. 2004. 'International Migration in the Americas: Emerging Issues'. Report of a conference organized by the Centre for Research on Latin America and the Caribbean (CERLAC, York University), Toronto (Ontario), Canada, September 19–20. March. 2003.

Brown, Dennis A.V. 2002. Inbetweenity: Marginalization, Migration and Poverty among Haitians in the Turks and Caicos Islands. Paper delivered at the Meeting of the Society for Caribbean Studies, University of Warwick (Coventry, UK), July 1–3, 2002.

Brown, Laurence. 2004. Contexts of Migration and Diasporic Identities. In *Introduction to the Pan-Caribbean*, edited by Tracey Skeldon, 118–135. London: Edward Arnold Publishers.

Bryan, Anthony T. and Stephen E. Flynn. 2001. 'Terrorism, Porous Borders, and Homeland Security: The Case for US-Caribbean Cooperation'. Coral Gables (Florida, USA): University of Miami (The Dante B. Fascell North-South Center), October 22. *http://www.oas.org/ezine/ezine4/art17.htm* (accessed May 2006).

Byron, Jessica. 2000. 'Migration, National Identity and Regionalism in the Caribbean: A Leeward Islands Case Study'. In *Contending with Destiny: The Caribbean in the 21st Century*, eds. Kenneth Hall and Denis Benn, 80–90. Kingston, Jamaica: Ian Randle Publishers.

Byron, Jessica and Diana Thorburn. 1998. 'Gender and International Relations: A Global Perspective and Issues for the Caribbean'. *Feminist Review*, 59: 211–232.

Chang, Ha-Joon. 2002. *Kicking Away the Ladder: Development Strategy in Historical Perspective*. London: Anthem Press.

Chang, Ha-Joon and Ilene Grabel. 2005 . *Reclaiming Development: An Alternative Economic Policy Manual*. (second edition) London: Zed Books.

Cortés Castellanos, Patricia. 2005. 'Mujeres Migrantes de América Latina y el Caribe: Derechos Humanos, Mitos y Duras Realidades [Migrant Women of Latin America and the Caribbean: Human Rights, Myths and Harsh Realities]'. Santiago,Chile: United Nations (CELADE, Population Division).

Duany, Jorge. 2002. 'Los Países': Transnational Migration from the Dominican Republic to the United States. Paper presented at the seminar 'Migration and Development: Focus on the Dominican Republic', Santo Domingo (Dominican Republic), March 7–9. *http://migration.ucdavis.edu/ceme/more.php?id=19_0_6_0* (accessed May 2006).

Edmondson, Locksley. 1979. 'The Caribbean within the Third World and in the Non-aligned Movement'. *Korean Journal of International Relations*, 19: 99–122.

————. 1974. 'Caribbean Nation-building and the Internationalization of Race: Issues and Perspectives'. In *Ethnicity and Nationbuilding*, ed. Wendell Bell & W.E. Freeman, 73–86. Beverly Hills (California, USA): Sage Publications.

Flint, Colin. 2002. Extra-territoriality, Reterritorialization and Hegemonic Power: The 'Hegemonic Dilemma' and Its Implications for Globalization. Paper presented at the Conference *Responding to Globalization: Societies, Groups, and Individuals*, Boulder (Colorado, USA), April 4–7.

Girvan, Norman. 2004. 'Agenda Setting and Regionalism in the Greater Caribbean: Responses to 9/11'. In *Caribbean Security in the Age of Terror: Challenge and Change*, ed. Ivelaw Lloyd Griffith, 310–333. Kingston, Jamaica: Ian Randle Publishers.

Graham, Pamela M. 1997. International Migration and Transnational Politics: Recent Developments in the Caribbean and Mexican Cases. Paper prepared for the 1997

Meeting of the Latin American Studies Association, Guadalajara (Mexico), April 17–18.

Grosfoguel, Ramón. 2004. 'La Racialización de los Migrantes Coloniales del Caribe en los Centros Metropolitanos: Una Introducción a la Historia de las Diversas Colonialidades en Cada Imperio [The Racialization of Caribbean Colonial Migrants in the Metropolitan Centers: An Introduction to the History of the Various Colonialities in Each Empire]'. *Caribbean Studies*, 32, no.1: 3–41.

———. 2003. *Colonial Subjects: Puerto Ricans in a Global Perspective*. Berkeley California. University of California Press.

Hazbun, Waleed. 2004. 'Globalisation, Reterritorialisation and the Political Economy of Tourism Development in the Middle East'. *Geopolitics* 9, no. 2: 310–341.

International Organizsation for Migration. 2002. 'IOM in the Caribbean'. Washington (DC). IOM Regional Office for North America and the Caribbean.

Lahav, Gallya. 2003. Migration and Security: The Role of Non-State Actors and Civil Liberties in Liberal Democracies. Paper prepared for the Second Coordination Meeting on International Migration of the United Nations Department of Economic and Social Affairs, Population Division, New York City, October 15–16.

Maduro-Jeandor, Ellen with contributions from F. Vierbergen and M. Jacobs. 2003. 'Schets van de Sociaal-Economische Situatie in de Nederlandse Antillen [Outline of the Socio-economic Situation in the Netherlands Antilles]', *Modus* 5, no. 1: 1–48.

Mills, Frank. 2002. The Transnationalization of Immigration Policy and Its Effect on Caribbean Microstates. Paper delivered at the twenty-seventh Annual Conference of the Caribbean Studies Association, Nassau, The Bahamas, May 27–June 1, 2002.

Mushakoji, Kinhide. 2003. Trafficking, Migration, and Gender Insecurity. Report of a seminar organized by the International Movement against All Forms of Discrimination and Racism (IMADR), Hyderabad, India, January 4. Osaka, Japan: Hurights. *http://www.hurights.or.ja/asia-pacific/no_31/05.htm* (accessed May 2006).

Portes, Alejandro and Kelly Hoffman. 2003. 'Latin American Class Structures: Their Composition and Change during the Neoliberal Era'. *Latin American Research Review* 38, no. 1: 41–82.

Puri, Shalini ed. 2003. *Marginal Migrations: The Circulation of Cultures within the Caribbean*. London: Macmillan.

Silié, Rubén, Carlos Segura and Carlos Dore Cabral. 2002. *La Nueva Inmigración Haitiana* [The New Haitian Immigration]. Santo Domingo (Dominican Republic): FLACSO.

UNECLAC/CDCC. 2001. Report of the Ad Hoc Expert Group Meeting on Intraregional Migration, Port of Spain, Trinidad & Tobago, November 9–10, 2000.

Port of Spain: United Nations (ECLAC/CDCC), May 21. *http://www.eclac.cl/publicaciones/Port of Spain/5/LCCARG645/ G0645.html* (accessed May 2006).

US Department of State. 2006a. 'Rice, Bahamian Foreign Minister Hail Success of CARICOM Meeting'. Washington (DC): Department of State, Bureau of Public Affairs, March 22. *http://usinfo.state.gov/wh/Archive/2006/Mar/23-899882.html* (accessed May 2006).

————. 2006b. 'The United States at the CARICOM Ministerial: Security and Law Enforcement'. Fact Sheet. Washington (DC): Department of State, Bureau of Public Affairs, March 20. *http://www.state.gov/r/pa/scp/2006/63437.htm* (accessed May 2006).

CONTRIBUTORS

ALLEN, Rose Mary lectures in sociology and social history at the University of the Netherlands Antilles, Curaçao; she holds a Ph.D. degree from the University of Utrecht.

ALLEYNE, Dillon lectures in economics at the UWI, Mona, Jamaica, and is presently engaged in a study of migrant remittances.

ARCHER, Carol is the Dean of the Faculty of the Built Environment at the University of Technology (Jamaica) and obtained her doctorate in political science from the City University of New York.

BROWN, Mikaila is the founder/director of AOW Consultants Inc. and gained her Ph.D. in social anthropology from Teacher's College, Columbia University, New York.

BURROWES, Marcia lectures in cultural studies at the UWI, Cave Hill, Barbados, and is a former Leverhulme Visiting Scholar at the Centre for Caribbean Studies at the University of Warwick, UK.

FIGUEROA, Mark is an economist and Dean of the Faculty of Social Sciences at the UWI, Mona.

GORDON-STAIR, Angela is a counselling psychologist and Head of the Counselling Service of the University Health Centre, the UWI, Mona.

GOULBOURNE, Harry is Professor of Sociology at the London South Bank University.

GRIFFIN, Clifford E. is an Associate Professor of Political Science at the North Carolina State University, specializing in Caribbean political economy and security issues.

HADEY-SAINT-LOUIS, Marie-Gabrielle was born in Haiti, is currently pursuing a Ph.D. at the University of Bordeaux, France, and is Head of the Department of Business and Public Management at the Technological University, Guadeloupe.

HENRY, Frances is Professor Emerita of Anthropology at York University, Toronto.

HICKLING, Frederick W. is Professor of Psychiatry in the Department of Community Health and Psychiatry at the UWI, Mona.

ISHEMO, Amani is Senior Lecturer in the Faculty of the Built Environment at the University of Technology (Jamaica).

JACKSON, Jason is currently pursuing a Ph.D. at the Massachusetts Institute of Technology; he has worked as a research economist at the Social and Economic Research Unit of the Caribbean Development Bank.

JORDENS, Peter is a consultant with PlanCaribe, Curaçao; his research interests focus on the political economy of development in the Caribbean.

KERR, Steven is the Manager of the Human Development Unit at the Planning Institute of Jamaica (PIOJ) and the Technical Secretary for Vision 2030 Education and Training Task Force.

KNIGHT, Pauline is the Director of Social Policy, Planning and Research at the Planning Institute of Jamaica.

MARTIN-JOHNSON, Suzette is a professional translator, currently pursuing a Ph.D. in Migration and Diaspora Studies at the UWI, Mona.

MORTLEY, Natasha Kay is a Research Fellow in the Faculty of Social Sciences, the UWI, Mona, currently pursuing a Ph.D. degree in Migration and Diaspora Studies at the UWI, Mona.

PALMER, Ransford is Graduate Professor of Economics at Howard University, Washington, D.C.

PLAZA, Dwaine is an Associate Professor of Sociology at Oregon State University.

POTTINGER, Audrey is a Senior Lecturer and consultant clinical psychologist in the Department of Obstetrics, Gynaecology and Child Health, the UWI, Mona.

REIS, Michele is a Lecturer at the Institute of International Relations, the UWI, St. Augustine, Trinidad and Tobago.

ROBERTSON-HICKLING, Hilary is a Lecturer in the Department of Management Studies, the UWI, Mona.

ROBINSON-WALCOTT, Kim is the editor of the *Jamaica Journal* and book editor at the Sir Arthur Lewis Institute of Social and Economic Studies (SALISES), the UWI, Mona.

THOMAS-HOPE, Elizabeth is the James Seivright Moss-Solomon (Snr.) Professor of Environmental Management and Director of the Centre for the Environment at the UWI, Mona.

VALTONEN, Kathleen is Senior Lecturer in Social Work at the Department of Behavioural Sciences, the UWI, St. Augustine.

WILLIAMS, Easton is the Manager of the Population Unit in the Social Policy, Planning and Research Division of the Planning Institute of Jamaica.

WILLIAMS-BROWN, Sharon is a counselling psychologist at the University Health Centre, the UWI, Mona.

WHYTE-GIVANS, Sophia is Consultant-Researcher and Speech Writer to the Director-General of the Planning Institute of Jamaica.

INDEX

Printed in the United States
134239LV00005B/2/P

9 789766 373511